AMERICA II

"These are the times that try men's souls. The summer soldier and the sunshine patriot will, in this crisis, shrink from the service of their country; but he that stands it now deserves the thanks of man and woman. Tyranny, like hell, is not easily conquered; yet we have this consolation with us; that the harder the conflict, the more glorious the triumph."

Thomas Paine, 1776

(The Crises Papers)

AMERICA II
JACK THE TURTLE

Black Chicken Publishing
2016

America II by Jack the Turtle

Copyright © <2016> All rights reserved, including illustrations. However, the author encourages copying and distribution in print, electronically, or by photographic or other media so long as the copies made are unaltered from the original, and are not made for monetary gain in any form. First Printing: <2016>

ISBN <978-0-692-66794-1>

<Black Chicken Publishing>First Printing: <2016>

Dedication

For my wife, my children, and my grandchildren.

…and for my country.

Contents

Foreword xi
Preface... xvii
   Just what was the American Dream?....................................... xvii
   Causes and Effects.. xix
   The road to hell is paved with good intentions....................... xxi
   Knowledge vs. Insight... xxii

PART 1 - The Road to Here 25
   The Government takes over control of the nation's economy.26
   Earlier levels of government involvement in the nation's
   economy... 27
   The Gold Standard.. 29
   Protecting against inside-dealing in banks
   and bank "runs"... 31
   The Federal Reserve Banks 32
   War and its impacts on government economic policies 34
   The U.S Becomes a Creditor Nation 35
   1925-1940.. 39
   1940-1955.. 66
   1955-1970.. 86
   1970-1985.. 108
   1985 To Now.. 139
   Summing up.. 166

Part 2 - The Road to the Future 171
   The First Step... 172
   The Second Step 174

Part 3 - Defining the Problems 176
   The Scientific Method for Problem Solving............................ 177
   Symptoms in General 178
   Symptoms of an Ailing Society.. 179
   Some Symptoms of a Society in Decline 180
   The problems and their basic elements................................... 183
   The four control mechanisms 264

Part 4 - Posing Possible Solutions 291
   Acknowledging Axioms
   & Defining Acceptance Criteria 293
   Lawyers as Lawmakers..305
   Who IS up to the job, and who can we believe?....................308
   Providing citizens with tools for rebuilding
   The American Dream 311
   Amending the Constitution..323
   It will take both time, and a new political party
   to get the job done 328
   But, more than laws and Constitutional amendments will be
   needed 332
   Well, we might try <u>education</u> on a <u>massive</u> scale!.................333
   Just say no! 338
   Measuring and Valuing work 372
   Wrapping up 377

Part 5 - Implementing Mechanisms..378
   Government Implementing Mechanisms...............................381
   Enforcement at the Government Level..................................388
   Implementing Options for Citizens 395
   Pocketbook Voting 397
   Strikes 400
   Peaceful Civil Disobedience 407
   Armed Resistance 409
   Limits on Citizen Implementing Mechanisms......................410

Part 6 - Proving the Solutions 411

Part 7 - Free Will..413
   Graph #1 - Human Speed of Travel.......................................426
   Graph #2 - Population Growth 427
   Graph #3 - Advances in Pneumatic Tire Durability 429
   Graph #4 - Government Forms Overlaying Population Growth
   What is the most important question we all must answer
   correctly? 434

Appendix - The Constitution 435

Constitution for the United States of America 436

Foreword

(Why I bothered…and why you should too)

If you are reading this, it is most likely that we share a concern about what's happening today in American society, and to a lesser extent what's happening in a lot of other societies around the world too.

At the outset, I started writing America II as a way of leaving behind for my children and grandchildren a view of the world as I saw it. My hope was then, and remains, that they may embrace the approach I have laid down for solving problems throughout their lives, both at home and as part of the communities and nation that they are part of.

When I decided to publish America II, I elected to do it using a pen name. I selected Jack the Turtle because it seemed to fit so well.

In part I was modeling it after Dr. Seuss' turtle Mack in his "Yertle the Turtle" children's book. You remember Mack. He was the turtle that finally got fed up with Yertle (the turtle king) stacking more and more turtles on Mack's back so he (Yertle) could climb up higher and see further places to rule. Finally, Mack burps, and shakes the stack of turtles that king Yertle has been perched on, and the king is brought back down to earth like the rest of the turtles.

In part I wanted to keep readers focused on the content of my writing, rather than focusing on anything about me personally. I also thought that using the pen name might add a level of mystery that might attract a few extra readers. Once captured they could help spread the word that there was a book out there that offered a really different perspective on solving the problems we have to solve if we are to succeed long term as a free and prosperous society.

Finally, I picked Jack the Turtle, because, like the tortoise in the fable of the tortoise and the hare, I have a tendency to start slow, but finish stronger.

I got a late start in becoming involved in what was going on in the world around me as far as politics and such are concerned, but now I think that I (and a lot of others like me) need to get involved, and stay that way; until the deadly problems we are now ignoring get brought out into the open and are solved. In my judgment that isn't happening today.

America II is the story of a great nation that is now, for the first time since its birth, failing to live up to its promises to a majority of its citizens. America II is a story of what one middle class citizen "Jack the Turtle" sees as being required for that promise to be restored, and for America to again be a beacon for all nations to follow.

Over the past 20-30 years' time I have witnessed changes in our society that have seen fear replace optimism and enthusiasm in the hearts and minds of many, and perhaps even a majority of America's citizens. For many years now I have felt marooned in the middle, trapped between two competing ideologies that are so caught up in their own limited agendas favoring one segment of society over the others, that they have lost all sight of what once made America great. It seems to me that those two competing ideologies are knowingly or otherwise hell bent on destroying what is left of the Great American Dream.

I don't want to give too much away here, but I think a short bit on credentials might be in order. First, I am old enough to have witnessed first-hand much of the history discussed in the pages that follow. So my bona fides are based on first-hand experience. Secondly, it is probably equally important to note what I am NOT. I am not a member of some think tank, not a big name writer or scholar, not a past or present politician, not a past or present bureaucrat, not a past or present big time business leader, in fact not a past or present celebrity in any field at all. I'm just a typical working middle class American watching with great concern as my nation appears to be heading down a dead end road that holds ever less hope and opportunity for future generations.

One thing I hope to provide is an alternative to the never-ending stream of "conventional" arguments about the condition of our country, by the politicians and established talking heads on TV who claim to be speaking on behalf of America's middle class workers. As you read through what follows, it will become very clear that none of them are speaking for me.

If you share my belief that none of the established politicians, "experts", and talking heads on TV are speaking for you either, you may well find within these pages a number of ideas that we already share. But even more important, you may find in this work a practical means of using your knowledge to make the American Dream come alive again, not only for you and your family, but for all Americans everywhere.

In the first chapter of this work you will see just how and when America got off track; how the American Dream became a shell of its former self, and became unavailable to so many American citizens; how and why the two major political parties now sharing power are completely helpless to ever come together and act to restore the dream; and finally what must instead be done for the dream to be restored.

We will first take a tour of the last seventy-five years of American history that will illustrate clearly where, when, and why events conspired to bring us to the present point in time, holding on to a badly tarnished American Dream.

The historic recap is presented in order to provide an insight into the cause and effect nature of political events and policies that have brought us to a point in time when there are more Americans unemployed and under-employed (forced to work beneath their skill and education level for poverty level wages) than at any time in our nation's history (including during the great depression of the 1930's).

Next we will examine together what must happen in order for the dream to be restored. I will postulate that only two things must happen, but if <u>either</u> of these is not done, I will argue that the dream will vanish altogether, and with it the America that was once the envy of the entire world.

One way or the other I will try to persuade you that America's fate will be sealed within the next two decades. Within that timeframe either the Dream will be fully restored, and with it America's claim to being the greatest nation on earth; or the Dream will die out completely and America will quickly be reduced to just another once great nation with visions of past glories lost, inhabited by citizens with few dreams worth noting any longer.

I believe that you will find the discussion on what our problems <u>really</u> are to be especially thought provoking. My perspective on the problems facing America is, you can be assured, quite different from the perspective of anybody serving in government (at any level) anywhere in America today. It is also equally different from the perspective held by all the "experts" and talking heads you see endlessly on TV. You will be offered verifiable evidence and examples to support the perspective being offered for your consideration. I believe it's going to get you thinking a whole new way about what we need to do as a country going forward.

Dyed-in-the-wool Democrats and Republicans will both love parts of what is in here, and hate parts of what is in here, but neither of these two parties is really at liberty to work on solving the problems that you will see revealed in these pages. As you read through this, you will see why that is (sadly) true. To remind you, those are the problems that caused the dismantling of the Great American Dream.

If that seems to put us on the horns of a dilemma, think again. I will argue that there is a road to the future that holds out a brightly shining American Dream that does not rely on today's politicians waking up to the horrible, unintended consequences of their past acts, facing facts, coming to understand the problems facing America (they really don't have a clue now), or acting to make things better.

Read this book and you will come to understand not only what went wrong, but also what's needed to get things back on track; and what you can do yourself to make the American Dream reappear for you and your family, and how you can make your life come out more like you want (and originally expected) it to. Then loan the book to a friend and ask them to read it and pass it along to someone else when they are done with it.

Forget about getting the book back. It's not important that the book be returned.

It's important that the dream be returned.

And, please do it soon.

The clock is winding down on what's left of the Great American Dream, even as you are reading this.

Jack

Preface

Whatever happened to the American Dream?

Somewhere along the way, over the past 75 years' time, we, as American turtles, lost sight of what it originally was, and what was required in order for it to be kept intact, and routinely realized by average middle-class American working turtles. Now many of us American turtles, perhaps even a majority of us, are individually and collectively feeling its loss. Many, if not most, Americans, especially those comprising the "middle-class", are expressing real concern that the loss may be a permanent one.

As you read through this, it will become apparent that the demise of the American Dream, in its original form, was entirely predictable, given a historical perspective of a series of events that brought us to the present point in time. And it will hopefully become equally obvious what must be done to restore it.

Just what was the American Dream?

To begin with, it might be useful to define just what the American Dream was considered to be back in the "old" days.

The American Dream was always (and is) just that. A dream. Its uniqueness lay in the fact that, as grand as it might be, it was fully possible for many, if not most, Americans to see their dreams realized, in full, in their lifetimes.

Dreams are individual kinds of things, and the American Dream was no exception. Each individual's version of the American Dream actually embodied a mix of elements, and those elements might vary somewhat, depending on whom you might be asking the question of. One citizen's American Dream might have more or less total elements than another citizen's American Dream, but every citizen's American Dream version included four "core" or foundation elements.

It is these "core" elements that were part of <u>everybody's</u> idea of the American Dream, that we will be considering, and measuring changes in over various periods of time, as we go along throughout the chapters of this work.

Included in everybody's original idea of the American Dream were the following four ideals and expectations:

1. The American Dream included an expectation of equality of opportunity to succeed financially, depending on each individual citizen's willingness to strive against adversity, and sacrifice present pleasures, in return for future improvements in their standard of living.

2. The American Dream included an expectation of equal treatment and protection under the laws for all citizens engaged in those activities identified in the American Declaration of Independence as being (the original) rights every citizen of this country was endowed with at birth. These included the right to life, liberty, and the pursuit of happiness. The first ten amendments to the U.S. Constitution were put in place to ensure that no one or no government could interfere with any honest citizen's pursuit of his/her God given rights.

3. The American Dream included an expectation that each successive generation would have greater opportunities for improving their standard of living, than the previous generation had enjoyed.

4. The American Dream included an expectation that the powers of the Government would be used to guard the previously mentioned rights, and opportunities, of all American citizens, against encroachment and assault from all quarters, whether coming from within or from outside of the nation's borders.

In order for dreams to become reality, they need a real and sound foundation to build upon. These four elements provided the foundation for the American Dream. When these four elements were present, most Americans felt that they could achieve whatever they set out to achieve, and were willing to strive themselves to make all of the other elements of their dreams happen on their own.

The dreams of American citizens differed from the dreams held by citizens of most other nations, in that dreams <u>came true</u> for citizens of this country much more often than did the dreams of citizens of other countries.

Dreams held by citizens in the majority of the rest of the world's countries, seldom were based on the same "core elements" that provided the foundation for the American Dream. And, the dreams of citizens of other countries were far less likely to be realized in full, no matter how great or limited they might be.

But, in America, the basic tenants (foundation elements) of the American Dream were fulfilled so routinely, that for a citizen of this country to see his or her dreams realized in full was not seen as something unusual. Rather, realization of the American Dream occurred so routinely, that, over time, it came to be viewed almost as an American's right, to have his or her dreams realized, in full.

By itself, coming to believe that success was a birthright didn't cause all of the problems that we are currently experiencing. But, this attitude on the part of some turtles hasn't been helpful either.

Causes and Effects

It is said that politics is "the art of compromise".

If it is true that politics is an art, and not a science, it may also be true that political acts may be viewed differently if viewed from a scientific perspective. Science requires always that things be (provably) true and precisely what they are. Politics requires only that things <u>appear</u> to be true, and/or be <u>accepted</u> as true, regardless of what the actual truth might be.

Perhaps applying a more scientific approach to defining the problems facing America at this point in time, can be useful in identifying what is needed in order to both solve these problems, and restore the great American Dream to its original luster.

At this point in time, it's at least worth a shot.

Newton's third law of physics states that "for every action, (between bodies and/or forces) there is an equal and opposite reaction". His first law (inertia) states that "a body once in motion tends to stay in motion, unless acted on by an outside force". Still another well-known scientific axiom (not Newton's) states that "nature abhors a vacuum". The same laws related to physics, noted previously, can be seen to apply equally well to the social interactions that occur between governments and those being governed. For example, if in the instance of Newton's third law we introduce government and citizens as opposing bodies, we would get the following: "for every government action, there is an equal and opposite citizen reaction".

And, if we define a particular government body or program as being a "body", and restate Newton's first law with that change in place, it becomes: "A government body or program once in motion, tends to stay in motion, unless acted upon by an outside force".

And finally in the third instance, if we replace the word "nature", with the word "government", the restated law becomes "Government abhors a vacuum".

Being natural and universal laws, the outcomes of applying them are, in every instance entirely predictable. That's one of the benefits relating to working with natural and universal laws. Unlike manmade laws that may be subject to "interpretation", laws of nature (universal laws) can only be read one way.

There's no "subjective interpretation" that can explain away gravity, or cause its effects not to behave in an entirely predictable manner, given any set of variables one might wish to introduce into consideration.

It may therefore be useful to go back in time and see how, by applying our knowledge about these (universal) laws, as they relate to interaction between governments and those governed, certain past events might well have been predicted, at the outset, to have caused the demise of the American Dream.

Of course, everybody has 20-20 hindsight. But, that's not the point.

The point is that much of the damage that has been done to the American Dream, was damage that was entirely predictable before the steps were taken that inflicted the damage....and the damaging steps were taken anyway, often with full knowledge of what the results later might be.

In hopes of gaining a better understanding as to how such things can happen, in the very first chapter we will review a chronology of the most significant factors involving citizen and government interactions, over the past seventy-five years' time, which have predictably led to the American Dream being in its present state of disrepair.

The road to hell is paved with good intentions

It is a middle-class American turtle's nature to be forgiving of those who may have mistreated us. Mostly, we are able to think positively about the actions of our fellow turtles, and usually we can be counted on to give them the benefit of the doubt.

But, sometimes we get so upset, especially when our own kind appear to have obviously mistreated us, that our naturally charitable nature fails us, and we just get plain angry. When that happens, our responses are usually limited to fighting back (biting) or withdrawing into our shells and sulking.

It's not easy being a turtle.

Throughout this work, I will typically take the position that those turtles who (in hindsight) erred, and in so doing did great damage to America, nonetheless for the most part, did so with good intentions toward their fellow turtles. Sometimes that won't be the case. There <u>are</u> some bad turtles out there. But, in most instances, the errors made, were (hopefully) more mistake than malice.

Knowledge vs. Insight

Americans are bombarded daily with an almost unbelievable amount of information. Most of it is brought to us by work contacts, schools, radio and television, plus other sources from books and newspapers, to direct mail, to on-line computer services, all of which are capable of supplying enough information to cause information overload for many of us American turtles. The amount of collective knowledge available to us is indeed great.

Within the confines of this work, you will see restated a lot of data that you probably had been exposed to before, but may by now have forgotten. Actually, you probably didn't completely forget it. But some of it may have been pushed down to the bottom of your memory queue, by vast quantities of other, newer, more spectacularly presented data, received by you on a daily basis.

When information overload occurs, what often gets lost is <u>insight</u>. Insight to see past events in a broader perspective, and to determine, based upon that perspective, how you came to be where you are now in your life, where your life is headed, and what you can do to make your life come out more like you want it to.

Fully engaged in the battles of day-to-day living, including earning a living, and confronted with mountainous amounts of unfiltered data, some of it true, some of it false, some of it ambiguous, it is easy to succumb to the alligators-and-the-swamp syndrome*[1]. It becomes increasingly difficult to sort through it all, separate truth from falsehood, see what needs to be done, and implement a plan for doing it.

In the broadest sense, my purpose in creating this work has been to provide you with a (perhaps different) insight into the past events that have shaped American society into its present form; and to aid you in using that knowledge to make the American Dream come true for you and your family.

Some of what follows may appear provocative, depending on your present political beliefs. It's not my intent to provoke. Rather it is my intent to lay the foundation for a useful discussion as to how the American Dream can be fully restored. At least the version of the American Dream as I know it. In order to know how to fix it, it will be helpful to understand how it got broken in the first place.

To the extent that your view of the American Dream resembles my view of the American Dream, this additional perspective may be of use to you.

I hope it is.

---

[1] "when you are up to your ass in alligators, it is sometimes difficult to remember that you originally came there to drain the swamp."

PART 1 - The Road to Here

This section is a fairly long one. Hang in there though. In order to understand where we are now, we need to really understand what all brought us to the present point in time.

There have been seven significant changes in American society, and in the relationship between American citizens and their government, that have occurred over the past seventy-five years' time, that have contributed greatly to our being where we are now, holding onto a tarnished and crippled American Dream.

In this chapter we will look at how these changes occurred, over time, with the goal in mind of seeing them in a perhaps different perspective, and by doing so, perhaps also coming to better understand what we have to do to restore the original luster to the American Dream.

Government actions touch all citizens; often in ways that were never expected. It will be seen that of the seven most significant changes in our society, which have served to reduce the American Dream to a shadow of its former self, government actions were involved either directly or indirectly in each one.

Let's begin this review by stating that it is not meant to just be an indictment of any government action, policy, or party. Our main goal will be to fix the dream, not to just fix the blame. But, in order to restore the missing elements, and keep them from getting lost again, it is important to understand how such things as the loss of the core elements underlying such a great and valuable dream could ever happen in the first place.

The Government takes over control of the nation's economy

One significant change between the citizens of America and their government relates to the government's assuming total control over the nation's economy. This didn't happen overnight, and wasn't due to any single cause. Rather, it occurred over about a seventy-five-year span of time, and, it might be argued, occurred almost as much by accident, as by plan.

The beginning of our present troubles can be traced back to the early part of the 20th century, when the Federal government began expanding its role in safeguarding the nation's currency and banking systems, and began using its law-making powers to effectively "manage" the entire economy of the nation.

Since then, in time periods that average roughly fifteen years in length, the Federal government has increasingly taken measures that have by now resulted in their achieving almost total control over all aspects of the nations, and indeed, the world's economy.

It should be stressed that all the evidence points to the probability that most of those involved at each point in time appear to have had honorable motives. It just didn't ultimately turn out the way everybody planned.

Many of the bad things that happened to the American Dream resulting from government controlling the economy, can, to a large degree, be attributed to the "law of unintended consequences" playing a significant role in the outcome. Throughout, we will witness the effects of the "law of unintended consequences" that continually interjected itself into the outcome.

The government's assuming total control over the nation's economy was at minimum, a contributory factor in bringing about the other six changes that we will discuss in this section, and may well have been the most significant single source of (hopefully unintended) damage to the American Dream.

Earlier levels of government involvement in the nation's economy

By way of comparison to how government has expanded its role in controlling all aspects of the nation's economy, we will first go back in time all the way to the Civil War between the North and South in our country. During this period, and in the fifty years that followed the end of the Civil War, economic crises were plentiful, and government acted often to calm the crises when they arose. The government's actions with respect to controlling economic matters during this period will be seen to have primarily centered around protecting citizens who had money stored in banks from losses due to:

1. self-dealing by bankers
2. printing money not backed by gold
3. counterfeiting of paper currencies
4. "runs" on banks deposits, which often caused banks to fail

Immediately following the Civil War, and for about fifty years thereafter, these four areas of concern occupied most (but not all) of the government's concern in economic areas. Of course, the federal government still had to be concerned with how to raise enough money to pay for its operations, and did so mostly through a variety of non-income based taxes, duties and tariffs on imported goods, and other fees, occasionally borrowing money by way of selling bonds to banks and wealthy investors, both foreign and domestic.

It should be noted that operating the federal government during this period was less expensive than it is now, due largely to the fact that the federal government didn't involve itself in many functions that it is now involved in. Throughout this section we will explore why, when, and how, the federal government got involved in so many different areas of the economy, that it had not been involved in prior to the turn of the 20th century.

Prior to the enactment of the Constitution in the late 1700's, some banks, printed their own forms of paper money, and held in their own vaults gold (and silver) in amounts (supposedly) equal to the value of paper currency that was printed and circulated.

Invariably, before the Constitution was enacted some banks were found to be printing and circulating more in (paper) currency value, than could be found in gold and silver in their vaults. It became pretty much "buyer beware" in terms of whose bank a citizen might allow to hold his or her gold, and how much actual gold was being held for paper currency redemption in the bank's vault.

Exchange rates were also a problem. Some shaky banks "dollars" might not be considered a good risk, and so those taking them might require more of the shaky bank's "dollars", in return for goods, than would be charged if a more secure bank's "dollars" were being used for the purchase.

In the mid 1700's, counterfeiting of paper currency was another big problem. There were, at times, so many different denominations being printed, by so many sources, that entrepreneurial engravers and printers had pretty easy pickings. Individual banks seldom had the capacity to identify forgers, or prosecute them, and there came to be a lot of paper money in circulation that was not backed by anything except the forger's smile.

In the mid 1800's near the end of the Civil War, the South's government had printed enormous amounts of paper currency, with nothing at all in the way of gold to back it. "Confederate" money, as it came to be called, was paper currency that was backed not by gold, but by the South's government's promise that it would later be backed by gold, after the conflict was over, and the region's wealth was restored. Those accepting confederate paper money in exchange for real or personal property ultimately discovered that their paper currency was totally worthless.

Northern banks and businesses (and foreign governments) refused to accept "confederate" currencies in exchange for purchases and/or loans. After the war was ended, the federal government moved to restore a uniform currency and exchange rate between all the states of the union.

The Gold Standard

After the Civil War, in a further attempt to restore a fair rate of exchange in the southern states, restore the credibility of the banks, stabilize exchange rates, and get a handle on counterfeiting, the Federal government acted to strengthen enforcement of existing laws that required all paper currency to be printed by the U.S. government, and purchased with gold or silver, from the U.S. treasury, by those banks wishing to circulate paper currency.

The U.S. policy of tying the value of paper currency to a precious metal, was itself patterned after the British government's having done the same thing earlier, and was originally specified in the Constitution. The British Pound was, until the early 20th century, backed by gold or sterling silver, and was designated as "pounds sterling".

National vaults were established to hold the gold and silver currencies. The most famous was the vault at Fort Knox, Tennessee, but there were some others as well. The Constitution gave Congress the right to set the value of gold and silver. The price of gold was not allowed by law, to "float" according to supply and demand. Only the American government could decree (for American gold sales) the price gold could be sold for, and all gold used to back paper currency was mandated to be stored in the federal government's treasury vaults.

This policy came to be known as "the gold standard", and it remained in force for almost two centuries after it was first implemented. The value of silver was further fixed with respect to the value of gold, and it too, was not allowed to "float" according to market supply and demand.

These two government actions (monopolizing the coining of all currencies, and the establishment of the gold standard) worked pretty well to stabilize the currency, nationwide, eliminate inflation in paper currencies not backed by gold, and re-establish a perception of banks as secure depositories for the general citizenry.

These policies didn't work out quite so well in terms of stopping counterfeiting activities. With only one printing plate per denomination to have to worry about, the best engravers didn't have to spread themselves so thin.

Also, with a single plate per denomination, whatever phony currency was good enough to escape detection, was now good all over the country (and world), rather than just in a specific region, served by a given bank. This allowed counterfeiters much greater freedom in terms of expanding their operations nationwide, and worldwide. (The law of unintended consequences).

In an attempt to minimize the danger to the economy that occurred due to forgers copying U.S. government currency plates, and printing money not backed by gold, in 1865, the government enacted a law authorizing establishment of a currency enforcement group known as the "secret service". That group's activities still, today, include protecting the integrity of the nation's paper currencies. The secret service's role also includes providing protection for members of the executive branch, and the secret service is now involved in international currency operations as well. Things went along pretty good for a while.

Protecting against inside-dealing in banks, and bank "runs"

Late in the 19th century, and early in the 20th century, self-dealing by bankers was determined to be a significant problem. It wasn't a good thing when bankers acted together to lend themselves the depositors' money for outside (private) business ventures. The thought here being that the bankers might not be all that objective when considering loans to themselves.

Some of these inside loans were pretty thinly disguised. A bank executive from Bank A would loan money to a bank executive from Bank B, and vice versa. The bankers weren't strictly speaking lending their own banks money to themselves, but the net effect was about the same, and just as dangerous.

Periodically, some bankers were also found to be guilty of allowing the bank's contingency reserve holdings to be drawn down to an unsafe level, by making loans with money that prudence dictated should have been reserve fund money. In the event of a large depositor making an unexpected withdrawal, the bank with an inadequate contingency reserve, might find itself without enough cash on hand to meet the depositor's withdrawal request. When a bank couldn't honor a withdrawal request in full, at the time it was presented, the word quickly spread to other depositors, and a "run on the bank" might (and often did) ensue.

A "run" on the bank occurred when all of the bank's depositors asked for all their money back, at the same time. Since most of the bank's money was out on loan to other individuals and businesses, there was generally no way that a bank could immediately return all of (every) depositor's money to them, if everybody decided to withdraw their money at the same time. (Remember the Christmas story of the run on the Building and Loan in Frank Capra's "It's Wonderful Life"?).

Banks typically kept a certain percentage of their total deposits available in a contingency reserve, to accommodate those withdrawing money in nominal amounts, and to cover losses from loans that went bad. A "run" on the bank resulted in the bank closing its doors when it ran out of money with which to accommodate depositors who requested a withdrawal of their funds. Once word went out that the bank was in trouble, the rush by depositors to get their money out of the bank, became a stampede.

The end result of a "run" was that the bank in question was put into receivership. Depositors might have to wait months or even years to get their deposits back. Some depositors received less than full value for their deposits when they were eventually paid. Some depositors received little or no money back at all, if the bank's financial condition was very bad.

A "run on the bank" was often a catastrophic event, not only for the bank's owners, but for the bank's depositors as well, since no workable means existed at the time to allow the government to restore the bank's financial health quickly. Not all bank depositors were wealthy individuals who could stand such losses when they occurred. Many were average citizens saving for a home, or retirement. Homes were not typically financed at 5% down, there was no Social Security to meet retirement income needs, and few, if any, businesses maintained private retirement programs for their employees, at this point in time.

The Federal Reserve Banks

In part to prevent these types of disasters, the Federal government intervened and established a "central bank" body charged with helping banks in distress. The Federal Reserve Act, enacted during this period (1913), established a group of twelve privately owned, regionally distributed banks that had the power to work with the Treasury to create additional money whenever it was needed for meeting extraordinary needs. The stockholders of the various Federal Reserve banks were primarily wealthy domestic and foreign investors, and commercial banks that from time to time got money from the Fed.

The Federal Reserve Bank actually constituted the third attempt by the U.S. government to establish a "central bank". The First Bank of the United States, and the Second Bank of the United States had been formed following the Revolutionary and Civil Wars, but each failed to gain the acceptance and support of the banking community in general. After the failure of the Second Bank of the United States, exchange rates were, for a time, set de facto by a Boston Bank that was considered the soundest in the country. However, the Boston bank lacked the ability to coin money on its own, or to make large loans to banks in trouble, both of which functions would be needed by a "central" bank.

At the outset, the Federal Reserve was essentially that of a money creating and policing organization. The original idea behind the establishment of the "Fed" as it came to be known was to provide a mechanism for aiding banks in short term distress, by "loaning" them funds, backed by treasury bonds, if an unexpected run on the bank's reserves was to occur. As time went by, the Fed expanded its role far beyond that limited goal.

Banking laws relating to self-dealing were further strengthened, disallowing self-dealing by bankers, and disallowing collusion between executives at different banks loaning money to each other as well.

For the most part, these government actions were effective in achieving their objectives. Some scoundrel bankers still managed to self-deal, and collude with other like-minded bankers, but the instances of both of these types of activity dropped dramatically, and instances of depositor's losing most or all of their money due to "runs" on the bank, and outright bank failures, were fewer and farther between.

War and its impacts on government economic policies

Between 1865 and 1925, the U.S. found itself engaged in other military conflicts. The most notable were the Spanish-American War and World War I. Between 1865 and 1925 there were also a series of economic recessions or depressions, some pretty serious. In 1907 there was a banking panic, when an inordinate number of banks failed. In one 30-year stretch there was a depression like clockwork, every ten years (1873, 1883, and 1893). In 1921 there was another bank crisis of significant proportions. And, in 1917, along came World War I, the "war to end all wars".

Paying for wars, handling banking crises, and restoring economies following depressions was seldom cheap; and paying for ours, during this period, was no exception. As extraordinary expenses relating to military actions, banking crises, and economic recoveries mounted, the government sometimes found that it needed more money, out of the total that was already printed up and in circulation, than existed in gold and silver value in the nation's vaults.

The government acted to cure the deficit caused from financing the recoveries from depressions and paying off war-related debts in two ways:

First, in 1913, the Constitution was amended to enact a law requiring all citizens to pay a percentage of their gross income to the federal government. This tax came to be known as the "income tax". There were no deductions calculated in before assessing the tax. Low income Americans were exempt. It was originally set at less than three percent of each citizen's gross income, and no-one involved really expected it to ever get any higher than that. In fact, it was presumed at the time, that the "income tax" might even be repealed in a few years-time, when its revenues were no longer needed to retire loans made by the government to pay off war-related expenses.

Secondly, the government acted to change the dollar per ounce price that gold (and therefore silver) was valued at, by revaluing the price upward.

The biggest benefactor of the "upward revaluation" policy change, was the U.S. government itself. Once the value of an ounce of gold was decreed to be more than before, the value of each ounce of gold already stored in the various national vaults, became greater (on paper anyway). The most notable effect of this policy change was to allow the government to print many more paper dollars than they could previously have printed, without having to add any gold to the treasury to back up the paper currency at redemption time; and to use the dollars thus created to help pay off the nation's war-related expenses, finance economic recoveries following depressions, and supply additional dollars thereafter needed by an expanding economy, after wars and depressions ended.

> It will be seen in retrospect that this was the point in time when the government shifted its emphasis relating to monetary policy away from being a protector of citizens deposits held in banks, to that of being a provider of paper currency whenever an extraordinary need arose.

The U.S Becomes a Creditor Nation

One of the most significant economic effects of WWI, was to elevate the U.S. from the status of being a debtor nation, to that of being a creditor nation. While WWI was an expensive proposition for the United States, it was a significantly more expensive proposition for the European countries involved. England and France had borrowed heavily from the U.S. to finance their own war efforts prior to the U.S. entering the fight. Once the war was over, the U.S. government insisted on repayment of the war debts run up by our allies. At the end of the war, our allies were financially strapped, and not well equipped to begin immediately paying off their war-loans to the U.S..

Germany, who lost the war, was ordered by the victors to pay restitution to the winners. The payments were termed "reparations". Germany was broke, like the other European countries involved in WWI, and not well equipped to immediately begin paying restitution to the allies. Within a year after beginning repayments to the allies, Germany defaulted on its reparation payments.

The failure of Germany to meet its reparation payments to the allies as they came due, made it difficult for America's allies to repay their war debts to us as they came due. (Cause and effect). The U.S. was new to the business of being a creditor nation, and had little experience dealing with circumstances wherein nations owing us money didn't pay up on time. The U.S. government took a hard line position, demanding payments when due, and making threats when payments were either not paid on time, or not paid at all.

In response to the U.S. government's hard line on debt repayment, the U.S.'s European debtors, who had been allies during the conflict, cranked up their economies, using devalued currencies (currencies not backed by anything at all), and exported cheap goods to the U.S., as a means of getting enough income to repay their war-debts to the U.S.

Beginning in the mid-1920's, the U.S. government acted to protect U.S. businesses from the threat of cheap imports, by imposing steep tariffs against goods coming in from Europe. The goal was noble, but the outcome was unexpected. American businesses were protected, but prices escalated for foreign goods used by American industry, and the European nations also responded with tariffs against American goods coming into their countries. Exporters on both sides were adversely affected, since the tariffs served to make their goods more expensive in the importing country, and that served to reduce to some degree the number of people who could afford to buy them.

The worldwide "trade war" that resulted from our government's initial tinkering with the paper-gold exchange rate, demanding immediate repayment of allied war-debts, and establishing high protective tariffs designed to protect American businesses from cheap European imported goods, built up over time. Not all countries imposed higher tariffs in retribution, at equal levels, or at the same time. But, like a malignant growth, the animosity and retaliatory trade practices continued to grow throughout the latter part of the 1920's, into the early 1930's, ultimately with disastrous worldwide consequences.

Near the end of this cycle, in the early 1930's, the now infamous Smoot-Hawley Tariff was enacted. It is often credited with being the single most important factor in causing the worldwide economic depression which followed soon after its enactment. But, in truth, the Smoot-Hawley Tariff was probably more like the straw that broke the camel's back.

Tariffs had always been a significant part of American foreign trade on both sides. In fact, one of the reasons that no "income tax" was needed during the first 150 years of U.S. history was due in large part to our government's taxing all the imported commerce used to build this nation. A whole set of events preceded the Smoot-Hawley Tariff that set the stage for the depression era. The most significant causes of the great depression of the 30's was a combination of well intentioned, but disastrous, government policies relating to:

1. Devaluation of paper currencies and inflating the currency supplies to pay off war debts

2. U.S. insistence upon immediate repayment of war-related debt and reparation payments from Germany and U S allies

3. Establishment of high tariffs by the U.S. during the mid-1920's, in order to protect American businesses from competition by cheap European imported goods; when European Nations sought to raise money for repaying war-debts to the U.S., by exporting their goods, made with cheap labor, and paid for with devalued currencies, into the U.S.

The Smoot-Hawley Tariff got a bum rap.

1925-1940

The Roaring Twenties

While much of this was going on, some entrepreneurial types were taking advantage of the currency inflation. As prices spiraled upward for items bought by everyday citizens, due to worldwide inflationary pressures, companies making these products saw their sales increase dramatically. A widget that sold last year for $1, might sell this year for $2. Even if the company sold the same number of widgets each year, the company's sales doubled in dollar volume, and assuming the company's profit margin stayed the same, the company's profits doubled in absolute dollar amounts each year too.

As publicly traded companies sales and profits were seen to be rising rapidly, by stock market investors, including some banks buying for their own portfolios; individual citizen investors felt increasingly comfortable buying stocks at today's prices, in expectation that they could sell them sometime in the near future at a healthy profit.

The government benefited from the profits being made in the stock market, and the increased profits, in absolute terms, being reaped by business. The "income tax" took its share of every dollar increase paid to workers, profits reaped by stock market investors, and businesses whose profits were soaring.

The banks benefited from the loans made to stock market investors, when the stocks held as collateral paid dividends, and when the stocks were sold at a profit, and the principal and interest on the loans was repaid.

Most workers were happy, because the unions saw to it that as company sales and profits went up, workers' wages and benefits went up too. As long as there was money available for the gamblers (investors) to buy the stocks with, repay their bank loans used to buy stock with, for consumers to buy the products with, and for the factories to pay their workers higher wages with, the currency inflation spiral appeared to benefit everybody involved.

But the perception of good times ahead was based upon a false premise: namely that there would always be enough demand for the stocks, and enough money to pay for the ever increasing costs of goods being purchased, and stocks being traded.

The Crash of '29, and the Great Depression (1932-1939)

The great stock market crash of 29 occurred because the banks had lent ordinary citizens savings, to gamblers in the stock market. The gamblers in turn, couldn't repay the loans when the stock market went south. Net result, without the protection of any kind of savings insurance, the ordinary citizen lost all his or her savings when the banks went broke, and closed down. Not a pretty sight.

Even before the great stock market crash of 1929, some in the Government had expressed alarm at the amount of borrowed money that was being thrown into the stock market. The stock market during the late 1920's was, in essence, a market whose actions were largely based upon, and guided by, the "bigger fool theory". The bigger fool theory states that no matter how foolish one buyer is, and/or how little the purchased item is actually worth, there will always be an even bigger fool come along somewhere down the road, to later take the first fool out at a profit.

Even as some government officials were expressing concern over the amount of money leaving banks to finance gambling in the stock market; the Federal Reserve arm of the same government was acting, before the stock market crash, to try to provide a means of increasing the amount of money available to the banks, in order to keep the banks supplied with enough money to allow the banks to keep lending money to investors "on margin".

Trading on Margin

Throughout 1928 and most of 1929, banks provided easy credit to stock market investors, who purchased stock with the borrowed money. The typical stock purchase made with borrowed money called for the bank to establish a safety margin of sorts by requiring the borrower to put up a certain percentage of the money for stock purchase personally.

The bank further generally required that in the event the stock price went down (for "long" purchases), the bank could require that the borrower immediately increase his or her stake in the loan, by paying off some predetermined amount immediately upon demand. Lending on margin against stocks was a very risky business. In essence if an investor with established credit wished to borrow money to buy some stock valued at $1000, the bank might establish a "margin" of $100, representing a percentage of the total price of the stock that had to be paid up-front by the borrower, with the stipulation that a margin "call" could be made for some additional amount of money to be put in by the borrower, immediately and on demand, in the event the stock's value dropped.

The bank didn't require that the borrower's down payment could not, itself, be made with money borrowed somewhere else. Many crafty investors found ways to finance 100% of their stock purchases.

The whole deal really rested on the bank accepting the borrower's notion as to how the stock would increase in value, and how he or she would then be able to repay the entire amount, with interest, with the stock itself being the sole collateral for the loan. In the event a banker got nervous about a particular loan for which the only collateral was the stock itself, the banker could make a "margin call" and the borrower was required to make an immediate repayment to the bank of the "margin" amount.

If the borrower couldn't repay the margin amount (immediately) when requested to do so, the bank could foreclose and take possession of the stock itself. Of course, once a foreclosure action was taken, if the value of the stock itself was not enough to cover the principal on the loan, the bank was out of luck, and would have to absorb a loss in the amount of the difference between the amount owed by the borrower, and what was received upon selling the stock.

An interesting thing about the great crash of `29 was the fact it was partially precipitated not by the banks running out of money to loan, but by many investors betting that (that) would happen sooner than it actually did.

By early 1929, it was apparent to many stock market investors that foreign investment in U.S. stocks was tapering off, and that worldwide production was in danger of outstripping demand for goods being purchased by U.S. consumers.

Selling Short

Many stock market investors were astute enough to see that the game couldn't continue indefinitely, and began planning a way to get out of the market, months before the great crash of `29. But, turtle nature being what it is, instead of just selling their holdings at a profit, paying off their bank loans, and walking away from it all rich, many decided to gamble further, and try to make even more money while the stocks were falling in value.

They began "selling short", often on margin (credit), betting that stocks had reached their peak in value, that banks were nearly out of money to loan for increased purchases, that worldwide inventories were overbuilt, and that the prices of stocks, in general, would therefore soon begin to drop dramatically. If that happened, the "short sellers" were well positioned to reap additional profits as the stock prices fell.

"Selling short" for those of you turtles out there that aren't coupon clippers, is a process by which investors can make money on stocks whose prices are falling. Essentially it works like this:

An investor looks into his or her crystal ball and determines that a particular stock is overpriced, and will soon fall in price, possibly due to other investors making the same determination, and starting to sell off their holdings of that particular stock. When the daily number of "sell" orders rises for a particular stock offering, that stocks price typically starts to fall, somewhat proportional to the increase in "sell" orders being received by the brokers from their clients.

The "short seller" borrows some shares of stock (not money, but actual certificates of stock) from a broker, and immediately sells them (probably to or through the same broker) at today's price. He then has the money from today's sale in his or her pocket, to do with as he or she pleases.

The debt owed to the broker who lent the stock is not related to the price of the stock.. Instead, the "short seller" signs a note saying he or she will repay to the broker the same number of shares of stock borrowed, on or before a particular future date in time... regardless of what the stock may be worth in the future.

If the stock price falls, as the "short seller" is betting it will, he or she takes a part of the money they sold the borrowed shares for, and repurchases the same number of shares at the lower price, and repays the number of shares borrowed, to the broker that the shares were originally borrowed from.

The difference between the higher price the "short seller" got when he or she first sold the borrowed shares, and the lower price paid to buy back the same number of shares at the lower price, constitutes the "short sellers" profit.

Timing is Everything

By October of 1929, a significant number of influential stock market investors had decided that stocks were priced all out of reason to the actual value of the companies offering them, that banks were about out of money to loan, that worldwide inventories were overbuilt, and that the market was therefore poised to drop sharply. As a result, they (in significant numbers) began "selling short". But their timing was off.

Instead of falling as the big gamblers predicted, the stocks they sold "short" continued to climb in price. What many forgot was the old saying to the effect that "for a stock sale to occur, there must be someone else buying that feels just as strongly that the stock will rise in price in the future".

The brokers began making margin calls to cover the "short sales" that weren't going as the investors had gambled that they would. The investors now had to sell parts of their holdings at a loss, to cover the margin calls. The excess of selling over buying, in order to cover margin calls, then caused the stocks being sold to start falling in price.

The falling stock prices, caused by "short sellers" covering their margin calls, hurt the portfolio values of other investors holding a "long" position (those betting the stock price would go up) in those same stocks. Those betting that stocks would continue to rise (stocks often also bought on margin with borrowed funds) then started to get margin calls when the stocks they borrowed against began to fall in price, rather than rise.

These ("long" position) investors too, then had to start selling some of their other holdings in order to meet "margin calls" by their banks. This group's selling then caused the stocks being sold to cover their margin calls, to fall in price, further accelerating the number of margin calls occurring throughout the system. Finally, at about this stage in the game, foreign investors in U.S. stocks also began selling their holdings at an accelerated rate. Stocks reacted by falling still further in price. In relatively short order, panic set in, and everybody started selling everything they had to just try to get out alive.

Banks holding large loans covered by stocks whose prices were falling rapidly, began seeing "runs" on their deposits by those fearing that their money would not be there if they waited for things to shake out.

The Federal Reserve Bank(s) reacted cautiously to the emerging crisis in the banking system. Perhaps thinking that the dislocation was a temporary phenomenon, the Fed was most notable by their absence during the early stages of the bank crisis. It has to be noted here, that this was the first time since the Fed had been formed in 1913, that a crisis of such proportions had presented itself. In 1921 a short-lived recession had occurred, and related to it a banking crisis of lesser scale…but nothing of this magnitude.

Whatever the reason, the Fed elected at the outset to let the markets and the banks try to sort things out on their own. By the time the Fed got really involved, the crisis had grown to such a scale, that Fed intervention was insufficient to bring things back to normal in the short term. Hundreds of banks, large and small, were placed in government receivership.

The biggest losers of the stock market crash of `29, and the related high number of bank failures which followed the stock market crash, were the average citizens who never participated in the folly, but saw their life savings lost; as bank after bank went bankrupt, when the banks could not recover the citizens money that they had loaned to the gamblers; and the stocks that the banks had accepted as collateral became worthless.

Fixing the Blame, but not the Problem

After the damage was done, the government blamed the whole thing on the banks, and foreign governments. Actually, there was plenty of blame to go around.

It is fact that the U.S. government's actions in arbitrarily revaluing upward the gold held in the treasury, had been a catalytic agent in precipitating the worldwide inflationary spiral that caused the stocks to rise falsely in value.

It is also fact that the U.S. government's insistence on immediate repayment of war loans and German reparation payments fueled the initial dumping of cheap foreign imports into the U.S.

It is also fact that the U.S. was the first to levy very high tariffs against European foreign goods coming into the U.S., as a means of protecting American businesses from the cheap European imports, and that these actions resulted in reciprocal tariffs being set up against American goods exported to European countries, which ultimately resulted in an all-out worldwide trade war.

It is also fact that treasury officials knew well in advance of the crash that stocks were seriously overpriced, and that the federal bank auditors knew that the banks were overextended in terms of lending against stocks whose value was inflated, but did not act to defuse the growing crisis.

It is also fact that the Federal Reserve's election to not intervene strongly, at an early stage in the banking crisis (*which was the primary reason it was established in the first place*) was a direct cause of the failure of many hundreds of regional banks.

The government nonetheless denied that they were in any way responsible for what happened.

> The "roaring twenties" represent the period in time when the capital markets in the U.S. fundamentally changed the basic nature of their function from that of being a place where businesses sought capital for seeding new ventures and growing established companies, to that of a place where money was invested in stocks primarily based upon an expectation that the value of the stock itself would rise or fall by some margin, over a prescribed period of time, based mostly upon hype-driven factors.

The banks that failed could not deny their part in the debacle. Their failures spoke more loudly than the denials of their executives. But the government didn't fail. It was badly crippled, but still functioning. Then the government set about to "make sure something like this never happens again".

Band-Aids to Stop the Hemorrhage

Part of the government's actions related to prosecuting bankers who were involved in some questionable loans to friends (instead of loaning it to themselves as they had in the past). Part of their actions related to establishing another government body to protect depositor's savings.

The Federal Deposit Insurance Corporation (FDIC) was established to dispel worry on the part of those who still had some money left, and encourage them to again put their money in a nationally chartered bank.

The FDIC carrot was a promise by the government to reimburse depositors, from the U.S. treasury itself, up to a prescribed limit, in the event the bank the depositor's money was in failed in the future. This was not a retroactive type action. Those already hurt by bank failures in the late 20's and throughout the 30's were not reimbursed for their losses. The new "depositor's insurance" only applied to deposits made after the FDIC was created.

The government acted to again require Nationally chartered banks to return to the previous policy that required the banks to hold a larger percentage of their total funds available in a contingency reserve, to meet unexpected withdrawals and bad loans.

The Federal Reserve also began in earnest by 1933 (three years after the crash on Wall Street) to infuse failing banks with treasury funds sufficient in scale to keep them afloat.

But the government's "corrective" actions were too little, and too late. The combination of the stock market crash of 1929, coupled with failure of hundreds of U.S. banks, and further coupled with the escalation of worldwide inflationary pressures caused by devaluing paper currencies in countries all over the world, and capped off by an all-out trade war between trading nations, proved to be more than even the U.S. economy could bear.

Given that both the banks and the governments were broke, worldwide, and the stock market was a shambles, the normal sources of capital for business expansion and restructuring weren't there. World trade in farm goods dried up. Banks began foreclosing on farmers unable to repay their loans for annual operating expenses.

Factories, overbuilt to supply goods worldwide began mass worker layoffs, as demand for their goods fell sharply. Without foreign markets to purchase their goods, factories became unable to repay their operating loans, and banks again foreclosed. Workers lost their jobs by the millions.

By 1932, the U.S. economy was in dire straits. Given that the United States had, at the time, become one of the largest markets in the world, for all types of goods, the effect of the U.S. economy sinking into severe decline had a predictable ripple effect on the economy of every nation that traded goods and services with (or in) the United States at the time.

The eight-year period from 1932 through 1939 (inclusive), during which time the markets sorted themselves out, and the government acted to restore confidence in the banks and the nation's financial health, came to be known as "the great depression".

And it was a depressing time indeed.

Worldwide.

The Terrible 1930's -
Climbing out of the Economic Depression

While government officials held themselves blameless for events leading up to the stock market crash of 1929, and the deep economic depression that followed the devaluation of the nation's currency supply, and the ensuing global trade war, the citizens whose lives were severely disrupted by these events weren't in such a forgiving mood.

The Congress and administration changed hands. The new President promised a "chicken in every pot, and a car in every garage". The President also stated that "the only thing we have to fear, is fear itself".

That was a lie.

There was still much to fear, including joblessness, starvation, lack of warm clothing, lack of medical attention when needed, and a lack of shelter to ward off cold winters for whole families and entire communities.

And, for the next eight years' time, those fears were frequently realized.

The nation was starting over, almost from scratch. There were not many factories producing at anywhere near capacity, and fewer citizens than ever, with money enough to buy any goods that were produced. As economic problems worsened, the general public became more and more depressed over their circumstances, and their seeming inability to alter them.

The new President understood the need to restore a positive frame of mind, as the first step toward full economic recovery. Though born to privilege, he seemed also to understand the desperation felt by the working men who had lost not only their jobs, but their self-respect, due to their inability to provide for their families.

The new President acted to restore a measure of hope to those displaced through no fault of their own. He urged the congress to establish a number of government supported work projects, designed to improve America's infrastructure, and at the same time, get displaced workers back to work, and restore their self-confidence.

> The "Great Depression" period in our history was also the point in time when the government first began to expand its charter; from that of being solely the guardian of each American's fundamental rights; to that of assuming some measure of responsibility for each individual citizen's economic welfare, at some prescribed level.

There was little money in the nation's treasuries with which to support any new programs, and much money would be needed. At the urging of the president, Congress acted to allow further devaluation of the currency supply (still tied to and backed by gold) to create the money with which to pay for the government work programs. Between 1929 and 1932 the Treasury again revised upward the price of gold from $20 per ounce to $35 per ounce. That constituted a revision downward for paper currency in value of about 43%. That is, each existing dollar became worth only 57 cents, in terms of its ability to be redeemed for gold or silver.

On the bright side, the currency devaluation allowed the government to print more than 40% more dollars in paper currency with which to pay for the new government programs. Depressions are counter-inflationary. That is, prices for everything go down, during a true economic depression. This meant that the government could buy more goods and services with the same number of dollars, than they could have bought with the same number of dollars before the crash. And by devaluing the paper currency, there were now almost twice as many paper dollars available to them to spend.

The Congress also acted to significantly alter the "income tax". Citizens lucky enough to still have an income, saw a much larger amount of their income taken by the federal government. The progressive nature of the income tax provided that the more money a citizen earned, the higher would be the citizen's tax rate.

Again, it was fully anticipated that once the nation's financial health was restored, the income tax could probably be repealed or at least scaled way back to almost nothing. And, Americans being the kind of people that they are, those with the highest incomes, and therefore the highest tax rates, didn't complain too loudly. Most of those who were well off were willing to contribute disproportionately toward helping their fellow citizens who were less fortunate get back on their feet.

And, the banks didn't complain about the inflation in the nation's currency supply, though they knew at the time, that it was an unsound financial policy both in the long and the short term. Without the inflation in the currency supply, many banks couldn't have stayed afloat, and they knew it.

Additionally, there was no danger this time around of retaliatory practices by foreign investors and/or governments. Foreign nations were hurting even more than the U.S. was. None of our former trading partners was in a position to be vindictive. Everybody was too busy just trying to stay alive. It is said that desperate times require desperate measures, and these were desperate times.

Everybody involved at the time, (banks, government officials, and individual citizens) probably understood that the choices being made were of the nature of "choosing between the lesser of evils". It is likely that the majority of those involved in bringing about these changes in the relationship between individual citizens and their government expected the extraordinary measures being taken at the time in order to restore the countries financial health to be temporary in nature.

It just didn't turn out that way.

(A government body or program once in motion tends to stay in motion, unless acted on by an outside force).

European Consequences of the Great Depression of the 1930's

Almost unnoticed in all the confusion at home, things were going even worse in some other countries around the world, most notably countries in Europe. While the worldwide economic decline hit America hard, coming as it did right on the heels of World War I, America was at least a winner in that war. Germany's economy had been virtually destroyed during WWI, and Germany had not had sufficient time to be rebuild their economy to any degree, when the "great worldwide depression" hit.

Following the example of America (and other nations as well) the German government resorted to inflating their nation's currency supply in order to fund government work projects, including restoring the nation's military machine. But Germany was a nation more dependent on its neighbors than was the United States.

The United States was blessed with natural resources sufficient to supply all of its own internal needs. Germany wasn't. When the United States inflated its currency supply, the only ones that had to approve of the measure, and be willing to accept its consequences, were the American citizens and American businesses affected by the devaluation. However, when Germany devalued its currency supply, the measures were subject to approval (or disapproval) of every European nation that Germany depended upon for trading in the goods needed to rebuild their country after WWI.

In part, due to some remaining hard feelings over Germany's actions in WWI, and in part because they didn't assign much worth to the German paper currency, which was not backed by much gold, many European nations either refused to accept German paper currency in payment for goods purchased, or required many more German (marks) in payment, when they did accept German currencies at all. The result was an unparalleled level of inflation in German paper currencies, which came to be termed "hyperinflation", which hit its highest level in 1923.

The German currency situation was "confederate money" all over again, but on an even grander scale. At one point in time it took a wheelbarrow full of marks to purchase a single piece of bread. Not a loaf. Just a single piece. German paper currency ultimately became worthless to the extent that not even German citizens would accept it. "Black" markets sprung up to allow citizens to exchange goods and services without the use of German currencies.

Just as the economic distress in the United States precipitated a change in the U.S. government in the 1930's, the economic distress in Germany precipitated a change in the German government in the 1930's. During the period of the great depression, a Corporal in the German militia was elevated to the equivalent of the Presidency in America.

The Corporal Takes Over Europe

Adolf Hitler was, if nothing else, a man of action. Hitler was cunning, shrewd and clever, if not overly intelligent. Other adjectives that have often been used to describe Adolph Hitler are mean spirited, manipulative, and devious. Because of the times, and where he was born, he became a ruthless, bureaucratic, war-mongering demagogue. If he had been born in America, after WWII, he would probably have just become a lawyer. (Just kidding. A little turtle humor there at the expense of our attorney population).

In Germany, as was the case in America, desperate times called for desperate measures. And Germany was desperate beyond anything America had known. Unable to persuade other European nations to willingly accept German currencies, Hitler began using the military might at his disposal to coerce trade agreements with Germany's neighbors.

Ultimately, more drastic steps were taken by the German government, and its military might was used to capture the other neighboring European countries outright, thereby allowing free use by Germany of the monies in their treasuries, their manufacturing plants and capacities, their citizens as slave labor, and their natural resources.

In Germany, as had happened in America, most government officials, banks, and individual citizens went along with Hitler's plans at the time. It is probable that there, as in America, everybody saw their actions as taking the form of "the lesser of evils". Most involved probably, at the outset, rationalized the extraordinary measures, and intended to make things right with the captured countries after the economic crises was under control.

It is doubtful that Hitler, himself held any such magnanimous thoughts about how things would go after the financial crisis was over. But the average German citizen probably felt a bit uneasy at times about the use of military might being brought to bear against their European neighbors, in order to resolve the immediate financial crisis.

None of which excuses the bad behavior on the part of those in Germany that resorted to, endorsed, or willingly (or even grudgingly) went along with, such policies as a means of restoring the countries financial health.

> ...the road to hell is paved with good intentions.

While no one denies that Germany's troubles were mostly its own doing, there is a certain fatal element involved in what happened to Germany following World War I. One has to wonder how the German people might have responded to a despot like Hitler, if there had been enough time after WWI, to rebuild Germany's economy, before the great worldwide depression of the 1930's came bearing down on them. They might have tried to tough it out more like we did. <u>We</u> didn't attack any other countries and confiscate their treasuries and natural resources, or kill and/or enslave their people, (at least not during the great depression of the 1930's).

Or, maybe not. We'll never know.

The Control of Oil

It is generally acknowledged that a significant reason that America and the allies prevailed during WWI, without greater loss of life on the side of the allied forces, was that our side controlled the flow of oil-related products within the conflict.

The German war machine ran out of gas (literally) during WWI, allowing the allies an easier victory than might have otherwise been forthcoming. This happened because the allied forces had access to sufficient petroleum reserves and refining plants to just keep pouring it on. And Germany didn't.

Germany's government saw the squeeze on oil coming, and attempted to keep supplies coming to their military. The allied forces effectively shut off the oil routes to inland Europe, and essentially starved the German war machine into submission. Both sides learned a lesson from this experience, and resolved to exert control over worldwide oil supplies in the future, especially those supplies coming from newly found reserves in middle-eastern countries, and North Africa. Not only did this make sense from a war machine standpoint, but it had become obvious that petroleum was a necessary element in the building of industrial strength in every area, war related or not.

Beginning at the end of WWI, and continuing through most of the 1920's, Germany wasn't in a very good position to compete in the race to control the middle east's oil supplies. They were broke, after losing the war; and had seen much of their military machine disassembled by the allies in retribution for their war actions. Germany thus wasn't in much of a position immediately following WWI to bargain from a money standpoint, or to use military force to coerce middle east countries into dealing with them.

The Seven Sisters

But three western allied countries were well positioned to make a run at controlling Middle East's oil fields, and they proceeded to do so. The three allied countries were the United States, Great Britain, and Holland.

Each of these countries already had within its borders an oil company giant, with significant resources of its own, willing and eager to expand its share of the worldwide oil market. Each also had powerful military resources that could be brought to bear, in the event middle eastern governments proved difficult to reason with.

In the United States, Standard Oil was the major player. In Britain, British Petroleum was equally strong. In Holland, Royal Dutch (Shell) Petroleum was about the same size and strength of the other two.

In 1928, these three companies joined with four more American oil companies (Texaco, Gulf, SoCal, and Mobil) and formed the first oil cartel, named appropriately enough "The International Oil Cartel". They were more often referred to (not always affectionately) as "the seven sisters".

These seven companies met and agreed, without first consulting with the middle-east countries involved, about how the oil reserves of the Middle East would be divided up amongst themselves.

There were some difficulties encountered along the way to gaining control of the oil fields of the middle eastern countries. One difficulty was that, divided as the Bedouin tribes might be that occupied much of the middle-east (about many subjects), there was something of a consensus among them, that their countries resources should not be unduly exploited by western countries.

Some of these feelings went back in time all the way to the religious Crusades, when western European Nations first invaded

Persian countries, took over their trade routes, and plundered their resources.

Some Bedouin tribes even vowed to go to war against the western countries, and their own western-backed internal rulers, who they determined were not operating in the best interests of the majority of their country's tribes and citizens.

The western governments of the countries housing the seven giant oil companies worked behind the scenes to smooth the way for the oil companies to get free reign over the oil reserves in the middle east.

In part, they sought to back rulers, in each affected middle-east country having substantial oil reserves that were willing to work with the oil companies involved to "develop" the country's oil reserves.

The allied governments involved advanced significant funds to chosen rulers in countries rich in oil deposits, to help them build infrastructure needed to process and export the oil, once extracted from the ground. The western governments also funded military operations for the rulers in the oil rich countries whose resources were being "developed". The military establishment was ostensibly put in place to protect the infrastructure developed with western dollars.

Some powerful Middle East rulers, supported by western financing, came under criticism from their own people, who felt that their country, its citizens, and its natural resources, were again being exploited, without the general citizenry benefiting proportionally. Some groups of highly-motivated, middle-east individuals took up arms against the ruling factions in their own countries, ostensibly to halt the exploitation. The ruling faction's military might then was often turned against the country's own citizens, to stop the dissent, and was sufficient for many years to hold the dissidents at bay.

A lot of middle east citizens paid with their lives for trying to resist the ruling factions supported by western governments who in turn were supporting western oil companies. For almost a half of a century following WWI, the seven previously mentioned oil companies, and their related governments, were successful in controlling Middle Eastern oil fields. But not without building up a lot of resentment on the part of many middle east citizens who felt that they were being taken advantage of by their own governments, and that their country's resources were again being plundered by the west.

The oil companies' motives were clearly profit driven. Nothing wrong with that. That's what businesses do. The western government's stated motives were to keep oil from falling into the hands of evil military powers, and to assure adequate supplies of low cost oil for sustaining strong industrial growth. The western-backed, middle-eastern government's stated motives were to use money from oil-development to bring their backward countries into the modern world.

Everybody had worthwhile motives, at least on the surface, but it didn't work out nearly as slick as everybody hoped it would.

Not by a long shot.

The resentment that many middle east citizens now harbor against western governments and western-based businesses, stems from this period immediately following WWI, when western countries and companies set into motion plans to control the oil reserves in that region of the globe.

The great depression era was the point in time, when the U.S. government first elected to collude with individual businesses to monopolize **other** countries natural resources in the name of "national security".

This policy effectively made it impossible for those middle-east countries whose resources were being taken for use in the west, to control their own destiny, and to function as if in a "free-market". environment.

Happenings of the period along the Pacific Rim in Asia

The Middle East's oil fields were not the only natural resources coveted by western countries, among them Britain, France, and the United States. Since early in the 20th century, the American Government had intervened on behalf of businesses extracting natural resources from other countries, half a world away, along the pacific rim in Asia.

The "gunboat diplomacy" used to attempt to persuade China to allow "development" of its resources was well documented, though depicted as an internal "rebellion". The "rebellion" was rooted in China, as in the Middle East, in disenchantment by the country's citizens, with foreigners assuming control over the country's resources. Korea, Manchuria, Java, Sumatra, Burma, Borneo, Siam (Thailand), Laos (French Indo China), and the Philippines were other Asian territories and countries that had natural resources desired by western-based businesses. The Philippines by this time had been acquired formally by the U.S.. However, in these countries, there was a measure of competition for the natural resources coming from another nation in the region that was also bent on industrializing.

Japan.

Japan, at various points in time, over the past several centuries, had invaded and occupied much of what is now considered the "Asian Pacific Rim". Japan's "holdings" at various points in time had included Korea, Manchuria, and much of what is now mainland China, with established outposts also in Malaysia, and the Philippine Islands. At one point in time, Japan's attempted occupations even included some of the outlying northern areas now owned and controlled by Russia.

And Japan, unlike the middle-east countries being courted for their oil by western businesses and governments, not only had its own ideas about who should control the region's resources, it had a significant military machine of its own with which to both enforce its will on its neighbors, and repel outsiders competing for power in the area. Japan, perhaps even more than Germany, had few natural resources of its own, and required most natural resources essential to building an industrial base, to be imported from its neighbors in the area, and further away. Japan had fears that if the U.S. based businesses gained control of the areas resources that Japan would be at the total mercy of the U.S.

At precisely the same point in time that the U.S. government was criticizing the attempts by Japan to subvert the Asian countries along the Pacific Rim, and exploit their resources and cheap labor. U.S. based businesses, with the help of the U.S. government, were doing much the same thing, in many of those same countries, and were also working at the same time to take over control of the middle east's oil fields.

Competition for the region's resources escalated both in business board rooms, and in the back rooms of the governments who wanted to control the wealth and power they represented. On the block, to be taken by the highest bidder (or strongest army) were great quantities of tin, magnesium, bauxite, manganese, and rubber, together with landed ports of call in close proximity to cheap labor. The stage was being set for another large scale conflict, at some point in time, in the not too distant future.

Nature intercedes to make things worse

As if our self-inflicted economic problems were not enough to deal with in the 1930's, nature dealt yet another blow. It stopped raining in the south-central part of the United States. The nation's "bread basket". The "bread basket", became the "dust bowl".

Farmers unable to grow crops without rain (irrigation being mostly unavailable yet) went broke and abandoned their farms and holdings, migrating to cities in hopes of finding work. Usually without much luck. Banks foreclosed on farm properties, but were neither able to work them, or sell them for enough to pay off the loans for which they had been the collateral. Most of these properties sat idle for more than a decade, waiting for a combination of resourceful immigrants, capital, and an economy strong enough to support the re-opening of the farms lost to drought and bankruptcy.

The government steps in to protect against natural disasters

In the 1930's and 1940's the government formed a plan for damming up the rivers of the drought stricken region in the central part of the country, in order to provide a means, in future years, of supplying irrigated water to the regions farms, and inexpensive electricity for homes and industry.

The Tennessee Valley Authority and the Army Corps of Engineers ultimately combined to bring about this end, over a thirty-year period of time. Over a protracted period of time, their efforts resulted in converting the Mississippi, Ohio, Tennessee, and Missouri rivers to a series of contiguous lakes.

There was considerable electric generating capacity put on line, the rivers were made more navigable, a measure of control over flooding along the lower Mississippi river valley was achieved, and the reservoirs thus created provided a source of water supplies for homes, industries and farms that was more reliable than rainfall and wells alone had been able to provide in the past.

The same principal was ultimately put into practice, with respect to virtually every major free-flowing tributary in the lower 48 states. In the northwest, the Bonneville Power Authority similarly dammed up the Columbia River and its tributaries, supplying cheap electricity to the entire northwestern section of the country. Other dams were built on the Colorado River in the Southwest, the most notable among them being the Hoover dam, which provided the electricity needed to fuel the rapid growth of Southern Arizona and Southern California.

A lot of jobs were created to supply the workforce needed to build all of the dams (and highways, and ports, and other infrastructure projects) initiated during the 1930's.

More Unintended Consequences

The dam-related benefits that accrued came with a price however. The river channeling and flood control dikes that worked to lessen flood damage along the lower Mississippi river, actually made flooding and flood damage worse, upriver, especially above St. Louis. The dams inhibited upstream spawning runs of the fish in the dammed up rivers, and whole fisheries died out, while the people who previously depended on those fisheries for a living were put out of work. The flood control dikes provided a false sense of security to many families who built homes (and whole communities) in what had previously been avoided as flood-plane lands in the upper river basins. When higher than normal runoff occurred, dams on the lower parts of these rivers caused water to build to abnormally high levels upstream. When this happened, the upstream dikes would periodically fail, and wipe out whole communities, and counties, and parts of whole states. When this happened, the Federal government would be called on to restore things to normal at taxpayer expense.

Again, the law of unintended consequences takes its toll.

At no time after the 1930's, did the government ever suggest that the flood-ravaged communities be relocated to a non-flood-plain area (if they were to be rebuilt at taxpayer expense).

> During the period that began with the great depression, the government established itself as the insurer of last resort for aiding citizens and businesses in recovering from the effects of natural disasters (floods, rains, droughts, hurricanes, tornados, fires, earthquakes, etc.). This was often the case even when the affected citizens or businesses were partially or completely responsible, themselves, for their losses. This was another "new" type of use for taxpayer dollars.

Some Government Programs designed to aid Individuals (as opposed to businesses)

The great depression era saw additional government programs put into place, designed to aid U.S. citizens. Many had had their savings for retirement wiped out by bank failures. The government responded by enacting a new program designed to supplement retirement. It was called Social Security. When it was enacted in 1935, the tax on earnings was set at one and a half percent of the first $3000 earned.

Many families had lost their homes, when the income earners job was terminated, and payments could not be made. The government responded in 1934 by enacting a program that offered banks a guaranteed repayment on behalf of the borrower, should the borrower not be able to pay off the mortgage (for any reason). The law that authorized the establishment of the Federal Housing Authority (FHA), was another outgrowth of the depression era.

Finally, the government acted to stop management exploitation of out-of-work and desperate workers by passing the Fair Labor Standards Act in 1938. The FLSA had several points to protect labor, but the one of most immediate interest to workers was the requirement that employers pay a "minimum wage" to whoever worked for them. Absent the minimum wage requirement, some businesses tended to take advantage of the desperation of those who were out-of-work, and willing to work, literally, for crumbs.

The Pound Falls

In 1931, Britain succumbed to enormous pressures to stimulate its own disaster-ridden economy by inflating its own paper currency supply. Much of the new currency was put to use increasing Britain's military strength. The military buildup was, in turn, fueled by Nazi Germany's moving aggressively against its European neighbors on the European mainland.

For over 200 years, every currency in the world had been pegged in value to the British pound sterling. Britain ruled the seas for much of that time, and it was often said that the sun never set on Great Britain, due to its far-flung colonies. When the British pound was devalued, and the price of gold and silver in Britain was allowed to "float" with market supply and demand, the thud of its fall was heard around the world.

Sir Isaac Newton must have turned over in his grave. Though it is little known, Sir Isaac was not just known for his adeptness at physics and mathematics. Newton was also for many years, beginning in 1717, the Master of the British Mint.

But, desperate times dictate desperate measures, and Britain was experiencing even greater unemployment than the U.S. was during the great depression. Riots in the streets threatened to topple the Crown. Faced with such dire circumstances, Britain opted for devaluing their currency, as a means to getting some of it in the hands of British citizens, thereby forestalling an open rebellion, stimulating their stalled economy, and providing sufficient currency in circulation for gearing up their war machine.

The devaluing of the British Pound Sterling was not an insignificant event, relegated only to importance in England. At the time the pound was uncoupled from gold and silver, the British Pound was the key currency in international trade, worldwide, and was the currency by which every other currency was measured in relative value, including the U.S. Dollar. If the pound was no longer the standard, what would the standard be?

1940-1955

Public Works aren't enough

By 1940, it had become all too apparent that public works programs, by themselves, would be insufficient to restore the U.S. to full employment. In fact, in 1937 there had been a serious backsliding in terms of recovery towards fuller employment, and a mini-depression within the larger "great depression" had wiped out most of the employment gains made between 1932 and 1937. By 1940, "net" improvement in reaching the goals set for full employment in America was far less than the government had hoped for back in 1932, when the public works projects began.

WWII

By 1940, Hitler's armies had conquered most of mainland Europe, and were threatening to conquer the rest, including Great Britain. Britain's government had initially adopted a position of placating Nazi Germany, in hopes of being spared themselves. The pacifist approach didn't work, and Germany began bombing the British Isles. Britain was (and is) an ally of the U.S., with common holdings in some areas.

War is a messy business, but on the plus side, both Britain and Germany, due to gearing up to make war on one another, had at least solved the problem of how to achieve full employment for their citizens.

Meantime, along the pacific rim in Asia, Japan was making similar inroads into mainland China, Korea, and what was then called Indochina (Siam, Laos, and Surinam), and flexing their muscles in the Philippines and Malaysia too.

Initially, the U.S. avoided direct involvement in Britain's war with the government of Germany, choosing to only lend money, and to provide military supplies and encouragement. In the pacific area however, the U.S. began moves aimed at halting the growth of Japan as an industrialized power, and aimed at solidifying its own position in terms of laying claim to the natural resources coming from that part of the world.

In the late 1930's, the U.S government provided assistance to some small countries comprising "Indochina" by way of subsidizing mercenary forces operating there. The most notable example was probably the providing of airplanes and related support for a group of U.S. mercenaries that came to be known as the "Flying Tigers". The Flying Tigers provided air support to resist the invasion of Burma and Laos from the north by Japanese forces attempting to use the "Burma Road", which was the main land-based supply arterial leading from China south to countries located on the Malaysian peninsula. China, Korea, and Manchuria were already at the time occupied by Japanese troops.

In June of 1941, The U.S. deployed warships in the Straits of Luzon, and in what was then called the "Burma Straits", placing a militarily enforced embargo on shipping into Japan, effectively stopping the flow of industrial resources coming into Japan, by way of the Indian Ocean, around the end of the Malay Peninsula. Included in the industrial supplies that were stopped from coming into Japan was oil from the Malaysia, Indonesia, Micronesia and a smaller amount from the Middle East.

The embargo by U.S. warships both threatened and angered Japan, who possibly felt that their claims in the area were better founded, and of longer duration, than were the claims of the United States.

The dissolution of the League of Nations (a forerunner of the present United Nations) left Japan with no worldwide forum to hear their arguments relating to the embargo. It probably would not have mattered anyway. The League of Nations had never had an army or any money of it's own, and depended on Western European nations for much of it's funding. Like its follow-on organization (The United Nations), the League of Nations was mostly a forum for aggrieved nations to sound off in public about the wrongs they felt were being done to them. (Moreover, neither the U.S. nor Russia had ever been League of Nation members.)

But, back to the chase. As seen earlier, the ability of the allied forces to withhold oil from Germany, had effectively starved the German war machine into submission during WWI. The same tactic seemed about to result in greatly limiting Japan's ability to compete for resources in the Asian Pacific Rim area of the globe.

Japan, with its back to the wall, and unable to get meaningful support for its position from the League of Nations, decided to come away from the emerging battle either carrying their shield, or being carried on it.

December 7, 1941 was indeed a day that would live in infamy. But, when Japan bombed Pearl Harbor, the stage had already been set for some time, for another worldwide conflict. Germany, Great Britain, and Italy, had already armed themselves to the teeth, and were at war with one another. The European underground movement was already in place, resisting the German and Italian military forces that had overrun the various European countries.

The expansionist (oil-related) policies of Great Britain, Holland, and the United States in the middle- east and northern Africa were already in direct conflict with Germany's, Italy's, and (to a lesser extent) Japan's needs to secure a supply of petroleum for their war machines, and industry in general. And, like Germany and Britain, Japan had already gained full employment by way of gearing up its military machine.

America's actions in placing a military-backed shipping embargo that resulted in stopping the flow of industrial commerce into Japan, was really just a match lit to the fuse of a stack of dynamite that had already been neatly stacked in place for nearly a decade. In retrospect, once the sea embargo was put into place against Japan in mid-1941, and given the impotency of the League of Nations at the time, Pearl Harbor, or at least an action like it somewhere in the Pacific, should have been an entirely predictable event.

Once the United States (formally) declared war on Japan, sides were quickly drawn up. The U.S. allied itself with all the resistance movements in place in Europe, and with Great Britain and Russia. Japan, Germany, and Italy had previously formed an alliance (the Tripartite Pact), so the U.S. declaring war on Japan meant that the U.S. was in effect declaring war on Germany and Italy at the same time.

World War II, the second "war to end all wars", between the "axis" and the "allies", lasted four years, cost hundreds of billions of dollars, cost millions of lives, ushered in the nuclear age, generated (more than) full employment in the United States for the first time in a quarter century, and gave birth to more government programs and bodies than had ever been dreamed of before, in every country involved in the war.

Women in the Workplace

The second World War also ushered in the beginning of the time when it would be necessary for both husband and wife to work outside the home, in order to make enough money to support the family. Industry had been forced to use women in industrial jobs normally occupied by men. The women worked out just fine, and were willing to work for less to boot. Soldiers coming home from the war were given their old jobs back, displacing the women who had performed them during the war. However, women were thereafter increasingly brought into new positions, at lower pay than their male counterparts. Over time the willingness of women to do equal work for less compensation had the effect of placing pressure on Unions to reduce their demands for pay increases.

More Devaluing of paper currencies

WWII again saw the U.S devalue its paper currencies, by again restating upward the value of gold already held in the nation's vaults. The U.S. was still, immediately following WWI, on the gold standard. During this period the printing on the paper currencies were changed to denote that each bill was a "silver certificate". Now people demanding redemption of paper currencies could be paid in silver, rather than in gold.

This change was needed to offset the fact that in the previous two decades, foreign businesses and foreign governments had taken large quantities of gold from the U.S. treasury as payment of debts due to them. Silver was easier to come by than was gold. The treasury sought to halt further outflows of gold by requiring currency redemptions in "specie" (the word economists use to describe precious metals) to be taken only in silver.

For some time, the U.S. "gold standard" had actually allowed redemption in either gold or silver metal, being patterned in this respect after Britain's measure of the value of a pound sterling. However, after the introduction of "silver certificates", paper currency could only be redeemed in Silver. The price per ounce of silver remained fixed in relationship to the price of an ounce of gold.

During the period from 1929 through 1932 the value of gold had been revised upward by the U.S. Treasury from slightly over $20 per ounce, to a bit over $35 per ounce. This resulted in devaluation in the value of paper currencies of about 43%. The action was needed to allow for printing more paper currency to cover the costs of the public works programs, and welfare programs implemented in the 30's. These programs were well intended, and were aimed at helping the U.S. recover from the great depression.

Even the (43%) currency devaluation proved inadequate to get the U.S to full employment status (or anywhere near full employment status); but it did result in putting a lot more paper currency in circulation.

The devaluation of the currency by about 43% had the predictable effect of causing prices for just about everything to go up by about 57%, over the same period of time. Cars that sold for $750 in 1929, sold for about $1200 by 1938. No major change in performance or size, just an increase in the total cost, associated with inflating (and devaluing) the existing paper currency supply.

U.S. Dollar becomes the key world currency measure

Back in 1931, Great Britain had effectively taken itself off of the gold (or sterling) standard, allowing gold and silver prices to "float" with market demand. Most European countries did likewise within the next decade. The purpose in each case was to legitimize greatly expanding the paper currency supply for the country in question, and to provide sufficient money in circulation, to pay for restoring war-torn countries, pay off war-related debts, and provide enough new currency to reinstate economic growth, following the onset of the worldwide depression.

Since every country involved was doing it, nobody much objected. However, whereas before the British Pound Sterling had been the value benchmark for the world, (including the American dollar), everybody now had to look for a new way to relate the value of their currency to the value of each other countries' currency.

The British Pound Sterling had become the benchmark for measuring all currencies against when Britain ruled the seas, had a commanding worldwide presence (colonies), was the world's foremost military power, and was the world's strongest and most stable banking nation.

When Britain abdicated its role as keeper of the currency prior to WWII, the United States assumed the mantle of keeper of the currency for the world. The U.S. dollar was initially accepted by all the other nations, as the currency to be measured against, for much the same reasons Britain's Pound Sterling had previously held the same title; namely, we were the strongest military nation on the planet, we had possessions and territories worldwide, our dollars were still backed by precious metal, and our banks were (even during the depression) the soundest and most stable available at the time. The favorable outcome of WWII for the U.S. and its allies, served to solidify and make (semi) permanent the American Dollar's claim to being the world's key currency, and the currency by which all other currencies would be measured in relative value.

War Bonds

The costs relating to paying off just war-related debts and expenses was staggering in itself.

During the war, the government had asked U.S. citizens to carry much of the burden, by way of contributing their own limited income towards "war bonds". Now the war was over, and the bonds were being redeemed by the holders, who wanted to buy houses, cars, and get their lives back on track.

Veteran Benefit Programs

The government had also initiated additional benefits for veterans returning home from the War. Homes were made available to veterans for no money down, and low interest rates, available over long periods of time (up to 30 years). Veterans were also entitled to a (virtually) free college education by way of the "GI Bill".

The benefits offered to veterans applied to all service members, not just to those families who had soldiers in the conflict. The "VA" loans, and "GI Bill" as they came to be known, continued for many years after the war ended, and applied to those coming into the armed services long after the war was over. Each of these programs had very high up-front costs, that wouldn't be paid back for a long time …decades, in some instances.

(A government program once in motion, tends to stay in motion, unless acted on by an outside source.)

While the motivation for providing veterans these benefits was honorable, it constituted another instance where laws were enacted to benefit one segment of the nation's citizens, at the expense of other segments. Those individuals-precluded for reasons of age, sex, poor health or physical disabilities from participating in the armed services were especially badly served in this instance, in that their taxes were used to subsidize benefits that would never be available to them personally, through no fault of their own.

Foreign Aid

On top of these costs, the winners in the WWII conflict met and agreed to help pay the expenses associated with the losers reconstructing their countries too. This was just the opposite of what happened following WWI. Following WWI, the victors required the losers to repay the winners for damages done, and to further repay all expenses that the victors had incurred in fighting the war.

Foreign Aid generally took the form of loans to countries needing help. The payout to the countries being helped was again immediate, while the payback period might extend over decades. Foreign aid turned out to be a very expensive welfare habit to feed or break. Many nations receiving foreign aid were unable to repay the loans (or even the interest on the loans) made to them, and these loans were either forgiven completely, or "rolled forward" into another later loan of greater amount.

The "rolling forward" method was preferred by government officials, since this process allowed the nations who were unable to pay back their loans, to never appear to be in default, thereby "saving face". When foreign aid recipients couldn't pay their loans on time when they came due, the U.S. would extend them another loan sufficient in amount to pay back the original loan, plus any interest that had accrued.

The net effect of this method of forgiving loans to "foreign aid" recipients was that the U.S. was owed ever more by the countries that could not pay back their loans, while the countries in default came to expect that their loans would be "rolled over" anytime that they were unable to repay them. It is unlikely that, at this point in time, anyone even knows how many (hundreds of) billions (perhaps trillions) of dollars of foreign aid "loans" have been defaulted on over the years, and which have never, to this day been repaid by the countries receiving them following WWII.

Land Banks

During this period too, the government again sought to preserve a healthy economy for the farming sector of the country, which had helped us win the war. During WWII, our farmers were subsidized, in return for creating enough food to feed not only the citizens of the U.S., but contributing food to all of our allies too. Tremendous quantities of land had come under cultivation during the war.

Now that the war was over, other countries were again free to begin cultivating their own crops, and feeding their own citizens. The amount of food that was needed from the U.S. (worldwide) was much less after the war, than it had been during the war.

The alternatives, if you were someone who made a living farming, weren't pleasant to contemplate. There were zillions more acres under cultivation in the U.S., than were needed after WWII.

If supply and demand took its natural course, the marketplace would dictate that those selling for the lowest price would sell the most crops. Under that scenario, some (maybe most) farmers might not be able to clear enough to pay off the loans on the increased land holdings they had bought and put into production during the war.

In response to government pleas and the needs of the war effort, some farmers had taken out (government guaranteed) loans to buy up a lot of farmland that had been idled during the depression, and put it into cultivation. A lot of the additional land needed for farming during the war, was no longer needed, but the farmers now had big loans still outstanding against the land purchases.

Because of their strategic importance during the war, farmers had gained a lot of clout in government that they hadn't had prior to the war. They pressured congress to help them make the adjustment back to a peacetime economy. Perhaps fearing a return to the days when large numbers of farms failed during the depression and a return to the days of the "dust bowl", the U.S. government acted to preserve the financial foundation underlying the nation's existing farming industry.

Aside from government loan guarantees, one of the methods they chose was to enact the "land bank" program. The Land Bank program was a program where the government paid farmers *not* to plant crops on their land. Farmers would provide the government with sales receipts showing how much income they received for the land that they *did* plant and harvest, and the government would then pay them a proportional amount per acre for each acre they owned, that they did *not* plant or harvest.

Essentially farmers could plant only half of their land, but receive the same amount of net income, as if they had planted it all, and harvested it all. And many did just that. This policy further resulted in creating an artificial supply-demand relationship for many farm goods. By having many farmers decide in the same year not to grow a particular kind of farm product, the total quantity of that product produced might be far less than it otherwise might have been, and that caused the end-consumer price for that product to rise well above what it might otherwise have been.

The "land bank" and government loan guarantee programs had a double-whammy effect on the U.S. citizens who were paying the bills: First, there were the high costs associated with guaranteeing farm loans, and paying the farmers for not growing anything on their land. Second, there were the higher consumer costs for food resulting from the artificial supply-demand relationships caused by not letting market forces work to lower prices.

Finally, aside from the first two unintended effects noted above, there was the unintended effect of creating resentment on the part of the non-farming population, who saw the government's farm policies as unduly enriching a small segment of the population, at the expense of the majority of citizens who never directly benefited from the subsidies, after the war ended.

The "land bank" program provided the means for a substantial number of farmers, to pay off very large real estate loans, with government money obtained from <u>not</u> growing anything, which in turn allowed them to later sell their unused land, and become wealthy in the process.

A non-farm analogy might be the government paying the average citizen for <u>not</u> living in a second home, when the government payments to you for not living in the home were sufficient in size to allow you to pay off the home (not yet lived in) completely within a few years' time, entirely with government (taxpayer) dollars. And, after the (not yet lived in) home was paid off; you could then choose to live in the home, give it to your children, or sell it for profit, as you wished. All after never having paid a cent toward its purchase price, or any interest on the loan covering it. The Government (read taxpayers) would have paid for everything.

It was during this-period in our history when the Federal government began as a matter of course, to subsidize some segments of the general population at the expense of the other segments of the population, and to pick helping some countries and not others. Pre-determining winners and losers, so to speak.

Income (and other) tax rates go (way) up

While the Social Security tax was originally intended to be self-supporting, and originally only applied to the first $3000 of income, the other programs listed previously, implemented during this period were never assumed to be able to pay their own way. Social Security aside, all the other programs implemented during this period were strictly payable by the taxpayers, from other tax sources.

Not surprisingly, income taxes were raised dramatically, as a way of paying the enormous costs of war and the new subsidy-type programs enacted by the congress. Following WWII, the top personal income rates in the U.S. rose to the 90+% level. Taxes on businesses were also increased, and taxes related to profits generated through capital investments (stocks, bonds, partnership investments, etc.) were likewise increased dramatically.

Those investing in businesses through making capital infusions by way of buying stock in a company or buying bonds issued by a company, saw any profits (dividends and/or interest) related to their contributions taxed <u>twice</u>. First the profits generated by the capital infusions were taxed at the business level, since the dividends paid out to the investors were not allowed to be deducted by the business as a business expense. Then, once the reduced dividend was received by the investor as income, it was taxed again as a "capital gain".

This was a questionable application of logic at best. If the business borrowed the money needed for expansion from a <u>bank,</u> the interest payments (bank's profit) could be deducted by the business from its total income, before paying corporate income taxes on the rest. However, if the business got its expansion from issuing stock or bonds, the interest payments (in the form of dividends) to the investors who were <u>not</u> banks, could not be likewise deducted from the businesses income before paying corporate income taxes on what was left.

The high personal and business and investment (capital-related) taxes assessed by the U.S. government provided significant incentives for individuals and corporations to consider expatriating (moving out of the country) some or all of their personal and/or business income.

The very high tax rates assessed against (all kinds off,) income in the U.S. during this period, resulted in some individuals and businesses beginning to relocate to other countries. Once operations in other countries were established, a springboard for multi-national company operations was a natural follow-on step. It then became possible or multi-national companies to thereafter play off one country against another in gaining monetary concessions that could be passed through to the company owners (stockholders).

> ...here we again see that, for every government action there is an equal and opposite citizen action.

Adding Fuel to the Fire in the Middle-East

On May 14, 1948 the Jewish Peoples Council voted in the Tel Aviv Museum to formally create the State of Israel. Land in what had been up until that date the British controlled region of Palestine was claimed for exclusive use of members of the Jewish faith. For about 40 years immediately prior to this event, Jewish and Palestinian citizens had jointly occupied the same area under British supervision. For many centuries prior to that, members of the Jewish faith had been forced to become assimilated into other societies, countries, and cultures, with mixed results. Members of the Jewish faith had long sought a homeland of their own.

The land claimed by the council included part of the historic city of Jerusalem, where Jesus of Nazareth had lived, taught, and died by crucifixion. The newly established homeland for the Jewish people was intended to roughly coincide with what had been their homeland in biblical times.

The creation of the state of Israel was also sought by many in the world community as a means of offsetting atrocities against members of the Jewish faith at the hands of the Nazis. After suffering such a horrendous wrong, the world (led by Britain and the United States) sought to make it right by providing the Jewish people with a long sought-after homeland of their own.

The state of Israel was created by dictate, without first obtaining the consent of the Palestinian people already living in the area now being set aside for the new Jewish state. Not too surprisingly, the Palestinians already living in and around Jerusalem were not pleased when told that their homeland had been taken over exclusively by and for members of another religious sect.

By way of comparison, try to imagine the reaction if the Mexican Government acted to take over the state of Texas, and told the Texans already living there that they would either have to move and/or take orders from the government of Mexico. If you've ever visited the lone star state, you know how well that would have set with the Texans already living there. (Oh wait. That actually happened, didn't it?)

The U.S. government allied itself with the new state of Israel early on (immediately). By itself, this action on the part of the U.S. government to legitimize the new state of Israel was sufficient to cause countries in the middle-east whose populations were in the majority followers of Islamic religions, to unite together, and to side against the U.S. in all foreign policy matters.

The benefits to the U.S. from having a strong ally, and base of operations, in the Middle East were expected to be significant. However, Israel's tenure in the region was not assured. Military and terrorist actions sprung up (initiated by both sides) immediately between Israel and her Palestinian citizens, and Islamic neighbors.

The Palestinians themselves were now outcasts in what used to be their own land, and were dead set on having returned to them the area that they had previously occupied off and on for centuries. A resistance organization was formed that took the name "Palestine Liberation Organization", or PLO for short.

The PLO sought funding from Islamic countries in the region that were sympathetic to their situation, and used the funds to establish guerilla groups that attacked Israeli citizens and settlements, and citizens of western countries who endorsed the new state of Israel.

These terrorist actions on the part of the PLO were partially intended to intimidate Jewish settlers into leaving the country, and partially intended to draw worldwide attention to what they considered the unfairness of the world's western nations banding together to support the takeover of their homeland by another religious group. The attacks by Palestinians on Israeli military personnel, had they been limited to such, would possibly have been understood and maybe even condoned by many observers of the conflict. However, the PLO's targets were not always military, but instead sometimes (too often) included unarmed civilians, including women and children.

Wars are always messy, and civilian casualties are always involved. However, in most wars, it was generally a goal, to the extent possible, to spare civilian non-combatants. The holocaust during WWII and the nuclear bombing of Hiroshima and Nagasaki were notable exceptions. In the case of the PLO, however, as had been the case with Hitler's Nazi regime, the civilian casualties were planned. Because of this, much of what had previously been sympathy for the Palestinians, worldwide, quickly turned to condemnation, and deservedly so.

The U.S. government acted to provide the state of Israel with sufficient military might that the Jewish citizens of the new state could establish themselves in their new country, and defend themselves from attacks by their Islamic neighbors, and the PLO.

U.S. foreign aid also provided funding for establishment of homes, businesses, and entire new settlements for Jewish citizens in the newly set aside state of Israel. When American supplied military might was used effectively by Israel against their Islamic neighbors, feelings of resentment against the U.S. government grew, in countries in the region who remained sympathetic to the plight of the Palestinians.

More Wars

The U.S. was barely out of WWII, when disagreements with Russia over politics, territory and trade caused the onset of the "cold war". The "cold war", as it came to be called, involved American armies in military actions all over the world. Sometimes American soldiers were directly involved. Other times the U.S. government just provided funding, and let other government's citizens fight the military battles. Either way, the "cold war" would ultimately expand to become America's most expensive war, in terms of dollars spent.

The most prominent event marking the onset of the cold war was the decision by Russia to build a militarily defended wall between East and West Berlin. The wall dividing the city's east and west sectors became known as "the iron curtain". The city of Berlin, itself, was entirely within an area ceded to Russia. However, during the treaty making process, the western half of the city of Berlin was given over to the U.S. and NATO forces to manage.

Go figure.

The Russians elected to try and starve the Americans and NATO troops out of the western section of the city, by not allowing U.S. supply trucks to use the highways coming into the city from elsewhere in Europe. This resulted in the largest peacetime airlift in history. Eventually the Russians gave up, and allowed trucks to carry commerce into West Berlin, and West Berlin flourished, while East Berlin struggled behind the Berlin Wall.

America and Russia were separated more by ideology than by the Berlin Wall. Russia had elected after the revolution in the early 1900's to become a socialist society. America was capitalist all the way.

After WWII, America elected to rebuild its economy based upon supporting private enterprise, and was successful enough to not only build the best standard of living in the world for its citizens, but to support similar efforts of other countries around the world through foreign aid. Russia elected another path, and sought to gain full employment by rebuilding its military might. Its economy too was successful enough to allow Russia to extend foreign aid to supporters of the socialist philosophy.

The Russian approach was not nearly as successful as the American approach when it came to providing a high standard of living for Russian citizens, or for the citizens of countries Russia supported through foreign aid. As a result of the "cold war", the world was divided into three ideological camps:

- The Capitalists, championed by America and its Western European allies
- The Socialists (communists), championed by Russia and China
- The "non-aligned" nations, championed by the United Nations

While the capitalists and communists vied for favor with the larger, more established, and most resource intensive, countries around the world; the non-aligned nations who were not so blessed with resources, played the capitalists off against the communists, and curried favor with whoever offered them the most foreign aid at the time. Not surprisingly, the non-aligned nations didn't get a lot of respect from either of the other side(s) in the cold war.

They did, however, get a lot of <u>money</u>. From <u>both</u> sides.

A New Paradigm For Wars

Prior to and during WWII, Korea had been occupied by Japan. Once the war was over, and Japan had exited the country, there was a leadership void. Some Korean citizens wanted to reform the country along capitalist lines. Others wanted to reform the country along communist lines. Predictably, a regional war broke out between these factions. Equally predictably, those wanting communism sought aid from Russia and China, and those wanting capitalism sought aid from the United States, and our European allies.

> A new model for conducting war evolved, which was thereafter followed in regional conflicts all over the world by countries who wanted to go to war with other countries, but did not have enough money to do so. The new paradigm called for the warring countries to align themselves ideologically with either Russia and/or China, or with the United States and its allies, and then supply the manpower to fight the war, but get the financing from the ideological ally who was a major economic power.

In previous wars, it was pretty much a "gloves off" situation, where whichever side was winning, just kept coming, until the other side was unable to continue, and had to give up. But, beginning with the Korean War, imaginary lines were drawn up over which neither side was allowed to advance, regardless of how well they were doing in the conflict.

The new war model thus ushered in the concept of "limited engagements". In a "limited engagement", an army that was losing a battle had the option of withdrawing back behind an imaginary boundary, and the opposing army was precluded from following beyond the designated boundary line. Kind of like saying "King's X" when you were playing children's games. In Korea, the boundary line was set at the 38th parallel.

The effect of armies playing by the new rules of "limited engagement", was to provide a format wherein typically no side ever won, and no side ever lost. When things got too hot for a side that was in danger of losing, they retreated behind the designated boundary line, and were thereafter free to take as much time as necessary to regroup, rearm, and begin another offensive, without having to worry about the other side coming after them in an offensive action, while they were resting up for the next round.

Still another new wrinkle in the "new" war paradigm was the option granted to allies to either take part or sit it out, and, if they took part, to retain the option as to what form their contribution would take.

Officially, the capitalist side in the Korean War was supported and financed by members of the United Nations. The UN had no money or army of its own, but the capitalist countries involved agreed to let the United Nations "manage" the "police action" for all the capitalist forces involved in the conflict. Nevertheless, individual nations within the UN could still elect to side with either the communists in the north, or the capitalists in the south. Russia and China sided with North Korea. Western nations predictably sided with South Korea. Some countries elected to send only money, others only materials, some fully equipped troops, and still others only moral support. The Korean war was the first war in modern history where a country who was "officially" at war with another, could elect to never take part in the actual fighting, or be otherwise involved in the war at all.

Finally, the new war paradigm provided that wars would no longer be called wars. They were thereafter typically called by such names as "police actions". The role of the financing countries became "military advisors" The actual combatants continued to call each other by derogatory names, as might be expected.

Typically, under rules of "limited engagement", wars became wars of attrition. Whichever side had the greatest will, and staying power, ultimately prevailed, regardless of who had the best army, or was the best equipped. Other times neither side gave up, and each just retreated behind the boundary and bided their time. Korea's "police action" fell into the latter category.

The new war paradigm was bitterly resisted in Korea by the commanding general of the U.S. forces, General Douglas McArthur. McArthur was a warrior of the "old school", which called for all-out effort, and never quitting short of victory or death. McArthur's penchant for speaking out about what he believed were illogical aspects relating to the new war paradigm, ultimately saw him relieved of his command and sent home.

The shooting period of the Korean war lasted almost four years, cost untold billions of dollars, cost more than a million lives, (both sides combined) and ended in a stalemate. Actually the Korean war never ended. The Korean War is still going on today, after fifty years of both sides biding their time, and waiting for an opportunity to resume with an advantage over the other side. Both sides now have nuclear arsenals at their disposal.

The new war paradigm established during the Korean War set the precedent for every war that would follow, except one, to the present point in time.

1955-1970

Legacy of The Texas Railroad Commission

A significant event that was little noticed at the time it happened in 1960, actually had its beginnings, as did so many other things we are now living with, during the Great Depression period.

With all the cutbacks in industrial output during the great depression of the 1930's, U.S. oil production far exceeded national demand requirements. At one time, oil sold for ten cents a barrel (excluding the cost of the barrel) in Texas, which was the largest U.S. oil producing state.

To save its oil producers, the state of Texas appointed the Texas Railroad Commission to do something to restore the profitability of oil drilling for the state's oil producers. The Railroad Commission was already responsible for conservation related to land appropriated to the railroads, and was therefore possibly in a position to make policy relating to managing natural resources in general.

The Texas Railroad Commission established a conservation program designed to create an artificially high demand for oil, by creating an artificially low supply of oil. When demand exceeds supplies, prices go up. And oil producers were in real need of a way to get higher prices for their oil.

The Texas Railroad Commission enacted rules that restricted the number of days per week that wells could be operated to produce oil. At one time, oil production was only allowed three days a week. That effectively cut oil production by more than half, and caused an artificially produced shortage of oil. Oil prices quickly rose by more than double, in response to the contrived shortages, and the Texas oil producers were saved from bankruptcy. Which was good. On the downside, the increase in the price of oil caused oil-intensive production processes to be more expensive, and goods produced by these processes increased in price too. This came at a bad time for some, since it started during the years of the great depression (those unintended consequences again).

Most government programs have winners and losers The winners in this instance were the Texas oil-producing companies. The losers were the Americans forced to pay more for goods produced by oil-intensive industrial processes, and the oil field workers idled through government intervention in the free enterprise market process.

In many respects the actions of the Texas Railroad Commission in creating an artificial shortage of oil, in order to prop up oil prices, for benefit of the oil producers, and at the expense of the general citizenry, mirrors the federal government's similar program that later created an artificial shortage of productive farmland, in order to prop up the prices of food, for the benefit of the farmers, and at the expense of the general citizenry.

> There's a pattern developing here. See if you can spot it.

The work of the Texas Railroad Commission didn't go unnoticed outside of the U.S. One person who took note of how effectively it worked in terms of increasing prices even when supplies actually exceeded demand, was a Venezuelan attorney named Perez Alfonzo.

Venezuela had considerable oil deposits of its own, but had great difficulty in developing their oil fields in a manner that yielded a decent return on the drilling and exploration efforts involved. In part Venezuela's difficulties in marketing their oil related to Venezuela's having been largely excluded from purchases by the "seven sisters" who at the time controlled the output of more than 90% of all the producing oil wells in the world. They didn't need Venezuelan oil, and mostly left Venezuela to fend for itself in the worldwide oil market.

Given the worldwide glut of oil at the time the Texas Railroad Commission enacted it's "conservation" policy relating to cutting back on the output of producing oil wells, there was little opportunity for Perez Alfonso to do much with the information, but wait for times to change.

And, times did eventually change. Following WWII, the world needed much more oil. For everything. Perhaps most significantly, the United States who had, prior to WWII, only imported 3% of its total petroleum requirements, was, by 1960, importing 25% of the oil it needed (it's now over 50%).

By this point in time, Middle East and North African oil fields had been developed to the point that their oil reserves were significantly in excess of what was needed, worldwide. The middle-east's oil glut served to keep middle-east, Venezuelan, and North African oil producers competing aggressively in the world markets to sell the oil being produced. The pressures brought about by middle-east, Venezuelan, and North African oil producers competing with one another in order to sell their products, kept oil prices so low, that the middle-east, Venezuelan, and North African producers were essentially working, just to survive, while western oil consumers got the benefits of the cheap oil.

But, as the paradigm for war had changed with the Korean conflict, the paradigm for the control of oil was about to shift.... dramatically. In the fall of 1959, Venezuelan attorney Perez Alfonso dusted off his notes, taken years before relating to the Texas Railroad Commission, and scheduled a meeting with Abdullah Tariki, representing middle-east oil interests, and they began planning a way to take control of their own destinies.

On September 9, 1960, Perez Alfonso hosted a meeting in Switzerland, attended by representatives of the governments of Venezuela, Saudi Arabia, Iran, Iraq, and Kuwait. At that meeting the attending countries officially formed the world's <u>second</u> international oil cartel, named the Organization of Petroleum Exporting Countries, or OPEC for short.

Their plan was simple; following the Texas Railroad Commission's formula for improving oil prices during the depression, on behalf of Texas oil producers; members of OPEC would voluntarily cut back on oil production to a point where worldwide demand for oil again exceeded the worldwide supply of oil, and prices could therefore be successfully increased, this time for the benefit of OPEC members.

The modern world's second international oil cartel was formed to provide a means whereby middle-east oil producing nations could compete effectively, on their own, with the first international oil cartel comprised of the "seven sisters". Due to internal squabbling within the ranks in the early years, the Organization of Petroleum Exporting Countries got off to a slow start in the 1960's, but within a decade, OPEC would prove a worthy adversary for the Seven Sisters.

Labor Unions get a larger piece of the pie

Labor Unions emerged very strong from WWII. The Unions had always prospered by creating an artificial supply-demand relationship between available workers and the needs of industry to employ them. Perhaps the Texas Railroad Commission got its ideas re: artificially reducing supplies, in order to raise prices, from the labor unions.

During the period following the Korean War, and throughout much of the "cold war" labor unions worked diligently to get legislation enacted that required any business contracting to do major construction or manufacturing work for a (U.S.) government agency to use union members exclusively, or, alternatively, pay non-union workers prevailing union wages. Once enacted, such laws provided the labor unions with tremendous leverage in terms of dealing with the government, which by this time represented almost 25% of the country's gross national product in terms of purchasing power.

By choosing not to expand the union's membership, or by not authorizing particular local union groups to bid on particular projects, the labor unions were able to demand, and get, much higher hourly rates for their members, than would have been possible if both union and non-union contractors were permitted to compete for government business based upon differing wage rates. This contributed significantly to increasing the costs of running the government.

Union dealings with the government tended to spill over into private industries, and the unions used the precedents set in government wage negotiations to get similar concessions in other industries, including most of the major industries in the country, like farming, auto manufacturing, steel production, textiles, and most construction trades.

The high wages being paid to union employees caused all goods and services produced in the U.S. to increase steadily and rapidly in price. Between 1940 and 1960, prices on average for U.S. produced goods rose by more than 100%. During this period in time, the U.S government maintained protective tariffs on foreign produced goods imported into the U.S. The protective tariffs allowed U.S. businesses to pay higher wages to American workers, without fear of their products being undersold in the U.S. market, by foreign products, produced with cheaper labor.

In the 1950's and 1960's the labor unions ruled, and their members enjoyed the highest average standard of living of any production workers on the planet. The government provided support to labor unions in the way of strike mediation. The National Labor Relations Board would periodically step in and force mediated solutions when labor strikes in a given industry threatened to spill over into other areas of the overall economy, or when striking workers had been out of work for excessive periods of time.

The greatest beneficiaries of the NLRB strike mediation efforts were the Unions. Union members could seldom stand to stay unpaid for as long as management could afford to stay unpaid. Company management and stockholders were generally well enough off to live off of savings for extended periods of time. Years even. The average Union member had fewer reserves to fall back on, and was likely to be more desperate, sooner, to see a strike end, and paydays resume.

During this period of time, the NLRB also enforced laws that required businesses to give striking workers back their jobs when strikes ended. Prior to the turn of the century, management had almost total control over laborers and labor in general. Child labor, sweatshops, 80 hour workweeks, company stores, and unsafe working conditions were the rule in the late 1800's.

During the first half of the 20th century, labor unions, backed by government actions and laws, worked to eliminate most, if not all, of the excesses visited upon labor by management, to a point where labor and management were about at parity with one another. After 1950, the pendulum continued to swing past center, and labor began to visit excesses on management, with the blessings of the government.

Labor unions acted to make it more difficult, and more expensive, for outsiders to obtain union membership. As demand for labor grew, while unions purposely held membership growth down, another contrived shortage, this time one of qualified labor, was created. With demand for labor exceeding availability of labor, costs of labor increased, and with it the costs to the public of everything produced by labor.

The Cold War Heats Up

Between 1955 and 1970, both ideological camps stepped up their attempts to influence other nations to adopt their ideology. The pattern continued to be one of soliciting member nations by way of foreign aid inducements.

The stakes got higher during this period due in large measure to the high costs of building nuclear arsenals. Russia and the United States spent trillions of dollars (each) developing ever more destructive weapons, and ever more efficient ways of deploying and delivering them to intended targets.

The idea here was to increase the total amount of destructive power that each side could deliver to the other to the point that, again, as in the case of "limited engagements" there could be no clear winner.

While the U.S. and Russia were the primary contestants in this race (which came to be called the "arms race") other nations also began arming themselves with nuclear weapons capabilities. In the bargain, the world became a much more dangerous place to live in.

War, the "old" way

In the late 1960's, some of the countries bordering on the new state of Israel, combined forces in an attempt to remove the Jewish people by military action. By this point in time, the state of Israel had received enough foreign aid, principally from the United States, to fully arm itself with modern weapons of war.

The countries bordering on Israel were, for the most part, dependent on Russia to supply them with military equipment and training in using it. In this respect, the conflict mirrored all the others around the world, following the onset of the cold war. That is, one side got funding from the U.S. and (sometimes) the allies of the U.S., and the other side got funding from Russia and China.

But there the similarity ends.

The government of Israel believed in the "old school" of conducting war. Ask no quarter, and give none. They also refused to recognize imaginary lines representing country borders, and rules of "limited engagement". When Egypt, Jordan, Syria, Iraq, and Lebanon began marshalling troops to mount a military offensive against Israel in 1967, Israel responded by attacking first and throwing everything it had into the fight right from day one. Israel's attitude was either we win it all, or lose it all right here, and right now. No limited engagements. No wars of attrition.

Israel's attack was executed with precision planning, and total disregard for all the "rules" that other countries had become accustomed to conducting war by. The fight lasted a total of six days. When it was over, Israel occupied not only the land it had previously held, but the entire Sinai Peninsula, the Gaza Strip, the land along the west bank of the Jordan river, and the Golan Heights, overlooking Syria.

All that, in just six days' time.

The countries who lost parts of their land in the conflict, complained to the United Nations, who demanded that Israel return the land it had captured. Israel refused.

The "six-day war" (Israel still called a war a war) served to give the defeated countries additional incentive to gear up militarily to a point that a return engagement might have a different outcome. Russia provided more funding, arms, and "military advisors" to Israel's neighbors. The United States did the same for Israel.

After the six-day war, the conflict between Israel and its neighbors settled into a holding pattern. Terrorist attacks against citizens, and government officials increased, but, significantly, from the time of the six-day war forward, no neighboring country of Israel attempted another frontal military assault.

Israel had proven itself a force to be reckoned with, militarily, and the Israeli government had proven themselves to be resolute, hard-nosed defenders of their new homeland.

Following the six-day war, Israeli's were still not _accepted_ by their neighbors, but they were almost certainly _respected_ by their neighbors.

And, Still One More War

Throughout the 1950's the French had been involved in a "Korea" of their own. French Indo China was becoming a hotbed of discontent, with the citizens of that area seeking to evict the French, and establish control over their own destinies.

France had initially established itself as a colonial power in the area in the mid 1850's, and continued its expansion in that area of Asia up until 1914 when WWI broke out. After WWII in 1945, part of what had been called French Indo China, had been renamed.

It was now called Vietnam.

France was (and is) a U.S. ally, and the U. S. was asked by France to support them in their attempt to hold onto their old colonial outpost. In the late 1950's, the U.S. government provided weapons, money, and combat assistance in the way of U.S. military troops called "military advisors", to France, in Vietnam.

The leaders in the northern part of Vietnam had elected a socialist/communist form of government, whereas the leaders in the southern part of Vietnam had elected to follow a capitalist/democratic form of government, possibly influenced by France's presence there. As happened in all other regional wars after WWII, the initiating parties quickly sought to align themselves with the strongest economic powers supporting their philosophy. The North Vietnamese aligned themselves with Russia and Communist China, while the Southern Vietnamese aligned themselves with the U.S. and its western allies.

By 1960 France lost interest in the conflict, and abandoned the government of South Vietnam. The U.S. allies from WWII, were, in the main, not particularly interested in joining the U.S. in a regional war outside their immediate (European) area. In part this was due to their having no economic interest in the area. In part it was due to having more pressing matters closer to home. Whatever the reasons, U.S. European allies mostly distanced themselves from the fray in

Vietnam at an early point in time. That left primarily just the U.S. to support the South Vietnamese position. In mid-1963, the President of the U.S. had expressed personal doubts about the U.S. continuing to be directly involved in Vietnam. In late 1963, that President was assassinated in Dallas, Texas. The man who took his place was committed to not only staying in Vietnam, but winning the battle, through attrition, if necessary.

Throughout the mid to late 1960's U S. involvement in the Vietnam War increased. By 1970, the United States had nearly 500,000 troops in residence in Vietnam as "military advisors" to the South Vietnamese Government and military.

The financial costs to support American involvement in Vietnam quickly mounted to the level of the cost of fighting WWII, and then just kept on growing. The cost in lives lost, on both sides, also continued to mount steadily.

The Business Exodus from the U.S. Accelerates

The number of U.S based businesses relocating major parts of their operations, especially manufacturing operations, to foreign countries increased sharply during this period of time. The high costs of labor in the U.S. were most often cited by the government for businesses moving offshore. The more likely reasons for the offshore flight of U.S based businesses, were the very high corporate and personal tax rates in the U.S. at the time, and the very high rate at which profits related to capital investments were taxed.

In fact, even if foreign labor costs were the same as or higher than labor costs in the U.S., businesses would have elected to relocate in order to get the tax breaks involved, since taxes constituted a greater portion of overall business costs, than did labor.

In the U.S for example, the cost of labor in making an electronic component represents only about 3% of the price of the product, while taxes represent more than three times that amount. Labor costs got the bulk of the blame, but high U.S. personal and business taxes were the real culprit that began the flight of U.S. based businesses to offshore locations.

The "Great Society"

Following the assassination of the president in 1963, the new president, upon taking office, almost immediately declared "war on poverty". At the urging of the President, the Congress enacted several new programs designed to help poor Americans.

Among these were a new unemployment law that federalized unemployment payments; a program designed to help children of poor families get wholesome lunches in schools; a program to subsidize families with dependent children by way of providing coupons that could be used to pay for food and other necessities; and a program to subsidize housing payments for those who could not afford housing due to low incomes, and the ever increasing cost of housing.

During this period, Congress also approved the first of several new laws designed to halt discrimination in hiring based upon race, creed, or sex. The new civil rights laws, which culminated with "affirmative action", aimed to make up for the discrimination suffered by some in the past, by requiring employers to give "preference" to some members of society, over other members of society, in future hiring and promotion actions.

Both the up-front costs, and the continuing costs of funding the "Great Society" social welfare programs enacted in the 1960's were extremely high. The use of taxes for these purposes came to be termed "transfer payments" by the government. The transfer was essentially from those having more money, to those having less money or no money at all.

The tools used to effect the transfer were taxes of various kinds, and laws establishing new bureaucracies to redistribute the money.

Once gathered in the form of taxes, transfer payments had no strings attached for the recipients. There was no requirement that recipients perform any work, in order to receive the payments. Later on, access to these programs were determined to be a "right" that less fortunate citizens were "entitled" to by virtue of their being citizens of the United States.

Handling of the "transfer payments" involved a large number of government employees at every level, whether local, county, state, or national. The "welfare bureaucracy" provided a base of employment that greatly enlarged the number of citizens employed by the government at some level.

> It was during this period of our history that programs designed to redistribute personal income by taking income from those with more and giving it to those with less came to be defined as "entitlements". All citizens were deemed "entitled" to a share of the nation's wealth, without regard as to whether or not they helped in producing it.

The Space Race

In 1960, the U.S. had fallen behind Russia in terms of rocket science. The Russians, as a by-product of the arms race, had evolved powerful rockets, designed initially to deliver nuclear warheads across great distances, very quickly. Both the U.S. and Russia had determined early on that the fastest way to deliver nuclear payloads was to attach them to rockets that were capable of rising above the Earth's gravitational pull. Once having developed this capability, it was a fairly short leap in imagination, to figure out that replacing a nuclear payload, with a capsule large enough to house a person, could allow mankind its first opportunity to orbit the Earth in a spaceship.

However, bridging the gap between imagination and realization would prove to be a significant undertaking. The difficulties associated with preparing the equipment-set necessary to put a person in space (as opposed to a non-living nuclear payload), and return the person (alive) to Earth were daunting. And expensive.

When the Russians beat the U.S. in putting the first person into free orbit around the planet, the U.S. president committed the U.S. government to putting a man on the moon by the end of the decade. That meant by 1970. The U.S. was the first to land a man on the moon. And, it was accomplished as the president had decreed.

The pilots that would ride the first rockets into space, and to the moon, were called astro<u>nauts</u>. The cost to win the space race was also astro<u>nomical</u>. Hundreds of billions of dollars were spent during the 1970's toward this end.

The Costs Mount Up

The arms "race", the "space race", the Vietnam Conflict, the cost of supporting "cold war" allies, the public welfare programs associated with the "great society", the costs of enforcing the new "affirmative action" law, and the recurring costs associated with having to buy our way out of occasional recurring economic downturns now called "recessions", resulted in the government's having to pay out an enormous amount of money during this period. More money than even the high rates of taxes that were in effect at the beginning of this period could cover.

The senior senator from Illinois, expressing concern over the mounting costs of government, is credited with admonishing his fellow senators during this period, with the statement:

"A billion here, a billion there, pretty soon it adds up to real money".

But congress was on a roll, and the senior senator from Illinois' words of warning did little to stem the tide of government spending during this period in our history.

More Devaluing of Currencies

In order to pay for the increasing costs of government, and government sponsored programs, it was necessary for the government's income to be increased each year. Again, during this period, an election was made to further increase by dictate, the value of the nation's gold deposits in the various treasury vaults. The upshot of this was, as usual, twofold:

1. It allowed the treasury to print more paper currencies. This was a benefit because the amount of gold in the nations treasuries had been depleted, and, at this point in time, the United States treasury still operated under a law that required every dollar printed to be backed by an equivalent amount of gold in the treasury. If gold was revalued upward, then each ounce of gold in the treasury could, by law, have more dollars printed against it, and put into circulation.

2. It caused the value of each dollar printed to be less than it was before the gold was revalued upward in price. In other words, it now took more dollars to buy an ounce of gold. Since the dollar's value was pegged to gold, the price, in dollars, of everything previously purchasable with gold went up proportionally. Since everything-was purchasable with gold, the price of everything went up proportionally.

Of course, the increase in prices in everything being purchased with dollars put significant pressures on wages to also be increased. When wages were increased, income taxes took a greater bite out of wage-earner's paychecks each month. This cycle of money "creation" was the method used by the government to pay for the additional government expenses being incurred annually, while America was still on the gold standard.

Lowering Income Tax Rates

The requirement of citizens to pay ever greater percentages of their total income to the government, whenever their wages were increased, due to the price of gold being revalued upward, and more paper dollars being put into circulation, in order to pay for increased government spending, caused resentment on the part of the majority of middle-class workers. They were doing the same work, at the same job, for the same employer, and facing increased prices for all the necessities of life like food, shelter, medical treatment, transportation, and clothing, but increasingly had less, rather than more dollars with which to pay for them, due to the government taking a higher percentage of each tax payers total income for their (the government's) own use, due to the "progressive" nature of the income tax formula.

Taxpayers began initiating measures of their own, at the local and state levels, to vote out of power, officials who increased taxes at these levels. Businesses increasingly left the U.S. shores to do manufacturing in countries who took less of their profits in the form of taxes.

Sensing a tax revolt, and seeking to avoid one, the Congress of the U.S. responded by periodically incrementally reducing the rates at which income-based taxes were assessed. The reductions were seldom (if ever) of a magnitude sufficient to give back all of what had previously been lost, and further were always lagging at least a year or more behind when the taxes were increased at the worker level, due to workers' wages being increased. The workers thus never recouped all of what was lost, and each year workers continued to fall slightly more behind in terms of having spendable income available to them.

Additionally, the congress did not make such reductions in income tax percentages equal for all, when such reductions were made. Instead, Congress without exception gave higher percentages of tax reductions to some individuals and businesses, than were given to others.

It didn't much matter which political party was in power at the time. Both political parties adopted use of the tax system as a tool for redistributing taxes along whatever lines their philosophy favored. When citizens got tired of one party redistributing tax money along lines they didn't like, for too long a sustained period of time, the voters would send the other party to congress for a while. Bottom line though was, that whoever was in power politically at the time, used the same process of distributing taxes more to some individuals and businesses, than to others, as they saw fit. No attempt at equality or fairness was ever made in this regard, by either of the two major political parties.

After giving individuals a tax rate "cut" in 1965, the congress turned around in 1968 and attached a "surtax" to the income tax on individuals. The tax "cut" was to take effect in the 1966 year, and would be reflected in tax returns filed in April of 1967. The "surtax" was equal to 10% of whatever the "base" tax was calculated to be The "surcharge" was retroactive, and also affected all taxes calculated for the year in which the surcharge was enacted (1968).

The end result of these actions on the part of congress was that the average worker enjoyed just one year of slightly reduced taxes, and then saw his or her taxes again rise to a level that was higher than they had been before the tax "cut" went into effect.

Not surprisingly, in 1969, workers began demanding (much) greater annual increases in their wages. The increased wages led to increases in prices of everything produced by labor.

> "For every government action, there is an equal and opposite citizen reaction."

Increasing Taxes on Capital

Regardless of who taxes were collected from, the total amount required to run the government had to come from somewhere. During this period, while congress was acting to appease individual voters and businesses by periodically making an incremental reduction in the "ordinary" income tax rates, the congress acted to gather back the taxes lost to them through tax rate reductions on businesses and individuals, by increasing the taxes charged against profits generated through capital investments. "Ordinary" income was deemed to be income gained through people working. "Capital gains" income was income resulting from money working.

Depreciation allowances were reduced for businesses investing in plants and new equipment. This caused businesses who invested in such things to show profits that were artificially higher for tax purposes. Since the amounts allowed as depreciation deductions, before taxes, were reduced by government dictate, each business making capital expenditures saw its reported profits increase, and its taxes therefore increased.

It should be noted that the difference between income and expenses needed to operate the business didn't actually change at all. The actual profit available to the business (difference between income and expenses) remained exactly the same. However, the apparent profits (not allowing the business to deduct capital related expenses before paying taxes) were increased, so the government received taxes on income formerly allowed as a business deduction.

At the same time, congress attached higher taxes to profits made by way of financing capital purchases by businesses. The largest and most successful businesses typically sought much of their capital for expansion of plants and equipment through the stock and bond markets, as a means of lowering their overall costs for such capital.

Stock offerings allowed those willing to lend money to a corporation to do so in a way that provided for repayment of the stock price later, from profits of the corporation, when dividends were paid. The stock certificates themselves were a form of currency, and could be bought or sold through established markets (NYSE, AMEX, etc.). Those purchasing stocks were accepting risk at the same time. The company might stumble in the future, and their "loan" (price of the stock) might never be fully recouped.

Bonded indebtedness was also an alternative to ordinary bank loans. Money obtained by corporations wishing to expand, by way of selling bonds, was paid back to the bondholder at a pre-negotiated rate annually (whether the corporation was profitable or not), and the corporation had the option of buying back its bonds from the initial purchasers at any time. This could allow the corporation to cut down its overall cost of the borrowed money, in the event the company did well, and could retire the bonds early.

Bonds had the additional advantage to the corporation, in that once paid off, the bondholder had no further claims to profits generated by the corporation from that point in time forward. Stocks, on the other hand, required the company to pay dividends as long as the company existed, profits were being made, and the stock was still outstanding.

Sometimes individuals formed partnerships for investing in a specific type of investment. It might be industrial, service oriented, for development of real estate, developing new technology, starting up a new company, or a variety of other reasons. These types of investment capital served to get most new businesses their original startup capital. They were generally riskier than investing in a major established corporation, but some of them (i.e. like a Microsoft or an Intel, or a Yahoo) periodically achieved great returns for those willing to invest at this level.

Whatever income came back to those investing in stocks, bonds, and development partnerships, was termed capital gains. Capital gains were (and are) essentially income generated from investing in activities relating to helping businesses get the capital needed for startup and growth.

Typically, it has been the case in business that risk and reward are intentionally proportional., That is, whoever was willing to accept the higher levels of risk involved in helping a company startup or grow, should be entitled to a higher reward, if the investment bears fruit, than would an individual who invests in less risky ways like putting money in a savings account at a federally insured bank.

By the government's actions at taxing profits coming from higher risk capital investments, more than profits coming from low (or no) risk other types of investments, the government was making a statement that it was discouraging such investments. In other words, "if you attempt to make money by helping businesses startup or grow, you will be penalized by having to pay higher taxes".

It appears that the rational for taxing capital investment-related profits at a higher rate, may have been that government officials felt that most middle-class citizens would see this as a tax that only others, perhaps more financially fortunate than themselves, would ever be faced with paying (at least directly), and that therefore the majority of citizens would support the capital gains tax.

Paradoxically, at the same time that the government was sending this message to investors, the government was itself getting in the business of providing startup and growth assistance to private businesses. During this time the Small Business Administration (SBA) worked to make it easier for small businesses needing seed and growth capital, to get loans at reduced interest rates from existing commercial banks. Again, not all applicants were treated equally under SBA rules. Certain segments of the society were given "preference" over other segments of society when SBA grants and loan guarantees were dispensed.

In this instance, the government was again working to directly interfere with the free markets. SBA loans and grants were not awarded on the basis of which candidates had the most promising businesses, and which had the best chance of succeeding. SBA loans and grants were awarded based upon which subset of society the applicant belonged to that the government wished to assist. All taxpayers paid equally into the fund administered by the SBA, but not all taxpayers had equal access to the funds, once under the control of the SBA.

The government's approach to subsidizing businesses through the SBA was decidedly anti-free-market. High risk loans often carried lower, rather than higher, interest rates. The government (read taxpayers) accepted high risks, and received low returns, essentially reversing the true risk-reward relationship that exists in markets that are free to set prices for borrowed money based on things like risk levels.

For the banks involved in making and "administering" SBA loans, no risk at all was involved, since the loans were guaranteed by the U.S. government (read taxpayers), yet the banks were still able to charge somewhat higher rates to SBA borrowers, than they charged to borrowers whose loans carried a lower degree of risk. This was the government's way of inducing banks to participate in the program. No risk at all for the banks, but higher than average rewards.

Guaranteed.

Businesses receiving SBA grants (which never had to be paid back) and SBA guaranteed loans, were allowed to deduct any interest paid on their loans, prior to figuring their taxes. Had these businesses received their startup and growth capital from the sale of stocks or bonds, as most businesses had to do, the interest would not have been deductible. SBA-backed businesses thus enjoyed many government provided "breaks" that other businesses were precluded from participating in. The government stated that the SBA's primary function was to help keep America at the forefront of the free-market system.

For Every Action,
There is an Equal and Opposite Reaction

Non-SBA-backed businesses responded to the increases in taxation of capital in two ways:

1. Affected businesses increased their prices for their goods enough to make up for the profits lost to capital taxes. This had a double-whammy effect on the average middle-class citizen. First, their purchasing power was reduced, since everything cost them more. Secondly, it put pressure on the companies they worked for, to reduce the wages of their workers, in order to remain competitive with foreign goods.

2. Affected businesses relocated more of their capital intensive operations to countries who offered them better deals in the tax areas. In the process, many found an additional benefit to moving out of the U.S. in the form of reduced labor costs. Finally, many who took this route found that there was not a driving need to provide benefits like Social Security, medical benefits, life insurance, etc. to workers in other countries, mandated by the foreign governments where they relocated their operations to.

Number 2, above, raised the double whammy on the American middle-class worker up to a triple whammy level. Not only did it result in pressure to reduce the pay to workers here in the U.S., it resulted in pressure to eliminate more of the jobs that remained behind in the U.S. , and to relocate more of them to other countries.

Realizing that the U.S. government could itself act to counter the loss of taxes due to companies relocating some or all of their business to other countries, by attaching high tariffs to goods made by them offshore; the largest businesses, who had operations both in the U.S. and elsewhere, (in the process, causing a new business category to be coined "multi-nationals") lobbied congress to enact "fair trade" laws that disallowed high tariffs against their goods being re-imported to the U.S., once made elsewhere.

A General Agreement on Tariffs and Trade was worked out between the multi-nationals, and the various governments who benefited from them in one way or another. The initial GATT treaty was enacted and approved during this period in our history. Since then there have been numerous attempts by individual industries, and governments to amend the original GATT treaty in a way that would increase the benefits accruing to certain businesses, industries, or governments, more than to others.

> During this period, it will be seen that the government greatly accelerated the rate at which laws were enacted which were expressly designed to favor one segment of our society over the others. This process, which had formerly generally been looked on with disfavor, experienced a paradigm shift, and from this time forward would be viewed as the preferred means of enacting laws within the United States. No one political party was more guilty or innocent of effecting this sea change in the way laws were enacted in the United States.

It will also be seen that it was during this period of change in the United States, that the rate of large domestic companies initially electing to relocate at least a portion of their labor-intensive operations to other countries, reached its highest level, and that this was facilitated by governmental actions that benefited those doing the relocating.

Business was especially quick to catch on to the change in the "rules" by which the government doled out money, as were some other groups that were seeking monetary assistance from the government. By 1970 lobbying of government officials by single individuals, businesses, and industries each having a single selfish focus, was well along on it's way to becoming the fastest growing growth-industry in the world.

1970-1985

Confusion Reigns Supreme

By 1970 the frequent changes in direction in the federal government's monetary and tax policies was causing ripples in government at other levels, and the administration teamed up with congress to settle things down. Every move by the government to take more of the total money in circulation for its own uses, had quickly been countered by individuals and businesses in a way that negated the ability of the government to achieve its goals, long term.

Additionally, the U.S. was reaching a point in terms of printing paper currency that threatened to hit the limit of paper currency that could be printed according to the requirement that all paper money had to be backed by precious metal in the nation's treasury vaults.

Yet, more money was needed, and the government acted to make sure that it was available. The trick was how to do it (inflate the currency supply) without touching off a serious inflationary spiral, in terms of prices for goods increasing, and workers demanding high wage increases to keep up with the increasing cost of goods. Nobody wanted a repeat of confederate money, or Germany's "hyperinflation" to occur.

The government acted in two ways to achieve their goals.

1. In 1971, the president asked for, and the congress consented to, enactment of a law that "froze" prices and wages at the current level.
2. In 1972, the president requested, and the congress consented to, creation of a law that took America off of the gold standard.

The gold standard part worked as expected. The price of U.S. gold rose almost tenfold, overnight, and the mint was freed up to print whatever amount of new paper currency the government felt was needed. And, since government programs needed a lot of money to finance them, a lot of new paper currency was printed up. A <u>whole</u> lot.

The first part of the government's plans didn't work out so well. Inventive businesses quickly found loopholes in the wage-price "freeze" law, (some of which had been put in there on purpose to help some "key" business types) and raised prices even more than usual. The thinking on the part of business was apparently that the congress might act to close the loopholes, and so they should increase prices enough while they could, to make up for perhaps not being able to do so again, in the near future.

> For every government action, there is an equal and opposite citizen reaction.

As a result of taking America off the gold standard, the value of American dollars fell dramatically all over the world. With each dollar worth less, all goods imported and commodities brought into the U.S. immediately were increased in price sufficiently to offset the fall in the dollar's value.

Since the U.S. was now more dependent than ever on foreign materials to feed our manufacturing businesses, the cost of virtually everything produced in America went up sharply. Between 1971 and 1973 alone, the average price of commodities rose by 65%.

The economy faltered badly, since workers were now beset by a very dangerous set of conditions, all of which worked to their detriment. Under the law, their wages could not be increased. The price of everything they bought was still increasing sharply, and the government was continuing to take an ever larger share of their income for taxes. Workers had no money to spend. With no money to spend by U.S. consumers, businesses both here in the United States and abroad, began to see a sharp reduction in demand for their goods, and began laying off their workers, and closing down plants.

By 1973, the entire U.S Economy was hurting badly. People looked to elected officials for answers, but found none. The government, faced with a complete shutdown of the economy, reversed itself 100%, and declared wage-price controls "anti-free-market", and abandoned the program. The recession of 1974-1975 that followed the imposition of wage-price controls was the worst since the great depression of the 1930's.

COLAs

Pent up wage demands from the wage-price control period resulted in workers being granted much larger than typical annual wage increases. A new term "COLA" began to find its way into wage and price negotiations COLA stood for Cost of Living Adjustment.

Having been burned before by the government's failed attempt to create an economic utopia by dictate, workers and businesses began inserting language in wage and purchasing agreements that guaranteed that they could increase wages and product (and service) costs at least as much as inflation in the nation's money supply caused prices to increase each year.

Of course, the government still had the progressive income tax to assure that they got their share of the new money that went into the marketplace in the form of wages and business profits, but that by itself did not guarantee that the money would be spent wisely, or as citizens expected it to be spent.

The argument was then made, and accepted, that most government programs should also have COLA's built into them, as a means of making sure that those affected by these programs were taken care of too. Not only programs like Social Security received COLA's, but a whole slew of programs that had originally been intended to be temporary in nature received COLA updates too.

> A government program or body once in motion tends to stay in motion unless acted on by an outside force.

The cost of operating the government spiraled upward sharply. The government's printing presses poured new currency into the system to pay the bills. The cost of goods and services in the private sector mushroomed rapidly. The progressive income tax continued to take ever increasing percentages of individuals' income, as increased wages paid to workers for doing the same work, at the same job, for the same employer, pushed individuals into higher tax "brackets".

Between 1968 and 1986 (a span of just 18 years total) the cost of an average home in any neighborhood in America went up by more than **400%**. So did the price of automobiles, food, medical treatment, clothing, and just about everything else. This was a larger percentage of increase than had occurred at any time in the United States, at any time since the Civil War. It wasn't as bad as confederate money, or Germany's hyperinflation of the 1920's, but it was close. Too close for comfort.

It was routinely the case that wage increases lagged behind price increases. This was virtually assured due to the nature of the COLA procedure. Prices would increase randomly all year long. But not until the middle of the following year did the government release its figures indicating how much prices had risen on average due to inflation in the nation's paper currency supply by the Treasury.

By the time the next wage adjustment was made for the average worker, based on the government's figures, almost two years would have elapsed between the time the worker saw prices increase, and when he or she actually began seeing an increase in their wages to offset the price increases. By then, of course, prices had already increased again (twice), and those increases would not be factored in for another one to two years' time.

It only took a couple of cycles like this for workers to catch on, and to begin demanding double the amount of COLA percentages as wage increases, as a means of not continuing to get behind the price-increase "curve". By 1980 wages and prices for consumer goods in the U.S. were increasing at more than 13% each year, according to government figures.

And, the government figures themselves were suspect to many people, and little trust was placed in them by individual workers, or businesses. It was assumed that the government would present figures designed to make citizens believe that the government was doing a good job of controlling inflation. Folks suspected that the government understated inflation, as a means trying to control it. In 1980, when the government's official figures indicated that inflation (CPI Index) was around 12%; interest rates were actually averaging between 16% and 22%, thus giving some idea of the extent to which businesses placed credibility in the government's figures, at the time.

OPEC

As if our problems relating to government indecision in the wage and price areas weren't enough, while all of this was going on, OPEC decided that it was payback time. By 1973, OPEC had gotten its act together, and its members finally agreed to a production cutback plan and successfully implemented it. The cost of petroleum based products and everything made that used petroleum in any way went up dramatically.

The cost of crude oil went from less than $10 a barrel, to a high, at one point in time, of $41 a barrel, then settled in at around $22-$28 a barrel (It's now over $70 a barrel). Gasoline for use in automobiles tripled in price over a two-month period of time. Not only that, but even at the higher prices, there was not enough gasoline being produced to meet the current demand. Americans began waiting in long lines to get enough gasoline to get back and forth to work. Vacations were put on hold. Tempers flared.

The government laid the blame at the feet of Middle Eastern nations now reaping high prices for their oil. No-one in the government mentioned the government's multi-decade support of the seven sisters, and/or the government's support of dictators in middle east countries that previously allowed the United States to profit from taking the oil from these same countries for a song before the dictators were overthrown, and the countries formed OPEC to get back some of what had previously been lost to them.

At the time the "seven sisters" organized to lay claim to the oil deposits in the middle east, there was no United Nations, no worldwide news coverage of business events to speak of, and no television.

Technological advances in the area of gathering and communicating (quickly) what occurred around the world, made it more difficult to take over a country, and subvert its resources. In prior centuries, citizens were more likely to accept at face value what they were told by their government. By 1970, citizens had the option of seeing first-hand what was going on, and forming their own opinions. The Seven Sisters and the governments backing them had little choice but to accept the OPEC mandates when they were passed down in 1973.

It has been calculated that the OPEC embargo of the early 1970's was responsible for the single greatest transfer of wealth between nations in the history of the world. For the first time since its founding, the United States was faced with a situation wherein a country whose resources had been taken by the U.S., successfully took them back. And, not a shot was fired in the process.

America Calls it Quits in 'Nam

In 1975 America officially withdrew its troops from Vietnam. Congress and the administration gave in to pressure coming from groups who had disagreed with America's reasons for being involved in what they considered another countries civil war. After nearly two decades of involvement, hundreds of billions of dollars spent, more than 50,000 American lives lost, and a hundred thousand Americans wounded, we quit the war.

Television had a large role to play in the decision to quit in Vietnam. At a time when the military conflict was going badly for the south Vietnamese position, TV routinely showed the unpleasant side of the conflict, including the hardships suffered by non-combatants.

Television reporters also returned with stories, backed by films, of America's military excursions into Laos and Cambodia, during the conflict, which excursions were "out of bounds" according to the rules of limited engagement, and which excursions were flatly denied by the American military and the American government.

American soldiers returning home from Vietnam did not enjoy the same kind of thanks and hero's welcomes enjoyed by American soldiers returning from prior wars. Additionally, a significant number of veterans returning from Vietnam were suffering physically from the harmful effects of having breathed in fumes from chemicals discharged from planes in an attempt to defoliate jungle areas around inland bases. Initially, the government denied that the sickness was due to chemicals like "agent orange", but eventually was forced to admit that it was the cause of the sickness, and that they had known at the time it was employed that it would harm those ingesting it, but that the decision had been made to use it anyway, and not warn (even our own) soldiers in advance.

One outgrowth of Vietnam was the introduction of a (much) higher level of distrust of the government by American citizens. By 1972, it had been proven beyond a reasonable doubt that the American military commanders, administration officials, and congressmen and congresswomen had lied, both big and often, to the American citizens, about the conflict in Vietnam.

Over time, the antagonism that existed during the conflict, between dissenting citizens and the soldiers that fought in Vietnam, at the individual level, subsided. The soldiers who fought and died in

Vietnam were ultimately viewed as good American citizens attempting to do their patriotic duty, but who, in the process, were decidedly poorly served by their government. The government officials involved in the deceptions, however, served to cover all government officials with a thick coating of public distrust.

Watergate

During the 1972 Presidential elections, a group of individuals associated with the election committee of one of the parties was caught trying to conduct a break-in and electronic bugging of an office of the election committee of the other party. The room that was broken into was located in the Watergate Hotel in Washington DC. At the time, not much was thought about it. Pretty much just boys being boys in the political arena where dirty tricks were the norm, rather than the exception.

After the election, the case gained notoriety when it was discovered that some people on the President's White House staff might have been involved, at least in a peripheral manner. When this possibility was followed up on by two newshounds from a prominent Washington (DC) paper, it was strongly denied by the administration, including strong denials by the president himself.

Over time, it was determined that White House staff, and the President himself, had known about the covert activities of the Watergate "burglars", and a big deal was made about the President, and a whole bunch of his closest advisors, having lied about not knowing about it when they were asked earlier.

The Watergate event took on a life of its own. It wasn't so much that anybody was shocked by the event itself. Politicians for ages had been known to spy on the other side. What stuck in everybody's craw, was that the President of their country, and most of his immediate staff, had gotten caught for the second time in as many years, lying outright to the people they were elected to serve. It may be argued that Vietnam made Watergate possible. And, it may be argued that Watergate resulted in the greatest disillusionment ever, in the way American citizens viewed their government officials.

The political fallout from Watergate was extensive. The president was forced to resign, faced possible criminal prosecution, and was pardoned by his successor. The vice president was indicted and convicted of criminal acts and went to prison. The attorney general, the top law enforcement officer and upholder of justice in the land, was indicted, tried, and sent to prison. Most of the president's closest advisors were convicted of being accessories to criminal acts, and perjuring themselves before Congress and the American people, and were also sent to prison.

Politicians lying wasn't anything new. Actually, it happened so often that people didn't usually even take notice when it did happen. Americans have always accepted a small amount of corruption and lying from their elected officials, and, for the most part elected to look the other way when it happens. Acceptance of a small amount of lying and corruption has always seemed a small price to pay for getting someone to take jobs that few people wanted, and even fewer could handle in a constructive manner.

But Americans also expect their politicians to at least be discreet when abusing their positions of power. That is just good manners. And, when a politician gets caught red-handed, with his or her hand in the cookie jar, or in a lie, Americans expect an admission of guilt, an apology, and a promise not to do it again. Promptly.

Americans don't like to be treated with condescension by their elected officials, or as if they just fell off a turnip truck. Americans know the score, and they don't like it when their elected officials treat them as if they are stupid. When elected officials break these unwritten rules in terms of owning up to mistakes in judgment and misdeeds, the citizens who elect them most often relieve them of their official duties, and send them packing.

Watergate proved that beyond any doubt. But, in the process, many American's came to feel that a majority of their elected officials at the highest levels of government held themselves above the laws that they held others to, and that they didn't identify with or respect the ideals of the citizens that elected them to office, and that they could therefore not be trusted. The majority of citizens coming to hold such views could, and ultimately would have serious repercussions for America.

The Cold War and the Defense Industry

White all of this was going on, so was the cold war between the socialist and capitalist ideologues. Hundreds of billions of dollars were spent annually for defense systems. The companies involved in some way in feeding the pentagon's needs for new weapons, and new ways for using them effectively, were among the healthiest in the world.

In part, this was due to the fact that these businesses not only sold their most current weapons technologies to the U.S. government, but they also provided prior generation weapons systems to the U.S. government, which the U..S government then sold to other nations as a means of bringing in money to pay the government's operating expenses.

This was a doubly good deal for the weapons producers, in that the U.S. government (taxpayers) provided all the R&D and growth capital that they could ever need, and these businesses did not have to compete for R&D and growth capital dollars in the typical fashion that businesses in other industries had to. And, the U.S. government's ongoing selling of old weapons systems to other governments (at a markup) meant that the weapons producers could reap very high margins on the older weapons systems, since the tooling required to produce them had already been paid for and depreciated in years past.

And, the government won doubly too, in that not only did they get a markup over what they paid the defense contractor for the second generation weapons that the U.S sold to other countries, but they got another reward when the higher than usual profits of the defense contractor were paid in the form of corporate income taxes.

It came to be the practice that defense contracts with the government had included in them COLA's, which served to guarantee that weapons costs would escalate by at least as much, if not more, annually, than the rate at which the government inflated the paper currency supply. Most increased in cost at a rate that far exceeded the paper currency inflation rate.

The government chose to look the other way when defense contractors openly cheated in the services provided, products delivered, and bills sent to the government for work done by them. While the Congress went through the motions of policing the contractors by way of putting in place various "watchdog" committees, these acts on their part were completely ineffective in stopping, or even slowing abuse by the defense contractors. It may be surmised that the reason such activities were ineffective is because the government benefited directly from the abuses when they occurred, and had no real intention of curbing them.

When defense contractors did things like charging $700 for a toilet seat, or $400 for a hammer, a high percentage of the overcharges went into the defense contractor's profit, and the government then received some of it back in the form of corporate income tax. Not legally speaking a "kickback" from the contractor to the government, but disturbingly close in its appearance.

Likewise, when the contractor, after including the cost of a few $400 hammers, attached a $25 million price tag to a fighter jet sold to the government, who in turn marked it up 25% over their cost when selling it to another foreign government, the government again benefited twice. First when they taxed the contractor's high profits, and second, when they pocketed the difference between what they paid the contractor for the jet, and what they charged the foreign government for it.

Obviously, the higher the cost paid by the U.S. government for the weapon, the higher would be the profit to the U.S. government, even if the markup percentage remained the same. If they paid only $12 million for the fighter, their 25% markup would only bring in about $3 million in profit. But, by paying $25 million for the fighter, and using the same markup percentage, the income to the government was doubled, to about $6 million a unit.

Periodically, the congress would make a show of fining a defense contractor in public hearings, and publicly berating the abuse and the abuser. Typically, the fine amounted to a few percent of the overcharges, and then the next year's defense budget would provide the abusive contractor with enough extra money to effectively wipe out the effects of the fine. Americans watched all this on television, saw through the smoke, haze, and deceit, and their distrust of government officials increased.

Environmental Concerns

The seventies and eighties saw significant growth in the number of citizens concerned about damage being done to the environment. Groups of individuals organized to lobby Congress over what they saw as abuses to the environment being made by various industries.

Initially, the "environmentalists" as they came to be known, were paid little attention to by the government. The government was also lobbied intensely, and very persuasively, by various industrial groups, who paid heavily into the election campaigns of candidates who promoted their views. The environmentalists were not as well organized, or as well funded, and, predictably, their causes were not championed by many elected representatives, at any level of government.

Over time, sensing that industry would always have the dollar advantage in terms of buying the cooperation of elected officials, the environmentalists decided to use a combination of tactics that had proven in the past capable of bringing down some of the most powerful political figures.

First, they gathered documented abuses on film (like in Vietnam). Then they persuaded television networks to show the abuses to the public at large (like in Vietnam and Watergate). In this manner, the elected officials had to combat visual images of environmental abuse with words alone. Now, although the industrial lobby retained the monetary advantage, the game was at least being played on the environmentalists' home field, and they began to make some headway. Watching whales get harpooned for perfume oil, and baby seals have their heads bashed in with clubs so that their fur could be made into coats, and whole mountain ranges denuded through clear cutting, was powerful stuff.

As a result of the actions of the various environmental groups (who were portrayed as "extremists" and "tree huggers" by the industrialists, their lobbyists, and the politicians supported by the campaign contributions of the industrialists); a number of laws were passed, and an agency was put in place to monitor industrial impact on the environment, to clean up past environmental messes left behind by industry that might endanger life, and to prosecute offenders in the future. Its name, appropriately enough, was the Environmental Protection Agency, or EPA for short.

The EPA was a lightning rod from day one, and continues to be one. At various points in time, it called to task other government agencies for allowing industries regulated by them to abuse the environment. This served to alienate other government agencies who were accused of not doing their jobs properly.

Industry saw the internal squabbling as an opening to "divide and conquer", and put its lobbyists to work supporting the administration of those agencies whose actions were criticized by the EPA.

Two government agencies drew more than average heat from the EPA. The U.S. Forest service and the Bureau of Land management were taken to task for allowing lumber, mining and livestock interests to over cut and overgraze public lands, and to "patent" (buy) public land for virtually no cost.

Bureaucracy being what it is, it turned out that one of the hardest jobs the EPA would have would be regulating its sister agencies within the U.S. government. Both the USFS and BLM were responsible for bringing in a lot of money especially in the way of "user fees" paid by lumber cutters and livestock growers.

Predictably, the USFS and BLM found champions for their current method of operation in the lumber, mining, and livestock industries, who lobbied heavily on "the hill" (in the U.S. Congress) to allow these agencies to keep things as they were. The EPA found champions for their views with the various environmental groups around the country. Neither side came away with all that they wanted. The viewing of the environmentalists' side of the story on the evening news, prompted elected officials into modifying some government regulatory programs relating to usage of renewable natural resources.

Clear cutting of entire mountain ranges was reduced. Policing actions relating to effluent discharges into the air and streams was initiated, and new industrial plants were required to allow oversight by EPA prior to and after construction. A few bodies of water, like Lake Superior, were restored, and some fisheries were partially restored too. Whaling and killing of furbearing mammals was cut back and regulated. Factories installed "scrubbers" in their smokestacks, and air became cleaner in some areas.

The EPA had less success in getting old messes cleaned up. Industry resisted paying the costs associated with cleaning up toxic waste sites, and used their legislative clout at all levels of government to drag out the cleanup process over years, sometimes decades, of time. The EPA also drew a lot of heat when it required industries to periodically file "environmental impact statements".

Environmental impact statements were aimed at industries whose activities were being engaged in (in) areas that the EPA determined were especially fragile, from an ecological standpoint. It was harder to gain public endorsement of a 1" minnow being threatened with extinction, or a small owl being threatened with extinction, than it was to get people to endorse the stoppage of the killing whales or seals, or clear cutting of whole mountain ranges. When the EPA stopped industrial activity as a means of threatening very small creatures, it was often held up to outright ridicule by those who opposed its actions.

When an industrial activity was suspended by the EPA for purposes of protecting something like a ladybug, or small owl, additional cries of "too much" were heard by those whose jobs were adversely affected. Paradoxically, some of the same individuals who cheered when the EPA shut down some stream polluters responsible for killing off a strain of minnow, in the process temporarily putting some workers of the polluting mining company out of work; complained bitterly when the EPA shut down the cutting of old growth forests to save some small owls, and temporarily put some lumberjacks out of work.

It became apparent that concern for the environment was very much a case of whose ox was getting gored at the time. Like the old saying goes: "everybody wants to go to heaven, but nobody wants to die to get there".

It is not possible to say with absolute certainty, but it is highly probable that, absent the EPA's actions, there would by now be no harvestable amounts of many species of fish in the seas, no old growth timber left in the mountains, no national parks free from the scarring effects of mining, and few, if any streams of unpolluted water for fish to live in, and for people to enjoy. It's been a fight, every step of the way for the EPA, and the industrial adversaries still lined up against them are formidable.

It remains to be seen if the EPA can, and will, be able to survive the onslaught with their mandate still intact. On the plus side for the environmentalists is that television remains available to them, and the network owners have thus far deemed it worthwhile to continue to show the public visual images of abuses to the environment as they occur. A picture of a game fish choking and dying in heavily polluted stream water is still worth many words. On the plus side for the industrial concerns is that people tend to vote with their pocketbooks, and pictures of people out of work, begging on street corners for food, perhaps due to EPA sanctions having been imposed on a business or industry, are worth many words too.

Perhaps the primary thing Americans learned from observing the EPA's battles to bring the needs of industry into harmony with the needs of the environment, was, how <u>money</u> had a tendency to alter the government's resolve. Cynicism toward government as a solver of environmental problems grew.

Social Programs

Social Security had started out one and a half percent of gross wages, up to a maximum gross wage level of $3000. Between 1970 and 1985, the percentage of income taken grew to over 12%, and the upper gross pay limit grew to $40,000 a year. That constituted a change from a maximum of $45 per year in the 1930's, to a maximum of about $4,800 per year by 1985, or about a **10,600%** increase from the inception of the program. (It has since gone up a lot more to 12.5% of $90,000+, or about **23,000%** since the inception of the program).

The government hastened to assure workers that their employer was paying half the tab, and that only half was actually coming from their paychecks each payday. This was untrue, of course. The worker paid all of the money into FICA. In truth, employers simply learned right off the bat to reduce workers' salaries and hourly wages enough to make up for the company's FICA contributions.

For every government action, there is an equal and opposite citizen reaction.

The increase in Social Security taxes was made necessary because the government had never built in a waiting period for workers to receive Social Security payments. Almost from day number one of the program, workers were provided pension supplements, when they had paid little or nothing into the program.

Making things worse by this point in time was the impact of the government's past economic policies aimed at paying for ever growing costs of government in part, by inflating the nation's paper currency supply, and causing wages and prices to spiral upward rapidly over the previous thirty to forty years' time, since Social Security had been enacted. As those old enough to have fought in World War II came to retirement age, after having worked for a decade or two at jobs with COLA's, they expected to have a retirement supplement that reflected their ever increasing payments into the program over the years. As inflation caused everything else to go up in price, Social Security had, itself, been modified to have similar COLA's built in for recipients.

By the 1980's, Social Security was being called on to pay out monthly supplements in the $800 per month range, every month until the retiree passed on. If the retiree lived thirty years after retiring, the payments would add up to almost $300,000. Given that most recipients had contributed only about $80,000 to the program, including "employer" contributions, and that not a single penny of their contributions had ever been saved up, or invested, but instead had been spent by the government the month in which they were collected, to pay someone else's benefit, Social Security was continually on the verge of bankruptcy.

Almost annually, congress came up with several programs to "save" Social Security, each one requiring another increase in payroll taxes, and each one promising to keep the program solvent forever. Over time, it became apparent to most Americans that Social Security was an experiment doomed to ultimate failure. As money-strapped families began to decide to have smaller numbers of children, a mathematical certainty arose that Social Security would fail.

By 1980, given that people were living longer due to better health programs, and improved medical treatments, and families were having fewer children, due to having less income left over after taxes with which to provide for a family, it became obvious that at a point in time long before the middle of the 21st century, that each contributor to the program would have to pay in enough to support one recipient, in full. This was quite a departure from what had been promised at the outset of the program, when there were more than 25 people putting money in, for each one that was taking money out.

Nevertheless, congressmen to a man (or woman) vowed to preserve Social Security "for future generations".

> A government program, once in motion, tends to stay in motion unless acted on by an outside force

Medicare and Medicaid

As average life expectancy rose, and costs of medical treatments rose, the combination of these two conditions prompted Congress to act again. Two new programs were enacted, loosely related to Social Security, designed to allay fears of retiring persons that their social security incomes would be eaten up with medical bills.

Initially, medical payments were made by Social Security, after that program was expanded to include early payments for workers who had to quit working early due to medical disabilities. The Social Security Administration indicated to congress that one reason that Social Security was constantly running out of money for retirement payments, was due to having ever higher percentages of what came in, being paid out for medical claims.

Rather than again increasing social security taxes sharply, and possibly starting a tax revolt, Congress started a new tax to "supplement" medical payments for qualified persons of advanced age. Taking their cue from the social security program, Congress wisely initially set the tax rate to be quite low. So low in fact, that from day one Medicare and Medicaid were in the red, paying out more than they took in. This was not done in ignorance. Congress knew from the start that they were under funding these two new programs. However, they apparently reasoned that over time, the Medicare/Medicaid tax rate could be gradually increased, as had been done with social security and the income tax. Experience showed that raising the tax rate a small amount annually had worked with the income tax, and Social Security, in terms of "conditioning" the public, and desensitizing them to the tax increases. Sort of like rats being conditioned to accept ever greater electric shocks, in exchange for pellets of food.

Medicare and Medicaid were programs administered by the federal government, who was a group not known for its efficiency. Abuse of the new programs by unscrupulous medical practitioners was quick to occur, and spread. It was $400 hammers all over again, but in the medical, rather than the defense industry. Providers of every stripe, increased their charges for Medicare/Medicaid treatments, and commonly sent out multiple bills for the same single treatment. And the government paid them. Several times, in some instances. Providers got used to passing through double digit annual increases for their services to all patients, assuming that either the insurance company's or government would end up paying them.

And, for the most part, time proved the providers right in these assumptions.

The government looked the other way while the price gouging occurred. As with the defense contractor abuses, congressional oversight committees held hearings periodically, and publicly castigate a few abusers. But, this was apparently mostly just done for show. As abusive medical providers reaped high profits from overcharging for their services (like $25 for a Tylenol capsule while staying in a hospital, when the hospital was getting them free), the government received back a part of their earnings in the form of income taxes.

Medicare taxes once gathered in as payroll deductions could only be spent specifically on Medicare related expenses. However, once the government received back a portion of the Medicare profits from abusive providers, in the form of income taxes, the government was free to spend the (general fund) money on anything it wanted to. Not perhaps, legally speaking, laundering Medicare money into general fund money, but identical in its outcome. (...if it walks like a duck, quacks like a duck ...)

Given that many providers were in the above 25% tax brackets, the government's looking away as abuses to the system occurred, resulted in the government getting about a 25% kickback. But, no matter how they worked it, there never seemed to be enough money, for either the providers, or the government. Providers continued to increase their rates in the double digits each year, and the government continued increases in both the payroll tax rate, relating to Medicare/Medicaid, and the top level of gross income that was taxable.

Entitlements

At the outset, social security was never intended to take the place of a full retirement Income. It was intended to be an added supplement that could mean the difference between just getting by, and having a full and rewarding life after retirement. Over time, however, the increases in social security taxes, and Medicare-Medicaid taxes reached a point where so much was being taken by the government, those workers had nothing left over with which to provide a retirement nest egg of their own for social security to supplement. Workers at large companies, and those covered by union contracts often had some retirement benefits through work, but for those who did not, it came to be that social security would be all that they had upon retirement.

Seeing the writing on the wall (both Social Security and Medicare-Medicaid were actuarially unsustainable over the long term) people fearful of being abandoned in their later years banded together to lobby congress for benefit assurances. The American Association of Retired Persons (AARP) was formed specifically for the purpose of lobbying congress on behalf of retirement age persons, at the expense of under-retirement age persons. Having members in every state, many of whom had nothing to do all day but write letters made the AARP a powerful lobbying group. Their motives were purely selfish, and they prided themselves on that fact. At least they were open and above board about it.

Congressmen and congresswomen feared the AARP political machine. The elected officials did not necessarily like the AARP, but they almost to an elected official respected its political clout. The AARP's primary goals were the preservation of Social Security and Medicare/Medicaid. They stressed that senior Americans were entitled to these benefits, and such programs thereafter became known as entitlements.

> Thus it came to be that Americans became <u>entitled</u> to rely on benefits from programs that mathematics showed to be unsustainable over the long term, and thus it came to be that American workers allowed the government to usurp the individual citizen's responsibility of providing for themselves in their declining years.

War Technology Trickles Down

By 1980, technology relating to miniaturization of solid state electronics originally developed for use in sophisticated weapons systems began finding its way significantly, into products developed for the non-military consumer market.

Automobiles, televisions, radios, record players, kitchen stoves, wrist watches, and all sorts of consumer products began being made smaller, cheaper, and improved over prior generation products, by way of introducing small solid state circuitry into their design.

Even among those involved in their development, few probably understood at the outset, the potential of these "chips" as they came to be called, and the extent that they could, and would, be used to reshape the world. Among the novel ideas coming out of the ranks of those involved in the potential use of "chip" technology, were a couple of college dropouts who developed in their garage a machine capable of performing calculations that were typically at the time performed on large scale computing platforms manufactured by the likes of IBM, Honeywell, CDC, Univac, and Digital Equipment Corporation.

The designers of the new gadget called it a "personal computer" or PC for short. The large computer manufacturers made fun of the new "toy", dubbed it something for "nerds", and went on about their business.

In its original form the PC was decidedly not something for the masses. But, over the next ten years' time that would change and the outfall of the "computer revolution" that was to come would impact every person on the planet more significantly than had all the technological change which had preceded it since man appeared on the Earth.

Chip technology was not only employed in the infant PC's that began about this period of time, but was also incorporated into machines used in manufacturing processes. Previously, machine controls were primarily designed with analog circuits which required larger chassis, more hard wiring, greater maintenance, and typically more human interface in operation as well. The newer solid state digital circuitry provided dramatic changes in all of these areas, and was cheaper to boot. Industry worldwide began retooling their manufacturing processes using machines controlled by solid state digital circuits and which were "programmable". Programmable circuitry provided that the same machine could be made to perform different work sequences under control of a computer program.

Due to "progressive" tax policies in the U S. relating to capital investments (money invested for things like research and development, and startup of new businesses), American tooling manufacturers were slower to get new machine tool products built around solid state circuits to market than were tooling manufacturers in some other countries. By 1985 manufacturers of everything from automobiles to small plastic products in the United States were tooled up mostly with manufacturing machine tools made by workers in other countries, and were dependent on these foreign companies for replacement parts, and major service too.

As "computer" technology spread, companies found that they could produce more products, with fewer workers, and proceeded to do so. In past times, workers threatened with a cutback in the number of jobs could look to unions to help persuade management not to lay workers off. By 1985, a combination of companies who had already moved part of their operations to other countries and the ease with which workers could be taught to interface with the new "computerized" manufacturing tools and processes, had served to take some of the leverage out of the unions hands, and put it back in the hands of management.

After 1980, when unions went out on strike, to protect workers' jobs from loss, the government looked the other way, and let the strikes continue until management won. Previous generations of workers had come to expect the government to protect them in a number of ways, that by 1985 the government had decided to not do anymore.

Specifically, prior generation workers had come to rely on the government maintaining tariffs on goods imported into the country that were sufficiently high to protect American businesses from being greatly undersold in the U.S. marketplace. Prior generation workers had come to rely on the government prohibiting companies hiring of permanent replacements for striking workers (called "scabs" by striking workers) and making companies return jobs to striking workers, when strikes were ended. And, workers had come to rely on government stepping in and forcing mediation in strikes that went on to a point where workers were hurting too badly, and/or when strikes were adversely effecting too many other citizens that depended on the "struck" company's products.

Between 1950 and 1980, unions had often abused their privileges, with government support, and management was pretty much forced to accept union demands. By 1980, the pendulum had again swung back in the direction favoring management, and would again continue on past center, to a point where management was in a position to abuse their privileges, and would do so.

Technological advances also changed the manufacturing paradigm in other ways. Development of huge aircraft for purposes of ferrying troops and military equipment over long distances was the precursor of development of similar aircraft for use in the private sector. Even prior to the OPEC oil embargo in the early 1970's, ships capable of transporting huge quantities of oil had been developed, and these were redesigned to accommodate other types of cargo as well in the period following the oil embargo. The evolution of trans-oceanic transport by air and ships, of massive quantities of cargo, freed manufacturers of primary products (steel, aluminum, plastics, etc.) from the necessity of locating their manufacturing facilities in close proximity to the source of raw materials.

And the networking of computers by way of satellite transmissions allowed widely separated offices of a company in different countries to communicate as effectively as though they were adjacent to one another in the same building.

By 1985, it was not only possible, but practical, from an economic standpoint, to transport raw materials half way around the world to a processing facility, and then transport the processed materials to wherever they might be needed. It was a short leap in imagination for manufacturing businesses housed in the United States to figure out that, given the new paradigm in transport logistics, they could move manufacturing operations to whatever country provided the lowest taxes and labor costs, import the needed raw materials, export the finished product, and still come out (way) ahead profit-wise.

The exodus of manufacturing jobs from the United States, to other countries where taxes on business were lower, labor costs were lower, and citizens (workers) expected a much lower standard of living than U.S. workers were accustomed to, was an entirely predictable event, once the government was seen to adopt a position of advocating "free-market" policies, which called for non-intervention in labor management disputes at any level.

"Trickle Down" Economics

In 1980 a new President was elected, after being governor of a state that had seen a grass roots tax revolution that resulted in taxes on individuals and businesses, at the state and local level, actually being reduced. The ex-governor, who was now President, had taken over the leadership of his state when it was operating in the red, and taxes were increasing faster than in any other state in the nation. When he left to become president, the state he had been governor in had seen tax rates reduced, government services made arguably more efficient, and the states operating budget was in the black. Voters elected him to try and do the same thing at the national level.

This happened at a time when inflation in the U.S. was estimated by the government to be about 12%, and estimated by everyone else to be much higher than that. The previous President had declared that the country was suffering from a "national malaise". The new President said that was not true, that the problem was citizens being held back by bad government.

The new President promised to reduce the size of government, reduce taxes at all levels, remove government's incentive to continually inflate the nation's paper currency supply as a means of stabilizing prices, reduce or eliminate taxes on profits generated through capital investments, and to bring the country's budget into balance. It was a tall order.

According to the new President, rather than having more dollars printed up and made available to the public with which to purchase things, a better approach would be to lower taxes of all kinds and encourage manufacturers to crank up their plants and produce as many products as possible, while letting competition among suppliers set prices accordingly. In theory, this would cause prices for goods (and money) to moderate, or even fall, rather than continuing to rise with the rate of inflation in the nation's paper currency supply.

In effect, the new President was encouraging government and citizens alike to return to a paradigm that existed before the Texas Railroad Commission did its work back during the depression of the 1930's. For several decades it had been accepted as gospel that the best approach was to use an economic model that called for taxes to be kept high and supplies of goods (and money) to be artificially held down, in order for prices to continually go up. The new President's recommendations flew in the face of the conventional wisdom of the day, and were roundly made fun of, by proponents of the existing economic model of the day. The new President's recommendations were labeled "trickle down economics" by the loyal opposition, and this catch-phrase was picked up on by the media, who joined in making fun of the new president's ideas. Even the new vice president had called the new Presidents ideas "voodoo economics" when they had been competing in the presidential primaries.

The new President in 1980 was elected by a very large majority, and declared that his election majority was intended by the voters to be a mandate for change. His majority in the election was apparently significant enough to convince a majority in congress to go along with his program, at least to some degree. During the first two years in office the new President got some of what he asked for. Tax rates were reduced, the capital gains tax was halved, and tax deductions were indexed to inflation which eliminated the government from getting to tax income resulting solely from inflation.

The President also asked for a line item veto, as a means of stopping the practice of legislators tacking on "riders" to important legislative bills that affected all Americans. This wish was not granted by the Congress, who had become accustomed to using "riders" as the means of fulfilling promises to campaign contributors. Riders, for those not familiar with the term, are amendments unrelated to the main topic of the legislation in question. Riders are a form of blackmail congress uses to get legislation funded when the legislation is unrelated to the general public good.

An example might be attaching an amendment to a bill fixing the rate for Social Security payments for the upcoming year, when the amendment calls for the government to spend a few million dollars on a project in a particular congressman's district, aimed at paying back a heavy campaign contributor, by way of funneling the contributor's business a job entailing building a new government building in a particular locality that the contributor lives in. The crude name for it is "pork barrel politics".

Any legislator can propose a self-serving amendment to any bill primarily relating to the broad national interest, which the president may feel forced to sign, and in doing so (perhaps unwillingly) puts the President in the position of having to accept funding for the hidden "pork" rider too. "Pork" has always the way politicians paid off campaign contributors with government (taxpayer) money. Nothing new about it as a concept. However, by 1980, pork barrel politics had grown to a degree that the general public was alarmed at its prevalence.

Congress was not ready to give up their addiction to pork, and the President's request for a line item veto was denied. The lack of availability of a line item veto for the president meant that congress could continue to spend at will, by attaching unrelated spending "riders" to legislation affecting the broader national interest, and the President had to either veto the legislation needed for the public good, in order to not approve the pork barrel spending riders, or approve the important legislation, and in the process also approve of the pork barrel spending.

Typically, these riders were attached to bills of great importance like a continuing resolution needed to authorize an increase in the government's debt limit or to a bill authorizing the annual COLA increase in Social Security payments, or something else that was equally important. If the president vetoed one of these, in order to dissuade the porkers, he was portrayed by his opponents as also being against the main issue to which the "rider" was attached.

For the most part, the new President's programs (that were enacted) worked as promised. The incentive for the government to continually inflate the paper currency supply was reduced slightly. Unemployment went down to levels not seen since the end of WWII. Capital flowed into new projects, and American businesses began to expand again. Income to the Treasury increased at record rates, as the economy gained momentum.

But, demand still continued to exceed supply as far as currency was concerned. Even though the economy was growing at record rates, the government remained stubbornly in the red, and the amount of red ink began to grow at an alarming rate. The reason was the lack of any mechanism to keep congress from spending at a higher rate than income was coming in to the government from taxes.

When the new President had been governor, and brought his state's budget into balance, he had had a line item veto, which allowed him to veto "riders" tacked onto major legislation of importance to the general public. That ability, at the governor's level, allowed him to let legislation affecting the general welfare through, while vetoing pork-laden riders, and in the process the state's budget was balanced. But, at the national level, he was denied this capability, and congress continued to "pork away".

The end result was that the nation's debt rose rapidly, as the Treasury continued to print money needed to finance the government's operating deficits each year. The new currency takes the form of treasury notes and bonds issued (sold) to the Federal

Reserve banks, in return for which the Federal Reserve causes the security issuers (i.e. governments) account at the treasury or a commercial bank to be increased by the face value amount of the new treasury bonds issued by the treasury to the fed. The government then uses the increase in its various bank accounts to pay for its operating deficits. The Treasury bonds issued to the Federal Reserve bank(s) at a discount are resold by the Fed to other investors for a profit (to the Fed) and these securities then become part of the "national debt".

Because of the Fed's actions relating to creating currency just to finance deficit spending by the congress, and it's use of its reserve regulatory powers to force banks to go along too, inflation was therefore not eliminated, but it was reduced slightly, since at least that portion of rising incomes at the individual and business level, caused by inflation, were no longer subject to taxation.

Congress claimed that the annual budget deficits were the result of the President's lowering taxes too much, (only Congress can act to lower taxes) and not a result of Congress spending too much. Exploding government deficits were used effectively by "spin doctors" (advertising firms) hired by members of Congress to show that, in the long run, "trickle down" economics was a flop.

In truth "trickle down" economics was (and is) the basis for capitalism. The opponents of cautious spending wisely chose to use the term "trickle down" in a derogatory way, and in the process discredited it, and the system it stood for. It had always been the case in capitalistic societies, that the investors who risked their capital in starting and building businesses that employed workers, received significantly more income from ventures that succeeded, than did the workers who invested (and risked) nothing in the venture. In the capitalist scheme of things, that was considered both just and fair. Those who worked hardest, risked ruin, and ultimately succeeded, should be entitled to the fruits of their labors if and when the venture ever succeeded.

Those not favoring this (capitalist) approach seldom acknowledged the price paid in terms of both human and monetary capital by those entrepreneurs who failed and were ruined in their attempts to become successful capitalists. In fact, for the past century, it has been the case that 5 out of 6 attempts to begin a new business result in failure, and possibly bankruptcy for the entrepreneur. In prior century's, the failure rate was even higher. New ventures that do succeed, typically take 13 years on the average to become successful.

Those entrepreneurs willing to take such risks, and work for little or nothing for so long, in order to get a piece of the American dream, were sometimes rewarded by disproportionate wealth, if and when the dream was realized.

Nobody in government cried much for the 5 out of 6 who lost everything in trying, but many were quick to fault those who beat the odds, and thereafter lived better than the workers they employed. A majority in Congress, for one, and several Presidents for another, routinely made a special effort to denigrate the successful capitalists publicly, discriminating against them in their taxing policies, in the process painting them to be un-American and unconcerned about the plight of those less fortunate than themselves. Then elected officials in Washington acted surprised when the capitalists chose to expatriate their companies and wealth to other countries, where they were welcomed.

During the Period between 1970 and 1995, the combination of government expansion of existing programs, paid for with inflated currencies, and government using the tax laws to "guide" individuals and businesses into practices favored by elected officials reached its peak. Indexing tax deductions to inflation failed to achieve its goal of stopping steady price increases as congress refused to act in a manner that balanced government expenses with government income from non-inflation-related sources. The national debt continued to grow rapidly. Temporary government programs were expanded, made permanent, and (re)labeled <u>entitlements</u>.

Americans mistrust of elected officials increased.

By 1995, price increases had outpaced wage increases to the point that the very great majority of families required both parents to work full time in order to afford a home of their own. Parental guidance was lessened in the home, and non-parents increasingly were placed in positions of teaching children things that had formerly been the responsibility of parents to teach.

1985 To Now

Wars

During this period, new wars continued to spring up frequently, and some old ones continued to flare up as well. At one point in the late 1980's the United Nations proclaimed that there were more than 55 shooting wars going on concurrently, around the globe. Perhaps the most significant war event during this period was the effective ending of the "cold" war between the Soviet Union, and the United States.

The USSR threw in the towel, and began a journey from socialism to capitalism. The many Soviet "satellite" countries that had previously come to rely on foreign aid from the USSR were thrown into a state of disarray, and many conflicts sprang up as these states began to identify new leaders, and establish new policies aimed at existing in a new and unfamiliar political/economic environment.

The USSR had nuclear weapons deployed in several satellite countries under its control, before the breakup of the USSR as a socialist federation. Primarily due to fear in the U.S. government about having to deal with new, small states with nuclear weapons, whose new leaders might be unpredictable; the U.S. congress voted to now extend foreign aid to Russia, in hopes that Russia's having money to spend, would make the newly freed up satellite countries allow Russia's leaders, who we were familiar with and trusted not to do anything foolish, nuclear-wise, manage the downsizing of the old USSR nuclear weapons stockpile. This worked pretty well, but, of course it also claimed a lot of U.S. taxpayer dollars in the process.

Concurrently, some of the USSR's old foreign aid recipients now saw the light of capitalism shining brightly, and now began coming to the U.S. directly in hopes of having the U.S. pick up their support, since the USSR was no longer able to do so. In several instances, the U.S. government elected to advance foreign aid to these smaller countries directly, causing a further drain on the U.S. Treasury.

With the close of the "cold" war, the U.S. became the unchallenged strongest kid on the block, worldwide. Between 1985 and 1995, there were a series of internal conflicts in smaller "third world" countries around the globe. Some involved use of military force, by at least one of the warring factions. Prior to the end of the "cold" war, warring factions would first align idealistically with the capitalists (U.S.) or socialists (USSR) to obtain financing.

After the end of the "cold" war this option was no longer available to third world nations, and increasingly, arms left over from the cold war would be seized by one faction, who used them indiscriminately against the other faction, as a means of forcing their will and policies on the other side.

When this happened, The United Nations, by virtue of being the principal public forum of the third world countries, would be called on to intervene, and would then ask non-third world countries who were members of the UN, to field a peacekeeping force (army) to quell the armed conflict, and provide an environment wherein governments could be formed through the elective process.

The end of the cold war, prompted by the dissolution of the USSR, and Russia's election to switch over to a capitalist economic model, placed a heavy load of responsibility on the United Nations to maintain control over military conflicts worldwide. The United Nations was long on desire, but short on money, when it came to rising to the occasion. Beginning in 1988, presidents of both parties elected to have the United States provide the means by which the United Nations could carry out its aims, while subjugating the U.S. military to control of non-American commanders. This was essentially a repeat of the policy adopted by the president(s) during the Korean conflict of the early 1950's. Predictably, there was disagreement over following this course of action, but it was followed anyway.

After the end of the cold war, the United States was by far the best equipped country remaining armed to provide the type of assistance the UN was seeking to bring into play, both in terms of military might, and, economics. And, repeatedly the U.S. did supply the bulk of the assistance needed, under the auspices of the United Nations. Other UN member countries contributed too, but the great majority of contributions made toward this end, both militarily and economically, were made by the United States. In fact, the U.S. typically contributed more than all of the other UN countries combined. Within a ten-year period beginning in 1985, the U.S. was called on to intervene militarily and economically in civil wars in Ethiopia, Kuwait, and Bosnia, and also was involved in short term military actions in Nicaragua and Granada, and provided some military assistance to Great Britain in a similar action in the Falkland Islands.

During this period too, attrition was taking its toll in the ongoing war between Israel and its neighboring nations. The inability of the USSR to continue funding the military buildup of Israel's enemies, and the inability of the USSR to continue providing satellite military surveillance to Israel's enemies took two of the most effective arrows out of their quiver. Seeing that military expansion of Israel and foreign aid to Israel by the U.S. government were likely to continue in place as before, Israel's enemy neighbors conceded to begin negotiating an end to the ongoing hostilities between them.

Banking History Repeats Itself

In 1981-1982 there had been a pretty serious economic recession. When the new President came into office in 1980, he promised to "get government off the backs of U.S. citizens", as a means of freeing up economic expansion.

One of the new President's policies was aimed at lowering the cost of borrowing money, in part by providing some competition with other lending sources. It called for allowing savings and loan financial institutions, to engage in the same types of lending previously only allowed to be engaged in by banks, and private investment groups.

The real estate construction industry had been badly hurt by the last two recessions, and was continuing to be hampered by stubbornly high interest rates. There is an inverse relationship between interest rates, and the health of businesses making things that typically have to be financed over a period of time. This applied to most large ticket items, like automobiles, and especially to homes and commercial buildings. The higher interest rates were, the less well interest-sensitive businesses fared.

Savings and loans had originally been authorized by congress when banks refused to make loans to people for homes to live in Savings and loans also typically were allowed to pay slightly higher (subsidized) interest rates to borrowers, than banks, in order to attract deposits that could then be used to finance home building. By 1980, S&L financing of homes had become the way most homes got built in America. But, by 1980, S&L's were having trouble attracting money for growth and expansion through stock offerings, since their dividends were not as attractive as those of banks, and other types of financing groups who were allowed to invest in higher risk, and therefore higher return, investments.

Congress modified the laws in a way that allowed S&L's to broaden the scope of their lending in the home market, so that they could not only invest in single homes, for homeowners, but could take equity positions in whole home and business development projects. Under the new rules enacted by congress, a S&L could partner up with a developer in terms of not only financing individual homes, once they were built, but in the buying of raw land parcels, putting in the infrastructure improvements (electrical lines, streets, sewers, water treatment plants, etc.). S&L's were even freed up to have credit card operations.

Prior to changing the S&L rules, the purchase of land, and infrastructure development had typically been paid for by real estate speculators, who absorbed the initial risks associated with such development. This level of real estate investing is among the riskiest of short term investments available to investors.

Over a long enough period of time, real estate has always appreciated. The old saying in the land sales business is "they aren't making any more of the stuff". However, once the land has been purchased and the infrastructure has been put into place, it is pure speculation, as to whether the property can be further developed, and sold to individual homeowners quickly or not. At this point, the first developers in the chain, those buying up the farm fields, and installing the infrastructure, are at the mercy of many elements outside their sphere of direct control. The country might go into a recession, interest rates rise, and home buying might be dramatically cut back for some time. An oil embargo might happen, or a war might come up. The main highway might be re-routed to the other side of town. Any number of things might happen to cause the semi-developed land to sit idle, for months or years, sometimes more than a decade.

This happened so routinely, that those engaging in this type of development were viewed by traditional lenders as feast-or-famine customers, and typically had to get financing through non-financial-institution sources. While the "field of dreams" prophesy: (if you build it, they will come), was a viable <u>long</u> term prophesy, it did not always materialize in the <u>short</u> term. Meeting quarterly payments of interest to S&L depositors was always a short term need of S&L's. Thus, using high-risk, long term investments for meeting short term bill paying was a risky approach.

Real estate investment trusts (REIT's) were the typical source of financing for initial real estate development, and the people that put their money in REIT's were typically people that had more money than most, and could afford to wait years, or even decades, for a return if necessary. When these trusts sought money in the form of bonded indebtedness, the bonds were backed by so little collateral, carried such a high debt-to-equity ratio, and carried such high risks of repayment, that they fell into the category of "junk bonds".

In its zeal to get the home and business construction industry going strong again, the congress enacted laws giving preferential tax treatment to REIT's, and gave S&L's permission to both invest in REIT's directly, and to enter into joint ventures directly with building contractors, to develop new projects from scratch (financing not only new homes in the projects for homeowners, but buying the land, and paying for the infrastructure improvements too). S&L's were similarly allowed to do this with commercial projects like developing industrial parks, and commercial high rise projects. S&L sales of junk bonds of their own soared.

Unintended results of this policy shift by the congress, in terms of allowing S&L's to broaden their investing, was to expose the ordinary depositors of S&L's to a much higher level of risk, and to cause interest rates for individual home buyers to go up rather than down.

The risk to individual depositors went up, because the S&L's were now free to invest depositors' money in higher-risk projects. The interest rates for individual home buyers went up because the S&L's now put most of their available money into the riskier projects, which had potentially much higher returns, which they hoped would persuade their stock offerings to be more attractive to stock market investors in the established stock markets. That left less money in the S&L's for individual borrowers to borrow for home purchases, and supply and demand then caused the price for the reduced amount of loanable money for individual homes to rise, in effect causing interest rates to go up, rather than down.

> The law of unintended consequences strikes again.

The Treasury arm of the government worked, during the period immediately following the "deregulation" of the S&L industry by the congress, to make certain that the S&L's had money available to them to invest in development projects. In part, this was done to be sure that new development projects got off the ground, and in the process, put construction workers back to work. In part it was done to make sure that the S&L's didn't run completely out of money to be used for financing individual homes, which was, after all, their original charter. This process was admittedly inflationary, but, only Americans were affected, and rationalizing the inflationary consequences was not difficult at the time. In these respects, the government's actions in broadening the investing options of the S&L's and inflating the currency levels to make sure that the S&L's had new money to invest in the newly allowed types of investments, paralleled similar government actions in broadening banks investment options, and supplying them with money to lend prior to the stock market crash of 1929.

Like stock market investors in the late 1920's, the S&L managers of the 1980's continued to invest in new projects well after all the real demand in the marketplace had been satisfied. S&L money invested in new projects beyond that point in time saw no returns coming back to the S&L's and their REIT partners, as a huge oversupply of partially developed land became available and sat undeveloped beyond the infrastructure point, and new commercial projects sat empty, once built.

Up until this point in time, S&L's had been able to meet interest payments for their depositors from money coming in from their development projects. Then, rather suddenly, there was not enough income coming in from development projects to meet the interest payments due to depositors, and the supply of money available to loan to homeowners wanting to finance a new home, dried up completely, touching off another serious round of interest rate increases. When the S&L's couldn't meet their commitments to their customers and depositors, they were placed into government receivership.

As had happened following the bank failures during the depression, the government responded by denying any responsibility for the failures of the S&L's, and set out to "make sure something like this never happens again". Congress held hearings and publicly castigated S&L owners whose businesses failed, prosecuting some who had self-dealt beyond the law. Congress also set up an organization called the Resolution Trust Corporation (RTC) to dispose of the S&L's remaining assets, at huge losses to the S&L's, and the taxpayers who footed the bills to the tune of an estimated **$500 billion dollars**.

That worked out to a cost, in increased taxes, in the amount of about **$10,000** for every family in the country. Being big hearted like they are, the politicians tried to hide the overall impact by using Federal Reserve Banks to create the money needed to underwrite the losses, and spread the payback of the loans over a long period of time, so that they would have time to slowly increase income taxes enough to pay back the Fed…and the taxpayers would not feel the pain until years down the road.

It was Deja vu all over again.

Welfare Programs

During this period, the various personal security programs previously enacted by the congress each encountered financial difficulties as the number of recipients continued to grow at a rate that was considerably greater that either the population in general, or economy in general was growing.

Congress was continually being asked for more money for things like Social Security, Medicare, Medicaid, food stamps, welfare subsidies in the form of childcare allowances, rent subsidies, farm subsidies, mining (mostly oil) subsidies, transportation subsidies, and block grants to cover the cost of programs mandated by congress which had to be paid for by state governments.

By 1990, America was beginning a decade that would see the advent of third generation welfare recipients. That is, the newest welfare recipients came from families that had for the previous two generations subsisted completely on government sponsored welfare payments of various kinds. And, the number of welfare recipients was growing at an alarming rate.

By 1990, the drain on the Treasury related to making payments to individuals, to enhance their personal well-being and security, was, when combined with the Congresses penchant for spending money that hadn't yet been printed, resulting in annual government spending deficits in the three hundred to four hundred billion dollar range, and was threatening to bankrupt the country.

In the early 1980's congress had increased Social Security taxes a lot, in hopes of reducing the probability of that program's going bankrupt in the near future. The tax increase served its purpose, and the SSA fund began to actually show a surplus each year. By the mid 1980's congress was getting desperate for ways to pay the government's bills, without further inflating the nation's paper currency supplies, and thereby touching off another round of price increases. The method they hit on was to "borrow" the surplus funds in the SSA account. The "borrowing" was repaid with freshly printed Treasury notes, which weren't payable until a time well in the future.

In this attempt, congress was essentially running up credit card bills, and then paying them off by borrowing the money from a second credit card to pay off the first credit card. Then, when it came time to pay off the second credit card, they simply re-borrowed the money to do it from the first credit card company again. In banking circles, this same procedure when done by using two accounts from different banks, is known as "kiting". Kiting checks is illegal, and is a federal crime. Again, Congress, by its actions, was showing the American citizens, that it deemed itself above the laws that it passed, which others were expected to obey.

While it possibly deserves a heading all its own, we'll throw it in here, since the subject of check kiting has already been alluded to. In the early 1990's a defecting government employee blew the whistle on members of the House of Representatives who were effectively kiting checks through the House post office. The practice was discovered to be epidemic in its proportions. Most House members were guilty of check kiting. Some of the kiters routinely even cashed checks for amounts that were not coverable any time in the foreseeable future, and used the kited funds for political acts that were illegal.

When this practice was revealed, most Congress members were angry at having been discovered engaging in practices that others went to jail for, rather than being contrite, and apologizing for their misconduct. Some members admitted their wrongdoing, and apologized to their constituents. Most of these were forgiven. Some weren't forgiven when the amounts of money involved proved too outrageous, and some got voted out during the next election.

Same old, Same old....

By 1990, congress was hurting for a story to tell that would please the American electorate. Spending was out of control, and Congress' attempts to lay the blame at the feet of past and present presidents were increasingly falling on deaf ears. Members of Congress (again) underestimated the ability of the American citizens to look through all the smoke and mirrors, to the substance of their dealings. Most Americans understood full well, and had for some time, that while the President proposes, it is the Congress that disposes. Presidents are not allowed to make laws. They can only accept or reject laws made up in the Congress, and presented for their signature.

In 1994, the party in the majority in congress changed hands for the first time in almost fifty years. Americans were letting Congress know that they had put up with about as much lying and corruption as they were going to.

Prior to the 1994 election, the person who was to be the new leader of the House of Representatives had drawn up a "Contract with America", which promised to address what his party saw as the problems facing the country. The contract called for reduced taxes, reduced government spending, less government intrusion in individuals lives, campaign reform designed to dislodge special interest vote payments through campaign contributions, term limits as a means of inviting citizens to not consider elected office a career choice but instead a period of public service, a return to spiritual activity in schools, and passing a constitutional amendment requiring congress to balance the federal budget.

The "Contract with America" was adopted and became the platform endorsed by most members of the Congress in the out-of-power party. At the end of the election, the contract had resulted in the out-of-power party being the in-power party for the first time in several decades. The new majority party began working to implement the contract that they had run on, with varying degrees of success. They lost out on close votes on all of the most important elements of the contract. Congress would not vote term limits on its members, would not reform campaign finance laws to preclude vote buying by single interest constituencies, and would not vote for a balanced budget amendment to the Constitution. In effect, Congress was reserving to itself the right to continue doing business as usual. All of the elements relating to the Contract with America, that were passed, were, of course subject to being changed later, or set aside completely.

Business Migration and Consolidation

Businesses continued during this period to migrate jobs out of America, and relocate operations to countries whose standards of living (and costs of doing business) were less than in the U.S. Key industries that had once employed millions of American citizens in good paying jobs, were by 1995, virtually all gone from the U.S. entirely, and were operating in foreign countries. Among the industries lost almost entirely to America, which had been invented here, and which were once dominated by America, were steel manufacturing, consumer electronics, computers, mass produced clothing, shoes, and machine tools.

Other industries that were previously dominated by American companies like automobile manufacturing were likewise relegated to followers in the industries that they used to lead. In order to keep the migration from being a complete exodus in the automobile industry Congress acted to impose "voluntary restraints" on foreign auto manufacturing firms, especially Japanese firms. The "voluntary restraint" was a threat to impose higher tariffs on foreign autos being imported into the country if foreign manufacturers didn't agree to sell fewer cars than actually possible in the U.S.

By the time voluntary restraints were enacted, the U.S. congress had already acted twice to shore up the auto industry. In the early 1980's congress had voted to loan billions of dollars from the U.S. treasury to one U.S. manufacturer that was on the verge of bankruptcy. The loan saved the automaker, and was repaid in full from later profits.

The Congress had also enacted a fairly steep tariff on foreign autos being imported into the U.S. The tariff bought U.S. auto manufacturers time to retool and improve their products to compete effectively with the foreign products, which were, at the time, not only better made, but often cheaper as well. Prior years U.S. tax policies had made it difficult for American auto companies to make enough money, or borrow enough money, to stay ahead of the game in the R&D areas, and as a result, American auto makers had fallen behind the curve in both innovation and product quality. The government's actions in this industry, in the 80's and 90's saved this industry from extinction on the American scene, but not before America lost 1/3 of its worldwide presence in the auto industry.

U.S. manufacturing companies faced with mounting pressure to gain market share, and faced with fierce foreign competition coming from countries having lower taxes, lower labor costs, and lower standards of living, and government policies at home that penalized Americans who invested in their companies for purposes of funding R&D and/or expansion, resorted to moving their operations out of the U.S., and buying up domestic competitors, as a means of staying alive and remaining profitable.

The corporate feeding frenzy saw small, entrepreneurial companies merged into large, stagnant companies at the fastest pace since just before the anti-monopoly laws had been enacted early in the 20th century. In the process millions (yes (tens of) millions) of Americans lost their good paying jobs with companies that they had worked long and hard to help build up, as merging companies sought to improve profits by eliminating redundant positions created by the mergers. Companies didn't need two presidents, VP's of engineering, accounting departments, etc.

Ultimately the merger mania that started in earnest in the mid 1980's would create a situation where one in three highly qualified people in the U.S. workforce would be under-employed, and forced to work in his or her later years for a small fraction of what they had been accustomed to working for, before they lost their jobs through corporate mergers.

In-Migration

Beginning in the early 1980's in-migration to the U.S. reached its highest level ever. Much of the in-migration consisted of illegal entries into the U.S. from countries where refugees were attempting to escape poverty. The U.S. had always been a magnet for such people, and had periodically in the past, had to severely limit the influx, in order to protect the supply/demand ratio of workers-to-work inside the nation's borders.

By 1990, the in-migration had become a flood. Net new arrivals to the U.S., not authorized under in-migration quotas, reached epidemic levels. Some state governments in those states most affected by the flood of illegal in-migrants, moved to take actions against the "illegals". The federal government beefed up its border patrol activities too. It didn't work. By 1995, illegal in-migration was being absorbed at the rate of approximately 230 new in-migrants per hour, 24 hours a day, and 365 days a year. In fact, between 1985 and 1995, illegal in-migration added more to the country's head count, than did the natural increase of births over deaths among legal citizens.

Undocumented in-migrants were generally willing to work at jobs paying minimum wage, and below minimum wage. Not surprisingly their presence in some manual labor industries served to alter the supply-demand ratios in a manner that stopped growth in wages completely, and non-in migrants involved in these types of work fell farther behind the wage-price curve as a result, causing resentment toward the in-migrant workers.

Unintended Consequences of Technology

Those businesses trying to compete while staying in the U.S. resorted to technology as a means of reducing their labor costs, and remaining profitable. "Productivity" became the new holy grail for U.S. based businesses. Productivity is the measure of how many man hours go into a given activity. The fewer man hours involved in an activity, the higher that activity's "productivity" is said to be.

Digital technology blossomed after 1985, and its impact in the area of "productivity" at all levels throughout all businesses was felt dramatically. Technology helped U.S.-based businesses compete with foreign businesses that were used to paying their workers the equivalent of fifty cents an hour, no overtime, and no benefits. In order to meet a challenge of this magnitude, U S.-based businesses typically had to find a way to employ machines in place of at least two thirds of their people. And, those U.S.-based businesses that chose to stay in the U.S., did just that.

The resulting worker layoffs weren't usually done all at once, and sometimes, if the company itself was growing, layoffs at one level were offset to a degree by hiring at another level within the business. But, the bottom line was an ever growing number of workers being put out of a job by U.S.-based businesses that elected to stay in the U.S. by way of implementing technological replacements for human workers.

Another consequence of the layoffs was that the displaced workers found themselves looking for work, of a comparable kind, that was increasingly hard to find anywhere in the country. And, it was not just a matter of being technologically up to date. One of the hardest hit worker categories was that of professionals in the electronic data processing industry. Within a ten-year period, beginning in 1985, the number of computer professionals employed full time by U. S.-based businesses fell by over 50%.

Even IBM, the founder and prior world leader in the industry was reduced from 450,000 employees down to 200,000 employees, a loss of almost 60% of its workforce. And, these were not minimum wage jobs being lost. Perhaps as many as half of the jobs lost by IBM workers paid over $50,000 a year, with full benefits, at the time the ax fell.

In order to find work at all, many of the laid off computer professionals resorted to becoming "consultants". Consultants typically made a fraction of what they made before their "real" job was eliminated, and most lost all forms of health benefits too. A disturbing number ended up working for a net earnings level that was a small fraction of what they had earned earlier. The government counted these people as fully employed. Those displaced did not consider themselves such, for the most part.

The layoffs at IBM were among the most troubling to workers nationwide, even to those who were not employed by IBM. IBM had been the last bastion of job security in the United States. If IBM could be driven to let its workforce go, then it could happen to any business. And, it did happen to most businesses that elected to stay in the US.

Of course, some businesses prospered from the technological paradigm shift, just as some businesses profited greatly from the great depression of the 1930's. However, on balance, it will be seen in historic perspective, that the technological revolution permanently displaced many, many, more workers than it would ever be able to provide <u>comparable paying</u> new jobs for in the future. And, like the effects of the great depression of the 1930's, the effects of the technological revolution that started in the early 1980s would be long felt by the population in general. Worldwide.

Almost perversely, the stock market(s) universally endorsed the displacement of American workers by the businesses that employed them. A businesses "productivity" was enhanced to some degree, with every job eliminated, assuming total output did not fall. Those businesses eliminating the most workers' jobs, and/or replacing human workers with machines, were seen as the businesses that would be most able to compete in the new "worldwide free-market economy" that seemed to be emerging. Thus, the stock market rewarded businesses who eliminated the largest number of their workers, by way of increasing the price of their stocks the most. This made the stockholders happy. It didn't make the displaced workers happy.

The government now acted to (again) close the barn door, after the stock had already gotten out. The government began sponsoring tax breaks for businesses that provided additional technological training to displaced workers, and using taxpayer dollars to set up similar programs for unemployed workers headed by government agencies.

Locking-in the gains made by Multi-National Companies

A grass-roots backlash against foreign-made products began forming in the early 1990's. Non-business groups formed to lobby Congress to employ protectionist measures designed to slow the flow of cheap imported goods into the country. Multi-national companies moved to assure that their products, now mostly made outside the U.S., could continue to be successfully sold back in the United States at a profit. It would be of little value to them to move their operations overseas in order to get the benefits of cheap labor, and reduced business taxes, if Congress acted to impose high tariffs on their products when they were re-imported back into the U.S.

By 1995 Congress had acted twice to appease the multi-nationals. A trade agreement affecting the western hemisphere countries was enacted that copied the trade agreement already in existence between European trading countries, known as the Common Market. The North American Free Trade Agreement, NAFTA for short, provided that existing tariff barriers between Canada, the U.S., and Mexico would be eliminated entirely over fifteen years' time. The government then proceeded to attempt to get other countries in the western hemisphere to join the NAFTA consortium.

Concurrent with the NAFTA effort, the congress moved to approve sweeping changes to the decades old General Agreement on Tariffs and Trade, GATT for short, that accomplished much the same thing in trading spheres in Europe and Asia, where a high percentage of goods imported into the U.S. were now being produced.

With NAFTA and GATT in place, the multi-national companies now had a completely free hand to operate their businesses without regard for the welfare of workers, on a worldwide scale, with the U.S. government's prior blessings. Multi-national companies could now play off one government against the others, one tax policy against the others, and one ethnic workforce against the others, at will, without fear of government's acting in a manner designed to protect the interest of workers. All on a worldwide scale.

The pendulum had now shifted to the extent that workers worldwide were again where they had been in the mid-19th century, when child labor, prison labor, company stores, and sweatshops were the order of the day. All of these symptoms of a system wherein management holds all the cards began to manifest themselves in countries worldwide, being somewhat more prevalent outside the U.S. In every instance, the governments wherein these abuses were taking place looked the other way. The government benefited from the industry at some level, and in developing countries especially, some benefits were seen as better than none.

Spaced Repetition and the Law of Unintended Consequences

Between 1970 and 1995 big business effectively drowned out dissenting views, by virtue of their increasing numbers, constant access to elected officials, and use of highly skilled and highly paid lobbyists and "spin doctors".

Spin doctors typically came from the ranks of big-time advertising firms, and are the same people conning us on TV into believing that some shampoo will restore hair growth. Between 1970 and the present, elected leaders have obtained the majority of their decision making input from this group, on topics they are involved in legislating. Trade between nations falls in this category.

The method used by multi-national businesses to persuade elected leaders of the wisdom of opening up America's markets to cheap imports, produced with child labor in another country, is essentially the same method used for selling shampoo. Psychologists call it "spaced- repetition ", and it is extremely effective as a brain-washing method.

Essentially "spaced-repetition" boils down to continually exposing the subjects' <u>subconscious</u> mind to some idea until the subjects' subconscious mind finally <u>accepts</u> the idea being submitted to it.

Psychologists tell us that the subconscious mind operates primarily at the visual level, encompasses little, if any, logical reasoning capability, and can, for the most part, only accept or reject (completely) ideas presented to it (sort of like the President?). However, the subconscious mind exerts tremendous influence over the conscious mind, which directly controls our actions. Once the subconscious mind accepts an idea, typically a visual image like seeing yourself driving an expensive car, or playing a sport well, whether the idea or image is good or bad, right or wrong, logical or illogical, (the subconscious usually can't tell which, and it doesn't really care), it thereafter exerts influence over the conscious mind in a manner that causes the conscious mind to direct its actions toward accomplishing the goal behind the idea or vision that has been accepted at the sub-conscious level.

Getting the subconscious mind to accept an idea that the conscious mind itself considers illogical is not an exercise for the uncommitted. Sometimes it takes years, even decades, before the subconscious mind will accept an idea presented to it, especially if the idea or vision has already been rejected at the conscious level. But, once the subconscious mind accepts an idea or vision presented to it, rational or not, the individuals conscious mind will thereafter be guided by the need to bring the subconscious mind's accepted idea or vision to fruition.

And, when an often rejected, but finally accepted, idea takes hold in the subconscious mind, the actions that result often call into play the law of unintended consequences as well.

An Example

Let's assume that you try to convince your subconscious mind that you should have a million-dollar home. You do this by keeping a picture of the home you want mounted over your desk at work, where you will be reminded of your ultimate goal each day. Initially, there may be resistance, at the subconscious level, caused by your conscious mind having already rejected the idea.

Your conscious mind, which operates at a logical and rational level, may respond with something like " let's see, you make $18,000 a year before taxes, and can afford a house payment of $500 a month. A million-dollar home would require a monthly payment of $10,000 each month. Nope, you can't have it!"

The subconscious mind might therefore initially also reject the idea, as a means of avoiding internal conflict within the individual, and direct your conscious mind to forget it, and get back to your $18,000 a year job, before you get fired for daydreaming. Which you do, because the subconscious mind has now directed your conscious mind to concentrate its energies in that manner.

But, you are determined, and you don't give up easily. Each day, for the next fifteen years, you visualize yourself living in the home of your dreams, in the process telling your subconscious mind "I want that million-dollar home". Each day, for fifteen years, for the same reasons, your subconscious mind replies "NO", and directs your conscious mind to have you get back to work at your day job.

Then, one day, when you're looking at the picture of your dream house, and in doing so presenting the idea of a million-dollar home to your subconscious mind, your subconscious mind just gives in and accepts the idea. "all right, all right, you can have the house, now leave me alone."

Once the idea has truly been accepted at the subconscious level, your life will change. Your subconscious mind will begin micro-managing your conscious mind, which will thereafter only allow thoughts and actions at the conscious level, that will help you reach your goal of having a million-dollar home.

That's when the law of unintended consequences most often kicks into play. Your family may disintegrate, your health may fail, your friends may vanish, and your reputation may go down the drain. You will almost certainly get your million-dollar house. But, at what total cost?

This process (train the subconscious mind as a means of controlling the conscious minds actions), has routinely been taught to Americans, and others, for at least the past twenty-five years' time, in self-help seminars, and in positive thinking classes, in self-improvement books, and visually, on television.

The thing it this, fellow turtles.... **It really works!**

Just about 100% of the time.

About the only time it fails to work is when the person dies before completing the actions called for at the subconscious level, or when the accepted vision hinges on a physical or mathematical impossibility.

Lobbyists have simply been using the same techniques to sell elected officials on programs designed to help their employers (multi-nationals) achieve their goals, that on other occasions they have used to make the rest of us believe that if we drink the right beer, or drive the right car, our youth, good looks, sex appeal, and athletic ability will return.

In the past dozen congresses, and within at least the last five administrations, the result of big-business' incessant "spaced-repetition" messages relating to opening up markets worldwide for their exploitation, has begun to bear fruit. NAFTA and the latest "enhancements" to the decades-old GATT treaty, were defined entirely by big business, posing as a benefactor to the government and American Citizens. Once solely defined by business, they were effectively promoted to elected officials, using spaced-repetition lobbying techniques, and, after decades of trying, were subsequently voted into law.

The subtleties of having themselves been brainwashed were lost on the elected officials, who didn't even know what had been done to them. In fact, many had difficulty explaining to their constituents why they voted for the elimination of protections for the workers in their country. Some seemed confused themselves, when explaining how, while they knew that the great majority of their constituents were dead set against lowering trade protections for U.S. workers, they nonetheless felt "compelled" to do so anyway, since they "had finally" become convinced it was necessary to eliminate worker protections, in order for America to remain competitive in the emerging worldwide "free-market" environment.

The newly embraced trade policies adopted and now promoted, by the U.S. government, will undoubtedly aid the worldwide competitiveness of multi-national companies, both foreign and domestic, in the short term. These government policies will also without question, result in lowering the middle class American turtles' standard of living substantially in the future until the middle class American worker turtles eventually have a standard of living comparable to that of worker turtles in other less-advantaged countries.

Again, the law of unintended consequences exacted its toll in acts committed by congress. American citizens, unable to understand why the majority of their elected officials would vote to give big business complete freedom to exploit workers, unless they were motivated by something other than the best interest of the people they were sworn to represent, voted to replace the party in majority in congress in 1994. As noted earlier, the new majority in congress elected to retain for themselves the necessary tools to continue doing business as usual, and for the most part, that is what happened. Citizen frustration and discontent with elected officials enacting programs that they saw as being detrimental to their future and the future of their families continued to grow.

Taxes and Subterfuge

Government programs had grown by the mid 1990's to the extent that taxes (in one form or another) now took slightly more than 50% of every dollar earned by middle-class working turtles.

Congress was between a rock and a hard place, trying to, on the one hand, continue funding government programs whose costs were escalating out of control, and on the other hand to keep taxes at a level that didn't prompt open rebellion on the part of the general citizenry.

In mathematical terms, lowering taxes, while increasing spending were considered mutually exclusive domains. That is, both could not inhabit the same space, at the same time. It was a mathematical impossibility.

Congress, un-persuaded by mathematical arguments, elected to continue business as usual. In the late 1980's a president who vowed that there would be "no new taxes - read my lips", signed into effect the single largest tax increase in the history of any nation on the planet. That president got voted out of office during the next election. The president that replaced him persuaded the congress, a majority of which were of his own party, to raise taxes even more. During the congressional election that followed the new president's signing into law the huge second tax increase in as many years, the citizens voted to change the majority in both houses of congress, to a party other than that of the sitting president.

The new majority in congress, beginning in 1994, was elected based upon promises made in the "Contract with America" noted earlier. The most important promises included in the "contract with America" were not kept, and the "new" congress resorted to subterfuge as a means of staying in power, while lowering government spending at the federal level to a point that would theoretically allow the government to be operating under balanced budget conditions by the first decade of the 21st century.

The means used by the "new" congress was to simply transfer the responsibility for several federal welfare programs over to individual states to handle. Supposedly the reasoning for doing so was that individual states were more capable than the federal government in these regards. The real reason was that there was literally no way that the federal government could both continue to pay the escalating costs of these programs, and concurrently ever hope to bring the federal budget into balance. The mathematicians were right. Doing both <u>was</u> a mathematical impossibility.

Elected officials at the federal level, thus abdicated their responsibility for handling federal programs, and passed the buck to the states to handle individually. States had no mechanisms in place to handle the new programs handed over to them, and, not insignificantly, had no tax base available and in place with which to pay for the programs handed down to them.

The federal government promised to help the states pay for the new programs being transferred over to them, by giving the states "block grants". Block grants were sums of money taken in by the federal government in the form of some kind of tax, that were then turned over to the states to use as they saw fit. The catch was that the block grants given to the states were not large enough to pay the costs of programs being turned over to the states. And, the federal government knew it when they did it. States geared up to increase taxes at the state level sufficiently to pay for the federally mandated programs, and taxes, overall, on the middle-class working turtles went up sufficient to cover the cost of having each state establish its own new bureaucracy to handle the programs congress had, by law, made them responsible for.

State governments initially resisted the "unfunded federal mandates" but the internal squabbling between elected officials at the federal and state levels did nothing to either lower the overall cost to the taxpayers of paying for the operation of government, or make government more efficient, or make it more responsive to the citizens it served. Elected officials at the federal level patted themselves on the back publicly for "returning power to the states, and acting to bring the federal budget into balance". Nobody else much applauded their efforts, which were seen by most middle-class working turtles as being generally ineffective, and more than a little disingenuous.

The more things changed, the more things remained the same. Trust in elected officials continued to decline. Elected officials were slow to pick up on the fact that the public saw through the smoke and haze, and viewed their attempts at subterfuge as little more than a shell game, aimed at hiding the government's true condition. The new president and most members of congress expressed disappointment that the public, in general, appeared to distrust them.

The government assumes control over the economy of the U.S., and all other countries

By the early 1990's, even the two huge, back-to-back tax increases enacted by the government in 1990 and 1993, combined with the congress mandating that states take over the operation (and costs) of running many federal programs, had proven inadequate to bring the federal government's budget into balance, or anything close to it. And, once again, the Federal Reserve was called on to enact policies that would force the treasury to pour more newly printed money into federally chartered banks, that could then be "borrowed" by the government, to pay the government's bills which were still greater than its income from taxes of all kinds.

Periodically, the government's inflationary practices would be sufficient in size, to alarm foreign holders of U.S. treasury securities, and dollars, and the value of American treasury notes and dollars themselves would be depreciated by foreign governments and foreign businesses. If this seemed by anyone in the government to be similar to what happened just prior to the great depression of the 1930's, it wasn't possible to tell from their actions. Congress continued to spend money that wasn't yet printed, and the Federal Reserve then acted to help U.S. banks to fund the deficit using the newly printed, devalued, notes and dollars.

This approach to financing annual budget deficits at the federal level had ongoing repercussions in the private sector as well. Prices for consumer goods continued to rise sharply, as manufacturers now based in foreign countries raised their prices to offset the fact that the U.S. government had, by their actions in further inflating the country's paper currency supply, made every dollar worth less than it had previously been worth. Thus, ever more dollars were needed for their products sold back in America, for them to just to stay even in the game.

The losers in this game (all government actions by this time had come to have winners and losers), were the American middle-class working turtles, who were now caught in a very deadly crossfire. On the one hand workers were seeing their jobs eliminated by way of giving them to workers in other countries, and/or merged or automated away at home, with competition for an ever dwindling number of good jobs forcing pay down at all levels; while on the other hand, prices for everything they needed were continually going up, due to the government's inflationary practices.

Foreign governments often felt called upon to come to the aid of the U.S. treasury, when the value of the U.S. dollar was seen to be falling rapidly. Products exported from their countries to the U.S. were in jeopardy of becoming overpriced (to American workers) if the dollar fell too far. That in turn, could cause businesses in their own countries to have to scale back, or shut down completely, since the U.S. market remained between thirty-five and fifty percent of the total market, for all goods, produced in every country; and no country could afford to lose the ability to sell their products in America.

Thus it came to be that by 1995, the effects of the U.S. government's funding government operations, using inflation as a primary tool or doing so, and the resulting continual devaluing of American dollars at a time when the United States dollar was still the key currency that all other currencies in the world were measured by, had led to a point in time when the Federal Reserve was in a position to control the economy of every country in the world, by its actions. And, the members of the board of Directors of the Federal Reserve were not even elected officials.

The reason that other governments felt compelled to go along with the Federal Reserve's policies, no matter how foolish, was because the American middle-class turtles constituted thirty-five to fifty percent of the worldwide market for all kinds of goods. The foreign countries could not act in a manner to hurt us, without hurting themselves even more.

Significantly, the American middle-class worker turtles were not similarly moved to use this leverage to their own advantage. On the one hand, the companies exporting American jobs were stabbing their former employees in the back, while, at the same time, asking their victims to be understanding of their problems on a global scale, and asking them to continue buying their products back here in the U.S. Products that were now being produced by the foreign workers that their jobs were given away to.

Surprisingly, most American middle-class working turtles went along with the game...

...Like lemmings marching over a cliff.

Summing up

Way back, I indicated that this would be a fairly long section. Congratulations for hanging in there! We're almost through with this part of the book. At the outset, I indicated that over the past seventy-five years' time, there had been seven significant changes in American society, and in the relationship between American citizens and their government, which were the principal reasons for the American Dream having fallen into a state of disrepair.

The pages preceding this one chronicled a number of possibly well intended, but, in retrospect often misguided, actions at the federal government level that have, by this point in time, all but dismantled the foundation underlying the American Dream, which had, in past generations, made the realization of American dreams, in full, routinely possible. At the risk of wasting paper, I'll restate them here for your review:

Included in everyone's original idea of the American Dream were the following four ideals and expectations:

1. The American Dream included an expectation of equality of opportunity to succeed financially, depending on each individual citizen's willingness to strive against adversity, and sacrifice present pleasures, for future improvements in their standard of living.

2. The American Dream included an expectation of equal treatment and protection under the laws for all citizens engaged in those activities identified in the American Declaration of Independence as being (the original) rights every citizen of this country was endowed with at birth. These included the right to life, liberty, and the pursuit of happiness. Some additional fundamental rights, including some property related rights, for all citizens of the United States, were enumerated in the first ten amendments to the U.S. Constitution, and a relative few more were added in later amendments to the Constitution.

3. The American Dream included an expectation that each successive generation would have greater opportunities for improving their standard of living, than the previous generation had enjoyed.

4. The American Dream included an expectation that the powers of the Government would be used to guard the previously mentioned rights, and opportunities, of all American citizens against encroachment and assault from all quarters, whether coming from within or from outside of the nation's borders.

Given that these were the foundation elements supporting each American's dreams, and given that by 1995 they no longer existed at all, anywhere except in the memories of those old enough to remember when they did exist; what is surprising is that Americans still dared to dream at all. Old habits die hard, and Americans still dreamed, but, absent these foundation elements, realization of the American Dream has now been moved out of reach for most middle class Americans. And middle class American's sense the loss, even if they don't always understand how it happened.

The loss of these foundation elements of the American Dream was facilitated by a fundamental shift in the relationship between individuals and government that is defined by the following seven changes within our society as a whole:

1. U.S. Government's assumption of control over the national (and world) economy.
2. Abdication of personal responsibilities by individual citizens.
3. Assumption of abdicated individual responsibilities by government bodies.
4. A decline in national pride.
5. The rise to power of multi-national companies.
6. Capitalism allowed to function without restraint by either government or unions.
7. Open collusion between business groups and government.

As you look back over this section, it becomes obvious that government actions were involved either directly, or indirectly, in precipitating these seven fundamental changes between the citizens and their government, and that government actions were directly involved in the loss of the four underlying foundation elements of the American Dream.

It cannot be logically argued that the government's taking over half of all available money from workers in the form of various taxes and lowering the value of the dollar through its inflation of the currency supply did not play a part in both parents having to work outside the home, which in turn had a negative effect on child rearing, with parents turning over more responsibility for raising their children to schools, day-care centers, and television sets.

It cannot be logically argued that the government's taking 12.5% of each individual's income to pay for social security, and more still (2.9% - to pay for Medicare and Medicaid), did not have a negative effect on families being able to set aside enough money to take care of aging parents and themselves when the time came to do so.

It cannot be logically argued that the government has not, over the past several decades, by its actions aimed at assuming responsibility for what used to be individuals' responsibilities and its taking ever more of the nation's combined income for its own uses, acted to make it financially impossible for the majority of individual citizens to meet what used to be individual responsibilities. Once the government seized the money earned by the individual, it also removed the individual's options relating to spending the money.

It cannot be argued logically, that Americans have not been encouraged by their government, to not take pride in being AMERICANS. The government's actions at hyphenating Americans (Hispanic-, African-, Japanese-, Jewish-, Native-, Senior-, etc.), and repeatedly passing laws aimed at purposely discriminating in favor of one group over another, have broken America out into divided selfish-interest camps, rather than promoting Americans as being just Americans... that being anyone that is a voluntary, legal, citizen of this country, regardless of ethnic background.

It cannot be logically argued that the governments past tax policies that severely penalized businesses in this country was not the single most significant contributory factor in the rise of American-based multi-national companies who bear allegiance only to stockholders, and have no allegiance to the United States as a nation or to their American workers.

And it cannot be logically argued that open collusion between government and business, aimed at furthering the interests of business and government (only) has not contributed to a situation that has resulted in the once enviably prosperous middle-class workers of America now being rapidly brought down to the lowest common denominator of worker prosperity worldwide.

Those Universal Laws

The universal laws referenced at the outset can, by now, be seen to be true indeed.

For every government action, there has indeed been an equal and opposite citizen reaction.

Sometimes the reaction was positive, but usually it was negative. When the government acted to seize more income from individual citizens, citizens reacted by abandoning personal responsibilities that cost money to meet. When government acted to seize business profits and penalize capital investments made in the U.S., and endorse "free trade" job giveaways, businesses moved their operations out of the government's reach, and in the process divested tens of millions of Americans of good jobs.

Government bodies or programs once in motion have absolutely stayed in motion; not (yet) having been acted on by an outside force. In fact, only one (wage-price controls) significant government program, once begun in the past 75 years, has actually been terminated. Rather, "sunset" laws have routinely been circumvented by way of having another government body assume responsibilities previously handled by a government body that was being "eliminated". Functionally, the "eliminated" activities have continued, exactly as though nothing had ever happened.

And, if nothing else was obvious, it has been-proven beyond any doubt that "government abhors any vacuum "There was never a time during the past seventy-five years, that government did not only insert itself into an area wherein it saw nothing being done, where it imagined something should be done; but government even acted at times, through its taxing policies, to first create the vacuums so that it could then move into, and take over, activities previously being done by the citizens themselves.

And, so where do we go from here? What has to happen for the American Dream to be restored and not again be subject to coming apart a second time in the future? That's what we will begin to talk about next.

Part 2 - The Road to the Future

Part 1 recapped how a circle of government and citizen actions and reactions brought us to a point in time, wherein the four underlying foundation elements of the American Dream no longer exist.

Caught up in the good fight of day-to-day living, events of historical significance have a way of being stored away in memory as isolated events. The purpose of studying history is to place isolated events in a broader perspective. Perspective leads to insight. Insight as to what caused the dismantling of the American Dream will be useful in charting a roadmap for finding our way back to a point in time when the American Dream is alive, well, and functioning as it did in earlier days.

Such insight will prove useful for those who still believe that the American Dream is a dream worth restoring. Believe it or not, not all turtles living in this country now feel that way. But, for those American turtles who do want to see the American Dream of old restored, we will press on.

Simple logic tells us that restoration of the American Dream would at least call for re-establishing the four foundation elements that have been lost, since they were both first and necessary prerequisites for assuring that all the other elements of each individual's American Dream at least had a chance of being realized.

But, fellow turtles, that, by itself, will not be enough. If the American Dream got dismantled once, it can be quickly dismantled again after it is restored, unless, the problems facing the American society, and the societies of other countries around the world, are identified, and solved. It was a failure to address the problems facing the world's citizens in virtually every country on the planet, and especially here in America, that caused the dismantling of the American Dream.

Thus, what is required to restore the American Dream is a <u>two</u>-step program:

The First Step

We must act to re-establish the four foundation elements that previously formed the foundation for Americans to build their dreams on. This will not be an insignificant task. Elected officials are loath to admit mistakes, and even more disinclined to abolish programs, once put into place. A lot of government programs have been implemented over the past several decades that had as their main premise discriminating in favor of one group of American citizens, over another group (or groups) of American citizens.

The list is far too long to go into here, but it includes hundreds of government tax and subsidy programs. Farmers, veterans, seniors, utilities, minorities, ethnic groups, individual businesses, individual industries, etc., etc., etc., etc., etc., etc., etc., etc., etc., etc., etc.... The list goes on (and on and on).

Equal treatment under the law, justice, and fair play, may, mathematically speaking, be either discrete domains, or shared domains. That is, they can be arranged so as to either exist together at the same time, or to not do so. The foundation elements underlying the American Dream were the basis for providing that these elements existed together, all of the time, and that they were equally available to all American citizens.

The present government model in America, requires them to not all exist at the same time. The present government model in America, in fact, requires some of them not to exist at all. Ever.

An act cannot be just and unjust at the same time. An act cannot be fair and unfair at the same time. Acts are either just or not, and fair, or not. Some may respond by saying "so what, life isn't always fair". Which saying may be true, but is nonetheless meaningless in this context. Government isn't life, and governments, at least the government established by the U.S. Constitution, originally had as its very most basic precepts that <u>while life might not be fair, government acts should be</u>. Citizens should be able to depend on their elected leaders passing laws that were both fair and just, for <u>all</u> citizens, every time.

It cannot be logically argued that, at this point in time, government laws are enacted with either justice or fairness in mind. There have been no laws passed within the past several decades in Washington that were not expressly designed to favor one group of Americans over other groups of Americans. Not a single one.

What is surprising is that elected officials in Washington, seem unable to understand that passing laws purposely designed to be unjust and unfair, might have a divisive effect on America. As this is written, elected officials in Washington continue to purposely look for ways to pass laws that favor one group of Americans over other groups of Americans, and continue to be perplexed as to why they are held in low esteem by their fellow middle-class American working turtles. As the chief contender said about the president he was running against in the 1992 presidential elections, "they just don't get it."

Without regard, at this point, to how it will get done, or whether the elected officials now in Washington are up to the job of doing it, let it suffice here for us to just agree that, in order for the American Dream to be restored, the four underlying foundation elements removed over the past several decades, will have to be put back in place.

And, that will be the easy part.

The Second Step

Assuming we American turtles have the resolve to re-establish the foundation elements underlying the American Dream, we will still be less than half-way home. In order to then be assured that it won't just quickly unravel again, the serious problems facing America, and most other countries around the world, will have to be identified, brought out in the open, faced up to, and solved.

It was the complete failure of the government to address the real problems facing us that caused the foundation underlying the American Dream to come apart in the first place. And, it will remain unraveled, or continue to quickly come apart again if (temporarily) restored, until the underlying problems facing our society are identified, faced up to, and solved.

That will be the hard part.

> If the second step isn't taken, it won't ultimately matter much if the first step gets taken or not.

In mathematical terms, parts one and two might be called mutually inclusive subsets. Both must be completed, and neither may exist for very long by itself, separate from the other. The truth of this may be viewed in what has already happened. The second part (identifying and solving our problems) was not paid attention to, and because of that, the first part ceased to exist too.

To remind you, the first part comprised the four foundation elements underlying the American Dream. Absent a foundation, the dream, predictably, crumbled.

That's it for this chapter. Sort of a way of making up for the first chapter being so long. Now, for those turtles who are still feeling brave, we will move on to a section wherein we examine the problems that have to be solved, if the American Dream is to not only be restored, but to thereafter remain intact, long term.

Part 3 - Defining the Problems

At the outset, we elected to adopt a scientific perspective in terms of viewing past events, and their outcomes, as a means of gaining a perhaps different, and hopefully valuable, insight as to what should be done in the future to restore the American Dream, and thereafter keep it alive and intact.

In keeping with that charter, the remainder of this work will assume that the best approach to take will be to follow the scientific method of problem solving.

"The scientific method", I can hear some of you turtles saying, "I think I remember something about that. It was in high school, I think. Geometry, I believe. Yes, that's it, I learned about the scientific method of problem solving in high school geometry". That's right, fellow turtles, it's the same one, and it hasn't changed since Aristotle originally thought it up, or when Sir Isaac Newton himself later used it, both when he was working on formulating his laws of gravity, motion, and inertia in 1687, and when he acted as head of the British Mint back in 1717, and kept England on the gold standard.

I don't want to assume too much, or insult any of you turtle's intelligence out there, but I know that it has been a long time since high school geometry for some of you, so I'm going to restate here the formula for solving problems, according to the scientific method…

The Scientific Method for Problem Solving

Step #1. Define the problem.
Step #2. Break it down into its smallest elements.
Step #3. Pose Alternative Solutions (hypotheses)
Step #4. Select the most likely alternative
Step #5. Implement the selected alternative.
Step #6. Prove the solution (test the results empirically)
Step #7. If the proof succeeds, stop. The problem is solved (QED). If the proof fails, return to step #1.

The reason for returning to step # 1, instead of step # 4, in the event the selected solution alternative doesn't prove out, is that the most common reason that solutions don't prove out in practice, is that someone defined the problem incorrectly at the outset. It is the case that if the problem itself is mis-stated, the resulting solutions will be ineffective. That's science. And, it applies to all kinds of problems, not just geometry, physics, astronomy, and so on.

For example, if your doctor advises you that he or she has diagnosed a malady as a stress-induced, nervous stomach, and proposes tranquilizers to remedy the problem, while your problem is actually a diseased gallbladder; the tranquilizers not only won't cure the problem, but you may die of the proposed cure that resulted from an incorrect problem diagnosis.

It also wouldn't help much to just go back to step # 4, and propose another treatment for a nervous stomach, like a different tranquilizer, or changing the size of the dosage of the medicine already being administered. The doctor would have to go all the way back to step one, and look for another problem definition, if your health problem was to be solved.

Unfortunately, some doctors aren't very good at problem diagnosis, or using the scientific method, and some just keep returning to step # 4, until the patient dies.

The political doctors in Washington have proven themselves to be among the worst in the world at problem diagnosis. In fact, diagnosing problems is, among all the activities this group engages in, the thing that they decidedly do least well.

Symptoms in General

Scientists and doctors have in common that they look to symptoms to identify problems. A scientist may use an observed change in a planet's orbit, to postulate that another body of significant mass is in the neighborhood, thus placing a gravitational pull on the planet. In fact, as I recall from Turtle Astronomy 101, something like that was what led to the discovery of the farthest planet from the sun in our own solar system.

Likewise, medical doctors look to symptoms of disease to help them diagnose the problems affecting their patients. Some of the symptoms doctors look for are pain, discharges of various kinds, loss of use of bodily functions, color changes, sensitivity to light or noise, changes in acuteness of the five basic senses, blood pressure fluctuations, temperature fluctuations, and so on.

Medical doctors are typically above average when it comes to separating symptoms from the problems themselves. A doctor, for example, would be quick to point out that use of antihistamines to reduce nasal discharge, was not actually curing the head cold that caused the discharge. And doctors recognize that pain is itself not a problem, but a symptom of a deeper problem somewhere in the body.

This is not to say that pain may not reach almost unbearable levels for the patient, and have to itself be treated as a means of providing some temporary relief; but it is to say, that if the underlying cause of the pain is not discovered and remedied, the pain will not go away long term. A doctor can provide morphine to a cancer patient to relieve the pain associated with the cancer, but if the cancer itself cannot be successfully treated or eliminated, the pain will continue, and the patient will ultimately die from the lethal effects of the cancer.

Symptoms of an Ailing Society

America is suffering from an alarming number of symptoms of a society beginning to collapse in on itself. Just as a patient with Aids or cancer typically expires from complications like congestive heart failure, or pneumonia, that take over when the virus or cancer has severely worn down the patients internal defense mechanisms; America is on the verge of becoming so worn down from fighting <u>symptoms</u> of decline, that it stands in danger of expiring not directly, from the underlying problems troubling the nation, but from concentrating exclusively on ways to alleviate the symptoms of those problems, instead of looking for cures to the problem(s) themselves.

Because of this, American turtles may occasionally gain temporary relief from uncomfortable symptoms from time to time, but absent anyone looking for cures to the underlying problems, the problems themselves continue to grow and spread. That being the case, symptomatic relief is predictably temporary in nature, and the symptoms recur periodically, and frequently. And, like physical symptoms, the longer the underlying problem remains unaddressed, the more difficult it is to treat the symptoms when they re-occur.

Finally, just as with physical symptoms related to deadly medical diseases, wherein failing to identify and treat the disease itself, ultimately results in the death of the patient, a continuing failure to identify and treat some of the deadly problems causing distress symptoms in American society, can, and may well, ultimately cause the death of the great American experiment. Fortunately, there is still some time to act, but time is of the essence, and growing shorter even as you are reading this.

At the risk of picking a fight, I'm going to present here a partial list of symptoms presently affecting broad segments of American society. I'm sure that there are more that could be listed, and I apologize, in advance, if I left one off the list that is near and dear to you. Please keep in mind that my purpose in presenting the list is just to provide some examples of the kinds of topics typically presented by elected leaders to the public at large, as problems, but which are, in fact, not problems at all. Instead, all of these are <u>symptoms</u> of problems that no-one in government is talking about at all.

Some Symptoms of a Society in Decline

1. High (real) levels of Unemployment
2. High levels of under-employment (people forced to work beneath their skill and training level)
3. Persistent budget deficits within government at all levels
4. High Taxes
5. Falling living standards and being forced to incur debt for everyday subsistence purchases
6. Persistent high levels of violent crime
7. Increased crime related to trafficking in controlled substances
8. Increased numbers of single parent families
9. Decline in "family values" (and loss of time for parental guidance in the home)
10. Foreign trade deficits
11. Unresponsive government (gridlock)
12. Corruption in government (bribes, kickbacks, self-dealing, fraudulent dealings, etc.)
13. Extraordinary growth in payouts to "entitlement" programs
14. Lack of adequate healthcare for some citizens
15. A need to provide for a permanent "welfare" class of citizens
16. Failure of educational systems to meet public needs and expectations
17. Extremely high levels of illegal In-migration
18. Environmental breakdowns (pollution, global warming, vital resource shortages, etc.)

I'm sure that there will be unemployed turtles out there that may respond by saying "if you were unemployed, then you would think that unemployment was a problem!" Same thing for under-employed turtles or turtles that aren't getting adequate medical treatment because they can't qualify for insurance coverage or can't otherwise afford treatment and so on down the list. But the topics listed here are, in fact, not problems at all. They are <u>symptoms</u> of problems that no-one is even talking about in government.

Elected leaders tend to refer to these symptoms as if they were, in fact, problems. Elected leaders then take individual positions regarding how best to address the topic at hand, and differences between different leader's views as to how to bring symptomatic relief are referred to as taking a position on the <u>issues</u> surrounding the "problem" of (insert the symptom name here). Issues are points of argument over strategy. Standing one's ground in arguments over strategy is referred to (among elected officials) as "taking a stand on principle!"

For example, an elected official might identify existing tax policy as something that was problematic. The official might then take a position that corporations should pay more in taxes, so that individuals might have to pay a bit less. Other elected leaders might then take an opposite view. Each side would then allude to the necessity of addressing the "issues" surrounding tax policy. The "issues" then become the relative merit of each side's arguments supporting their views on the subject.

Over time, in the above example, (tax policy), the elected leaders would eventually get around to voting on legislative bills that supported the strategy of each side. One side would see their bill enacted into law. The other side would not. The losers (and winners) would then make a big thing out of "standing on principle!"

Most likely, within a few months or years, the losers of this round would come to be in the majority and revisit the "issues" of tax policy, and win, and the tax policies of the previous winners would be reversed. Again, both sides would make a big thing about "standing on principle!"

The reason that neither side's changes to tax policy remain in effect for long, and that citizens periodically replace elected leaders predisposed to reversing a prior elected body's tax policies (which failed to bring long term relief), is that neither side began their quest with an accurate definition of the problem. Tax policy if done badly, may spawn many symptoms that visit discomfort on citizens. But, tax policy itself is a symptom of an underlying problem (or problems). That being the case, unless the underlying problems are identified and solved, it is not just unlikely, but a complete impossibility, that tinkering with strategies surrounding individual elements of a symptom like the tax system, will solve the problems.

> Given this approach to problem solving by elected officials, the only thing that is certain is that strategies relating to symptomatic relief will continue to be argued every year, and that the problems that are not being addressed will continue to get worse.

The problems and their basic elements

There are eight very significant problems facing American middle-class working turtles. The same eight problems, in fact, face working turtles worldwide. Some societies are more affected than others by individual problems, but all societies are now interconnected to a degree that what affects one, also spills over to some degree to affect all the others as well.

The first problem is unsustainable expansion in worldwide human population

This problem may be broken down in to individual segments that relate to how the expanding population causes an unsustainable drain on non-renewable resources, how the exploding population also causes the depletion of renewable resources at unsustainable rates, and how problems relating to population increases in one country may spill over to become problems relating to population increases in adjoining countries.

When the planet Earth housed 2 billion humans, it was still possible for most replaceable natural resources to renew themselves with like kind and quality resources, at sustainable rates, which were in balance with the need to protect the overall environment.

By the time our planet came to be home for 3 billion humans, it was occasionally the case that some renewable natural resources in common use by humans, like oil for energy, and wood for building materials, fuel, and paper manufacturing, began to show signs of being used up faster than they could be replaced, with like kind and quality replacements. Most living species threatened with extinction at this point in time, were plants, small fishes and insects that few people had ever heard of, and which most people didn't feel connected to.

At 4 billion humans, planet Earth was beginning to show definite signs of strain. Concerned groups began making public statements regarding the number of life species that were being made extinct annually, and further expressing concern over the rate at which both non-renewable and renewable natural resources were being used up. By this point in time, not all the plant and animal species facing extinction were unknowns to the public at large. The Atlantic and Pacific salmon were in severe decline, and Atlantic cod were all but gone. Old growth trees were disappearing rapidly. The rain forests in South America were being cleared at about the rate of a state the size of New Hampshire every year.

By the time the human population reached 5 billion, clean water and clean air had become extinct in and around heavily populated areas. By this time, it was the case that wind and rain had become insufficient to dissipate the "pollution" caused by man's converting mass into energy. Now, once made dirty, the Earth never got a chance to completely clean itself. The pollution moved with the air and water currents from one place to another, but never went away altogether. And, the remaining amount of mass available that was suitable for conversion to energy had by this time come into serious question in the scientific community.

We are now at 7.5 billion people….and growing…...rapidly.

The Rule of 72

Bankers use the "rule of 72" to determine how long a time, in years, it will take for dollars to double at a given compound interest rate. Here is how it works. Divide the rate at which the money supply grows (compound interest rate) into the number 72. The result is the number of years that it will take the original amount of money to double at the interest rate used as the divisor.

The "rule of 72" is an applied mathematical formula that not only applies to interest rates and money growth. It applies to any type of growth rate, and anything that can be similarly "grown". Specifically, it also applies to the rate of growth of the population of humans on planet Earth.

For example:

If the world's human population grows at a "net" rate (births less deaths) of 1%, the worldwide population will double in just 72 years. (72 divided by 1 equals 72).

The Bad News

The bad news is that the population of the United States is growing at almost a 1.5% compounded growth rate, and the Earth's overall human population is expanding at between a 1.5% and 2% "net" compounded growth rate. Our planet already has a population that is mathematically unsustainable over the long term, and, at current population growth rates, that population will double within the next 30-40 years.

Here in America we have been somewhat shielded from the effects of overpopulation. But, that is changing rapidly. Previously, the U.S. had sufficient natural resources within its boundaries to sustain all its citizens. Now, like other less-fortunate countries, the U.S. is having to face the fact that it no longer has within its borders sufficient natural resources to meet the needs of all of its citizens. Mineral deposits relating to iron, aluminum, wood, and oil are now being imported, not just to save money, but because we don't any longer have enough of them remaining here at home to meet the growing demand by Americans alone.

By scientific estimates, there remains enough (mostly as yet) undiscovered crude oil to provide for usage at today's rates, and given today's population, for another 75 to 100 years. In the event the world's population doubles to 14 billion in 30-40 years, and then doubles again to 28 billion within 70-80 years from now, the amount of crude oil yet remaining in the earth's crust, mostly still undiscovered, will allow us to continue using petroleum for energy, and otherwise, for about 35 years. Likewise, for wood, iron, and coal. Aluminum will do better.

Given this scenario, the quality of life, as we now know it, in the U.S. will end, no matter what else happens, sometime <u>during the lifespan of the next generation</u>, if the population of the U.S. and the population of the world in general continue to expand over the next thirty years, as they are doing now.

> Now, **THAT**, my fellow turtles, is a problem!

Overpopulation not only threatens our ability to live within our (natural resource) means, it poses threats to social stability. It is not just coincidence that citizens of less advantaged countries are seeking in record numbers to enter the U.S.

When citizens of Mexico, or Asia, or, for that matter, any other country elect to leave that country, and enter the U.S., illegally if necessary, a large part of the reason that they do so is a (correct) perception that the U.S. is presently better off both economically, and resource-wise than the country they are seeking to leave behind.

A large part of what illegal in-migrants into the U.S. are running from is the effects of overpopulation in the country they are leaving.

Lack of resources and/or an inability to develop existing resources in some countries may result in even a large country that has relatively few people per square mile, being overpopulated. A region is populated to an unhealthy degree whenever the available natural resources (and available jobs) in the region are insufficient to provide for sustaining the existing population of the region.

Note:

> Overpopulation may occur when a single person requires more to sustain life, than is readily available to the one person needing sustenance. Overpopulation does not require a high number of people in a given space. Overpopulation only requires enough people to over-deplete the resources available locally to sustain life.

In the United States, we have been slow to acknowledge this, due to having developed economically and technologically to a point where we have been able to provide in the past for meeting the needs of our expanding population by importing additional resources from outside our borders. However, this constitutes an artificial redistribution of resources that cannot be indefinitely sustained. At some point in time, those exporting oil to the U.S. will stop doing so, in favor of keeping the dwindling supply for their own citizen's use. Typically, this is where we have, in the past, brought into play something like a "manifest destiny" policy that allows us to take the needed resources from those who might be reluctant to sell them to us, using military might.

When the Earth's population was a fraction of what it now is, the practice of "might makes right" as regards taking another country's natural resources, could well serve to meet the conqueror's needs indefinitely. At least until another source could be found. However, at this point in time, even this (military) approach won't work for more than a decade or two. We are just flat running out of some natural resources, worldwide. But, back to the chase.

Illegal in-migration had, by 1995, reached proportions such that even if growth in the number of natural and naturalized (legal)

Americans were to stop completely, the population of the U.S. would still double within sixty years' time, just from the effects of illegal in-migration. Between 1980 and 2000, The U.S. population grew at the net rate of 230 illegal in-migrants per hour, 24 hours a day, 365 days a year. The flood of illegal in-migrants was (and remains) a direct result of overpopulation in the countries they are in-migrating from. Thus, it can be seen that the overpopulation problem generates multiple symptoms. Unsustainable natural resource depletion and illegal in-migration, are just two of them.

In problem solving the second step is to break out the problem into its simplest elements. However, in the instance of overpopulation, within the U.S., and (for the most part) worldwide, no-one in government is yet acknowledging that overpopulation is a problem. But it clearly is.

The second problem is that the middle-class working turtles of America, and the world in general, are seeing their labors systematically devalued.

Working-class turtles worldwide are facing an unprecedented systematic devaluation of their labors. This problem too has more than one element in its makeup.

Technology has made it possible to produce more of everything with less human labor.

For example, in a medium sized city in Japan, there is a factory that makes high-precision machine tools for sale worldwide. It's a BIG factory. The factory works 24 hours a day, seven days a week. There are two shifts. One is eight hours long, and uses human labor. The second shift is 16 hours long, and no humans are in the plant during this shift, except the night watchman. All production is done during the 16-hour shift when humans are not present.

During the first shift, humans unload the tools produced by the machines the previous night, service the machines, and load palletized raw materials on conveyers that "feed" the machines. Then, the machines are turned on, and everybody leaves. They even turn off all the lights, just to save a few dollars (yen).

In past decades, prior to the invention of the microchip, over a thousand humans used to be "machine operators", and work at good paying jobs in the plant that now uses human labor only to feed the automated processes.

"Productivity", that is the measure of how much product is produced per employee, effectively tripled at this plant. Not only that, but the products produced by automated processes are superior in workmanship to those produced by humans, and, the automated processes don't bring personal problems to work with them each day, don't require lunch or rest breaks, don't require health or dental insurance, and last, but not least, don't cost anything at retirement time. In fact, at retirement time, the automated equipment can be sold for scrap, producing not an expense, but some additional income to the stockholders.

To be sure, the ultra-modern factory noted above employs some very well-paid technical staff to get the factory set up in the first place, and to "program" the automated manufacturing processes. And, the technical specialists that are still on staff make more on average than did the average "machinists" that used to work there by the hundreds. Bottom line though, the plant now employs less than a third of the number of skilled production workers it did two decades ago.

And, it's not just a matter of re-training the displaced machinists to be computer specialists, in order to restore their jobs. If all the displaced machinists at the plant in the above example were to be successfully converted into PhD's in computers and electro-mechanical processes, only about 10% of them would ever become re-employed at jobs of that kind. The other 90% of the displaced workers would not be able to find work as technical specialists. They would either remain unemployed, or be reduced to working at a job that was below their skill and education level, for reduced wages (i.e., be under-employed).

American middle-class working turtles are being systematically devalued as workers by way of:

1. Elimination of middle-management positions ("flat" organizations)
2. Replacing skilled manual labor with automated processes
3. Exporting high-value jobs to countries with low standards of living.

Executives in U.S. based multi-national companies are under great pressure to always show stockholders increased sales, and (especially) increased earnings. Their rewards for succeeding in these regards can be significant. The typical American CEO may make over <u>1000 times</u> as much as the average employee in the firm he or she heads up. However, the price for failure on the part of the CEO to consistently achieve increased sales and/or earnings is swift dismissal.

Given that many multi-nationals are already of such a size that they have over half the entire worldwide market in their primary business, it becomes increasingly difficult for firms so dominant to continue increasing sales and earnings at record levels. Even if they somehow got all the rest of the business left in their primary field, they could then no longer grow in that business. But the stockholders don't care about things like that, and growth must continue, or the CEO's job won't continue.

Enter the merger. Once maxed out in one field, the "multi's" continue growing by buying other multi's and a lot of smaller companies too. Then the "consolidation" process starts. The "merged" conglomerate doesn't need two sales departments, two marketing departments, or two of most of what they now have two of. The result is a mass discharge of lots of employees who are now termed "redundant".

The thing is this fellow turtles: When half of the businesses, are buying up the other half, on an ongoing basis, the number of "redundant" employees that find themselves unemployed will always continue to grow, no matter how many college degrees the displaced workers hold, in perfectly matched work disciplines.

Much of the elimination of "middle-managers" and the trend toward "flat" organizations has been made possible through technology. With current technology, a manager can keep involved through tele-conferencing, E-mail, faxes, and cell-phones, with workers under him or her located in geographically dispersed locations throughout the world. Thus, when a merger involves offices in several countries, it is now possible for a single manager to handle multiple offices, by applying technology to the management effort.

Even if your company doesn't get "merged" into another one, there will increasingly be a need for fewer managers in the company, because of efficiencies made possible through new technologies. Fewer managers mean fewer opportunities for advancement up the corporate ladder. Fewer managers also means that those managers who do get displaced through "downsizing" or by way of being rendered "redundant" through mergers, may well be unable to ever find-re-employment as comparable level managers in another company.

Between 1985 and 2000 roughly 1/6 of all middle-managers in the U.S. lost their jobs. And, these weren't minimum pay positions. They averaged over $40,000 a year, with full benefits. Over half of those so displaced have never found comparable employment to date. Most of these are now re-employed at jobs that pay a small fraction of what they used to make (i.e., they are under-employed).

Between 1985 and 2000 roughly 1/6 of all skilled manufacturing production workers in the U.S. also lost their jobs or took significant pay cuts. Skilled production workers are (were) the backbone of the middle-class working turtle population. Like their middle-manager counterparts, over half of those displaced have yet to find employment at a comparable wage/benefit level.

To date, government has concentrated its efforts at helping this group by subsidizing "retraining" in high tech skills. There is no significant level of relief on the horizon for most of those displaced thus far that will come from "retraining" of displaced workers, unless what they are being retrained to do is live in poverty.

While many workers displaced through mergers, downsizing, and automation have gone back to school and gotten degrees in business, or in a high-tech discipline, a majority have graduated only to find that their "new" career is just as overpopulated as the one they were first displaced from, and also overpopulated with younger, equally well-trained, job-seeking candidates who are themselves out of work (and generally willing to work for less at the start). For the first time in our history, it is common for new graduates from college not to be able to find employment in their chosen field.

Supply and Demand

The economic laws of supply and demand are immutable. In every instance that supply exceeds demand, prices for supplies fall due to competition. (Remember the Texas Railroad Commission?) In part due to worldwide overpopulation, and in part due to technology obsoleting human labor in many areas, and in part due to technology removing previous barriers to operating in geographically distant regions, and in part due to government's worldwide following the pied piper of "free-markets", there is now a permanent distortion in the supply and demand relationship between labor and the number of qualified workers needed.

The glut of available labor, worldwide, has predictably driven down the average wage in every work area except top management positions, and, unless things change pretty dramatically, and quickly, pay for most forms of human labor can be expected to continue to fall in real (adjusted for inflation) terms.

Technological advances in the area of manufacturing production, farming, mining, and transportation have been responsible for putting tens of millions of middle-class American turtles out of work in the last two and a half decades. The effect of this paradigm shift has been to devalue human labor by equating it to measures of work performed by machines.

The ongoing exporting of high-value manufacturing jobs out of the United States, to other countries having lower standards of living for production workers, has also been responsible for putting tens of millions of middle-class American turtles out of work within the last two and a half decades. The effect of this paradigm shift has been to devalue human labor of American workers, by equating their efforts with those of foreign workers used to living on less than three dollars a day in pay.

Given all of the above, it can be stated with a high degree of probability that within thirty years from now, if human labor continues to be devalued at the present rate that it is being devalued in the United States, by way of downsizing, merger reductions of "redundant" positions, replacing human work with automated processes, and exporting high-value jobs to countries with low standards of living; the middle-class will disappear altogether, not only from America, but worldwide; and the average wage paid to an American worker will be pulled down to the level of the lowest common denominator of workers worldwide, being insufficient to sustain life at the relatively comfortable levels we now know and enjoy.

And, **THAT** is another very real problem!

Compound problems

Making things more difficult, problem #1 and problem #2 are on a collision course. Given the ever growing worldwide population, there will be a steadily growing number of well-educated workers seeking entry into the job market. Technology will continue to devalue human labor by making it possible for fewer people to do all the work that is needed in terms of producing goods and products, worldwide.

Unless things change from the way they now are, many of those being born in the last half of this century will not be needed for work of any kind, and will not (ever) be able to get a job that pays enough to sustain life in a worthwhile manner.

It is a fallacy that today there are too few good jobs, worldwide, for workers seeking high paying employment. There are now, as is typically the case, exactly the right number of good jobs in the world to do everything that really needs to be done. There are enough automotive related factory jobs to make all the cars that are needed. There are enough computer related jobs to make all the computers that are needed. There are enough construction related jobs to make all the new homes that are needed. There are enough farm related jobs to produce all the food necessary. And so on.

The problem is not that there are too few good-jobs in existence worldwide. The problem is that there are too many people for the number of good jobs that exist today, worldwide. Supply and demand then works to cause the price of all jobs for which there is an excess of workers over available jobs, to fall.

Current thinking in government is that individuals in the future will probably have several "careers". This is different from prior generations who trained for, and expected to work in a single field of endeavor for most of their working life. What this appears to recognize is that about as soon as a worker gets used to a new type of work, he or she will likely be displaced by technology, or job migration to other countries, and have to find another way to make a living. This is currently being touted by government spin-doctors as an exciting and refreshing change from the past.

Population growth calling for a need to continually create more jobs, is heading for a train wreck of magnificent proportions with technology gains calling for ever fewer human workers in each work area. The fallout of this wreck may be something along the lines of WW III.

> And that, if it occurred, would be a **real** problem!

Worker "retraining" will have limited beneficial impacts on this problem. At some point in time, in the not too distant future, it won't matter if an individual has degrees in business management, and medicine, and some high-tech engineering field, and marketing, and law, and accounting, and genetics and agriculture. There won't be enough good jobs, as we now think of them, available in any work discipline, regardless of how many disciplines the person has been "retrained" in. Technology will keep advancing in a manner that continually allows for all needed work to be done with fewer humans, while population growth continually generates more and more people needing good paying jobs.

We have been conditioned to think in terms of a "real" or permanent job being one that requires the worker to be actively engaged in some job-related activity for a minimum of 40 hours a week. Immediately following the Civil War, the typical "full-time" work week was about 70 hours. By the end of WW II, union workers enjoyed a 40-hour work week, while non-union workers averaged 48 hours a week. Since 1950 businesses have successfully resisted attempts to further reduce the number of hours constituting a full-time work week. Logic tells us that if the total amount of work that needs to be done remains constant, but the "work week" is shortened by some percentage, the end result would be creation of a similar percentage of new job openings.

Since 1950 the work paradigm has shifted dramatically, due in large measure to the government electing to fuel inflation as a means of funding government expenses. After 1950, when prices continued to rise much more quickly than wages, it became necessary for both parents in most families to work outside the home, in order to make ends meet.

Prior to 1950, only one member of the family had to work full time in order to make enough money to meet expenses. In that scenario, only five out of every ten adults needed a full time job, and there were typically an excess of available (good) jobs over available workers.

But, by 1990, price increases outpacing wage increases had made it necessary for 9 out of 10 adults to have a full time job, in order to maintain the same standard of living.

Not surprisingly, the flood of new people seeking jobs, coupled with technology's reducing the number of people needed to do most tasks, had by 1990, created a situation wherein there were an excess of available workers over the number of worthwhile jobs available to employ them.

Thus unemployment and under-employment can be seen to be symptoms of a combination of increasing population, excessive inflation of the money supply to pay government bills, technology replacing human labor, mergers and technologically inspired "downsizing" making large numbers of middle-managers "redundant", and high-value production jobs being exported to countries with low standards of living, all acting together to devalue human labor, worldwide.

Again we see the immutable laws of cause and effect at work. It cannot be logically argued that if the U.S. population had remained constant over the past four decades, and the invention of the microchip had not occurred, and merger-mania had been scaled back by the government, and government had not elected to inflate the currency supply in order to pay its bills, and exporting of high-value manufacturing jobs had not been encouraged by the U.S. government, we, as American turtles, would not now be having to worry about things like unemployment, under-employment, falling standards of living, or both parents having to work outside the home, in order to make ends meet.

Unemployment and under-employment did not first happen, and cause technology to advance at a rapid pace, inflation of the currency to occur, the population to grow, the job exodus to foreign countries to occur, and the overall devaluation of human labor (especially in the U.S.) to occur. The technological revolution, currency inflation, population expansion, exporting of jobs with the governments blessing, and overall human labor devaluation happened first, and caused the unemployment and under-employment to follow (and some other things too.)

Problem number three is citizens being systematically excluded from the decision making process in the most important decisions affecting their lives.

American turtles have become "conditioned" to allowing elected officials to make all of the most important decisions affecting their livelihood, and lives in general, for them. They have been encouraged to take this path both by the elected officials, and the puppet masters that pull the strings of the elected officials.

Back in Part 1, we reviewed the seven most significant changes in the relationship between Americans and their government. Number two on the list was: "abdication of personal responsibilities by individual citizens". It was followed by number three "assumption of abdicated individual responsibilities by government bodies".

It has to be emphasized, that government didn't usually take anything away from anyone at the point of a gun. It was typically more subtle than that. What happened was that the government's continuing inflation of the nation's currency supply to pay the government's operating expenses, caused commodity and product prices overall to go up rapidly for all Americans. Taxes were raised too. Both parents had to work to meet expenses, and pay higher levels of taxes. Social security and Medicare and Medicaid further decreased take-home pay. People stopped saving (there wasn't anything left over to save), stopped setting aside money for retirement, stopped staying home and raising their children, and put Mom and Dad in rest homes when they got old, rather than taking care of them themselves. Then the government set up programs to do all these things for them, using (a small portion of the) tax dollars taken from their paychecks.

This paradigm shift occurred over a forty- year time span. New government programs filtered on-line one or two at a time, every few years, rather than all at once. Insidiously, the government moved in to take over what had previously been individual responsibilities. Because it didn't happen all at once, people became "conditioned" to accepting the changes one at a time. However, over a forty year time span, the cumulative effect was to transfer many, if not most, of the most important individual responsibilities to the government, and along with them to also transfer all decision making relating to these responsibilities to elected officials and bureaucratic bodies.

Perhaps the most damaging aspect of this process was the "conditioning" of citizens that accompanied the confiscation of personal responsibilities by the government. Like pigeons being conditioned to accept painful shocks, in order to get small amounts of food from a pellet dispenser, Americans were conditioned to accept many other painful and damaging changes in their lives in order to get handouts of various kinds from the government.

Part of the process included getting American middle-class turtles to accept working through elected officials and bureaucratic bodies, exclusively, in order to address events affecting their lives in a dramatic fashion. Elected officials are pre-disposed to work harder for those who contribute toward their election campaigns than they work for those who don't contribute toward their election campaigns. In most instances, the greatest contributors are single interest groups that often have goals that are diametrically opposed to what the majority of voters in an elected official's precinct may be in favor of.

Occasionally, a candidate for some elected office is fielded that is not affiliated with either single interest groups, or one of the two major political parties. When this happens, candidates from the two major parties both attack the third candidate, the media downplays the third party candidate's chances, and the lobbyists supporting the major party candidates spend money encouraging voters to choose between the two candidates they are financing and who are both indebted to them.

Lobbyists for single interest groups typically contribute to both (Republican and Democratic Party) candidate's campaigns, as a way of assuring that <u>whoever</u> gets elected will be beholden to them. The idea here is to limit the voters' choices to one of two candidates, either of which can be expected to work on behalf of the single interest entity making campaign contributions to pay for the election effort. It is as important to the single interest lobbyists, as it is to the elected officials they support, that the general population agree to work exclusively through elected officials.

This makes it easier to control the outcome in a more cost-effective manner.

If there were, say, ten parties fielding candidates, the single-interests would have to grease five times as many palms in order to control the outcome, and the chances of some rebel in one or more of the parties ignoring them, and marching to a different drummer, would be greatly increased. The fewer political parties, the better, from the single-interest contributor's standpoint.

Back in Part 1 the method used by spin doctors to brainwash elected officials was disclosed (spaced repetition). The same method has been successfully used over the past forty years to condition most Americans to accept continually choosing between the lesser of evils, in terms of choosing elected officials.

Having been thus conditioned, American turtles have allowed elected officials to not only legislate away their personal responsibilities, but to also make decisions that affect their livelihood, and virtually every other aspect of their lives, including making decisions in areas that over forty years' time, the elected officials have proven beyond any doubt, that they are incapable of making good decisions in.

Some Examples

For example: Only elected officials are allowed to determine how much of the nation's aggregate income the government should be allowed to take in the form of taxes. Bureaucratic appointees not subject to voter approval are allowed to control the economy of the world through enactment of their policies and regulations (i.e., the Federal Reserve Board of Governors). Only elected leaders are allowed to make decisions relating to trade treaties and trade policies that affect the future of all middle-class American turtles. Only elected officials are allowed to enact laws that bind others, but not themselves. Only elected officials are allowed to make laws that usurp the rights and responsibilities of citizens, and turn them over to government bodies. Only elected officials are allowed to make laws that favor one group of Americans over other groups of Americans.

Mind you, this is all perfectly legal. The Constitution allows it to happen, and that's probably as it should be. The thing is this, fellow turtles, the government has proven itself incapable of making such decisions rationally, or in the best interests of the country overall, but, at the same time elected officials do not trust you to be directly involved in the decision making process.

Unresponsive government and corrupt government are outgrowths of American turtles having been conditioned to abdicate their personal responsibilities, and turn all important decision making affecting their future's over to government to handle. Absolute power corrupts absolutely.

By way of conditioning us to accept the superiority of the wisdom of elected officials, we are told that the combination of a need for citizens to have available more spendable income, middle-class taxes therefore needing to be lower, the need to provide for a strong national defense, the national debt needing to be reduced or eliminated, the need to provide a "safety net" for poverty stricken citizens, and a concurrent need to provide for meeting the financial and medical needs of an expanding older generation creates a very complex situation, requiring exceptional political skill, intellect, and courage to address successfully.

Oh really?

Perhaps the reason it all seems so complex to the heavy thinkers in government, is that those involved are, intentionally or otherwise, concentrating their efforts in the wrong area entirely. They have allowed themselves to be diverted away from the problems, and instead have focused their attention entirely on reducing the severity of symptoms of the problems instead.

In mathematics it is axiomatic that how the problem is defined, determines the types of solutions that will be proposed. It is absolutely the case that defining the problems is the thing that elected officials at the Federal level do least well. For example, when was the last time you heard an elected official mention the exploding population or devaluing of human labor as problems that needed to be addressed? And when was the last time you heard an elected official express concern over the fact that his or her constituents were being excluded from the decision making process in the most important areas affecting their lives? Like never?

Prior (and current) approaches aimed at involving citizens in the decision making processes, relating to defining social problems, and implementing laws as a means of solving them, have increasingly fallen short as the country's population expanded beyond the 100 million mark. Prior (and current) approaches called for backing candidates for elected office that (at least during the campaign) share your views in most areas, and hoping that whoever gets elected doesn't mess up too badly, or cause damage that can't be later undone. This approach worked better during the first hundred years the U.S. was in operation than it has worked in the second hundred years.

Especially over the past fifty years' time, the advent of single interest groups financing campaigns has now skewed the process to the extent that most elected officials in Washington barely give lip-service to their non-campaign-contributor constituents anymore; and as a result, the non-single interest, non-money contributors, comprising a majority of Americans, are effectively now without representation in Washington.

Elected officials will say that this is not the case, but consider just the few examples that follow:

American middle-class workers have been excluded from the decision making process regarding what percent of the nation's aggregate income should be set aside for running the government.

Middle-class Americans have been similarly ignored and excluded from the decision making process regarding how taxes should be assessed and collected, and excluded from the decision making process regarding what percentage of total income received as taxes, should be allocated to each government function.

Middle-class Americans have been excluded from the decision-making process when deciding whether to commit American military might, and American lives, in foreign wars in which the American people had no direct interest. We are not talking about defense of American shores from outside threats here, or actions in response to other countries declaring war on the United States by way of a surprise attack on an American military base, like what happened during Pearl Harbor. We are talking here about entering ongoing wars between two or more other countries altogether, or intervening on behalf of one side or the other in another country's internal civil war. We are talking about undertaking military actions in instances wherein there is enough time for all Americans to be consulted. Often there are <u>years</u> of time for deliberation before taking action. Even then, there has been no attempt to decide such matters by gaining a consensus of Americans (polling doesn't count .... voting counts).

These matters are decided only by gaining a consensus of elected officials, who have often admitted to voting contrary to the wishes of the majority of their middle-class constituents when making these kinds of decisions on their behalf.

American middle-class citizens are likewise excluded from the decision making process when deciding how much of their income, in the form of taxes, (and debt), should be given away to help citizens in other countries through foreign aid. The cumulative effect of over forty years of foreign aid has by now reached a level where the un-repaid foreign aid "loans" when counting the cost of continually "re-financing" them (rolling them forward) with borrowed money from the U.S. Treasury, represent about 10% of the nation's national debt, and 10% of the taxes collected from American citizens each year.

In 1995, the U.S. congress voted to give Mexico $50 billion dollars to help that government stay alive when they mismanaged their economy. Fifty billion dollars amounts to about $2000 being contributed by every single family in the United States. At the time, the U.S. treasury was flat busted, and the government's elected leaders voted to advance the $50 billion anyway, knowing that the only way it could happen would be for the U.S. treasury to inflate the currency by printing up 50 billion dollars in paper, thus further reducing the value of every dollar already in circulation by a couple of cents.

Fifty billion dollars is a huge amount of money that comes directly from U.S. taxpayers, exclusively for use by an inept government of another country altogether, and has a significant effect on American families who will ultimately collectively see every dollar of it come directly out of their wallets.

There are two really important questions here. First, how much of each American's income should they be forced to turn over to citizens of other countries each year? Second, is it appropriate to borrow the money to give to citizens of other countries, when we are, at the time, unable to pay our own government's bills here at home? Even though these decisions are arrived at over months of deliberation in the Congress, and even though there is more than adequate time to seek a consensus from the Americans most affected by these decisions, elected leaders refuse to share the decision making process with the citizens, and, in fact, here again, often admit to voting contrary to the way the majority of their constituents have asked them to vote, when such questions come before congress.

Middle-class Americans have been excluded from the decision making process in every instance that the nation's paper currency supply has been inflated to pay off bills run up by the government, even though immensely destructive effects on their lives were the result of these decisions.

Middle-class Americans have been excluded from the decision-making process in every instance wherein congress was considering enacting a law that favored one group of Americans over other groups of Americans.

Middle-class Americans have been ignored when it comes to the establishing of trade policies with other countries, even though the trade policies ultimately determine the security of their jobs, and the standard of living of their families. During debates on two trade policies (NAFTA and GATT) elected officials acknowledged that their constituents were almost uniformly against passage, but that "in good conscience" they felt obliged to vote for passage anyway.

And similarly, when it came to deciding whether there should be institutional checks and balances maintained at the federal government level to discourage either management or labor from taking undue advantage of the other, ordinary Americans have not been allowed to participate in the decision making process.

And when it came to establishing checks and balances between government income and government expenses, ordinary Americans were even more boldly and purposely excluded from the process. Both houses of congress voted publicly, on television, and decided that the public should not be allowed to decide state by state whether the federal government should be forced to live within its means. Again, acknowledging all the while, that they were being bombarded with requests from the people they represented, to offer an amendment to the Constitution that mandated a balanced budget, the elected officials declared that they could not "in good conscience" vote the way their constituents wanted them to vote.

(Does that spaced repetition work on these guys, or what?)

Over the past fifty years' time, ordinary Americans have been systematically excluded from directly participating in the decision making process in virtually all matters such as these that directly affect their lives and the lives and future of their families. The present decision making process places elected officials in a position of making decisions regarding the welfare of the great majority of their constituents in direct competition with the interests of single interest campaign contributors. In this competition, the middle-class constituents have lost every significant contest.

It is insufficient as an argument to claim that Americans retain the right to vote out of office officials that they believe are acting contrary to their interests. The current elective process is rigged in two ways against the individual citizens and in favor of incumbent elected officials and single-interest campaign contributors.

First, elected officials have available to themselves, on a daily basis, access to free media, and use of highly skilled spin doctors paid for by single interest parties that support the incumbent. It is spaced-repetition all over again. The incumbent's side of the story is replicated and spread widely, while challengers enjoy none of these benefits.

Secondly, the process by which potential challengers to an incumbent's position are selected is slanted to favor incumbents. The major political parties have committees to select those who will be favored with money and supported. The committees are invariably made up of party hacks who expect something in return for giving an individual a shot at running for office. Further, in most states, and for all national elective offices, the laws have been designed to protect the idea of a two party system, and purposely make it (very) difficult for an individual outside the sphere of influence of the main two parties "committees" to even be allowed to have his or her name placed on the ballot.

Both of these conditions conspire to perpetuate the status quo, as regards keeping most Americans from having any real chance of getting elected to an office that is involved in the making of the kinds of decisions we're talking about here. Incumbents understand that once elected, displacing them will be difficult for a challenger to do, regardless of how they vote, and they often vote contrary to the interests of the majority of their constituents, without much fear of having to pay at the ballot box in the next election. Of course, displacing incumbents is not anything like impossible, and it happens frequently enough that elected officials like to point to the "turnover" rate in their bodies. It is very difficult, however, to displace an incumbent, for the reasons stated previously.

In the U.S. senate for example, during the 1994 elections when a theory relating to "term limits" was being discussed, some of the senators who had been around the <u>longest</u> made a point of mentioning that almost half the membership of their body had changed hands within the last two elections. Which was true. But meaningless. The "turnover" is invariably accomplished, in the main, at the "junior" senator level. The "senior" level senators hang in there forever.

The reason for the turnover among junior senators is seldom discussed, but it is a safe bet that inability to affect an outcome on a matter before the Senate has a lot to do with turnover at this level. Even elected senators who are "junior" status are excluded from the decision making process. Once this becomes understood by the "junior" senator (or congressman), many elect to not stay on, since their input is never requested, and they are reduced to, like the rest of us, to having to choose between the lesser of evils in legislation that was defined entirely by other more senior senators, with the "help" of lobbyists.

The result of this biased system is that only those willing to do the bidding of the committees of the two major parties, who are in turn given their marching orders by the single interest groups that pay for their operation, and contribute the most to their candidate's campaigns, are even allowed in the game at all. Further, only those who, once admitted into the game, who have proven over a relatively long period of time that they are willing to "go along to get along" are allowed in the inner circle, where all the decisions are made.

Length of tenure typically decides things like committee membership and committee chairmanships in both houses of congress. No matter is even allowed to be discussed on the floor of either house, unless the chairman of the committee overseeing such matters agrees to let it be heard. And, there is always a "go along to get along" price attached to having your matter brought forward for discussion. The legislative proposals of those who are unwilling to bow to the party committee's directions, simply never see the light of day. After a few years of this, the best, brightest, most principled and least corruptible members of congress simply decide to quit, and go somewhere else where they can maybe make a positive difference.

Some stay on who are not willing to be manipulated, and do what they can. Which is very little. But most who stay on agree to play by the unwritten rules of the game which call for taking direction from committees who in turn are guided by single interest contributions. Understanding how the system is biased against them, average American middle-class working turtles have in increasingly great numbers stayed away from the "formal" elective process, and have instead established their own "informal" elective process.

Unwilling to always accept the "lesser of evils" when selecting candidates for elective office, and recognizing that the present formal elective process requires that candidates from the two major parties always be of a kind that has demonstrated a willingness to compromise on principle in order to gain the parties support and financing; and further understanding that the good-old-boy network of senior members will quash any idea that falls outside preservation of the status quo, before it ever gets to the floor for discussion; average American middle-class working turtles have, in ever increasing numbers, voted "none of the above", in state and national elections, which they can do from their living rooms.

It is a myth that Americans don't take time to vote in elections at all levels. Americans hold the voting franchise near and dear to their hearts, and virtually 100 % of eligible voters vote in every election, for all candidates, and upon all legislation presented to them, which affects them directly. There have been no exceptions to this in at least the past five decades. However increasingly, they refuse to acknowledge and legitimize the "formal" elective system, which they understand to be stacked against them, by voting in established booths, always for the lesser of evils; and instead vote "none of the above" from the comfort of their living rooms.

Members of congress have been slow to catch on to the fact that by now most Americans understand very well how they conduct business in Washington, and further understand fully that those conducting it have, for the most part, had to completely abandon principal as the price of membership into the elite decision-making circles of government. What is surprising is that the elected officials themselves don't seem able to comprehend why they are held in low esteem by average Americans.

Elected officials, proud of having been elected by a small minority of citizens in their district, promote the view that if average Americans choose to vote outside the established system, that they are effectively forfeiting their vote, because votes cast outside the established system don't count. They are wrong of course, but they don't yet understand how wrong they are.

But, the bottom line is this. At this point in time, American middle-class working turtles have been effectively excluded from the "formal" decision making process in those matters which most affect the outcome of their lives, and the lives of their families, and the lives of future generations of their families.

And, **THAT** is definitely a problem!

When citizens come to believe that elected officials no longer have their best interests at heart, and cannot be trusted to enact laws that afford them fair and equal treatment, it is only a short distance forward to a point in time when citizens can rationalize ignoring the laws passed by elected officials.

Law breaking is rampant in our society. Violent crime, drug trafficking, child abandonment, fraud, tax evasion; the list goes on and on. Citizens look to elected leaders to set examples for citizen behavior. When ordinary citizens determine that elected officials can participate in illegal and unethical actions and not be held accountable, the message is that lawbreaking is acceptable. Just don't get caught.

It is necessary to recognize that, in the main, crime is a symptom, and not a problem. In large part, crime in the United States is largely a by-product of a combination of citizens being excluded from the decision making process relating to the most important things in their lives, laws passed that are purposely designed to benefit some segments of society at the expense of other segments of society, government inflationary actions that have had disastrous effects on the economy, government actions that have encouraged two-earner families where children are raised outside of the home, and government actions that have encouraged American companies to export their high-value jobs to other countries, thereby causing poverty to spread at home; all topped off by some very bad examples of personal and leadership behavior being set by elected leaders.

When ordinary citizens come to believe that the major decisions affecting their lives and the lives and future of their families are outside of their ability to influence the outcome, a feeling of desperation sets in. The old saying that "desperate people commit desperate acts", is a true saying.

Violence is not inherently random. Violent behavior most often results from people trying to gain a measure of control, over their lives, over another person, over an injustice they feel has been done to them, or over something else that they feel is threatening them. When people sense that they are losing control over the events that affect the outcome of their lives, they feel threatened, and act to restore a measure of control. Violence is an entirely rational response to feeling threatened. If it were not so, no species would long exist on this planet.

We really only have two ways to go here. We can choose to arm ourselves to deal with the violence when it occurs on an increasingly frequent basis, or we can come together to act in a way that removes some of the threatening factors inducing the violent behavior.

Of course, not all violent behavior is threat induced. As noted at the outset of this work, there are definitely some bad turtles out there that will have to be dealt with in a penal setting. However, acting to remove the most threatening factors that presently induce fear into a large, and growing larger, segment of our society is (or should logically be) the preferred approach.

We must also recognize that not all fears are equal.

Fear of death is insignificant compared to the fear that a mother and father feel who have no job, no money and no food for their children. Fear of death is likewise insignificant compared to the fear that a young person feels who sees no way ever out of a circle of poverty that has gripped his or her family for generations.

There is a lot of **F**ear, **U**ncertainty, and **D**oubt permeating American society right now. The "FUD factor" has been used frequently by elected officials to get citizens to go along with the present government decision-making process. That is, "better the devil you know (me), than the devil you don't know (my opponent)". Or, "better the government programs that you know (the ones we have now), than government programs you don't know (any change in the status quo)".

At some point in time, possibly in the not too distant future, the cumulative fears of hunger, poverty, and being faced with eternal want, will become a FUD factor of their own that is sufficient to override the "status quo" FUD factor promoted by the politicians.

Should that happen, the paradigm would then shift back toward one where individuals assumed more control over the outcome of their lives.

When a measure of individual control over the most significant events affecting the outcome of their lives is restored, and the most feared threats recede, for American middle-class working turtles, violent behavior in our society will become immediately less by a significant measure.

And, only then.

Problem number 4, is that ongoing government currency inflation practices cause the value of existing dollars to fall, which in turn causes prices related to living standards to continually increase much faster than wage gains.... and living standards to therefore continually fall further each year for most middle class American citizens.

In 1950, the average production worker earned enough from working 40 hours a week (172 hours a month) to provide for meeting all the basic needs of a family of four. This included making enough to save up enough for a down payment on a two to three bedroom tract home, and making monthly payments on that home, including principal, interest, taxes, and insurance. It also included enough income, after taxes, to provide for making a car payment on a car that was three years or less old, and to cover such things as operating expenses relating to the car, food, clothing, school expenses, personal health and life insurance policies on all family members, paying of utilities (electric, gas/oil, refuse collection, water, sewer, etc.), money enough to take the family out to a movie once a week, money enough to pay for a week's vacation away from home each year for the whole family, enough money to set aside about 5% of the wage-earners gross pay for a rainy day or retirement, and enough to give about 1% of the wage-earner's gross pay to charitable organizations.

The average worker in the "service" sector earned about half as much per hour as an employee in the "production" sector. In the main, in 1950, there were enough "production" sector jobs for each family to have at least one member so employed, and thus it was the case that most families elected to have one parent stay at home full time to see to duties on that front, including, not insignificantly, child raising.

This financial condition applied to approximately 80% of all working-class turtles at the time. While this was going on in 1950, the government was mostly operating in the black, income taxes were taken out of everyone's paychecks, and so was Social Security. The option, in 1950, to pay for everyday subsistence items "on credit", from a family's standpoint, did not exist to any great degree. And, this capability was not especially missed, since the primary wage-earner in the family typically made enough to operate on a pay-as-you-go basis.

Now we fast-forward to the 1990's, and look at what has happened to the average middle-class working turtle's income. By 1990, eighty percent of middle-class families had to have both parents working outside of the home in order to have the same standard of living that one outside earner could produce in 1950, with much of what used to be paid for on a pay-as-you-go basis, now being paid for in monthly credit installments that never ended.

A significant percentage of Americans could not, by this point in time, even with both parents working outside the home, earn enough to (ever) make the down payment on a typical 2-3 bedroom home, or thereafter make payments on one. The majority of Americans had lost the ability to set aside money to pay for vacations, or for a rainy day or retirement. Credit was used extensively for purchases of everyday subsistence items like food.

Economists in the 1990's point to things like credit purchases being up at Christmas-time, and tremendous growth in the number of people leasing new automobiles as being signs of a healthy economy. These trends appear to have been accurately reported by the media, but they have done little to relieve the overriding feeling of pessimism that overhangs much of the middle-class working turtle population.

If there appears to be a contradiction here between how economists and working-class turtles view the same indicators, think again. There is no contradiction at work here. Given that real, disposable income for most Americans has been steadily dropping over the last three decades, it appears that the reason that credit purchases are up, is directly related to the fact that disposable income is down. In other words, people are using credit to buy things they used to pay cash for, because they had more money to spend in the past than they have now. People lease cars, because they can no longer afford to buy them, even over an extended five or six-year period of time. If this is accurate, it is the case that the very same forces that are at work in the credit markets that economists see as a positive sign, are viewed by a significant cross-section of the public at large as signs of an unhealthy economic situation, and one which they may (correctly) feel is likely to get worse, before it gets better.

Actually, both sides are correct in their interpretation(s). The economists see increased economic activity, regardless of its consequences, as a good thing. Middle-class workers see not only the economic activity, but the vanishing of an ability to extricate themselves from ever-increasing debt loads, and this makes the middle-class workers uncomfortable.

Taxes and Minimum Wages

At the time this is being written, considerable discussion is going on among politicians re: taxes. Both major parties are trying to outdo each other in terms of "setting the agenda" for the debate, insofar as how the existing tax law(s) should be modified, in order to give us middle-class working turtles a "tax-break". There is also another push on to make a token increase in the federally mandated hourly "minimum wage".

Media Interviewers of political figures, accompanied by groups of "expert panelists" spend endless hours discussing the pros and cons of various proposals for modifying the federal tax laws, advanced by various political figures. A lot of discussion centers on how taxes for middle-class workers can be reduced, while, at the same time, not causing the national debt to grow at an accelerated rate. Every politician, economist, and media guru has their own mathematical model purporting to show the validity of their hypothesis, based, of course, on their own assumptions. We are repeatedly reminded that the problem is enormously complex, and barely within the reach of these "experts" to grasp, and hopefully solve.

It is not true that the problem is complex. And anybody with the sense God gave a lump of dirt should be able to see what's needed to solve it.

In the instance of tax policy, those involved at the "policy making level" have uniformly diagnosed the problem as federal taxes being too high on middle-class working turtles here in America. So, all involved are busting their buns to bring us middle-class turtles a "middle-class tax break", and maybe throw in a few cents increase in the minimum wage for good measure. Paying for the middle-class tax break and the minimum wage increase will, as usual, be done mostly with smoke and mirrors. And, it won't work because the real underlying problem is purposely being not addressed at all.

The problem is not that American middle-class workers are paying too great of a percentage of their income in taxes (though that is probably true too). The problem is that American middle-class working turtles are receiving (far) too little gross income for the work that they do, and also, are continually having their work further devalued by either turning it over to automation, or giving it over to a worker in another country whose standard of living is incredibly poor, compared to the average middle-class American's standard of living.

Think about it!

If your family's gross income were to be immediately doubled, would you be all that concerned if the present tax rate took its share of the increased amount coming to you? You would still have about a 60% increase in spendable income available to you.

And, imagine what a boost that would give the Federal government. Its income from taxes (by whatever type of taxes like income-tax, flat-tax, or national sales tax) would increase dramatically too, and be (more than) enough to cover the government's operating expenses, "entitlements" (until we can wean ourselves away from them), funding of a safety net for the displaced and disadvantaged at present levels, and to start not just holding steady on the national debt level, but actually reducing it each year.

It is undoubtedly the case that if the total amount of tax dollars now being taken in from poor and middle-class citizens could, somehow, be immediately increased by 75%, all of the complexity surrounding how to balance competing interests for available tax dollars would just disappear, as if by magic.

Why? Because there would again be (as there often was in the distant past) enough money to do everything that was needed in government, at the appropriate level, and probably do it at a tax rate that was reduced from today's levels too. A reduction in the tax rate would be a pleasant bonus, if it occurred, and a possibility of reduced taxes should logically occur with 75% more coming into the government each year, but in an environment that did not require sacrificing one group's interests to the interests of other groups. If everybody immediately had 60% more spend able income, it wouldn't necessarily be such a big deal if tax rates were cut, or not.

Just look at the arithmetic.

Let us consider the impact if only those earning the absolute minimum wage could see their incomes double. For now, let's choose to disregard those who are out of work and are still looking for a job, those who have been out of work for so long that they have given up all hope of ever finding work, and those who are making slightly above the poverty level of income, but are seriously under-employed, and working for a small fraction of what they used to make. The government in Washington acts as if these groups did not exist at all, so, in order to compare apples and apples, we will, for purposes of this discussion, also pretend that they don't exist.

For our discussion here we will just consider those who are already employed, (this alone is sufficient to make government officials happy) but who are working at or very near the current minimum wage level of $7.25 per hour. This group (not including illegal in-migrants) may make up as much as 20% of America's total working population. It admittedly includes a lot of "first job" positions. But it also includes a lot of positions filled by someone who used to make $15-25 per hour before their job was automated, eliminated, or exported to another country. Elected officials are reluctant to acknowledge that this (under-employed) group is suffering too.

But, back to the chase.

Twenty-five million workers earning $7.25 an hour cumulatively generate about $310 billion in payroll dollars annually. Of this total, the government usually gets nothing at all (to keep) in the way of income taxes, since, at less than $16,000 a year, all of this income would be exempt from taxation at the Federal level. In fact, since this level of income qualifies the earner for "poverty" status, and "unearned income credits" (a form of welfare payments), this category of worker constitutes a considerable drain on the treasury each year.

FICA (social security), Medicare/Medicaid, and state and local sales taxes still apply (and aren't returned at the end of the year), but for our purposes in this discussion, we will disregard them, since no matter what the final gross pay totals, they can be considered proportional, and, disregarding them helps keep the illustration simple(r).

Now, consider the impact of increasing each such workers pay to just $10.50 per hour. Gross income for this group would now increase to $500 billion in gross income. And since these workers would now be above the poverty level, they would send about $18.75 billion annually to the treasury in the form of federal taxes (15% of the $125 billion in taxable income above the poverty level).

And, since these workers would now be above the poverty level, they would cease to be an "unearned income credit" welfare drain on the treasury, thereby freeing up $ billions more of what used to be welfare dollars for more productive uses.

What's more, two people in a household earning this amount ($10.50 per hour, each, or $21.00 an hour total) would have enough purchasing power in today's economy to buy a small home, own a good used car, and have enough money for nourishing food and decent clothes for their children.

Finally, think what a boost having a 60% increase in disposable income available to this group would have on the American economy as a whole. In large measure, that, or actually something about <u>twice</u> that good, was part of the American Dream of yesterday.

Actually, in 1950, this was the level of income typical of <u>one</u>-earner families. Realistically, we will first have to construct a model where two workers can get by, before we can hope to return to a point in time where a single worker can bring home enough to provide for meeting a whole family's basic needs. Sadly, neither the one-earner nor the two-earner model is increasingly available to tens of millions of American working families today.

Ratios and Comparisons: (circa 2005)

A home that in 1950 cost $12,000, today costs about $180,000. That constitutes a 1500% increase in dollars needed to purchase a typical 2-3 bedroom middle-class home. A "middle-class" family car cost about $1,800 in 1950. A similar family car today costs about $19,000. That constitutes a 1055% increase in dollars needed to purchase a family car. Gas in 1950 was 20 cents a gallon. Now it's over $2.50 a gallon, an increase of 1250%. A movie ticket in 1950 averaged fifty cents. Today a movie ticket costs about $5 on the average, constituting a 1000% increase. A loaf of bread in 1950 cost 14 cents. A loaf of bread today costs about $2.60, representing an increase of about 1800%. A pair of levis in 1950 cost $4. A pair of Levis today costs on average about $35, an increase of over 850%. A visit to the family doctor in 1950 averaged $6. A visit to a family doctor today averages $70, representing a 1050% increase. Shelter, food, transportation, medical treatment, clothing, and entertainment represent over 75% of every family's basic expenses. The average middle-class manufacturing worker in the manufacturing heartland of the U.S. had a gross income of a bit less than $4,000 a year in 1950. The average middle-class production worker in the heartland had a gross income of slightly less than $27,000 a year in 2005. That represents about a 570% increase in average production wage-earner income, on average between 1950 and 2005.

Summing up: Prices for the basics (food, shelter, transportation, clothing, medical expenses, and entertainment) have gone up an average of a little more than 1100% since 1950, while average production wage-earner income has gone up about 575%.

Given this disparity between the rapidly rising cost of living, and the much less rapid rise in average wages, it is readily apparent why the number of adults working outside the home went from 5 out of 10, to 9 out of 10, over the same period of time.

The primary cause of the measurable decline in the standard of living for the majority of Americans that has been occurring over the past forty years' time, and which decline is accelerating even as you read this, is the government's ongoing practice of inflating the nation's money supply. The government does this as a means of paying off bills that they have rung up, for which income to the government from taxes of various kinds isn't enough to cover.

> It is especially important that working people come to understand that government inflation of the money supply is the cause of prices increasing, rather than as government "economists" would ask us to believe, that inflation is a result of prices going up. First inflation of the money supply happens by the government, and then prices go up to offset the negative effects of inflating the currency supply. NOT the other way around.

Back in the first section of the book, we reviewed how printing up "money" (in any form, whether paper dollars, treasury "notes", negotiable treasury securities, etc.) when the "money" in question was tied to some acceptable standard of exchange that was deemed to have value, such as gold bars, caused the value of existing paper dollars already in circulation to go down. When the government acted to arbitrarily increase the value of the measuring standard (gold), the effect was to proportionally de-value the paper "money" already in circulation.

That is, if gold was arbitrarily increased, by dictate, from $20 per ounce to $40 per ounce, the effect was to immediately make it necessary to come up with twice as much value in paper money to buy an ounce of gold, or anything else that was purchasable with gold. Since, at that time, everything was purchasable with gold, the price of everything would go up (double) accordingly.

The primary reason for arbitrarily increasing the value of gold was to allow the treasury to print up more dollars. At the time, the country was on the gold standard, which required that every dollar printed have a like value of gold standing behind it in the treasury's vaults. The need for additional dollars for the government to spend was typically tied to some supposedly good cause like paying off war debts, getting dollars in circulation to revitalize a stalled economy before election time, or something of the sort.

The undesirable consequence of this practice was, that businesses and individuals holding dollars saw the purchasing power of the money they already had in their checking and savings accounts become less.

Businesses, who see both the purchasing power of their existing bank accounts become less, AND their costs of operating and expansion capital go up (loan interest rates and bond rates) react by requiring more dollars for their goods, and services, in order to make up the losses suffered from the government's inflating the currency supply. Then pressure on businesses to increase workers' wages occurs because workers are faced with paying higher prices to those businesses that have raised their prices for goods and services.

> Remember: "For every government action, there is an equal and opposite citizen reaction"

Not only American citizens holding dollars are affected when inflation of the U.S. money supply occurs. Everybody in the world holding dollars or taking dollars in exchange for goods or services is affected. Thus inflating the currency supply here at home causes the price of everything imported from other countries to go up too. It's a very vicious cycle.

The government wins (temporarily but not long term). Businesses win (both short and long term). Somebody has to lose. Guess who?

In 1972 the U.S. abandoned the principle of tying the amount of paper "money" in some form to a stated quantity of gold in the nation's treasury vaults. This did not, by itself make things worse. Money, in any form whether metal or printed paper, only has whatever worth buyers and sellers assign to it as a medium of exchange.

What gives "money" (in any form) its value, is the belief that it is strictly limited in supply, against a growing demand. Whenever the supply can be easily manipulated or "grown" by either side (buyer or seller, but most often the buyer) the value assigned to the "money" form becomes less by an amount proportional to how much can be easily added to the available supply.

A case in point might be the value of diamonds, which quickly dropped in value when a way was found to reproduce them artificially. Of course, diamonds in the "natural" state were always (and are still) very common and plentiful. What gave diamonds their high value for many years in the past was an artificial reduction in the supply, due to a single company (DeBeers) buying up all the diamond mines and only letting about 1 % of their inventory be sold all over the world each year, thus making diamonds APPEAR to be hard to come by. (Shades of the Texas Railroad Commission).

There are many other examples too, relating to various nation's (paper) currencies, including past instances in our own country. In the past, Continental dollars during our revolutionary war, Confederate dollars during our civil war, Reich marks during Germany's period of hyperinflation in the 1920's, U.S. dollars again in the 1970's and 1980's when prices rose over 400% here at home, and even more recently Mexico's Peso, all have been instances where national currencies fell quickly and drastically in value, when the government in question arbitrarily decided to just "manufacture" some more money with which to pay their debts.

For the past forty years, the U.S. government has been steadily and systematically increasing the amount of "money" in circulation for no other purpose than to pay their bills. As in every past instance in recorded history, the effects on the populace have been negative and damaging to the general standard of living of citizens in the country whose government was doing the inflating. When the government talks about "managing" inflation, what they are really talking about is walking the tightrope between printing up enough money to pay their own bills, while disguising their actions so as to not touch off a business and citizen reaction that might end up like it did in Germany in the 1930's. For those readers who might be too young to remember what happened in Germany back then, the result was a little thing called WWII.

In part, the government accomplishes this "balancing" act by promoting the idea that they are just reacting to increasing prices that are outside of their sphere of control, (given the global economy and all, don't you know?) and are really just printing up dollars to cover the increased cost of goods that somehow, mysteriously, keep rising. In another part, the government attempts to moderate citizen and business reaction to their inflation of the money supply by understating its negative effects.

Most businesses are sophisticated enough to not let themselves be suckered by government propaganda relating to what inflation REALLY costs, and act to protect themselves accordingly. But, a surprising number of otherwise intelligent citizens don't understand the real costs, and end up getting hurt. Badly.

The effects of inflation on workers and consumers are actually significantly greater than government "economists" let on. In fact, in order to "keep up" with inflation it is necessary for workers and consumers, who ultimately pay ALL costs associated with inflation, to increase their income at not once, but between TWO AND THREE TIMES the (government's stated) inflation level, each year.

The government never publishes the actual inflation rate (that is, the amount of "new" paper money they print up and force into circulation in order to pay their bills, after "borrowing" it back from the Federal Reserve banks they "sold" it to). So, workers and consumers are never provided with this information as a guideline that they can use when negotiating for wage and salary increases. Instead the government publishes figures that reveal only how much consumer prices (at the wholesale level) have gone up, as a result of their inflating the money supply.

This omission on the government's part is probably intentional. It is very important to those in government that the public at large remain in the dark about how much money they print up each year just to pay off their bills. However, in recent years it has become easier to estimate the amount of currency inflation initiated for these purposes. The annual government spending deficit is, in the main, paid off entirely by means of the treasury printing up government "securities" having a face value equal in amount to the annual deficit. These "securities" are then "sold" to private investors, or by means of a complex and somewhat convoluted process "sold" to the privately owned Federal Reserve banks, who pay for them with checks drawn on their own accounts, which are not allowed to be audited.

We never know if these privately owned Federal Reserve banks checks are good, but we do know that there have never been enough paper dollars printed in all of the time since we have been a country, to pay off the accumulated amount of the nations "national debt", or even pay it halfway off. In all of the time since our mint started printing up dollars, only about half as many dollars have been printed, as currently exists in the amount we refer to as our "national debt".

It is therefore a mathematical certainty that at least half of the value of checks written by the various privately owned "Federal Reserve" banks never had sufficient dollars behind them, to cover them. But the "Federal Reserve" banks are not subject to government control in any way, and are not subject to audits by anyone other than their own owners. We just have to take their word for it that they had enough U.S. dollars to make their checks good. At the same time, the Treasury's own records indicate that at least half of value of their checks could not conceivably have been good, because there was never enough currency printed up by our mint, to cover them.

Which brings up an interesting question: Given all of the above, it appears that our government has, for many years now, simply printed up enough "money" to cover their spending shortfalls. The methods by which they have moved this "money" into circulation have been purposely complex to make it appear that the "money" in question is legitimate, and has real value. Yet it also appears certain that there have never been any "real" dollars ever printed up to cover at least half of it. It has apparently all been done with smoke and mirrors through "electronic funds transfers" between the various banks involved, and the Treasury department.

OK, so, the cat's out of the bag. The government just prints up money to pay off about one-fifth of its bills every year, has been doing this for about forty years' time, and is actively still doing it today. And, the world is still turning, isn't it? According to the government, we are all doing just fine, money-wise, and we all have a rosy future ahead of us, in spite of their annual practice of inflating the (pretend) money supply, and its effect of lowering our living standards.

By government logic, even though we are all individually losing a bit of our financial security each year as a result of their inflating the money supply, we will all together, collectively, somehow make it up in volume as a country, somewhere down the road.

There is an old business adage about how losing a little on each transaction, but trying to make up for it in volume, is a recipe for disaster. However, our government doesn't believe in old-fashioned adages like this as a rule for running national economies, so we continue to operate as if the reverse were true.

Now, here is the interesting thought I would like you to consider: Instead of just printing up enough money each year to cover our annual spending shortfalls (the annual budget deficit) why not just go all the way, and print up enough to pay for ALL the government's spending needs? If we did this, there would be no need for taxes at all!!! We are already doing this for about a fifth of the government expenses rung up each year. Why not just do it for the other four-fifths too??

And while we're at it, we could print up enough extra currency to pay off the "national debt"... all at once. After all, it's just a matter of paper and ink. We already have the printing presses and printing plates. Or, alternatively, we could just write the Federal Reserve banks we owe the money to a check on the U.S. treasury to pay them back, just like they wrote us one on their banks to create the debt in the first place. One hand would wash the other. A debt created by them paying us off with a bad check, would be retired by us paying them back with yet another bad check. Poetic justice?

Of course, both domestic and foreign "investors" in U.S. Treasury "securities", including individual citizens foolish enough to invest in "government securities", would lose a bunch of their portfolio value. The twelve privately owned Federal Reserve banks would probably go broke overnight.

But, the rest of us would then be able to pay off our debts in devalued dollars, since our incomes would rise relatively about tenfold overnight, and we would be entirely out of debt. When your income becomes $900,000 a year, paying off your old $90,000 mortgage wouldn't be all that hard to do in a year or two, would it?

And the banks would have so much extra money to lend that they would be fighting each other to offer the lowest interest rates, otherwise their money would just sit there and rot, while they went broke.

Just something to think about the next time you look at your pay stub and measure it against your personal debt load.

But, back to the chase. We were talking about how inflation makes it necessary for consumers and workers to have annual increases equal to TWO TO THREE TIMES the government's stated increase in the "consumer price index". The reason is obvious once you do the math.

Let's assume that the government "grows" the money supply by 3% in the upcoming year, as a means of paying off government spending that taxes didn't cover. The effect of this would be to cause the value of every dollar already in circulation to be reduced in purchasing power to 97 cents .... just like it always has in every past instance since the concept of "money" was invented as a means of simplifying exchanges for goods and services.

(Cause and effect: Inflating the "money" supply being the cause. Devaluation of existing Dollars being the immediate effect.)

Now those foreign businesses already having U.S. contracts in the works for sales and services have just seen the prices they quoted reduced in value, by U.S. government action.... by 3%. Unfortunately, they already based their business plans on the assumption that the lost 3% would be coming in to them to be used in paying off their employees and suppliers, and now, overnight, it isn't there any more. What would YOU do if faced with this situation? Right! You would raise your prices going forward enough to make up for the loss incurred at the government's hands. Worldwide this would happen, has happened each year for the past forty years' time, and is happening even as you are reading this.

American businesses must then react to the foreign price increases by passing the increases through to their customers here at home. Their customers are American citizens, who now must demand wage increases needed to keep up with the price increases they are forced to pay.

Well, you say, that's not so terrible, I'll just ask my employer for a 3% raise to get back even in the game. Right? If you do, you will automatically lose the game!

Just look at the arithmetic.

First, the government's actions have just made every dollar you already have in the bank (or 401K, stocks, bonds, home equity, etc.)

worth 97 cents each. These same actions on the part of the government have resulted in businesses worldwide increasing the cost of their goods and services by (at least) a similar 3% amount. So, a widget that last year had a price tag of $1 now carries a price tag of $1.03. OK, now get out your calculators, and figure it out. How many dollars' worth 97 cents each, will it take to purchase a widget carrying a price of $1.03? (Hint for those learning "new" math in the 90's. Divide 103 by 97).

Wait a minute! Can that be right? Could it take 1.06 dollars? If so, that would mean that workers and consumers would have to receive TWICE the stated increase in the "consumer price index" increase, JUST TO STAY EVEN!

But, regrettably, that's NOT the worst of it. The "consumer price index" that the government's economists use to gauge how much prices have gone up as a result of their inflating the currency supply, doesn't take into account TAXES. Even without government inflation of the currency supplies to pay their bills, workers would have to get wage increases equal to TWICE the stated increase in the "consumer price index" to stay even in the game.

Again, the arithmetic is pretty simple. The "consumer price increase" is computed against GROSS income.... before any taxes have been subtracted. But taxes of ALL kinds (federal income, state income, FICA, Medicare, Medicaid, worker compensation taxes, unemployment taxes, local, county and state sales taxes, excise taxes, gasoline taxes, personal property taxes, auto lieu taxes, real estate taxes, "licenses" of various kinds, "user" fees, and last but not least, the percentage of everything we buy that represents taxes paid by businesses, that is collected back from their customers, etc, etc, etc.... you get the idea) now represent a bit over 50% of all income earned by middle class American turtles.

Thus the absolute increase in the "consumer price index" when calculated against GROSS income, would be equal to a bit more than TWICE AS HIGH a percentage, if compared to income after all kinds of taxes were subtracted. Now, add it all up. Inflation of the nation's currency supply has the effect of requiring individuals to need wage increases equal to TWICE the stated amount of increase in the "consumer price index" each year. Additionally, taxes subtracted from gross income ALSO have the effect of requiring individuals to need wage increases equal to TWICE the stated amount of increase in the "consumer price index" each year. The end result is that American turtles must receive between TWO AND THREE TIMES the stated increase in the "consumer price index" each year. ..... JUST TO STAY EVEN IN THE GAME. Those who don't, simply fall further behind each year by an amount equal to the difference between (about 2.5) times the consumer price index increase, and whatever percentage of wage increase they actually receive.

Government "economists" will say this is not so, and that just getting a 3% increase in wages would offset the 3% increase in prices. But you KNOW that they MUST be leaving SOMETHING out, don't you? Otherwise how do you explain the fact that even though wage increases have approximately equaled increases in the "consumer price index", as calculated by the government, over the past thirty years' time, and Federal income tax deductions were "indexed" to inflation (really they were indexed to the "consumer price index") in the early 1980's, the average American middle-class standard of living now requires two full time wage earners in the family to maintain, and the after-tax cost of living has increased at a bit more than DOUBLE the rate that wages (and net spendable income) have increased?

There are only two things you need to remember about economics, no matter how complex the "economists" would have you believe the subject to be:

1. Supply and Demand.
2. Cause and effect.

When demand exceeds available supplies (in anything, including money) prices go up. When the government's demands for more money to spend are met by simply "manufacturing" some more money (in some form, securities, paper currency, bonds (debt), or even simply increasing the amount stated to be in the treasury's vaults) the price of everything purchasable with money, in any U.S. currency form, ...Goes UP...worldwide. Quickly.

> Inflation is BY DEFINITION an increase in the money supply. Only the government is allowed, BY LAW, to inflate (increase) the amount of money, IN ANY FORM that is in circulation. It's in the U.S. Constitution. It is therefore obvious that only the government could conceivably be the CAUSE of inflation. While government "economists" would like us to believe that price increases cause inflation, the reverse can be seen with certainty to be the case.

Imagine what would happen if all of a sudden all the businesses in the world got (even more) greedy and suddenly all got together decided to increase their prices for goods and services by 100%, but our Treasury refused to print up money for citizens to use in paying the higher prices. What would happen? There being no money available to use for paying the higher prices, the businesses in question would either reduce their prices enough to match the available currency supply, or have to find another country to sell their goods and services in. America being roughly 35-50% of the total worldwide market (for everything, produced everywhere), the result would be a predictable immediate returning of prices to their prior level, or the businesses involved would quickly go broke from lack of sales.

Just because businesses demand more, doesn't mean we have to give in to their demands. We are running things, not them. And, deep down they know it. But big business has effectively brainwashed government politicians (and a lot of us middle-class turtles) into believing that we need them more than they need us. Not so. Every business individually needs customers and employees more than customers or employees need any given business.

We know why big business promotes the view that workers and consumers need them more than they need us. The question is why government economists continue to also try to convince us that we should go along with such an idea. Only two possibilities come to mind:

1. Perhaps they are just stupid, and don't know any better.

2. Perhaps they know better, but are purposely misleading us to keep us from understanding how they are running the economy into the ground… and the middle-class with it.

We may never know which of these is the case. But it is almost certainly either one of these or a combination of both. In any case, we must ask ourselves if this is how we want things to remain, and act accordingly.

The Emperor isn't wearing any clothes. We know it. So is it really to our benefit to continue to pretend otherwise, and, if so, what are the costs to our children and grandchildren that are associated with doing so?

Bottom line here, fellow turtles, is that middle-class workers' wages, in "real" terms, have been falling for over thirty years, are falling now, and can be expected to continue to fall, until the inflation-induced problems creating the falling wages are addressed, which isn't happening today.

| And THAT is definitely a problem! |

Problem number 5, is that American national pride and American national companies have been replaced by multi-culturalism and multi-national companies.

Over the past three decades, it has become increasingly fashionable to denigrate the American ideals that were, in large measure, responsible for building America into the world power it now is. Americans are continually encouraged to view themselves as citizens of a particular race, other foreign country, ethnic or religious background first, and as American citizens second.

This is exactly the opposite of the view that was popular over the first 150 years of this country's existence. New citizens in-migrating to this country during the first 150 years of our history were encouraged to think and act as Americans first, and consider themselves as prior citizens of some other country second. Similarly, in school, students were taught to pledge allegiance to the flag of the United States (only), and the republic for which it stood. The current school of thought is that we should celebrate our racial, in-migrant, ethnic, and religious differences to the same degree that we celebrate our being citizens of the United States of America.

For many American turtles, especially those who are third or fourth generation American turtles, it is hard to see the logic of encouraging separatism within the framework of the whole tapestry that constitutes American society. Most of those electing to come to America did so to improve their lot in life, believing that opportunities were greater to do that in the U.S. than they were back in the country where they in-migrated here from. If that is so, then most must have felt that, on balance, the U.S. society offered more than the society that they were leaving behind. And, it would probably now be generally conceded that (that) was an accurate view of things.

It is no surprise that there are no free lunches. To bet otherwise is to be often disappointed. In the past, learning English, and working to become an American like other Americans, was considered part of the price of admission into American society. It didn't guarantee success, but choosing not to do so almost certainly guaranteed failure. Now in-migrants are encouraged not to pay this price of admission. Instead generations of Americans already here before the newest in-migrants arrived, are asked to pay the price in the way of maintaining bi-lingual government operations at all levels.

During the signing of the Declaration of Independence, Ben Franklin volunteered that "we must all hang together, or we shall all certainly hang separately". That was the case then, and it's still the case today.

When, by enactment or "interpretation" of a law, the government encourages in-migrants to not consider themselves Americans first, and only coincidentally a previous citizen of another country, and/or member of some ethnic group second, the effect is to further divide a society that needs more than ever to become united.

Beginning in the 1950's U.S. government tax policies on individuals and businesses resulted in some citizens and businesses expatriating some or all of their assets to protect them from what they viewed as excessive taxation. Thereafter, the government continued to enact and enforce tax policies that, over the next forty years' time, resulted in an exodus of production-type jobs and businesses to other countries where the cost of labor and taxes were considerably less than in the United States.

Combined with the government tax policies which encouraged businesses to locate offshore, technology made it possible for corporations to manage businesses that were widely separated, geographically, with fewer and fewer managers.

The multi-national companies that emerged over the past thirty years' time, have been fundamentally different from the multi-national companies of prior decades and centuries, like the Hudson Bay company, or the East India Company, or many others too numerous to mention. The prior century's multi-national companies retained a feeling of nationalistic pride, associated with the country that they operated from. The multi-national companies (American-based, and other country-based) that have emerged in our generation have no such pride in their makeup.

The present-day multi-national company, regardless of country of origin, (and regardless of PR claims to the contrary) bears no allegiance to any country. Instead, the allegiance of multi-national companies today is wholly and entirely to the company's stockholders.

Increasingly the stockholders of U.S. based multi-national companies are citizens of foreign countries, who not surprisingly could care less about what happens to workers of the multi-national companies who aren't citizens of their own country.

American companies that are multi-national display "made in China" or "made in Malaysia" or "made in (you name it) outside of the USA" on their products as though displacing American workers was something to be proud of. The financial markets applaud these changes too, and reward companies exporting their high-value production jobs to countries having low standards of living, and consequently lower labor costs, by providing them with additional funds to be used for exporting even more jobs.

The multi-national companies argue, at least in part, that their moves offshore were initially made necessary because the U.S. government previously took so much of their income in taxes, and further taxed their capital investments to a point that they had to relocate to countries that were less oppressive in these regards.

This is partly true, but greed played a part too. At the time the exodus started, the U.S. also maintained sufficiently high import tariffs that even though American made goods cost more to produce than goods made in some other countries, the American-made goods still cost the U.S. consumer less to buy than a competitive foreign-made product, and Americans mostly were therefore able to not only support American manufacturers, but pay a bit less for American made goods as well.

There was a combination of factors that precipitated the exodus of production-based businesses out of the U.S., causing the displacement of millions and millions of American middle-class workers. Government taxation policies relating to business, combined with the natural, and healthy, profit motive inherent in the capitalistic process, and changes in government-based institutional barriers relating to labor/management disputes and anti-trust (mergers) to provide the incentives for the exodus.

By 1980, most of the biggest U.S. based multi-national companies had moved at least some of their production-based operations offshore, and they then began moving politically to secure the gains made through doing so. Congress was lobbied intensely to open up completely the U.S market to imports, completely free of any import tariffs at all, to be accomplished over a period of time. This would maximize their profits on goods produced outside of the country. In 1994, after much debate, congress agreed to businesses demands to not tax goods they produced outside the U.S., when the foreign produced goods were imported back into the U.S for sale to Americans.

The rise of the multi-national companies, bearing allegiance to no country or group of citizens other than their stockholders, is a relatively recent event. Prior generations and prior centuries had in their makeup large companies with worldwide operations. This is nothing new. What is new is the attitude of such companies that they should bear no allegiance to the country that spawned them, or the workers of their native country.

The United states was built, in large measure, by wealthy citizens and companies of foreign countries electing to invest part of their excess income and profits in a fledgling upstart of a country in the western hemisphere. Now wealthy citizens and companies from the U.S. are electing to likewise invest in other "emerging" countries around the world. Which is as it should be.

However, there is a large, and very significant, difference between how foreigners invested in building the United States, and how U.S. citizens and businesses are going about investing in the building up of the current group of "emerging" countries. When foreign investors put money into U.S. based businesses, they only invested money that was not needed to sustain the operations and workers in their country of origin. They invested in a manner that protected the citizens of their own countries.

The investments in "emerging" countries now being made by wealthy U.S. citizens and businesses, is being done with a total disregard for the welfare of the U.S. citizens being displaced in the process.

Over the past three decades a number of possibly well intended, but disastrous government policies have brought us to a point in time where American citizens and American businesses have come to think of themselves as owing allegiance first to some ethnic group, or some profit making enterprise, rather than owing allegiance to the idea that is America.

> And THAT is a problem!

Problem number 6 is discriminatory lawmaking; that being the enactment of laws designed to favor one group of Americans over other groups of Americans.

For at least the past forty years' time, there have been no laws enacted at the federal level that were not expressly designed to favor some Americans, at the expense of other Americans.

Enactment of some, perhaps even many, discriminatory laws has probably been well-intended. This is not always the case, of course. There have been numerous (hundreds of) discriminatory laws passed whose intent was not honorable. In the worst instances, discriminatory laws are passed for no nobler purpose than to pay off a political debt, or help a personal friend or business campaign contributor of an elected official skim off some taxpayer money from the public trough.

The most egregious examples are seldom if ever exposed, due to the way legislation makes its way through the congress. A bill of national importance (actually any bill, important or not) is allowed to have unlimited numbers of "amendments" attached to it, that have no relationship whatsoever to the matter addressed in the main bill. For example, a bill whose purpose is to address something like measures being proposed to clean up polluted air in metropolitan areas, may see attached to it an amendment by a single member of congress, that calls for the government giving $ 15 million to a particular construction business in the congress member's rural district, when the business in question has nothing whatsoever to do with affecting air quality, but the owner of which business just happens to be a personal friend of and campaign contributor of, the congress member.

These types of unrelated "amendments", designed to enrich personal friends and contributors to individual congress member's campaigns have earned the label of "pork barrel" spending. The idea here is to compare the process to swine feeding at the public trough.

While unimportant bills may also have such "amendments" attached to them, this happens infrequently. The idea behind attaching unrelated amendments to important bills is to force the President to accept the unrelated "amendment" if the president wants to accept the idea of the main matter forming the basis for the bill. Currently, the President is limited by law to either accepting completely, or rejecting completely, a bill, with all amendments attached. The present law prohibits the president from vetoing unrelated amendments, while accepting the main matter being addressed by the proposed legislation.

Were this all there was to it, it wouldn't be so bad. An "escape-proof" line item veto could be enacted into law that allowed the President to easily identify and veto unrelated "pork barrel" amendments, attached to important bills of national interest, thereby providing accountability at the presidential level for enactment of such unrelated amendments. The president could then no longer claim that he or she was forced to accept "pork" in order to sign into law bills affecting all Americans. And that would be a pleasant change. This might not be easily done, but it could be made to happen.

Over the past several congressional sessions, there have been bills introduced in both houses of congress that propose to provide the president with a "line item veto". Following the 1994 congressional elections, some freshman members of both houses of congress attempted to introduce a constitutional amendment that would provide the president with a line item veto. They were unsuccessful in their attempt. Individual members of congress who voted against giving the president a line item veto made eloquent speeches about why this would be unwise, and effectively give the president a voice in making laws affecting spending of government money, which voice they claimed belonged exclusively to congress as part of the constitutional separation of powers. The eloquent speeches were perceived by most American voters, as nothing more than Congresses' protecting its ability to perpetuate pork barrel spending.

During a later debate in 1995, a majority of congress members from both houses admitted that their constituents were in the great majority telling them that they wanted the line item veto to be provided to the president, but they then went on to say that "in good conscience" they could not vote that way. Members of congress felt free to vote contrary to the wishes of their constituents because they understood the difficulty in unseating an incumbent who has been blessed by his party's election committee, and financed by the single-interest groups that benefit from pork barrel spending.

Finally, in 1996, a "limited" line item veto was passed. The version passed by congress in 1996 allowed pork items to be bundled (hidden) in groups of items of a similar kind of spending, some of which were legitimate, and listed under misleading titles, making them easy to miss, (and be excused for doing so).

The bad news:

The bad news is that as discriminatory and bad as "pork barrel" amendments are, they are just an extension of a pattern in lawmaking in general that has become predominant over the past five decades. Not just the unrelated "amendments" to important bills affecting most Americans are discriminatory. The main bills themselves are also discriminatory in nature. And, sadly, this has not been done in ignorance on the part of members of Congress, but has been done on purpose. (The road to hell really is paved with good intentions).

By way of illustrating laws that were designed to be purposely discriminatory when they were enacted, I will here just list a very few of the best known. The list could be several pages, perhaps even several volumes, long, and I again apologize in advance, if I left off one of your favorites. The list is just for purposes of illustration, and I'm purposely limiting it to a few examples that just about all middle-class turtles are familiar with:

The Income Tax - designed to favor the poor and the wealthy, at the expense of the middle-class.

The Social Security Act (including Medicare and Medicaid) - designed to benefit the old at the expense of the young.

Affirmative Action - designed to benefit women and minorities at the expense of non-minorities and men.

NAFTA and GATT - designed to benefit management and stockholders of multi-national companies at the expense of production workers, worldwide.

The Land Bank Act (and many other farm subsidy programs) - designed to benefit farm businesses at the expense of food consumers.

The GI Bill - designed to benefit those who spent time in a military service branch, over those who did not spend time in a military service branch (regardless of whether the nation was at war or not during the enlistment period, and regardless of exclusions mandated by health, age, sex, etc.).

The Marshall Plan - designed to help citizens of foreign countries at the expense of citizens here in the United States.

A whole slew of Welfare programs - designed to benefit some more disadvantaged group of Americans (both individuals and businesses) at the expense of a number of some supposedly less disadvantaged groups of Americans (mostly the middle-class).

The United States has a long history of enacting laws to provide advantages to some at the expense of others. The Declaration of Independence and the U.S. Constitution prior to enactment of the Bill of Rights favored property owners over non-property owners, and allowed for the keeping of slaves.

It is worth noting that the U.S. Constitution was considered unenforceable until the Bill of Rights (the first ten amendments) was added. Those whose individual rights were not protected and/or who believed themselves unrepresented and excluded from the decision making process outlined in the main body of the Constitution prior to enactment of the Bill of Rights simply disregarded it as the law of the land. Only after those excluded at the outset were included by way of adding the Bill of Rights, did the U.S. Constitution become the <u>accepted</u> law of the land.

It appears to be human nature that lawmakers are wont to enact laws that favor those they wish to favor, at the expense of those they dislike. One lesson of the Bill of Rights is that Americans in general dislike being excluded from the decision making process, and dislike laws that are designed to favor either one group of Americans (or government itself) over other Americans, and ultimately act to remove the exclusions and the discrimination. This is a lesson that politicians over the past fifty years have chosen to ignore.

Some promote the view that Americans only dislike discriminatory laws that act to their detriment, but favor discriminatory laws that work to their benefit, at the expense of their fellow Americans. This is a cynical view, promoted by those whose interests are benefited from dividing American opinion, and setting sub-groups of American society against one another. Once such a division has been accomplished, the perpetrators are then free to resume engaging in "pork barrel" lawmaking, while those who would be most opposed to their actions, are having their attention diverted away from what's happening in the "back rooms" of Washington. Sort of a variation on the old shell game. "Watch this hand...."

No one political party has a lock on this type of behavior or lawmaking. Both of the present major political parties have been equally guilty of this type of behavior over the past forty years' time at least.

Discriminatory law making is a hard habit to break. Once congress enacts one law that favors one group of Americans, over other groups of Americans; it is somewhat difficult to rationalize not doing it a second time, when a second group asks for special treatment. The more times congress acts to favor one group over another, the more difficult it becomes to refuse any single-interest group's request, until at last, a point in time is reached that (that) becomes the only kind of laws that are enacted.

> Well, fellow turtles, welcome to that point in time. We are there.

A philosophical question arises here about what the purpose of government is. Is the purpose of government to provide <u>equal</u> opportunity to <u>all</u> citizens, or is the purpose of government to provide for assuring <u>some</u> level of outcome for only <u>some</u> of its citizens?

When the United States started out, the underlying premise was that the main purpose of government was to provide equality of opportunity, and to protect individual citizens from encroachment upon their freedoms from either their own government, or foreign powers. That remained the underlying premise for nearly 150 years after the U.S. came into being as a sovereign nation.

Over the past several decades, attempts have been made to modify that premise by including a tenet that government should also act to affect a prescribed level of outcome for some citizens, especially those seen to be disadvantaged in some way.

In mathematical terms these are mutually exclusive subsets. That is, both cannot exist at the same time, and in the same space. It is not-possible to have as a basic premise underlying government the equality of opportunity for all citizens while at the same time consciously acting to reduce the opportunity for some and increasing it for others, with the government being put in a position of choosing winners and losers.

The attempted modification in the premise underlying government actions (attempting to guarantee equality of <u>opportunity for all</u>, while concurrently guaranteeing the <u>outcome for some</u>) has been accomplished in the main through the process of passing laws that discriminate in favor of one group of Americans at the expense of other groups of Americans.

The "us-versus-them" mentality that predominates in America today is a logical outgrowth of what happens when a nation cannot decide what it wants to be when it grows up. The question of what should be guaranteed by government (opportunity or outcome) must ultimately be settled in favor of one over the other. There is no sustainable middle-ground.

This is an area where Americans at some point in time have to draw a line in the sand and in doing so say "This is who we are, and what we stand for".

Whether Americans opt for opportunity (capitalism) or outcome (socialism) will determine the outcome of the great experiment in government that has been (and is) America. Despite well intended arguments to the contrary, neither America nor any other country has as an option selecting individual elements from each philosophy and existing as a hybrid "sometimes capitalist - sometimes socialist" society. A nation, in order to survive long term, must go down one path or the other.

A nation can't exist for long "mostly capitalist, but a little bit socialist", any more than a woman can exist for long "mostly a virgin, but a little bit pregnant". History is replete with examples to show that this is true. The disintegration of the former Union of Soviet Socialist Republics is a study in what happens when a socialist government attempts to adopt isolated elements of a capitalist philosophy.

The reduction of Great Britain from being leader of the World, and setter of monetary standards for the world, to a position of being a has-been among the great nations of the world, is a study in what happens when a capitalistic society attempts to adopt isolated elements of a socialist philosophy.

There is no evidence whatsoever, to suggest that the outcome for the United States would be any different from that of the USSR or Great Britain if we elect to follow a similar path in either direction. There is an old saying to the effect that "those who cannot learn from history, are doomed to repeat it".

It's a true saying.

Discriminatory law making is the divisive agent of separatism in general. Discriminatory lawmaking, especially over the past half century, has created divisions among Americans based upon wealth levels, age, sex, and race and/or ethnic background. The end result of this has been to encourage Americans to think of themselves first as part of some hyphenated group, (i.e., Senior-, Hispanic-, African-, Retired-, Jewish-, Catholic-, Irish-, Italian-, Disabled-, etc., etc., etc.) and only secondly as Americans.

During the civil war between the north and south, when the question of slavery was being decided, the president volunteered that "a house divided against itself, cannot long stand". That was true then. It is true today. Ongoing, purposeful, discrimination in lawmaking is rendering America a house divided against itself.

And, THAT is definitely a problem!

Problem number 7 is a failure to fully implement technology for purposes of improving the political and economic well-being of American citizens.

Technology has provided the basis for significant change in many areas of our society. Technology has been made considerable use of in terms of improving our ability to produce more of everything with the involvement of less (per capita) human labor. Technology has also been used extensively to improve our physical health and longevity, to advance war-related goals, and for purposes of restoring health when it is lost through disease. Paradoxically, the ability of technology to positively impact these areas of our lives, has resulted in bringing about some very negative and unwelcome changes in the economic well-being of an ever growing number of Americans citizens.

A combination of automating what used to be manual tasks, when combined with a rapidly expanding population, has caught not only American middle-class working turtles, but worker turtles worldwide, in between two diametrically opposed forces, that threaten to crush them all.

In part, this may be happening, because those in leadership positions, at all levels, in both the public and private sectors, have allowed themselves to become trapped by conventional thinking. Conventional thinking holds that technological advances are limited in working to advance productivity, improving health and longevity, and providing new and improved means of effecting warfare. In all past generations this has been the case, and so it has perhaps been assumed that such will always be the case.

Technology itself has been responsible for now making it possible to overturn this conventional wisdom. Prior generations' advances in technology were admittedly limited to impacting these areas. But no prior generation ever had the advantage of using something as powerful as a micro-chip for whatever purpose they wished.

Today, computers are primarily used for the traditional purposes mentioned earlier. We have better weapons, and better ways of delivering both the weapons and troops to wherever they might be needed. Our understanding of the physical universe is much greater than ever before, and growing every day. Advances in medicine occur almost on a daily basis. The Internet has effectively made it possible for all computers, of all sizes and makes, to be joined in a manner that provides for sharing business and other information on a scale never before possible. Manufacturing productivity has never been greater.

All of which are worthwhile applications for technology.

To date there have been no significant attempts to employ technology for the purposes of bettering the political and/or economic well-being of citizens here in the U.S. who have otherwise been adversely affected by technological advances, or, for that matter, citizens of other countries who have been similarly affected.

Because of the micro-chip, there exist today numerous opportunities to break free from conventional thinking relating to using technology, and to begin using technology to improve economic well- being, and to improve social interactions between citizens within individual countries and their elected officials, and between citizens of different countries.

Polling doesn't count .... Voting counts

Technology has the potential for being brought to bear in a number of ways that can directly and indirectly improve the economic well-being of Americans. One such application area would be using technology in a way that allowed American middle-class working turtles to become more directly involved in the making of the most important government mandated decisions that affect their economic well-being and the outcome of their lives in general.

For at least the past forty years' time, American middle-class working turtles have been largely un-consulted by elected leaders in such matters, and often ignored when they were (infrequently) consulted at all.

It is highly questionable whether Americans voting directly in the past, on matters affecting their economic well-being, and their lives in general, would (or could) have done worse than elected officials have done, using the present model for governing. Technology has now, for the first time in the history of the world, made it possible for citizens to now begin moving to take back direct control over their own lives.

Pick an example. Income taxes, capital gains taxes, spending on social security, Medicare, defense, involvement in other countries civil wars, foreign aid, NAFTA, welfare, labor relations, etc., etc., etc., etc., the list goes on for pages. It is pure conjecture of course at this point in time to surmise exactly how these topics would have been handled if all citizens were more directly included in the decision making process, but it is a pretty safe bet that there would have been large differences in how at least some of them were handled.

The Internet has provided a basis for information sharing between individuals on a scale that is unparalleled in the history of the world, so far as we know. A large minority of individuals in the U.S. and worldwide presently have access to the Internet network. But, that is changing rapidly, and a relatively high percentage of a group comprised of some of the brightest most successful, and most influential individuals, worldwide, do have Internet access already. Because of this, unparalleled possibilities exist for positive interaction between citizens here in the U.S. and citizens elsewhere around the globe.

And every person who is "connected" associates with dozens, if not hundreds, of others who are not, and shares information directly with them.

Tabulating political activities

Political leaders at every level have been quick to seize on use of the Internet's World-Wide Web (www) as a means of enhancing communications with their constituents, which may (or may not) be a step in the positive direction. Of course, a lot of what's presently available on the (www) from a political standpoint is "spin" on ideas that the politicians want to sell down the chain to their constituents, in an attempt to convince them that they are working on their best behalf. But, it is at least another arrow in the quiver of those "connected" citizens who feel better because they are able to share their thoughts with their elected officials.

A logical, and beneficial, extension of this level of interconnection would be for elected officials to provide a way for constituents to not only express their thoughts on-line, but to have those thoughts and wishes compiled in a manner that allowed all of the elected officials constituents to see what others like them were saying to the elected official, without having the elected officials spin doctors- first "interpret" the messages. We are all aware that how the question is asked, can pre-determine the responses. (i.e., "Yes or no, do you still beat your wife?"). This level of interconnection between elected officials, and their constituents, could be not only worse than useless, but dangerously misleading, if the questions were first allowed to be "framed" by spin doctors so that the outcome was pre-determined.

Still another logical extension of this technology would be for the government to implement a system, available through the Internet, to provide for interested, and connected, citizens to view how their elected officials voted on every issue coming before congress. Voice votes have been made obsolete by technology. There remains no good reason why all votes taken in congress could not be recorded electronically, even allowing congresspersons the capability to dial in remotely and vote. This would eliminate congresspersons dodging important issues by being able to make up excuses for not voting on sensitive bills before their body, and would provide an additional benefit in that all citizens could see, immediately, just how their elected officials voted on all matters affecting their lives.

And technology could be used to track the comings and goings of single interest groups calling on elected officials, by keeping track of which lobbyists, representing which single interest called on which elected officials, how much money each contributed to "action" committees that ultimately ends up in campaign coffers, and so on. Using technology as a watchdog over elected officials, and those who finance them, would provide additional incentives for elected officials to be careful about whose interests they favored with their votes.

It is one thing to mandate that lobbyists declare their intentions when registering as lobbyists, but this alone will do almost nothing at all to reduce their influence over elected officials. Passing a law that requires lobbyists to reveal their true masters' intentions will be ineffective so long as there is no record of who, and how, and how often they peddled their influence to. Technology provides a way to really bring the single interest groups and their spin doctors into the full light of day, on a daily, and year-to-date, and congressional term-to-date basis, congressperson by congressperson, and for elected bodies overall.

Using technology in this manner provides a potential for more meaningful discourse between average middle-class American working turtles and elected leaders, on matters affecting their constituents' economic well-being, and which otherwise significantly affect the outcomes of their lives.

If this smacks of George Orwell's "Big Brother" in reverse, so much the better. While the FBI is presently lobbying congress to allow them unlimited ability to listen in to private conversations between anyone they wish, without benefit of a court order; the correct approach is (big surprise) just the opposite. It is the ordinary citizens who should have unlimited access to the goings on in back rooms of government, rather than the other way around.

But it doesn't stop there. The existing electronic network could be used (today) to allow all citizens to vote directly on all important matters affecting their economic well-being. Of course the Constitution would first have to be amended to allow citizens to participate directly in lawmaking at the Federal level. Currently, the Constitution reserves all decision making related to enactment of legislation to the Congress and President (only). The United States is (sort of) a Republic. In a Republic, as you turtles already know, citizens vote through elected members in legislative bodies. In the case of America, the members are typically (but not always) selected by way of voting for them in an election. In a Democracy, all citizens vote directly (on everything), and decisions are based upon gaining a majority of the popular vote.

When the U.S. was born, during the revolutionary war that started in 1775, which was further "formalized" by signing of the Declaration of Independence in 1776, it was already much greater in size than Great Britain. By the end of the revolutionary war, the size of the territory controlled by the United States government had swelled to something of the size scale of all of Europe. Towns and villages were often remote from one another. Some frontier outposts and forts were several days or weeks ride from a major metropolitan center. Reading and writing skills were not prevalent. (In this respect, maybe not so much has changed). There was no television available where citizens could directly see and hear what candidates had to say before voting. Elections required people traveling on foot and on horseback to vote, and to carry ballots and results. Election booths, and election processes, were highly subject to tampering.

These conditions, combined with an inherent distrust of the general public by the founding fathers, and philosophical arguments going all the way back to the Magna Carta, resulted in the founding fathers electing the "Republic" government model at the time the U.S. government was being established. Government by way of a "Democracy" model would, under the conditions present at the time the country was founded, just have been too difficult to make it work out. There would, at the time, certainly have been more opportunities for misuse of elective processes under a "Democracy" model, in the main, than were likely to occur under a "Republic" model. (The founding fathers were also somewhat elitist in their thinking, and suspected that a majority of citizens at the time were not qualified in many respects to be directly involved in running a government). In retrospect, most would probably agree that their choice was a both a rational and valid one at the time it was made.

Time has now changed many of the conditions, especially geographic and communications-wise, that served as part of the basis for the founding fathers decision to frame the Constitution entirely along the lines of a Republic.

Recognizing the danger to America as a whole that could occur if corrupt or deviant elected officials could not be removed, the framers of the constitution took pains to make provisions in the original document for citizens to take back their government from elected officials if they felt the need. The elective and impeachment processes relating to replacing officials are time consuming, but both have been used in the past, and they work. In one instance, that relating to amending the Constitution, a somewhat democratic approach is employed. While only the congress can actually enact legislation amending the Constitution, such actions can be precipitated by two thirds of the states petitioning congress to amend the Constitution, and after passage by the congress, three-fourths of the states must ratify the amendment before it becomes law.

But, mostly congress makes the laws with a minimum of direct citizen involvement in the process. When government did something stupid, like what happened leading up to the great depression of the 1930's in this country (and all over the world) lack of education, lack of television, and lack of any way for citizens to come together and directly act to take back the system from the elected officials possibly kept the government from being overthrown by the people at large.

It's not a given that the citizens at large could have kept us out, or thereafter gotten us out of the depression, once in it, any more quickly or in better shape than the politicians did, if they had been allowed to vote directly on solutions to the problem(s); but then there's also nothing to suggest that they could have (or would have) done any worse either. The thing is, they never got the chance to try. They were never consulted.

Still another area that technology could be used to benefit economic well-being would be to use mathematical modeling to challenge the conventional wisdom regarding how many hours should constitute a full time work week, assuming such a week's activity would produce enough income if worked (for now) by two people, to provide for meeting all the basic needs of an average size family, and to publish the results.

This information could then be used by the public at large to guide establishment of public policies relating to things like what the minimum wage should be here in America. Similar models could be used for the same purpose in other countries, to aid the people living there in their decision making along the same lines. This assumes of course, that public policy called for having a minimum wage. That might not be the case, if the public at large were allowed to vote on it.

Eliminating the middlemen

Technology provides the ability in many areas to eliminate middlemen whose being in the economic model proves to be a detriment to the economic well-being of the country as a whole.

Eliminating the "professional" politicians from the process of exclusively making the most important decisions affecting our lives and economic well-being, is certainly a possibility that could be made available by the use of new technology. And doing something along these lines holds the potential to not only disallow congress making future decisions that are damaging to the economic well-being of a majority of Americans, but we would also then have much more efficient means of going back and reversing past actions on the part of elected officials that we felt were precipitated by fuzzy thinking, or, worse, bad intentions.

Given that past generations of elected officials have been responsible through the laws that they have passed for bringing us to the point where something in the neighborhood of 50+% of all income earned by middle-class working turtles is now taken by some government body; using technology to bring about a reversing or amending of some of the past acts responsible for taking away our income before we even see it, could perhaps be the most significant way technology could positively impact our economic well-being. But there are also other ways technology could be made to help.

Conventional wisdom, and roads less traveled

The current worldwide "production - trade - sales" model for just about everything we buy today was defined in the early 1800's, at a time when the kind of technology we enjoy today was not ever a glimmer in the eyes of the scientific communities of the world. At the time the present marketplace model was defined there was no such thing as radios, television, telegraph, fax machines, automobiles, highways, airplanes, airports, cross-country mail services, overnight package delivery coast-to-coast (and worldwide), personal computers, modems, on-line shopping, or any other sort of an electronic "medium" for conveying information.

Distance between where producers of goods might be located, and where their customers might be located presented significant sales and marketing challenges to producers needing to get their story out to the buying public. Most selling was done one-on-one, face-to-face, between a prospective buyer of goods, and an agent (salesperson) for the producer.

Sending individual widgets to individual buyers was both inefficient and cost prohibitive under the "old" market model. Producers most often met these types of challenges by utilizing commissioned or independent marketing representatives to help them find businesses within a prescribed geographic area to buy their products in bulk lots, and sell to either smaller businesses in their region, or directly to consumers in the area.

Because of the sparseness of the population in some regions at the time (especially west of the Mississippi river) and the great distances that might exist between population centers, the marketing representative typically acted as an agent for more than one producer in a given region. This allowed the independent marketing rep to be more productive by being able to talk about more than one company's products when making each sales call. In those regions that had few population centers the reps first job on behalf of a producer was typically to identify one or two large businesses that could act as a "distributor" of the producers' widgets to other smaller businesses within the region. This practice made it possible for the producer to have fewer accounts to keep track of and fewer trade routes to ship goods over.

A side benefit of this model was that each element in the sales "chain" except the end-consumer, provided a means of spreading the overall cost of getting goods into consumers' hands over several businesses, and this, in turn, reduced the amount of money any one seller in the "chain" had to come up with at any single point in time.

Where non-perishable goods were concerned, this model also provided a way for producers to level out their production processes, making widgets at an even pace all year long, and shipping them in "lots" to those down the sales chain, while giving each member in the chain an incentive for taking more than might be needed at any single point in time. This helped the producers' cash flow, and leveled out production requirements.

Sometimes, the more things change, the more they stay the same. While the products themselves have changed often over the past couple hundred years' time, the process for getting them into consumers hands remains about the same, in the main, as it was a couple of hundred years ago, when the model was first introduced.

When new technologies have been applied they have been used more to benefit the makers and sellers of the products, than to benefit the end-users of the products.

We have already seen how producers employ technology to improve productivity, and eliminate jobs being done by humans. We have also seen how technology has been employed to allow producers to move their operations to places remote from their primary markets, which has, in turn, caused millions of middle-class American working turtles to lose their jobs. We have seen technology used to rush goods to middlemen in the sales chain using computers to manage inventories on a just-in-time (JIT) basis. Manufacturing Reps have been able to expand to become large businesses themselves, using technology to keep track of the ever increasing number of producers they represent, and potential businesses suitable for handling the producers' goods regionally and locally. Technology has thus been used by businesses at all levels to serve their own economic interests.

But, how well does this model serve the economic interests of America's middle-class working turtles? Not nearly as well as some might have us think. Each middleman in the chain between producers and end-consumers of the producers' products exacts a profit from their efforts. In the instance of "distributors" (especially of non-perishable goods) the profit comes from simply taking in products made by a producer, warehousing them for a few days, and then handling the final routing to a "retail" outlet that handles the producer's products. In the instance of manufacturers "reps", the profit comes from introducing the producers to prospective customers at the distributor or retailer level. At the retail level, the profit comes from storing the producers' goods in a way the end-consumers can examine them up-close before buying them. In the present market model, which began over 200 years ago, there are typically (at least) three middlemen involved in getting a producers' product into the hands of the end-consumer.

The current sales "chain" adds significantly to the cost of everything going through it. For example, of the cost of a typical product purchased at the retail level, after going through the various middlemen's hands, only about 25% of the sales price is needed to pay for the cost of labor, materials, and contracted outside work needed to build the product. Another 25% of the retail price paid for such a product represents the producers "gross" profit for building the product. The "gross" profit is then used to pay off non-production-related expenses of the producer, and the producer's taxes, before giving what's left to the stockholders in the way of "after-tax-net", in the form of dividends.

What this means is that approximately 50% of the price being paid at the <u>retail</u> level for most non-perishable goods is money that goes toward the overhead involved in keeping the present sales "chain" intact, and keeping the middlemen in place in the sales "chain".

Think about that!

Almost fifty percent of the money spent on most non-perishable products at the retail level does not contribute in any way to the value of the product being bought at the end-consumer level.

Consider: What would it do to your economic well-being if, all of a sudden, all non-perishable goods you purchased suddenly cost about half as much to buy? If the cost of goods fell by half, and your income were doubled, as indicated in the discussion re: problem number 4, you would effectively be almost four times better off in terms of spendable income, and it might be possible to consider perhaps having one parent elect to stay at home for purposes of promoting family interests on a full time basis. Technology could be used for the purpose of eliminating middlemen transactions that cause significant increases in the price of many (but not all) things a consumer buys from a producer. But for the most part, that isn't happening now.

Currently, the primary users of new technology to bypass middlemen aren't doing it to make their products available to end-consumers at greatly reduced cost. Instead the current crop of "factory-direct" sellers is using the new technology available to them to keep more of the middlemen's profit for themselves, and they most often spend the rest on expensive catalogs and TV "infomercials".

The end result is that today technology is still being used almost entirely to benefit producers and sellers of products, while passing on the huge costs of doing so through an outdated market model that includes groups of "middlemen" whose original functions have been made obsolete by way of current technology.... to a group of middle-class working turtles who are seeing their real pay, and purchasing power, decrease annually.

The government publicly decries the "rock and a hard place" most middle-class working turtles are caught between, the "rock" being falling pay levels, and the "hard place" being escalating prices caused by their own inflationary spending, and helping to keep alive the present 200-year old sales model. But, by their actions, they have chosen to endorse both of these detrimental practices. The reasons are. obvious.

The higher the price of products in the marketplace, the higher (in absolute dollar amounts) the profits of the companies producing them, and the higher the profits of all the middlemen businesses that exist between producer and end-consumer. The government benefits too in that income taxes collected on corporate income, and dividends paid to stockholders remain higher under the "old" market model.

The principals of these businesses and government bodies have a vested interest in keeping things just the way they are. The fear of having to find another way to make a living is a legitimate concern if you are a middleman, and your function might suddenly go away. And the fear of having to find a way to continue operating government offices if tax receipts were to suddenly be halved at the corporate level is a legitimate cause for worry if you are a government body, or someone relying on a government body for your welfare.

But, it begs the question as to what is best for the end-consumers of producers' products. The thing is this fellow turtles, if we want to avoid becoming a nation of "haves" and "have-nots", we will have to find a way to eliminate a lot of middlemen between us and producers of products, and between us and government actions that affect our lives and economic well-being. We have to become a nation of producers and consumers, instead.

The arithmetic is really pretty simple. Either we "retrain" a lot of "middlemen" to become producers, or we "retrain" all the other middle-class working turtles to live in poverty. "Middlemen" presently constitute about 5% of the nation's population. Everybody else makes up the remaining 95% of the nation's population. If the decision were up to you, which group would you choose to retrain? The solution becomes even clearer when we consider that the present "middlemen" hold an inordinate amount of the nation's wealth among themselves. It is simply easier for a well-off "middleman" to make the transition from "middlemen" to becoming a "producer" of something of value, than it is to retrain 95% of a population who have little or no accumulated wealth, to all somehow become "middlemen", or alternatively, live their entire lives in poverty.

Manufacturers' reps and distributors could probably at this point in time be eliminated from the chain for many non-perishable products in a way that caused product prices to effectively fall by about 40%. In the instance of "big ticket" items like autos and computers and appliances, the retailer could often also be effectively eliminated from the chain, and prices to end-consumers for these kinds of products could be reduced significantly from present levels too.

This is not to suggest that we suddenly eliminate all the Wal-marts and K-marts of the world, and try buying everything we need through the mail. It is to suggest that use of technology to eliminate a significant percentage of "middlemen" who do nothing to increase the value of products being purchased at the end-consumer level could serve to cause each middle-class American working turtle's income to stretch significantly further than it does today.

It is to suggest that we, as American middle-class working turtles have it within our power, by voting with our pocketbooks, and through initiation of laws that require producers to disclose the number of middlemen involved in getting their products to end-consumers, to act in a way that "encourages" producers to work actively at ways to get their products to us at prices that are significantly less than they now expect us to pay for them.

At this point in time however, technology is only being used to further the interests of businesses, middlemen, and government users of citizens' money, and these bodies have a vested interest in NOT using technology to modify the present market and government models in a way that improves the economic well-being of American middle-class working turtles. The government too is not particularly interested in providing citizens a way of tabulating the activities of elected officials and the lobbyists that peddle influence to them, and/or which improves citizen's abilities to provide unfiltered input into the decision-making process and to petition congress on matters of redress.

And, THAT is a problem!

Problem Number 8 is Government controlling the nation's (and the world's) economy for the benefit of government, and single interest groups dependent upon the Government, at the expense of American middle-class working turtles.

For roughly the past thirty-five years, the government has chosen to finance spending relating to government programs primarily by way of inflating the nation's paper currency supply. The effects of this have been disastrous on the American middle-class working turtle population. Problem number 4, the widening gap between worker pay, and the cost of living for American middle-class families, resulted primarily from government inflating the nation's currency supply. Obviously, unless it is stopped, the economic outlook for middle-class American turtles will be even bleaker in future years, than it is now.

The bad news is that there have been few signs that anybody in government is at all seriously interested in stopping this practice. Those who have tried to stop the practice have without exception seen their efforts fall (way) short of the mark.

A lot of discussion over "balancing the budget" goes on in Washington. In the past several laws have been passed that absolutely mandated government to live within its means. Remember Gram-Rudman? Upon seeing how easy it was for pork-minded colleagues to skirt around the intentions of their well-intended legislation, Messrs. Gram and Rudman decided that it was a hopeless task, and they ultimately left government service to do something that might prove more useful.

None of the laws passed to date have acted in even a small way to either cause the budget to come into balance, or to otherwise operate in a manner that would improve the economic well-being of most American middle-class working turtles. As this is written congress most recently showed its resolve in this area by voting a second time to NOT to allow there to be an amendment to the Constitution that mandated a balanced budget.

No matter. Really! The Constitutional amendment would have done nothing at all to cause Congress to act responsibly in terms of limiting spending. A few of the opponents of the balanced budget amendment were unusually candid in revealing why no such amendment, by itself, could ever work The reason is so simple it's obvious. Government can always just print up enough money to cover expenses, no matter how much they decide to spend. The budget would appear to be balanced (money available to pay bills being equal or greater than the amount of bills needing payment) but the nations' economic well-being, and the economic well-being of all middle-class American working turtles would continue to spiral ever downward.

Government essentially has <u>four mechanisms</u> that they can bring to bear to control every aspect of not only the economy of the United States, but the economies of every other country in the world as well. The reason that actions by the U S. government can also control other countries' economies is that other countries depend on the United States to be a market for a very significant amount of goods produced in their countries. Whatever happens to the U.S. market happens equally to every other market in the world, by virtue of the U.S. middle-class working turtles comprising between thirty-five to fifty percent of the total worldwide market for virtually every kind of goods produced.

The first control mechanism

The first mechanism the government has available for controlling every aspect of the nation's economy is the Federal Reserve Bank. The Federal Reserve Bank (usually referred to as "the Fed") isn't really a bank, in the usual sense, at all. Actually there are twelve Federal Reserve banks, and all are privately owned businesses, and are not owned in any way by the government and are not in any way subject to control by any of the three branches of the Federal government. You can't get a business, home or car loan there, and it doesn't honor major credit cards, but it (the Fed) absolutely controls the American economy and the economy of every other country on the planet by its actions.

The Fed directs the printing up of "new" dollars by the treasury, and getting them into circulation so that the government can "borrow" them and use them to pay off debts that have been run up, for which taxes by themselves were insufficient to cover. The mechanism by which all this is accomplished is purposely complex, in order to keep Americans from seeing what's going on. That process was described earlier, so we won't go into it again here. Of course, the Congress must occasionally help out by way of voting to increase the national debt ceiling, but Congress can always be counted on to do that out of self-interest.

When the government wants to make us feel good about things, like around Christmas, and around election time, the Fed typically acts to have a lot of "new" paper money put into circulation, so that we can all go out and buy things (mostly on credit), and feel good. Six months later, things are not only back where they were for most Americans, but the national debt has gone up as a result of the Fed's actions, and the interest payments start coming due (for both the government and the citizens that bought things using credit).

The government (Fed/Treasury) then pumps some more paper currency into the banks, which the government then immediately turns around and borrows back from the banks, for purposes of then giving the money right back to the banks, to pay the interest on what they just borrowed.

Is that a great system or what?

The thing is fellow turtles, every time the Fed forces more paper currency to be printed, and forces banks to take the "new" currency, which is backed by nothing more than some politicians smile and good looks, the price of everything you have to buy for your family goes-up proportional to the percentage of new "funny" money placed in circulation, out of the total amount in circulation.

In the discussion of problem number 4, the effects of the government's actions in inflating the paper currency supply were examined. At the same time prices go up, the purchasing value of every dollar you earn is reduced a like amount. Thus, every time the government causes the amount of paper currency in circulation to be inflated unnecessarily, every middle-class American working turtle loses twice.

Over the past thirty-five years' time, the government has inflated the nations paper currency supply so often, and to such a great degree, that as this is written, the government has no way of even knowing how much total money is in circulation. No kidding. They printed it up. But they themselves don't even know how much they have printed, and how much of it is still floating around the world somewhere. Nobody knows.

And this is the group we are counting on to save our economy. Mind you, these are not even elected officials. They are political appointees, and they serve at the pleasure of the executive branch. They are supposed to be independent, by virtue of being appointed for a specific "term" of service, during which even the top executive cannot remove them. But, you don't get asked to join the board of governors of the Federal Reserve, unless the president has obtained, in advance, your personal guarantee that you will vote the way he or she wants you to vote.

The Fed is made up of people whose sole function is to control the economy of the nation for the benefit of who? All American's? Hardly. To see whose interests are served by the board of the Federal Reserve, one has only to see what they did for a living before they became board members. Most were mega-businessmen, bankers of one kind or another, or economists. All were political insiders and friends of high-up elected officials who have agendas (pork) that they want to see addressed.

The bottom line here, fellow turtles is that the Federal Reserve's ability to cause paper money to be printed for purposes of paving off government debts is, when combined with congress' unlimited ability to authorize more debt and borrowing responsible for ALL inflation, and inflation causes prices to go UP, and the value of wages earned to go DOWN by a like amount.

In fact it is precisely BECAUSE the inflation FIRST causes the value of existing dollars to go down, that prices MUST (thereafter) soon go up, or those taking dollars in payment would lose profit from their sales that were there before inflation of the currency made each dollar worth less.

Remember: when the government inflates the currency supply by 3%, the immediate result is that every dollar already in circulation (in your bank account) is reduced in value to 97 cents. Then merchants have to raise prices to $1.03 to get back the 3 cents lost to inflation, and YOU have to thereafter buy goods that now cost $1.03, with dollars that are now only worth 97 cents each. OK, now do the math. How many dollars' worth 97 cents each does it take to buy something that now costs $1.03? Right! It takes a dollar and SIX cents, NOT a dollar and THREE cents. If your annual wage increase only matches the stated inflation rate, you automatically LOSE an amount equivalent to the inflation rate percentage in income annually! Now, guess why living standards have been falling for the last 30 years!

We have been conditioned to believe that some inflation of the nation's currency supply is inevitable, and that the causes of inflation are a complex mix of elements that even economists have difficulty understanding. The only question, we are told, is what the proper level of inflation should be to facilitate maintaining a "sound economy". This is not true. Inflation only occurs when more paper money is printed up, and put (forced) into circulation. At the time the Constitution was enacted, the government monopolized the coining of currency, in all forms. The government still holds that exclusive right today. Inflation is, by definition, a growth in the supply of currency in circulation. Only the government is allowed, by law, to print more currency and place it in circulation. Therefore, it is seen that the government is the sole cause of inflation. There is nothing more complex to it than that.

The government economists supporting the government's contention that some inflation is inevitable are basing their hypothesis on false premises. Government economists contend that population growth by itself would mandate that at least some new currency must be placed in circulation each year, or there would not be any way for those coming into the job market for the first time, to get paid. All the currency printed up prior to then would be needed just to pay off workers that had come into the job market before. The false premises upon which the government's ("there must always be at least some inflation each year") hypothesis rests assumes that product prices must always either stay where they are, or go up, whenever the absolute number of employees in the workplace is increased, and that the numbers of workers in the workplace will constantly increase. It is nowhere written (outside of government and some business circles) that prices and population must always go up. Of course, both businesses and government profit from ever increasing prices and growth in the number of consumers, but that alone is not sufficient reason to assume that prices must always go up.

It's possible that new workers in entering the job market for the first time might benefit more if their coming into the market worked to lower product prices more than it worked to lower money available to pay wages. This would be the exact opposite of what happens today.

As the workforce expands, the government disproportionably increases the currency supply. The reason for the disproportionate increase in the money supply relates to the government invariably sneaking in a few (hundred) billion extra for themselves when adding for purposes of giving new workers a way to get paid at current wage levels.

Actually either of two approaches can be made to work in a manner that doesn't cause the economic well-being of middle-class citizens to suffer. Prices can go down, and things can still work out. Some of the greatest fortunes in this country got their start during the great depression of the 1930's, when prices had dropped dramatically. Prices can (and will) stabilize when the amount of currency added to circulation equals whatever is needed only to support the private sector's growth.

The trick is to eliminate the government's capability to conspire with the Federal Reserve banks to just print up more money, for their own use, without first getting permission from those whose lives will be damaged if they do so. It may not happen in your lifetime that any of you turtles reading this will ever get to vote for an elected official who proposes to restructure the Federal Reserve in a manner that precludes its ability to flood the worldwide market with newly printed dollars, backed by nothing more than the promises and smiles of the Federal Reserve board of directors.

The second control mechanism

The second government mechanism for controlling the economy of the nation, and the world, is taxes. Whatever money out of the total in circulation is taken from the citizens and businesses for government use is thereafter unavailable for use by citizens and businesses.

For the first 150 years of America's history, there was no such thing as an income tax*[2]. Most of the first 150 years of our history, the government also operated in a manner that had the treasury showing a positive balance (being in the black) at the end of each years' operation. For at least the past fifty-five years, the government has collected more and more in the way of taxes, and very few recent years have seen the government operate in the black.

Taxes and tax laws have been the primary instruments by which elected officials take money in a discriminatory manner from those they dislike, and give it, also in a discriminatory manner, to those they like a lot. Politicians spent inordinate amounts of time explaining how they are just trying to help some deserving, but disadvantaged, group, and how they regret having to hurt members of other groups in the process. We are told that it is regrettably inevitable that laws always take the form of hurting some, in order to help others.

Politicians are not very good at defining problems, so it is not surprising that they are collectively also poor at breaking problems down into simple elements, or formulating alternative hypotheses for solving whole problems, or even solving individual small elements that comprise larger overall problems.

Science teaches that only by formulating as many possible hypotheses as possible during the problem solving process may we be assured of achieving a complete, and provable, solution to a problem. As we have seen, the social dislocations enveloping our society are not problems in themselves, but, instead, are symptoms of other problems (like this one) that nobody in government wants to talk about.

When government chooses to attempt treating social dislocations as if they were the main problem, they are on false ground to begin with. But, that aside, when they do go down this treacherous path, they make it much worse when they refuse to

---
[2] Except for a short time during the Civil War.

consider all possible hypothetical "solutions" available to them. At the top of every list of hypotheses for curing some social ill or the other should be this possible alternative.

"Alternative Number I - Do Nothing"

It's a great alternative, and if it had been selected often in the past, we probably wouldn't be in such bad straights today. Actually, that was the alternative most selected by politicians during the first 150 years of our history as a country, and choosing it often, brought America from a position of a puny little wannabe Republic, to the greatest economic power in the known history of the world. At least for a while.

The question again arises. Should the function of government be that of guaranteeing opportunity, or guaranteeing outcome? There are risks associated with going either way. If capitalism is not voluntarily tempered with a sense of community and charity, there will be citizens who suffer greatly from economic want and privation. If, on the other hand, government works to guarantee the outcome, electing a socialistic course, the outcome for those at the bottom looks better in the short term, but there will certainly be (a lot) more turtles down at that level, and as the disintegration of the USSR has shown, the socialistic approach ultimately crumbles under its own weight, taking all turtles down with it.

> We must ultimately choose one over the other. There can be no government mandated middle-ground where we attempt to guarantee opportunity for only some and guarantee the outcome for only some, and guarantee nothing at all for the rest. And my fellow turtles, that is essentially how the United States government is attempting to operate today.

Within the present American socio-political landscape there are three distinct sub-groups of turtles.

The overall turtle population distribution falls along typical bell-curve lines. At the top, there are between 5 and 10 percent of our citizens who are very well of financially. At the bottom are between 10 and 20 percent of our citizens who are very bad off financially. In the middle are between 70 and 85 percent of our citizens currently struggling more to keep from falling into the bottom group than to raise themselves up into the top group.

In the past the bell-curve was proportioned a bit differently in that the percentage of turtles that were least well off financially was a smaller percent of the overall population, and the group at the top was also smaller, and the majority of turtles in the middle were struggling more to get into the upper group, than for fear of falling into the lower group.

But, back to the chase.

For the past several decades the government has been using their taxing authority not just to pay for government operation, but to move the government into areas never intended by the founding fathers, and, more importantly, it has used its ability to collect and redistribute tax dollars to discriminate in favor of some Americans, at the expense of other Americans, and further to not only do this in a discriminatory way, but in a wholly unfair and unjust way. The most visible, and costly taxes collected by government are those related to income, Social Security, and Medicare. Together, at the individual level they represent about 30% of every American's gross income. Together at the corporate level they represent nothing at all.

Corporations do not, strictly speaking, pay taxes. Not ever. Of any kind. Corporations are indeed "taxed", in a manner of speaking only, for a share of FICA, and Medicare, and even on their income, but this is primarily a subterfuge to make it appear that individuals are taxed less than they really are. The taxes of all kinds, paid by business in one year, are added to the price of the businesses products or services that are sold the next year, and recouped from their customers. Thus individuals, in the absolute end, pay all taxes. The poor pay none, the rich and businesses collect back in the following year what they "paid" in the prior year in taxes. The middle-class turtle group pays for everyone else, rich and poor alike.

Bummer, you say? Maybe so, but, it is true.

Ironically, this country was founded on a basic belief that there should be no taxation without representation. Today, the middle-class working turtles whose ancestors fought and died for that principle are essentially without representation. The two major political parties represent the extreme opposite ends of the spectrum. The Democrats really represent only the least financially well off. The Republicans really represent only the most financially well off. Nobody at all represents the turtles struggling to stay afloat in the middle.

Perhaps it is time for a new party to be formed to represent the turtles in the middle. We could call it the MID-AMERICAN party. When asked what party a voter belongs to he or she could then reply either "I'm a Democrat", or "I'm a Republican", or "I'm a Mid-American", and everybody would know right off whose interests the voter had at heart. My guess is that most turtles would then place themselves in the Mid-American party, as the party of their choice.

It is not only possible, but likely, that if a party were to come about that represented the interests of the middle-class turtles of the country, there would be some changes made in a lot of areas, taxes being one of them. It's just a guess, but I think the "new" party would begin moving fairly quickly, and strongly, toward a model that guaranteed opportunity to the exclusion of guaranteeing outcome. Of course, I could be wrong, but it would be fun to see how it came out.

A "Mid-American" party would be entirely free to also look at what kind of tax collection system should be employed. The present politicians are so wedded to conventional thinking, and so used to using the tax policy to reroute taxpayer dollars to their friends and favorite causes, that it is unlikely that they would ever do more than tinker around the edges of the present tax structure.

We are told that deviating much from the present system would be an enormously complex undertaking, and that, bad as the present system is, we are better off trying to fix it, than trying to replace it (i.e., the old "better the devil you know, than the devil you don't know"). The old FUD factor. There is an enormous (and enormously expensive) system in place that has such a great fixed inertia, that politicians cannot imagine how to dismantle or replace it, while at the same time protecting their ability to pork away. And, as Long John Silver might have said to his mates on the Hispaniola,

"There be the rub, me laddies".

Scrapping the existing tax system and replacing it with a very simple one, is only a complex issue <u>if</u> keeping middle-class turtles from knowing how much they really pay in taxes, and protecting pork barrel spending and retaining the ability to favor one group over another, are determined to be both necessary and/or desirable elements of a tax system. If these were not the real reasons for keeping the tax system complex, replacing the present complex tax system with a very, very, simple one, would be a slam dunk.

Much of the present tax system is based upon what may well be a false premise. That being that the least fortunate among us wish to be supported, like charity cases, at the expense of the rest of us. It is conjecture at best to make such an assumption, and extremely insulting to those among us who may be less financially fortunate than others. This turtle has never talked to another turtle of less means and heard the less fortunate brethren complain about having to help his or her country, financially, militarily, or otherwise.

Those suggesting that taxes being set at the same level for all turtles, of whatever means, unduly penalizes the poor, since by virtue of being poor, the poor might have to pay more in taxes under such a program than they do now (they pay nothing at all now) are missing the point. <u>Twice</u>.

First, the poor aren't asking to be excused from helping their country pay its bills. Second, taxes that penalize some with the intention of helping some others are inherently unfair. And it is nowhere written (outside government) that turtles of less means wish to be the cause of other turtles being treated unfairly, even if it is to help them over some bump in the road. The present tax system was, without question, designed to purposely always be unfair to some Americans. A law cannot be fair in part and unfair in part. A law is either fair or unfair. The present tax laws are undoubtedly, and without question, unfair.

By its actions in using the tax laws to favor some groups of Americans, at the expense of other groups of Americans, the government has established itself as a champion of unfair dealing between itself and the citizens it is supposed to be serving. Actions have consequences. The consequence of the government's choosing to tax some citizens more than others has rendered the government incapable of being respected as an institution. Incredibly, elected officials continue to promote unfairness while expressing amazement that they are not admired as leaders. They just don't get it.

Should the opportunity ever present itself, and it were to somehow be left up the turtles in the middle to design a tax system with the goals in mind that the system be both fair and simple to administer, it would probably take less than a day to come up with a system that would be fair to all turtles, easily implemented, free from evasion, and which promoted opportunity over outcome.

But nobody in government trusts the turtles in the middle to make decisions like this, and the turtles in the middle aren't being asked for their opinions, and nobody is listening to their opinions when they volunteer them. In the meantime, the present tax system is being used to effect a continually shifting redistribution of wealth among Americans, and used to run the economy of the United States, (and indirectly the economies of all other countries) for the benefit of a minority of Americans, at the expense of the majority of other Americans (and everyone else in the world too).

The third control mechanism

The third control mechanism by which the government manages the economy of the U.S. (and other countries) is foreign trade policy. Foreign trade policy has multiple elements. Money grants and loans to foreign interests come from taxpayer pockets, and affect the ability of American middle-class turtles to make ends meet. Setting of tariffs is another element that government can elect to use for purposes of both bringing in income to the government from imported goods, thereby reducing the need for income (and other) taxes on its citizens, and to protect worker wages here at home.

In recent history the government's actions in the areas of foreign trade have been very costly to American middle-class workers, especially those employed in production-type jobs.

Since the end of WW II, the United States government has given away untold hundreds of billions of dollars to governments of other countries. The cumulative number of dollars given to other countries since WWII is in the hundreds of billions, and maybe more than that. At this point in time nobody even knows how much has been given away. Part of the reason for the lack of knowledge is sleight of hand bookkeeping by the government. Money given to foreign countries is mostly funneled through a "loan" process, which obligates the receiving country to agree to pay back the money, plus interest, by a certain point in time. Loaned amounts are not considered expenses to the U.S. government, but instead are put on the government's books as <u>assets</u>. An asset is something of value to the holder.

If the money given to foreign governments by way of foreign aid loans was (actually) treated as a <u>loan</u>, the U.S. treasury could expect the money to come back, plus interest. Also, if the foreign aid "loan" was indeed an asset of the government, it would have value and could be sold like any other asset. Most of you turtles who are homeowners have probably seen your home loan sold from time to time. Periodically, holders of home mortgages need some extra money, and may sell some of the loans held in their portfolio at a bit of a discount to another lender to get needed operating cash. When this happens you get a notice through the mail that the loan for which your home is the collateral has been sold to another lender, and you are provided with a new address to send your home mortgage payments to.

If the "loans" made to foreign governments by the U.S. government had value, and were really "assets" of the government, in the true sense of the word, they could also be sold by the government whenever the government needed some operating cash.

So, why aren't they? Ever sold, that is? The short answer is, because they are worthless for the most part, and everybody in the world knows it. Being worthless, it would be hard to find a buyer for any of them. Nobody wants to buy a loan (at any price) that has been "rolled forward" every time it comes due. Rolling forward is an indication that the borrower has no money with which to repay the loan. Who would want to buy a loan like that?

Since WWII, starting with the "Marshall Plan" the United States has annually given billions of dollars away to other governments using the above described "loan" process. In the very great majority of instances, the "loans" remain unpaid, many for decades, and some have been quietly written off entirely.

Often the loans have gone to governments that were known at the time to be highly corrupt. In fact, sometimes the reason for the loans was to purposely help the corrupt governments to become even more corrupt, when the officials of such governments could be induced, through corruption, to serve U.S. interests. Our history is replete with foreign aid "loans" being made to corrupt governments, and a percentage of the "loaned" moneys later appearing in Swiss bank accounts of the leaders of the corrupt governments the money was given away to.

The shah of Iran, the president of Iraq, the president of Nicaragua, the president of Mexico, the president of the Philippines, the president of South Vietnam, the list goes on and on (and on and on). Most of these "loans" to foreign governments are still shown on the U.S. government's books as assets of value. Does any turtle reading this really believe that loans like those noted here will ever be repaid?

The U.S. government has, in the past, often made loans like these even when the U.S. treasury was broke, and we didn't even have enough money to cover the operating expenses of our own government. This is accomplished through inflating the currency, printing up more dollars, and forcing banks to take them in as reserves, and then borrowing them back from the banks to "loan" to another country.

The Government then prints up some more money to pay the banks interest on the money that they borrowed and gave away to a foreign government, while often not ever being repaid even the interest on the money "loaned" out to the foreign government, let alone the principal amount of the "loan".

Is that another great policy or what?

This process has now been abused to the point that a conservative estimate would be that ten cents out of every tax dollar collected from middle-class American working turtles now goes for paying the interest on the accumulated total of foreign aid money "lent" out to other governments, that has not been repaid when due, but which the U.S. government is still repaying to the banks, both interest and principal, as part of the nation's "national debt".

Another important element of foreign aid "policy" is determining the proper level of tariffs for specific goods entering the country. During the first 150 years of our history, the commerce imported from other countries that was used to build this nation was taxed upon entry. The purpose was twofold.

First, to get money to pay for the operation of the government. Second, to protect domestic workers and businesses when the goods being imported were in direct competition with goods being manufactured here in the U.S.

By setting a tariff such that the overall cost of imported goods to someone here in the U.S. was higher than the total cost of buying a comparable product produced by American workers, the government acted to both protect American businesses, operating here at home, and to also bring in money to pay for running of the government. For the first 150 years of our history, taxing imported goods was a primary source of income to our government, and during this period of our history, there was no such thing as an "income tax".

Within the past twenty to thirty years, with the rise of "multi-national" companies, governments worldwide have been lobbied intensely by big businesses to stop the practice of taxing imported goods. The tariff free exchange of goods between different countries has been labeled a "free-market" approach. We are told that "free-markets" were the thing that made America's rapid growth possible, and therefore "free-markets" should be a model for all "emerging" countries to follow, if they wish to be as successful as the United States, economically speaking.

This is not true. In fact, the exact <u>opposite</u> approach, called "free-enterprise ", is what allowed America to grow so rapidly, and it is "free-enterprise", and not "free-markets" that other countries should be trying to achieve, if they wish to grow as we have.

Over the past two to three decades, big business has seduced governments' worldwide, using "spaced-repetition" to sell the siren song of "free-markets", as a replacement for "free-enterprise"

The difference between "free-markets" and "free-enterprise" is in what the "free" stands for. In "free-enterprise, the "free" stands for freedom of individuals to control the outcome of their own lives, protected by their government from outside (foreign) interference and unfettered by excessive government regulation here in the U.S. In "free-markets" the "free" stands for the freedom enjoyed by large companies with worldwide operations to exploit workers in every country of the world without restriction and with the prior agreement and blessings of all the governments of the world.

"Free-enterprise" and "free-markets" are not remotely the same thing, and, in fact are virtually diametrically opposed in their (real) goals.

Over the past twenty-five or so years, multi-national companies have worked incessantly to convince the leaders of not only the U.S., but every other country as well, that free-markets are the same thing as free-enterprise, and that therefore, given that the U.S. rapid growth as an economic power was based upon a free-enterprise model, countries worldwide should now embrace "free-markets", because "free-markets" are really the same thing as "free-enterprise".

It took over twenty years to get the job done, but as this is written, the leaders of the world's governments have mostly bought into the "free-enterprise is the same thing as free-markets" siren song, and have elected to go along with the "free-market" program.

Free-markets are great levelers, at least in theory. There has never before been a time in recorded history that any prosperous nation willingly chose to go the "free-market" route. Sometimes at the point of a gun, facing military might in the extreme, or otherwise being coerced from a trade standpoint, nations have opened their borders to tariff free imports, in the process typically upsetting their own economies. But there are no instances recorded where free-markets were willingly entered into, and the countries comprising the free-market trade group are all known to have benefited equally.

There are, however, many examples of "free-market" experiments that resulted in the production workers of all countries involved being pulled down to the same level of pay, that level being far less than the turtles in <u>some</u> of the countries were used to being paid before the "free-market" worked it's magic. The European Common Market is a good example.

Another such example would be the United States of America. Over the past twenty years' time, even without formally passing any trade policy laws, the U.S. Government has acted to encourage replacement of our past free-enterprise philosophy with the free-market philosophy that was designed by multi-national businesses, and sold through spaced-repetition to our elected leaders. Tariffs have been steadily reduced with our trading partners, allowing goods made in countries where the workers have very low (and very poor and inexpensive) standards of living, to compete in price directly with goods made by middle-class American working turtles, who once made enough to support a good standard of living here in America.

Most recently the government acted to institutionalize the switch over from a free-enterprise system to a free-market system. The general agreement on tariffs and trade (GATT), and the North American free trade agreement (NAFTA) were the mechanisms for institutionalizing the switch. The result has been an entirely predictable, steady, lowering of the standard of living for American middle-class working turtles over the past ten to twenty years' time, toward the (lower) standard of living of the workers in other countries around the world.

All multi-national businesses and the governments of poor countries have profited from the U.S. government having decided to replace the free-enterprise model, with the free-market model. The U.S. government and U.S. production workers have lost ground. It is the case in a "free-market" environment, that while all multi-national businesses will always win in both the short and long term, and the governments of poorer countries with large populations will also win in both the short and longer term, that governments and production workers in wealthy countries with lower populations must also then lose in both the short and long terms.

The reason is simple: We live in a finite world.

There is a fixed amount of (real) wealth available for distribution at any one point in time. In a free-market environment, the sum total of all wealth flows proportionately to the countries with the largest worker populations. This is great if you are a worker turtle in China or India. It's possibly not so great if you happen to be a middle-class American working turtle.

The goal of free-enterprise is to encourage citizens and governments of less well-off countries to strive for a higher level of wealth and achievement. The rising tide raises all boats theory. The goal of free-markets is to encourage citizens and governments of well-off countries, to voluntarily lower themselves down to the level of all other countries worldwide. The lowest common denominator theory.

Whatever their "reasoning" for doing so, the elected leaders of America have chosen to switch over from a free-enterprise model, to a free-market model. As they have done so, the result has been a predictable and steady lowering of the standard of living for middle-class American working turtles, and ever higher government spending deficits, resulting in part from lowered (per capita) taxable income being paid to American workers, and lowered tariffs coming in from imported commerce.

The fourth control mechanism

The fourth mechanism that the government uses to maintain control over the nation's (and as a result, the world's) economy, is controlling the outcome of labor-management disputes here at home.

Prior to the beginning of the 20th century, management was not restrained from mistreating workers, and frequently did just that. Due to high levels of in-migration, there was a significant out-of-balance condition that existed between how many people there were seeking work, and how many jobs there were that needed filling. Supply and demand thus worked to drive labor costs down to rock bottom, and provided an environment wherein workers would tolerate tremendous abuse in order to just keep their jobs. Sweat shops, eighty-hour work weeks, child labor, prison labor, and unsafe working conditions, were the norm, and were tolerated by the government. (Like they now are in some poor "emerging" countries with very large populations, and occasionally again here in the U.S. too).

Union movements acted to draw attention to the plight of common workers, and strikes were an effective tool for getting management to concede some points to labor. During the last quarter of the 19th century, and the first half of the 20th century, trade unions fought valiantly to bring American middle-class working turtles into the mainstream, to be treated with dignity, and paid a share of the total wealth they produced. By 1950, the American middle-class working turtle who was a union member enjoyed the best standard of living of any group of production workers that ever inhabited our planet, at least so far as we know.

During the first half of the 20th century, trade unions also worked diligently and successfully to lobby elected leaders in government to enact laws that institutionalized some of the gains made through their efforts The national Fair Labor Standards Act, and the National Labor Relations Board resulted from trade unions efforts to institutionalize gains made on wage and benefit levels for their employee members.

Congress was also effectively lobbied by the unions to keep import tariffs sufficiently high that increased wages paid to production workers here in America, didn't cause the finished goods produced here in America to be higher priced than goods imported from foreign countries. Finally, congress passed anti-trust laws designed to protect workers from the detrimental effects of monopolies, when one company began gobbling up all the others in its field.

Labor related laws enacted during the first half of this century admittedly benefited workers at the expense of both management and stockholders of large companies whose workers were, in the main, union members. It must also be noted that prior to this time, the looseness of laws relating to business had previously greatly favored management and owners over workers. This is not to suggest that two wrongs made a right. The problem that precipitated both wrong actions (laws favoring one over the other) was an initial failure to perceive the negative impact on workers that was sure to ensue if population was not held to a level that matched labor supply and labor demand.

When population growth outstrips the ability of the marketplace to fairly decide things like wages and benefits, the management side will always prevail, unless a way can be found artificially, to restore the balance.

Once having seen the population expand beyond the level that could be supported (equitably) using only supply and demand market pressures, the Unions fought to create an artificially lower supply of workers, in order to drive wages and benefits up, and then, not surprisingly the unions moved to institutionalize these gains by getting laws enacted toward that purpose.

The effort required by the Unions to artificially manipulate labor supplies downward, and manipulate prices upward through tariff protections, in order to make it possible for wages and benefits to go up, should not be minimized. The battles that erupted when management attempted to "break" unions by hiring "scabs" (replacement workers) when union workers went out "on strike" were often violent in the extreme. Both the strikers and their "scab" replacements were fighting, literally, for their own lives, and to keep their families alive. The "scab" was management's weapon in labor strikes. There was, at the "real" level, a large imbalance between total labor available to do work, and how many jobs the managers wanted to fill. There were often two or three unemployed people for every job that was available. (Of course there might have been more workers needed if management had only required workers to work sixty or seventy hours a week).

Given this disparity, management always had more hungry, unemployed, people wanting to fill positions of striking workers, than they had striking workers to replace. Hunger is a powerful motivator. Out of work "scabs" under different circumstances, might even have agreed with the striking workers, and might otherwise have refused to allow themselves to be used as replacements, thereby strengthening management's position while the strike was going on.

But, desperate people commit desperate acts, and the "scabs" families needed food and shelter just as badly as did the families of striking workers. Understanding that if management were free to replace striking workers with "scab" replacement workers, the Unions took to surrounding businesses against which they were striking, and using force and intimidation to keep replacement workers from reporting to work. A lot of strikers and scabs were injured, crippled, and killed, fighting over the few jobs that were available.

When the strikers were ultimately successful, not only workers who were union members saw their economic well-being improve, but non-union workers also benefited as management "voluntarily" upped the pay to non-union-members too, as a means of discouraging them from joining (and further strengthening) the unions.

The rising tide raised all boats.

Over time, it came to be the case that the Unions hard won gains won them the admiration of the majority of American middle-class working turtles, and union membership soared. Now, the government felt real pressure to act to institutionalize the gains made by the unions. When the unions were small, and represented few Americans, elected leaders could afford to ignore them. However, when unions came to directly or indirectly represent a majority of working Americans, elected leaders ignored them at their peril.

The power of the Unions was relatively short lived. Corruption within the unions tainted them in the eyes of non-union members. Unions also began to abuse their new powers, to an extent that most Americans could not support. At one time it was the case that a member of a carpenter's union working on a government job, could not plug in his own power drill, but instead had to wait for a member of the electricians' union to come and do it for him.

Combined with excessive demands, like the example immediately above, union leaders succumbed to corruption at the expense of their own members. Union leaders set up Swiss bank accounts and awarded contracts to friends who "kicked back" part of the proceeds from doing the work. Union leaders enriched themselves from the pension funds that all members were made to contribute into.

Union leaders then hired "goons" to punish detractors, and to continue to enforce their will on their own members, whenever a member got "out-of-line" or complained about the abuses on the part of the union leaders.

By the mid-1960's, the public was becoming disenchanted with unions and the abuses they were visiting on everybody else in society. The abuses suffered by businesses at the hands of unions was finding its way onto the evening news, which by this time was being displayed on television. By the mid-1970's, multi-national businesses had begun to respond to union demands by moving part of their operations to other countries. Somewhat surprisingly, with the government's blessing. The primary reason for doing this remained tax benefits, since labor was still a relatively less significant factor in profits than was taxes. However, once a business moved part of its operation to another country to save taxes, it was a nice additional benefit to see raw labor costs go down too, and, not insignificantly, to be free from union abuses.

By the mid-1980's, most big companies had at least part of their operations offshore, and increasingly when a threat of a union strike occurred here at home, management could achieve most of what it wanted simply by threatening to move more work to other countries. Unions had no ability to intimidate or force workers in other countries into honoring a picket line here in the U.S. Foreign "scabs" were an even more potent threat to U.S. union members, than were American "scabs".

Congress, sensing that unions were no longer untouchable on the one hand, and being lobbied through spaced-repetition by the lobbyists for multi-national companies to switch over from "free-enterprise" to "free-markets", began moving to de-institutionalize prior union gains made over the previous seventy years' time.

The laws relating to mergers and monopolies were left untouched, for the most part, but the government chose to "interpret" the laws differently, and companies began buying up other companies at unprecedented rates. Unions petitioned congress to consider the plight of displaced workers relating to mergers, but the government elected to take a hands-off position on mergers. Mergers were now considered "good" and enablers of "increased productivity".

Previous to this about face on the part of the government, mergers and anti-trust laws had been used to protect workers and acted as institutional barriers to management gaining absolute control over labor through monopolizing particular industries.

In the early 1980's, a pseudo-government operation involving air traffic controllers went out on strike for more benefits. Without getting into whether the strikers demands were realistic or not, it will suffice to say here that the U.S. government moved to use the military to help scabs replacing striking workers report to work without fear of intimidation by striking workers, and further acted to allow the firms being struck to give the striking workers jobs away, permanently to the replacement workers.

Later, these "temporary" actions, which were originally meant to be used only in the instance of the air traffic controller strike, were enacted into U.S. labor law and legitimized for all occasions when workers, in any industry, elected to go out on strike.

These actions on the part of the government, (allowing unlimited mergers, allowing permanent striker replacements, using military force to help replacement workers gain entry to businesses whose workers were on strike) when coupled with the government's endorsement of big businesses relocating to other countries without having to pay import duties or taxes on goods made elsewhere, and brought into the U.S. for purposes of being sold in the American market; effectively removed all the institutional barriers that had ever previously existed, that allowed workers to have a say in the outcome of their employment, their standard of living, and, in fact, the outcome of their lives.

The government's about-face took less than-fifteen years, total time, to complete.

Once the institutional barriers to management exploiting workers were removed, business began using their newfound might to increase profits, totally without regard to the effect on their workers lives, or the lives of their families. By the 1990's it had become routine to read in the papers, or hear on the news on a daily basis, of businesses laying off hundreds or even thousands of workers. Every day of the week. Every week of the year.

Elected leaders were quick to point out after its first year in operation that they could point to an additional (net) 100,000 jobs being created in the U.S. that could be directly attributed to passage of the North American Free Trade Agreement. The government's figures were suspect because of who compiled them, but even more disingenuous was the government's failure to concurrently disclose how the 100,000 "net" figures came about.

After passage of the NAFTA, an estimated 45,000 middle-class workers who were used to making $40,000 per year plus benefits, lost their jobs, directly as a result of NAFTA. While at the same time NAFTA resulted in creation of an estimated 150,000 new jobs at minimum wage, or sometimes slightly below minimum wage. The "net" number of people employed went up, but the average wage of those employed relating to NAFTA went down. A lot.

To government officials, this was a positive thing.

There were admittedly a few exceptions to the above-noted trend re: job "creation", wherein some higher paying jobs were created too, here in the U.S. However, for every good paying job created by NAFTA, there were three to four good paying jobs eliminated, or replaced with multiple poor paying jobs.

The four control mechanisms (hopefully)
Unintended effects

The Federal Reserve has continually inflated the nation's currency supply in a manner that has caused prices to significantly outpace wages for all middle-class American turtles. Americans now must typically have both parents work outside the home in order to have a standard of living that used to only require one parent to work outside the home. Effects on children and family life have been predictably poor as a result. The disparity between wages and living costs has never been greater (not even during the great depression of the 1930's).

Tax policies have been used over the past fifty years to unfairly enrich some Americans, at the expense of other Americans, with abuses coming about equally by both major political parties. The poor have sometimes benefited. The rich have sometimes benefited. The middle-class American working turtles have never benefited. They just pay the bills.

Foreign trade policies have been changed to provide multi-national companies the capability to exploit workers of all countries with the blessings of their governments. Companies have, not surprisingly, moved quickly to take advantage of these changes for their benefit.

Labor laws have been interpreted for the benefit of management, at the expense of the workers who built the companies. All of the Constitutional barriers that previously kept management from exploiting workers in the extreme have been removed by the

U.S. government, and American workers are now completely at the mercy of management, who has shown a total disregard for their welfare.

The four mechanisms employed by government to seize, and retain, control over the nation's economy. and, in fact the economies of all countries with whom the U.S trades goods and services, have been used over the past seventy years and especially in the past thirty years' time; in ways that have had a disastrous effect on the economic well-being of most middle-class American working turtles.

And **THAT** is a problem!

Reviewing the problems

The first problem is unsustainable expansion in worldwide human population.

The second problem is that the middle-class working turtles of America, and the world in general, are seeing their labors systematically devalued.

Problem number three is citizens being systematically excluded from the decision making process in the most important decisions affecting their lives.

Problem number 4, is that ongoing government currency inflation practices cause the value of existing dollars to fall, which in turn causes prices related to living standards to continually increase much faster than wage gains.... and living standards to therefore continually fall further each year for most American citizens.

Problem number 5, American national pride and American national companies have been replaced by multi-culturalism and multi-national companies.

Problem number 6, is discriminatory lawmaking, that being the enactment of laws designed to favor one group of Americans over other groups of Americans.

Problem number 7, is a failure to fully implement technology for purposes of improving the political and economic well-being of American citizens.

Problem Number 8, is the Government controlling the nation's (and the world's) economy for the benefit of government, and single interest groups that are dependant on the government, at the expense of American middle-class working turtles.

Part 4 - Posing Possible Solutions

And Choosing Among Alternatives

Once the problems have been defined, and broken down into their various elements, it is time to begin working on their solutions. If the problem definitions have been accurate, and what have been identified as problems really are problems, and not just symptoms of problems, the rest of the problem solving steps are pretty straight forward.

However, a word of caution here may be in order as a reminder. Just as it is important in the problem definition stage to be sure that the definitions center on problems rather than just symptoms of problems it is equally important from then on to maintain objectivity when posing solutions to the problems.

In part, this requires listing as many possibilities as possible, during the part of the problem solving process where we look at alternatives. While it is often the case that there may be more than one way to solve a given problem (remember those "elegant" v. "inelegant" proofs of geometry theorems back in geometry), only by posing as many hypothetical alternatives as possible at the outset, may we maximize opportunities for implementing an "elegant" solution to the problem.

For those of you turtles who don't remember the difference between "elegant" and "inelegant" proofs in geometry (or heaven forbid, maybe never even took geometry), I'll refresh your memories. An "elegant" proof, or solution to a theorem or problem, is one that is so simple that it becomes obvious, once it is disclosed. An "inelegant" proof, or solution to a problem, is one that is inordinately complicated, and which generally includes more steps in the logic chain, and is more difficult to understand, even after it is disclosed, even though it ultimately does serve to prove the theorem, or solve the problem.

Most turtles out there would probably opt for government programs to be simple, and easily understood. Most turtles out there would probably also agree that not many government programs now in operation exhibit either of those two characteristics. There is a reason for that. The reason is that most elected officials have had no previous formal training whatsoever in problem solving before they became elected officials. Unsurprisingly, they are collectively very poor not only at defining problems, and differentiating between symptoms of problems, and actual problems; but are equally poor at the step requiring posing and examining of as many alternative solutions as possible.

A combination of lack of any prior training in problem solving, combined with strong built-in biases going in, renders many elected officials effectively dysfunctional when it comes to trying to solve the problems facing America today. It's not so much that they are inherently bad turtles, or even stupid turtles, most are just very poorly equipped to solve the Country's problems.

Acknowledging Axioms
& Defining Acceptance Criteria

All problem solving requires reliance on axioms at some point in the process. Axioms are statements accepted as true without proof. For example, in plane geometry it is axiomatic that parallel lines in the same (flat) plane will never intersect. Of course, since planes extend out infinitely in both directions, no-one has ever been able to follow two parallel lines in the same plane out far enough to prove empirically that they never meet, so an absolute proof that parallel lines in the same plane will never intersect is not possible. But, the concept of "parallelism" combined with no-one ever being able to show even a single instance where parallel lines in the same flat plane did meet, has provided the basis for our accepting this statement as true, without requiring it to be formally and empirically proven.

In geometry, there are several axioms, upon which all the other proofs are constructed. Of course, if anyone were ever to prove by example that any of the axioms used in Euclidian (plane) geometry were not true, then all the other proofs built upon the axiom in question, would also then be rendered false.

In science a solution is accepted as true only if not a single instance where it fails can be demonstrated. In science, even if a proposed "solution" to a problem works 99.9% of the time, if there is even a single instance that can be demonstrated where the proposed "solution" fails, then the proposed "solution" is deemed "false".

A later part of the problem solving process requires that the proposed solution (once identified and implemented) be "proven". Though the "proof" process is a couple of steps down the road, it is at this stage, where we propose possible solutions, that we also identify the "acceptance criteria" that will be applied when "proving" out the solution. During this phase of the problem solving process, "if-then" statements are drawn up that later serve as the basis for examining whether or not the solution approach selected actually worked.

For example, in a socio-economic setting, a proposed solution to problems stemming from population growth, might have defined an acceptance criterion that states, "if the solution is valid then population growth will be reduced to 1.5% a year by the year xxxx".

Later on, in the "proof" stage of the process, this "acceptance criteria" would be applied to conditions in place after the selected solution were in effect. If population increases fell to 1.5% or less, by the year xxxx, the solution would be accepted as valid. If not, the solution would be rejected as false. If the "proof" failed, the proposed solution would be scrapped, and the solver would have to go back to step number one in the problem solving process and begin anew.

When solving problems, it is important to always include as part of the "proof" process, a requirement that the solution must be in agreement with all known and accepted axioms, in the field in which the problem solving occurs. In marketplace problems for example, all proposed solutions would have to be measured against the "supply-demand" axiom which states that when supplies exceed demand, prices fall. The corollary (reverse) of this is also true That is, when demand exceeds supplies, prices go up.

A present-day example

To see how true the supply-demand axiom is, one need look no farther than our government's continuing inflation of the nation's paper currency supply. The government has continually demanded more money than was already in circulation, to pay for its own operation, and to pay for programs it has enacted without regard to the amount of currency already in circulation when they were making their decisions. Their demands have been met by simply printing up some more paper currency to pay off their bills. The net effect of this excess demand, against the existing supply of currency, caused prices for everything, including money itself (interest rates), to go up sharply, for everybody.

In the early 1980's the president proposed a government economic model based upon the immutable, ages-old, "supply-demand" axiom of the marketplace, as regards the value of currency. The president proposed that by shrinking government demand for more currency to be printed up, and allowing the marketplace to thereafter on its own determine the purchasing power of the currency already in circulation, that prices would stabilize, and perhaps even fall somewhat. In other words, if government demand for available currency fell, then the existing supply of currency would stretch farther, and the price of currency (interest rates) could also fall. If the price of currency were to be reduced, the purchasing power of each dollar already in circulation would be increased by a like amount.

The president's ideas were soundly ridiculed by just about everybody. The "conventional" wisdom of the day refuted (chose to ignore) the "supply-demand" axiom, and stated that the exact opposite was true. That is, the conventional (governments) wisdom held that the greater the government's demand for currency to pay its bills, and the more currency printed up and put into circulation to pay them off, the less things would (somehow) cost. The government's "conventional" wisdom of the period ultimately prevailed, thereby making our economic problems much worse in the process.

There are lessons here for those willing to learn them. The first lesson is that it is sheer folly to pretend that axioms can be ignored when attempting to solve-problems; and that the solutions arrived at by way of purposely ignoring or violating the axioms will somehow still hold true.

The second lesson is to beware the conventional wisdom of the day; especially if the conventional wisdom is promoted by a government body. Conventional wisdom can be a trap that is very difficult to get out of. Question everything.

Conventional wisdom is often wrong, in the extreme. For example:

1. In the 8th century, conventional wisdom held that the Earth was flat.

2. In the 11th century, conventional wisdom held that the earth was the center of the universe, and the sun, and all the stars revolved around it every day.

3. In the 14th century, conventional wisdom held that self-government was a fundamentally flawed concept, which could therefore never succeed in practice. (Benevolent dictators were thought to be essential).

4. In the 17th century, conventional wisdom held that the Earth's gravitational pull would forever preclude mankind from traveling in space.

Not all the people proposing these ideas at the time were foolish individuals by any means. The proponents of these ideas, at the time, included some of the most respected scholars of the period, and some of the most successful and influential people of their times, including some who had made great contributions to science, business and trade, education, and government.

Time has a way of exposing false conventional wisdom; and false conventional wisdom can be a trap for people in all walks of life, at all levels throughout society. Conventional wisdom is not easily overturned, even in the face of compelling evidence that the conventional wisdom may be wrong. In the instance of the previous example relating to the Earth being the center of the universe, the person who first questioned this conventional wisdom publicly, was put to death for voicing his opinion. Sometimes challenging the conventional wisdom of the day requires the challenger to have a bit tougher skin too.

Though we like to believe that we live in a more enlightened time, it is still the norm that those initially questioning the conventional wisdom of the day are set upon and destroyed. The destruction of conventional wisdom "heretics" today does not usually take the form of burning at the stake, or beheading, as it did in earlier days, but instead more often takes the form of character assassination, and being subjected to ridicule both by opponents and media "experts", with a vested interest in preserving the status quo.

Objectivity

Speaking of axioms, it is axiomatic in problem solving in general, that the way problems are defined, determines the types of solutions that will be proposed (remember the doctor's nervous stomach diagnosis). That's why it's so important to differentiate between problems, and symptoms of problems, at the start of the process.

It is also axiomatic in problem solving, that no solution can be considered true unless it resists all attempts to defeat it through logic. That being the case, problem solvers are encouraged to consider all alternatives as equally possible, at the outset. Closer examination and subjecting alternatives to additional questioning and logical tests during the process of eliminating alternatives will result in the narrowing down of the list.

It is almost always self-defeating in the long term and often in the short term too; to exclude possible alternatives from the list of possible solutions to a problem, based upon personal bias. That is to say, it is counter-productive to limit alternatives that pre-determine the outcome based not on logic, but on desire.

Imagine how Einstein's theory about how matter and energy are related might have turned out if Einstein held a preconceived notion that matter and energy were separate and unrelated entities. He never would have considered an equation like $E=mc^2$, which, as all you turtles out there know who took a physics course, turned out to be the right answer. (Einstein later determined that another equation re: matter and energy would also be needed to take into account the effects of curved space and gravity).

The point is, that it is important to consider as many different alternatives as possible during this stage of the problem solving process, and to then apply logic, instead of emotion, to weeding out those alternative solutions that are based upon a flawed hypothesis.

Data Gathering - Defining the "Scope" of the Problem, and Prioritizing

Part of the process of proposing and selecting of possible alternatives requires examination of relevant data. Data includes examining symptoms of the problem, and quantifying the extent of the symptoms. When working in the area of government, or almost any other socio-economic area, this can be tricky. The reason is that those that the data is being gathered from may wish to skew the outcome by selectively offering only that data, taken out of context, which suits their needs for your review.

A primary purpose for quantifying the symptoms is to aid in determining how to measure the dosage when administering a solution. A secondary purpose for quantifying the symptoms is to help the problem solver determine priorities when more than one problem is present at the same time.

Medical doctors do this part pretty well in general. If a patient has multiple symptoms, of what might be multiple problems, the doctor needs to determine appropriate solutions for each problem, and to prioritize his application of therapies, and to determine where problems overlap. In emergency situations, like treating victims of an auto crash, the doctor may view several problems that all require attention, and will ultimately have to address all of them, but must do so in a way that maximizes the benefits to the patient. First the patient may have to have a heart re-started, and pulse and breathing restored, before the doctor can take time out to worry about stitching organs back together, setting broken bones, and performing plastic surgery and skin grafts.

Doctors rely on other doctors, and many different diagnostic techniques, some machine assisted, to diagnose problems. They then break each problem down into its simplest elements, and propose alternative solutions. When doing this part, they often refer to data accumulated during this visit, and data from prior medical records to narrow down their choices. It wouldn't be good to inject an unconscious patient with penicillin, if the patients past history indicated a serious allergy to that drug. Also it wouldn't be advisable for the doctor to reject a particular anesthesia simply because he or she had a religious belief that called for no use of drugs for pain. All alternatives should be considered.

When it comes to making a country work, or curing the ills of a society, it is likewise good problem solving practice to consider as many alternatives as possible, and to ferret out good supporting data when considering which alternatives deserve serious consideration, and which should be scrapped.

When it comes to gathering data, quantifying symptoms, and prioritizing solutions, doctors of the nation's ills have routinely fallen short of the mark. The proof of this is that the problems continue to exist, and grow, despite all the tinkering with laws that occurs in Washington.

As we have seen, the main reason their efforts have fallen short of the mark is that they have failed to define the problems correctly. But, even assuming that elected officials were to recognize the problems facing the country, all the present evidence suggests that they would fail anyway, because they have a tendency to use inaccurate data (often on purpose) when attempting to quantify symptoms, and prioritize treatments.

Imagine how attempts to apply Einstein's theory of relativity might have worked out if Einstein had been forced to use questionable (government-supplied) data as regards the speed of light. Einstein might go the Congressional Budget Office (CBO) and be told that the speed of light was 125,000 miles per second, while being told by the Office of Management and Budget (OMB) that the speed of light was 250,000 miles per second.

If Dr. Oppenheimer used Einstein's theory of relativity, and the CBO's figures for the speed of light, the first atomic bomb might have taken New Mexico off the map. On the other hand, if Dr. Oppenheimer used Einstein's theory of relativity, and the OMB's figures for the speed of light, the first atomic bomb might never have detonated at all.

Without regard to which of these possibilities might have been better for us than what did happen when 186,000 miles per second was used, it should suffice to say here that having reliable data available during the process of evaluating possible alternatives, is very important.

Or, as they say in the computer world:

"Garbage in - Garbage out".

Which philosophy might be OK, if you are in the trash collection business. But, if you are in the business of making decisions that affect the economic well-being, and the outcome of the lives, of all the citizens of a country, it leaves a lot to be desired.

Whose data can be believed?

There are many sources of data available to us turtles today. In fact, there is so much information available, from so many different sources, that it becomes problematic deciding which to use in making decisions. When "buying into" a data source, it is probably wise to proceed as when buying other things. Caveat Emptor. Buyer beware.

There are few unbiased sources of information available. Even school text books are often "revised" to present information from a "different point of view". Producers of entertainment shows on television and radio and television talk-show hosts, like everybody else, have their built-in biases, which are often reflected in the information presented on their shows.

Elected officials have "agendas" (sometimes hidden) that result in bias being imparted into information that they pass along. A significant percentage (almost half) of congresspersons were formally trained in Law School before becoming congresspersons, and are adept at "framing" data to make it appear to be something other than what it really is.

Single interest promotions are always self-serving, and often purposely misleading of the facts. Economics is a relatively simple subject that those involved in it take great pride in making appear very complex, and confusing. Political "analysts" make a living primarily by presenting half-truths, and outright lies, as "factual data" in hopes of achieving something on behalf of whoever pays their salaries.

Example

Recently a paper manufacturing company portrayed itself on television as "the tree growing company". The advertisement showed employees of the company, accompanied by local children, planting evergreen trees in an area that had just been clear-cut. The message gave the impression that the company planted many more trees than it cut down. Which was true. But meaningless. The trees cut down by this company in the last forty years were each two to four hundred years old, and each represented many, many hundreds of board feet of lumber. The seedling-trees being planted by this company were three to four months old. It would take ten thousand of them to equal even <u>one</u> old-growth tree in terms of board feet of lumber, and it would be three to four hundred years before the seedling(s) began to represent a like kind and quality replacement for what had already been cut down.

Question(s): Can we believe this company's data about how long it takes to renew the number of trees of like kind and quality taken out of logged-out areas? Can we believe the data of the government agency that provided the tree cutting company with public trees to cut, about how long it takes to renew the number of trees of like kind and quality taken from public areas? On a larger scale, can we believe any single interest's data, about any topic near and dear to their hearts?

Example

In the fourth (calendar) quarter of 1995, Democrats and Republicans were arguing over adjustments to the Medicare and Medicaid "entitlement" programs. The Democrats were proposing to increase spending in these areas by 65% over a seven-year timeframe. The Republicans were proposing to increase spending in these areas by 62% over the same seven-year period of time. The Democrats issued statements through news conferences that the Republican plan aimed to "gut" these programs. The Republicans issued statements through news conferences that the Democrats plan was nothing more than a repeat of past "tax and spend" Democratic politics. Neither of these were true statements. Both parties' plans included ongoing increases in Medicare-Medicaid spending, and the plans were, in fact less than three percent apart over a seven-year span of time, in what would be required to fund them. That made a difference of less than one half of one percent a year between the two party's proposals. (Both parties were recommending increases that were 3+ times the going inflation rate).

Question: Can we believe either Democrat or Republican leaders' data with respect to Medicare and Medicaid? If not, can we believe their data with respect to any subject at all?

Example

In each of the 1994 through 2003 years, approximately 2% of the middle managers in America lost their jobs through technology aided mergers between some of the largest multi-national companies in the world. The federal government endorsed every merger. The majority of middle managers displaced through mergers were unable to find <u>like kind and quality</u> work after being displaced. As this occurred, financial (stock and bond) markets endorsed the mergers, and government economists advised that the economy was doing well.

Question(s): Can we believe that the government's data that indicates that mega-mergers are good for employment? Can we believe that the federal government really cares about the economic well-being of workers displaced through mergers? Can we believe the government economists views that mergers are good business for middle-class working Americans?

Example

In each of the Presidential election years of 1992, 1996, 2000, and 2004, the presidential contest was awarded to a man who received about 45% of the total votes (cast in voting booths). During that presidential election, only about half of "registered" voters voted (formally). The president was elected by a vote of (about) 45% of (about) 55% of the total population. That comes out to about 25% of the population. The winner declared that "Americans have spoken" and that the vote provided him with a "mandate" for change. Bottom line, 55% of those voting formally wanted another candidate for president. Over 70% of the total population did not want any of the candidates whose names were on the ballot to be president. The winner's "mandate" for change was based upon the fact that 75% of the country wanted someone else to be president, and <u>not</u> him!

Question: Can we believe any elected official who claims a "mandate" for his or her actions, when the election shows that a majority of eligible voters for the position, actually wanted someone else to get the job, or, alternatively, didn't want any of the candidates listed on the ballot to get the job?

Example

Prior to the 1994 "mid-term" elections for congresspersons, a poll, paid for by the Republican national committee revealed that the ten items comprising the republican "Contract with America" were favored by a large majority of those polled. Later, after the election was over, and Republicans had increased their membership in both houses of Congress, the polling company admitted that it had "rigged" the wording of the questions being asked, in order to pre-determine the outcome, and further had falsely reported to the public the wording of the questions actually asked of those being polled.

Question: Can we believe "polls"

We could go on (and on, and on) but I think that you turtles get the message. The only data you can believe, is that which comes to you through your own investigative efforts. It is essential that data be filtered through at least a "common-sense-reasonableness" filter, before accepting it as a basis for problem solving.

Lawyers as Lawmakers

Between forty and fifty percent of all congresspersons received their university training in the subject of Law. Lawyers are particularly unsuited to work that requires knowledge of problem solving. The reason is simple, Law School prepares its students to be many useful things, but being a problem solver is not one of them.

Most attorneys are intelligent, ethical, and honest. But then so are most clergymen and most professional athletes, and they wouldn't necessarily make very good problem solvers either. More than intelligence, honesty and ethical behavior are required in order to be an effective problem solver.

The emphasis in law school is on manipulating the rules of procedure, to make things appear other than what they are. One does not attend law school to learn about the law(s). One attends law school to learn how to effectively use technicalities associated with the rules of criminal and civil procedure, to achieve a pre-determined (desired) outcome. One also attends law school to learn how to be an effective advocate for a given position, and in the process learn how to be adversarial without being (too) offensive.

A fairly recent highly publicized criminal trial relating to an ex-football star accused of murdering his ex-wife and a male friend of his ex-wife's, provided Americans with an opportunity to see what law school is all about. Both sides (prosecution and defense) spent an inordinate amount of time and money arguing to the judge, outside of the presence of the jury, about what evidence the jury would be "allowed" to see and hear. It's worth noting here that the purpose of all this wrangling is (was) to purposely not allow the whole truth to come out.

The attorneys for both sides were expert, and both sides were successful to some degree. The result of their successful efforts was that the jury was absolutely precluded from knowing the "truth, the whole truth, and nothing but the truth".

Without going into how useful it may be from the standpoint of protecting an individual's rights who has been accused of a crime, it will suffice here to say that, as shown by the above noted trial, a primary purpose of law school is to teach lawyers how to conceal the truth, twist facts to appear to be something other than what they really are, and to keep the whole truth from ever coming out. All in the name of justice, and protected by attorney-client privileges.

This is an extremely useful knowledge set, and it serves our criminal justice system and our adversarial legal system in general well, for the most part. Our legal system is admittedly imperfect, but so are all the others around the world, and ours is probably as good as, if not better than that of any other country.

But, this type of thinking so deeply implanted in law school is counter-productive when it comes to dealing truthfully and openly with the public as an elected official and further, it renders it's followers among the least able when it comes to identifying problems and finding solutions. Lawyers are deal-makers, not problem solvers. To lawyers the ends always justify the means. Justice and fair play are not important to lawyers. Winning is. Would-be lawyers pay serious money to law schools to teach them to think in this way and only in this way.

Another serious failing related to lawyers, when it comes to being legislators, is the lawyer tendency to believe that all things can be accomplished through the enactment and enforcement of a law. Experience teaches otherwise, but lawyers never learn. Thus, once elected to a legislative body, lawyers cannot resist the temptation to try to bend society's will by enacting laws designed to make people live the way the lawyer (author of the legislation) thinks they should.

History is replete with ill-conceived laws that failed to achieve the desired end result, some even that were made part of the U.S. Constitution itself. Prohibition, Wade v Roe (abortion), the "drug wars", laws regarding school prayers, affirmative action (discrimination), 55MPH Speed limit, Wage-Price Controls, no-smoking laws, no-littering laws, pornography laws, etc., etc., etc. The list goes on and on. The reason that none of these types of laws ever work is that they attempt to address through legislation, matters that can't be successfully addressed through legislation.

There has never been a successful attempt in the known history of the world to legislate morality according to some pre-determined point of view. The lesson is clear. Humans resist, at <u>all</u> costs, any attempt by anyone to dictate morality to them. But attorneys, especially, see this history of failure to achieve the desired results through legislation, as a challenge to be overcome, rather than a lesson in human nature and human behavior. And, because of this, attorneys continually revert to passing laws in a forever doomed attempt to make society come out the way they think it should.

Don Quixote would be proud of them.

Who IS up to the job, and who can we believe?

So, if we can't depend on the conventional sources for information and decision making, who can we turn to? Who can be trusted to propose solutions to the problems we face today that are insidiously taking away the American Dream from ourselves and our children and our grandchildren?

Why us of course. We will have to do it ourselves.

By way of trying to assist along those lines, I'm suggesting here some ideas for proposing solutions that I think will allow us to do a better job in this area, than our elected leaders have been able to do in the recent past. I recommend the same methodology to those elected leaders who may be interested in restoring the American Dream, but admittedly I hold little hope that they will be either listening, or receptive.

Anyway, here they are:

Ten Tips for Proposing Solutions to the Problems facing America:

1. Always include the four basic foundation elements of the American Dream as axioms against which all proofs must be measured (assuming that restoring the American Dream is a desirable goal).

2. Look at all alternatives, not just the easiest, most popular, or cheapest to implement in the short term. Specifically, remember that the U.S. Constitution was designed, on purpose, to be amended as the country's needs changed.

3. Always include the "do-nothing" alternative as a possible solution.

4. Don't cheat. Remember that solving one problem at the expense of making another problem worse does not constitute a valid solution. For example, in Newton's instance, it would not be acceptable to accept a proof for the law of inertia, which invalidated the law of gravity.

5. Remember to identify "acceptance criteria" when picking solutions. If the solution is a valid one, the adverse symptoms will become predictably, and measurably, less over a predictable amount of time. If the symptoms don't disappear over the predicted timeframe, denounce the solution as invalid, and go back to step number <u>one</u> to see if the problem has been correctly defined. (Don't just extend the timeframe and throw some more money at it, in hopes that it will somehow work out).

6. Remember that scrapping invalid solutions is just as important as implementing valid solutions.

7. Remember that solving problems, especially socio-economic problems, is not a popularity contest. Those who are the problem will not be pleased when and if the problem is solved.

8. Do not allow yourself to be distracted by diversions while looking for solutions to problems. (like concentrating on temporary middle-class tax cuts or token increases in the minimum wage when the problem is your job being given away to someone in another country).

9. Remember to always frame alternative solutions to problems in a way that the effectiveness of the solution can be measured objectively...using data that can be verified.

10. Challenge conventional wisdom. When conventional approaches to problem solving fail, over a long period of tune, to achieve the promised results, it will usually be the case that the conventional wisdom itself is wrong. Remember that for centuries physicians used to use leeches to "bleed" contagious diseases out of their patients. The exact <u>opposite</u> of prior centuries of conventional

wisdom proved to be what was needed. Immunization requires injecting modified disease cells <u>into</u> the body to help it build up immunity.

It will not be the purpose of this work to attempt to propose a complete solution to all the problems facing us today. Given the problems already defined herein, some solutions are obvious. Even so, it will first be necessary to construct a level playing field for implementing solutions, lest the solutions, once implemented, be quickly set aside by those with an interest in seeing to it that the problems either remain unsolved, or that the problems can be quickly reinstated, (especially if they <u>are</u> the problem).

Providing citizens with tools for rebuilding

The American Dream

As we begin to consider possible solutions to individual problems, one of the "outfalls" from such thinking, will be the discovery that some new tools may be needed by citizens when they set about to rebuild the American Dream (and keep it rebuilt). It is the case that when an inventor invents a new "widget", the inventor will then need to also come up with a means of producing the new invention. The inventor cannot just go down to a hardware store and buy a "widget maker", since "widgets" did not previously exist.

The U.S. Constitution provided the tools necessary for the initial building of the great American Dream. And, if things were now, as they were at the time the Constitution was originally written, the existing Constitution would be all that would be needed to rebuild the Dream. But things are not now as they were then. Much has changed in the world since the Constitution was first laid down on paper, and enacted into law.

Part of the way that the world has changed has to do with the number of people being governed under the constitution, and the many different functions government has taken for itself, and away from those being governed.

Part of the way the world has changed has to do with government enacting into law many laws designed to protect government from intervention by those governed, and laws designed to shield elected officials from their constituents. These laws, all passed after the Constitution was first put into place, have effectively turned the tables completely from what the founding fathers intended. Instead of a government "of the people, by the people, and for the people", law makers over the past seventy-five years have passed laws that have rendered our government one "of the government, by the government, and for the government".

If the American Dream is to be restored, the "people" will have to have a shot at getting back into the game. Right now, the "people" have been relegated to spectators in the game. It will be necessary, as a first step, to let the "people" back into the game, and provide them with Constitutional tools that level the playing field.

It will be also beneficial to put into place some guidelines that maximize the opportunities for "elegant" solutions to be implemented "Elegant" solutions, you will recall, are those that are so simple that they become obvious once disclosed, though they may not have been obvious before then.

A significant problem with most legislation enacted today (and for at least the past fifty years as well) is complexity. It is typically not because the topic being covered by legislation is itself complex, that the legislation drafted to cover it becomes unwieldy. Rather, it is because the legislation is purposely worded to provide more favorable treatment to some citizens, than to other citizens, that this occurs. Providing language in legislation that "targets" specific groups for favorable treatment, while providing the means for bureaucratic employees at the same time to deny equally favorable treatment to others, often causes legislative bills to be (very) lengthy, ambiguous, and difficult to interpret. One very efficient way to make it difficult for elected leaders to pass discriminatory legislation would be to amend the U.S. Constitution as follows:

Constitutional Amendment Number 1

"No legislation proposed before either house of congress may exceed two single-side, typed, letter-size (8 ½" x 11") pages, in its entirety, including all appendices, amendments, references, and enabling language which are to be included in full, with all print to be double spaced and no smaller than 12 point Helvetica-equivalent type, and all pages to have 1 " margins on all sides. Legislation proposed through petition or referendum must also comply with this law. "

This amendment would require bills to be straight forward, and easy to comprehend. This is a necessary, but not sufficient, step in eliminating discrimination from law making at the federal level. It is not sufficient, because a bill could still be introduced that met this requirement that blatantly sought to favor one segment of society over other segments of society. But, at least the discrimination would then be out in the open for all to plainly see.

A second amendment to the U.S. Constitution that would serve the national interest, and promote honesty in government at the federal level would be the following one:

Constitutional Amendment Number 2

"All legislation introduced in either house of congress must address a single topic. No legislation may be submitted before either house of congress that includes an amendment that is not directly related to the main topic of the legislation being proposed. Legislation proposed through petition or referendum must also comply with this law."

This amendment would eliminate the past practice of "pork-barrel" politics whereby congresspersons attach unrelated "riders" (sometimes now called "earmarks") to important legislation as a means of avoiding presidential vetoes over spending for special-interest friends and contributors of the author of the "rider".

A significant benefit of these two amendments, when combined, would be that there would be no further need for a "line-item" veto. Both the president and the proponents of enacted legislation could, and would, be held accountable for their actions. No more excuses.

Constitutional Amendment Number 3

"Congress shall enact no legislation, and the president shall not sign into law, any legislation that in any way favors any citizen or group of citizens more than any other citizen or group of citizens. Laws enacted through petitions or referendums shall also be subject to this requirement. This amendment shall apply equally to all laws, past, present, or future, including future amendments to the Constitution, but shall exclude the existing Constitution and its amendments as of (the date of enactment of this amendment). This amendment shall be the only law allowing for ex post facto operation in its enablement, unless the Constitution be further amended later to include other specific instances of ex post facto law operation. All natural and naturalized citizens of the United States of America shall have standing to sue in the courts for relief of discrimination under the laws, under this amendment. "

This amendment would allow for mandatory removal of unfair laws already on the books, at all levels, and eliminate the need for "sunset" laws that have proven easy to circumvent, and which have allowed government programs, once in motion, to remain in motion". This amendment would allow laws to be challenged by any citizen, in the Federal courts, thereby providing the "outside force" necessary to halt ineffective government programs that congress and the executive branch are wedded to.

Of course, that might all go for naught if congress and the executive branch conspired to "stack" the Supreme Court with "status quo" judges, who had the option of remaining in office for life. This has happened more than once in the past. To avoid this happening in the future, another amendment to the U.S. Constitution needs to be enacted to the effect:

Constitutional Amendment Number 4

"Federal Appeals court judges and Judges appointed to the Supreme Court shall be appointed for a combined term not to exceed eight years in length. If a sitting federal appellate court judge resigns before serving the maximum eight years' allowable time, he or she shall be eligible for re-appointment to the court, but the total time served by a justice may not, for all terms of appointment, and for all federal appellate courts combined, including the Supreme Court, exceed eight years duration."

This provision in the Constitution would preclude the citizens at large from being held captive for an extended period of time by a recalcitrant appellate and/or Supreme Court. When the Constitution was being drawn up, there was a shortage of learned judges available to sit on the court, and virtually none at all who understood the brand new U.S. Constitution. That is clearly not the case today. Today one out of every 250 people (men, women, children, and babies, legal and illegal citizens alike, all included) in the United States is an attorney. We have law schools, attorneys, and judges coming out of our ears.

The President and Congress would remain involved in the selection and confirmation of appellate and Supreme Court judges, but limiting the terms of Supreme Court justices would enhance the probability that sitting justices were attuned to current conditions in society, and would eliminate opportunities for the executive branch and congress to saddle the country with a group of justices whose ideology might long outlive that of those responsible for their being elected to the court. By tying the maximum term for Supreme Court justices to that of the president that nominated them, the president's ability to "stack" the court in a way that allows his or her ideology to continue influencing interpretation of the laws decades after he or she is gone from office, would be minimized.

Another important amendment to the Constitution would restrict the government's ability to coin and borrow money for their own use, to the detriment of all others, to wit:

Constitutional Amendment Number 5

"The federal government shall not in any way, or by any means, without prior authorization as determined by a majority vote 51%(+) of all American citizens, natural and naturalized, who are eligible to vote, cause or allow the total value of currency of all kinds, and money in all forms, including treasury securities and debt instruments of every kind, including but not limited to bonds and debentures, in existence, to grow in value at a faster rate than the growth rate of the population of natural and naturalized citizens of the country, and the private sector portion of the GDP combined. The population growth rate and private sector portion of the GDP shall be determined annually and figures relating to each shall be subject to audit by a different private auditing firm each year. The government may not take for its own use, by any means whether directly or indirectly, more than 20% of the value of any amount of new currency (money) or government issued (or related) debt instruments put into circulation by any means, annually, or otherwise."

In order to dissuade the government from simply continuing spending by way of increasing taxes, when the supply of currency is limited to growing at the same rate as the overall (legal) population and rate of growth in the non-government related economy, another Constitutional amendment will be required, which supersedes existing tax laws.

Constitutional Amendment Number 6

"Taxation without representation being a primary causative agent in the decision to form this nation, the method of collecting taxes, and the total percentage of the nation's gross domestic product that the federal government at all levels, in all branches, and for all functions for which it is in any way responsible, shall have made available to it to accomplish its work, shall be determined by a majority 51% (+) vote of all American citizens, natural and naturalized, who are eligible to vote. The method of collecting taxes and the percentage of gross domestic product to be made available to the government may only be voted upon during presidential or congressional elections as citizen referendum measures. No national tax policy may be enacted without obtaining a simple majority vote of all eligible voters."

The amendments relating to limiting inflation to the rate of population growth plus real growth in the GDP, and allowing citizens to decide the method of taxation, and the amount of GDP (and newly printed currency) that the government could claim for meeting its expenses eliminates the need for a separate amendment to mandate that government balance its books. When the money runs out, the spending stops; automatically. The government would be forced to live on whatever the people decided it should have. Not a penny more.

Borrowing shouldn't be much of an easy or inexpensive option either. The interest payments on borrowed money would simply reduce the total amount remaining for other purposes (just like it does for individuals). Thus, borrowing should make less money available rather than more, and become less desirable. Limiting the government's ability to print up new currency for only legitimate reasons, like fueling real growth in the productive sector of the economy, wouldn't be of much value, if the government could then turn right around and take it all back for its own use, thereby driving up interest rates for others who might need to borrow from banks for homes, cars, business expansion, etc.

Therefore, in addition to limiting the amount of new currency going into circulation, it is necessary to limit how much of any new currency, and the overall amount of currency in circulation, that the government can reserve for its own use. Of course, the government might, when faced with such limitations on its ability to tax citizens and print and borrow money, elect to revert to taxing imported commerce as a way to raise more operating cash. This could be dangerous, and might touch off another trade war if it were to occur, but, on the plus side, if they elected to take this route, it could also serve to later re-create a lot of good paying jobs for citizens here in the U.S.

Wars and revolutions will continue in the future, as they have in the past. In our history there have been numerous military actions engaged in by American soldiers whose main purpose was something other than protecting the American national interest. In some instances, American troops were sent into harm's way for no purpose more vital than making a sitting president "look presidential" when an election was coming up. Which is fine. So long as that's what the majority of Americans want to have happen. Otherwise it's not fine.

And let's not forget, wars cost money. Lots of money. It was inability on the part of our allies to repay us for fronting their costs in WWI, combined with Germany's inability to pay for the damages it caused during that war, that provided the foundation for both the great depression of the 1930's and WWII. We're _still_ trying to pay off the debts rung up way back then, for everybody involved, on both sides. Given that wars have high costs in both lives and money, it seems fair that those paying the bills in terms of both lives and money, should have a say in deciding both whether, and when, we should go to war. That's not how it works now. An amendment to the Constitution is needed to allow Americans a greater say in deciding their own fate in this regard.

To wit:

Constitutional Amendment Number 7

"In the absence of a frontal assault on the nation's borders or the borders of its territories and/or possessions, or a verified threat to the same, the President may only commit to military actions and the Congress may only commit to funding of military actions when first authorized by a simple majority vote of all legal citizens, whether natural born or naturalized in a national citizen referendum on the question. Authorization shall require a favorable vote by a minimum of 51+ % of all legal U.S. citizens eligible to vote. . This provision may be temporarily set aside for a period of no more than 90 days-time, in the event the nation is determined to be at war with another country in a war that threatens to cause any U.S. state, possession, or territory to be directly invaded with foreign troops or air or sea-related weapons of war. "

This provision in the Constitution would combine with the provisions limiting inflating the currency supply, and setting tax policy, to give citizens a permanent say in what wars were conducted. A President could, if we were invaded, immediately (temporarily) set aside the tax structure, and conceivably even take everything available for 90 days-time to beat off aggressors. However, beyond the 90-day period, the citizens would again be in control of funding, and whoever controls the funding, controls the ability to make war.

Another amendment recognizing the need to utilize technology for purposes of strengthening the fabric of the nation, and involving citizens in the decisions affecting their economic well-being, and the outcome of their lives is needed.

Constitutional Amendment Number 8

"Current and reliable information being provided to the citizens being a foundation element of a free and democratic society, Congress shall in an on-going manner act to use up-to-date technology to provide auditable records of their activities, including but not limited to recording of all votes, making available voting records of all members on all legislation, insuring that members of congress receive accurate copies of all correspondence submitted electronically and otherwise from all sources, maintain accurate records of all personal visits including tabulating of same by subject matter, and when applicable noting company affiliation of visitors, and making the tabulated records easily available, free of charge by way of up-to-date technology to all interested parties. Congress shall further be charged with responsibility for implementing and maintaining an electronic vote tabulating system that provides access for all citizens to electronically, in a secure fashion, from home directly record their votes during all elections for federal office, voting on all referendums submitted for ratification and which provides a means for citizen petitions to be compiled electronically and submitted for congress' consideration; said system to be subject to audit by a different private auditing firm annually. "

By adding these eight amendments to the Constitution, several desirable effects should be forthcoming.

First would be that the playing field would be leveled greatly, and individual citizens would be encouraged to rejoin the "formal" voting system that many have now abandoned in favor of just voting "none of the above" from their living rooms.

Secondly, these amendments would serve to acknowledge that the passage of time, and the forward march of technology, have transformed our country into something quite different from the one that existed when the Constitution was first written, and that, because of these changes, individual citizens now need to have more direct input in the decision-making process in those areas that have the greatest impact on the outcome of their and their families lives, thereby providing them with a feeling that the ultimate outcome of their lives is (much more than at present) in their own hands. When hope and control are present, desperation becomes less.

Third, it simplifies things for us all.

Fourth, it eliminates single-interest domination of the lawmaking process, by enlarging the number of people that have to be "sold" on an idea by lobbyists, since all citizens, rather than just a few elected officials, would have direct input relating to the outcome of all life-changing legislation, and all self-serving legislation would be openly labeled as such.

By themselves, these eight amendments to the Constitution would go a long way in restoring the credibility of the government as an institution, and making it a government that truly was (is) a government "of the people" These eight amendments to the Constitution might also go a long way in solving major portions of some of the eight problems comprising the list of most significant problems facing us today as a nation.

But perhaps most importantly, these amendments provide the necessary tools for restoring the American Dream, and keeping it restored. Some more laws below the constitutional level might need to be passed, some changed, and some scrapped to get the whole job done. These amendments to the Constitution would provide the tools needed to make that happen. And that would be a good start.

Amending the Constitution

Of course, many entrenched elected officials would feel threatened by enactment of these amendments, and could be expected to fight them all the way. We will be told that "amending the U.S. Constitution is not something to be considered "lightly". Which is true. But, at this point in time, several amendments need to be added if our society is to survive long term.

The U.S. Constitution has already been amended twenty-seven times. A few more amendments won't be excessive, especially if their sole purpose is to make the Constitution itself more responsive to the needs of the citizens it was designed to serve.

Sometimes in the past, Constitutional amendments were even made that rescinded amendments made previously. The founding fathers did not fear amendments themselves. In fact, the first ten amendments were enacted all at once in the form of the "bill of rights", by the very same people that drew up the Constitution in its original form.

The main body of the Constitution is designed to define explicitly the powers reserved to the government. Implicit in this is the assumption that powers not expressly reserved for the government are powers available to others. Though it was implied in the main body of the Constitution, that powers not reserved to the government were vested in the people, even the framers of the Constitution felt uncomfortable about not saying so right out front.

The Constitution was only ratified after the framers agreed to go back and add specific language specifying some of the most important citizen rights, if the holdout states would ratify the initial document. The first ten amending articles to the Constitution had that purpose, and became known as the <u>Bill of Rights</u>.

In fact, by far the most amendments added to the Constitution have been added for purposes of enumerating and expanding specific citizen rights. It would not be far off the mark to say that the main body of the Constitution is primarily concerned with defining the powers the government keeps for itself over the states and individual citizens, and that the majority of amendments are primarily concerned with defining and/or expanding the rights held by individual citizens.

There are some exceptions, like the income tax amendment, and the prohibition amendment, and a few amendments fixing the number of congresspersons and clarifying internal changes of power upon death or disability of a federal official, but most of the amendments concern themselves with defining and protecting individual citizen rights.

The Constitution is not a very long document, being about fifteen pages in length, more or less, depending on how small the print is that's used to reproduce it. Unlike many laws passed today below the Constitutional level, the various sections and articles are fairly short and to the point. When you have some extra time, you should read it. I will include a copy as an appendix to this work.

It will be the case that those whose interests are improved by keeping things as they are now, will try to convince us that amending the Constitution for these reasons "establishes a dangerous precedent", and we should therefore fear doing it (the old FUD factor).

The framers of the Constitution were a mixture of scholars, businessmen, philosophers, farmers, and soldiers. Most were students of the law, but not formally trained in it.

Specifically, most were students of the "nature" of laws, and how laws worked to organize societies. Most were familiar with the teachings of Plato and Aristotle, who previously spent considerable amounts of their time pondering the relationship of governments to those being governed.

The ancient Greeks viewed government forms as cyclical in nature. That is, a monarchial form tended to become transformed into an aristocracy, as the monarch was forced through numbers to share power with an elite propertied class (that could finance armies and protect themselves by use of force if necessary). Aristocracies in turn tended to become Oligarchies, where the privileged few pursued their own interests at the expense of the underprivileged many. Oligarchies tended to dissolve into Democracies, as the mass of individual citizens got tired of being exploited, and overthrew the leaders, establishing a system where everybody got to vote on everything. Democracies typically were short lived, being sharply divided by too many individual interests. Democracies fairly quickly deteriorated into Anarchies, where there was no law, and every individual did as they pleased at the expense of all other individuals. Anarchy is typically followed by the rise of a dictator who is able to restore order. The dictator establishes him or herself as monarch, and the cycle starts again.

As a way of disrupting the cycle, and establishing a form of government that could be sustained indefinitely, Plato sought to describe an ideal society through his work "The Republic". His contemporary Aristotle agreed with the goals, but disagreed about achieving them. The propositions postulated by Plato and Aristotle were further examined by several other politicians and philosophers and at least one scientist of note, and expanded on.

Among the list of those who pondered the relationship of governments to those governed, that started with studies of the works of Plato and Aristotle were John Locke, John Calvin, St. Thomas Aquinas, Baron Montesquieu, James Otis, John Adams, James Madison, Thomas Jefferson, and a young English college professor whose book Principia Mathematica became quite the rage back in 1687. In 1717, the young English professor would later become the Master of the British Mint. That's right, it was Sir Isaac Newton. Newton's discoveries of the natural laws of gravity and motion had a profound effect on philosophers and politicians by suggesting that there was an order to the universe that should be copied in establishing governments among men, and that God had already ordained such laws relating to man's natural, God-given rights, if we could but seek them out.

Those who caution that amending the Constitution in a manner that seeks to lessen some powers of Congress, and increase the powers of individuals, are simply mindful that once an oligarchy (which is the stage we are at now) begins to deteriorate, the next most probable stage is democracy, which in turn quickly typically deteriorates into anarchy (which few turtles would like to see us resort to). Thus when they state that Constitutional amendments should not be considered lightly, they are entirely correct in so thinking and saying. But, fear of possibly slipping into anarchy should be used to temper the wording of amendments, rather than used as an excuse for refusing to amend the Constitution further at all.

Fearing change is an exercise in futility. Change is constant. Everything in the world changes a little bit, every day. Today's great plan often turns into tomorrow's recipe for disaster, unless we are prepared to modify it along the way. Change or die might be a better philosophy to go by.

The U.S. Constitution provided a plan for building and maintaining a free nation. Like any plan it must periodically be revised and updated, or it, and the society it serves, will ultimately die out. The framers of the Constitution understood this, and specifically provided in the original document a means for it to be amended whenever necessary (Article V). It's necessary now.

Risk is inherent in the process of government. It can't be avoided. Changing the Constitution is admittedly a risky business. However, leaders (should) become leaders by way of exhibiting dexterity in problem solving, in the areas addressed by government. An old management adage to the effect that "the sole job of management, is to translate uncertainty into calculated risk, and then act to minimize the risk, and maximize the profits to the organization", could apply equally well to those whose charter it is to manage the business of our country.

Congress and the President are supposed to always balance the risk against the rewards when it comes to enacting legislation that affects the lives of all Americans. The outcome of their actions can seldom be guaranteed. There are no guarantees in life, and that holds true for government too. Risks can be minimized by way of making sure that the data used to make decisions, is accurate data. When accurate data is available upon which to base decisions, the risk of implementing solutions to problems can be minimized. Not eliminated, just minimized.

Within the past twenty years' time, all three branches of government at the federal level have become "risk averse", meaning afraid to take risks of any kind. This especially applies to risking sharing any of their powers with each other or with the public at large. Again, there are, and always will be, risks. The risk of sharing no power at all when making the most important decisions affecting the lives of citizens has to be balanced against the risk of sharing power at some level. Providing citizens with more power than they have now is admittedly risky. The alternative, at this point in time is, however, even more risky.

Right now, Congress and the executive branch of government are not only refusing to share any of their decision making powers, they are routinely acting to try taking back powers originally provided to the citizens in the Constitution. Average middle-class American turtles sense that government has fallen prey to becoming a tyrannical oligarchy, and are (rightly) concerned that unless they are allowed back in the game, as far as participating more directly in the making of the most important decisions affecting the outcome of their lives is concerned, their future is bleak indeed.

It will take both time, and a new political party, to get the job done

Amending the Constitution is not easy. First, a bill has to be introduced in Congress to amend the Constitution. Then both houses of congress have to pass it by a two-thirds majority. Once passed by both houses of Congress, the amendment must then be ratified by a three-fourths majority of the legislatures of all the states.

The framers of the Constitution were not able to envision a world like we live in today. The long distance communications in particular that we enjoy today were totally unthinkable at the time the Constitution was written. The framers of the Constitution never anticipated a point in time where citizens might actually be able to work toward a consensus among the entire citizenry, other than by forming a "chain" of communication from town hall meetings, to state legislature meetings, up to Federal (Congress) meetings. Thus, the Constitution only provided for its own amendment through such a "chain" of upward communication.

Past paragraphs have discussed how the upward communication "chain" envisioned by the framers of the Constitution has been tied into knots by a consortium made up of Democrat power brokers, Republican power brokers, and the puppet masters that pull their strings. This has resulted in effectively taking the average citizen out of the communication process, except by way of working through the (status quo) options offered by one of the two major parties. Increasingly, as we have seen, a bit more than half of all American middle-class workers have chosen not to recognize formally, or legitimatize the lack of choices, by agreeing to continually pick from a selection that only represents "the lesser of evils", and have instead increasingly voted "none of the above", from the comfort of their living rooms on election day.

The bottom line here is this. Given that the existing congress is primarily made up of Democrats and Republicans, both of whom are irrevocably wedded to the present system, which serves their interests, but not the interests of the middle-class; it is unlikely that any one of the previously mentioned amendments would ever be introduced in either house of Congress, let alone passed and sent to the states for ratification. Admittedly, some progress can be made in solving sub-elements of the eight biggest problems facing us today, without amending the Constitution as noted.

In upcoming paragraphs, we will explore some of these options. However, many of the problems facing us today cannot be otherwise solved. And, just as importantly, none of the solutions to the sub-problems that can be solved without resorting to amending the Constitution, will likely stay in place long after being implemented, unless the turtles in the middle are able to gain some additional measure of control over their own lives and economic well-being.

If the country is to be righted and the American dream restored, and the dream not again be dismantled by a Congress that has been bought and paid for, the American middle-class will have to organize and support a third "centrist" party representing their interests.

Previously, I recommended naming the new party the Mid-American Party, but whatever name is chosen, the objectives would be the same. The new party would be the party representing the American middle-class, which now has no representation whatsoever in Washington, or elsewhere. The middle-class has been bled almost to death, and repeatedly sold down the river, by both the Democrats and Republicans, always to further their own agendas, and never with any regard for those in the middle who pay all the bills.

Both the Democrats and Republicans talk about helping the middle-class. But both the Democrats and Republicans then turn right around and VOTE to bleed the middle class even more for purposes of meeting their own agendas. Both the Democrats and Republicans apparently think the middle-class citizens are there only to serve their interests. Both the Democrat and Republican politicians apparently think the middle-class workers of America are primarily ignorant peasants, dull of mind, and lacking in the courage and the will to take control over their own lives. Of course, they would never say these things publicly, but by their actions it is apparent that this is how they must actually perceive the great middle-class working community of this nation.

For about the past forty years' time, the American middle-class workers have seemingly been trying to prove them right. But that can change, anytime the great sleeping giant representing the American middle-class chooses to awake and stop playing the game by rules defined by the two special interest parties representing only the rich and poor of the country.

True, the middle-class has been routinely fooled by both of these groups in the past, but that's not a guarantee that they can always be fooled. The president during the civil war reminded us that "you can't fool all of the people all of the time". The Democrats and Republicans apparently don't believe that. Instead, most of them got their political training at the P.T. Barnum School of Politics whose motto is the well-known "there is another sucker born every minute".

But I would offer another, more appropriate motto for the middle-class party banner, namely "Fool me once, shame on you - fool me twice shame on me". In order for the interests of the majority of Americans to be represented, a new political party representing the interests of the American middle-class must be formed, take over the government, and restructure our laws and amend the Constitution to prohibit minority special interest groups like the rich and the poor (Republicans and Democrats) from using their minority status to control the lives of the majority of citizens in this nation.

The easiest (for the time being) alternative is to do nothing, (it's always an alternative) and let conditions for the middle-class citizens continue to deteriorate to the extent that an internal revolution, using guns, is eventually required for the middle-class to take back what has been taken from them.

The more logical (and less violent) choice is to form another political party, and relegate the two present special interest parties (Democrats and Republicans) to splinter groups, which they already are in fact, in terms of voting power, at all levels of government.

Once in power, the new party should not be expected to be vindictive and purposely work to rub the noses of Democrats and Republicans in the dirt, even though they might both deserve some of that as repayment for the past bad things they have done to the middle-class Americans who have been paying the bills they have rung up to pay off their special interest friends.

It is logical to assume, that, since the middle-class majority has all along been paying the bills for both of these groups, the middle-class majority has already demonstrated a naturally charitable nature, and could be expected to continue helping both of these two special-interest groups to a reasonable extent in the future, as they always have in the past. The only change would be that it would be the party representing the middle-class Americans, instead of one of the two small special-interest parties now controlling things, that got to decide what "reasonable" meant.

But, more than laws and Constitutional amendments will be needed

It is important not to allow ourselves to fall into the old attorney trap of thinking that all of our problems can be solved through enactment of laws, at the Constitutional level, or any other level. Actually, the biggest problems are probably largely outside the scope of any law to address successfully. Laws (good laws that is) are only supposed to provide a foundation, and framework, upon which other personal actions can build.

An example might be the huge problem facing us (worldwide) in terms of unrestrained population growth. Part of that problem can, on a country by country basis, be addressed by enactment and enforcement of laws. Part of that problem can't be successfully addressed through enactment of laws.

In-migration laws can be established that limit the amount of population increase in a country from citizens of other countries moving out of their native country, into another country. Walls can be built to enforce the in-migration limits This has been accomplished successfully more than once in the past. The great wall of China was constructed to keep foreigners, and foreign invading armies, out of China. It has worked successfully toward that end, for more than two thousand years. More recently, the Berlin wall was constructed to keep West Berliners out of East Berlin, and vice versa. It worked too. Thus in-migration can be limited through enactment (and enforcement) of laws, and by putting up physical barriers. But that is much less than half of the overall problem relating to population growth.

The greater element relating to population growth has to do with population increases occurring because more people are being born than are dying each year, coupled with technological advances enabling average life spans to increase. Of course we could pass laws prohibiting more than (x) children to a family. We could attach tax surcharges to families having more than the prescribed (x) number of children. We could pass laws terminating life for citizens unable to take care of themselves. We could pass laws rationing fuel and food so that large families suffered more than smaller families. We could pass laws limiting the size of family dwellings, so that large families would be cramped while small families would have room to spare.

There are three things wrong with these approaches. First, they would not work (for every government action, there is an equal and opposite citizen reaction). Second, they wouldn't be fair. Third, they would be complex and difficult (if not impossible) to enforce, verify, and administer. Passing laws is not a solution to this part of the population growth problem. So what might work?

Well, we might try <u>education</u> on a <u>massive</u> scale!

Instead of pussyfooting around the problem, ignoring it, denying it, pretending it doesn't exist, pretending it is not important, pretending that it is inevitable, or pretending that we will all somehow manage, through some as yet unknown technology breakthrough, to just keep sailing along, resource-wise, when there are 20 billion people inhabiting the planet; we might try bringing the problem out into the open.

If we can spend tens of billions annually on something like controlling access to a few narcotics, which affect a relative handful of people, why not at least consider spending as much or more, educating our population, and that of other countries, about the much greater dangers inherent in excessive population growth, which affects everyone on the planet?

The instinct for self-preservation is among the most powerful most animals, including us humans, exhibit. When we encounter danger, our natural reaction is to protect ourselves, and our families. In this respect most humans are more alike than they are different. Given the facts, most people would voluntarily act to reduce population growth if they were able to understand the disastrous consequences for not doing so to them, personally, and to their families, and in fact, to the future of humans as a species on this planet.

This is an area of common concern (preservation of the species) that we share with people all over the world. It is therefore a problem area we might (and should) be able to cooperate in solving. Part of the educational effort, should there ever be one, would include helping people all over the world understand that overpopulation does not necessarily involve lots of people living in a small space, but rather that overpopulation exists whenever there is an imbalance between the number of people and the amount of locally available resources (and jobs) available to meet their needs.

There will probably continue to be ongoing debate regarding birth control and abortion, and anything else that might be used at the individual level to cut back on population growth, and with, or without, control mechanisms some people might never get with the program. Some religious organizations might resist, and direct their followers to do likewise. But, the very great majority of individual turtles probably would see the benefits of going along voluntarily. Recent experience relating to broad segments of at least one prominent church that historically espouses unlimited reproduction, has been seen to backfire, as members of that faith quietly just decided on their own to implement birth control measures within their own families. Public condemnation would make those who chose to continue toward contributing to the problem, rather than becoming a part of the solution, pay a price for doing so. And, paychecks and welfare checks certainly wouldn't stretch as far for families electing to practice unlimited childbirth.

The bottom line here though, is that laws alone will not be enough to solve the population growth problem, or to even alleviate the symptoms associated with it, long term.

The second great problem facing us (devaluation of human labor) can likewise not be completely solved through enactment of laws. Government could, if it so desired, return to a point in time where government interceded to balance the interests of management and labor. Tariffs could be raised, minimum wages could be increased, management could be made to give striking workers their jobs back after strikes ended, and the anti-trust laws could be used to stop mergers that resulted in job loss to workers of the merged company.

If this path were taken the current degradation in wages for American workers could be stopped, and possibly reversed over time. But, actions like these by the government would cause campaign contributions to stop abruptly for those voting for such measures, and other countries would probably respond as they did in the late 1920's by imposing high tariffs of their own on goods made here in America, thereby touching off another worldwide trade war. American exports would suffer, and the foreign element of some American manufacturer's sales would be reduced, causing some worker layoffs to result.

Finally, government siding with labor over management at any point in time for any reason would now be unacceptable to American-based mega-businesses, who might then elect to move even more of their jobs out of the country as a way of showing both the workers, and the government, which way the cow ate the cabbage (who's boss).

Enactment of laws designed to improve the plight of American workers would clearly not be acceptable to either management of American-based businesses, or the governments of nations with which we exchange trade. Because of this, the current U.S. Congress, whose members' political campaigns are largely financed by these groups, cannot be expected to take such actions. Instead, current elected leaders can be expected to dance around the problem, periodically arrange for the peasants to be thrown a token crumb in the way of a temporary tax cut, or a promised future increase in social security, or something of the like, while the problem continues to grow and eat away at the fabric of our society. We can expect no meaningful help from any existing branch of government headed by either Democrats or Republicans.

That just won't happen.

So, what's a middle-class American working turtle to do? Here, I have some good news for You. Even without amending the U.S Constitution, enacting any laws, or writing letters to any elected officials, this problem is absolutely solvable. Fairly painlessly, and relatively quickly.

There may be other solutions to this problem, but I will hazard a guess that no other solutions will be as elegant as the one I will offer here for your consideration. It is foolproof.

- It cannot be defeated by any government actions.

- It does not require any action at all on the part of any elected official, which is good because most of them have been brainwashed, and are powerless to help.

- If elected officials don't like it, there is nothing they can do individually or collectively to stop it from being implemented.

- It doesn't give any foreign government a reason to retaliate against our government from a trade standpoint.

- American-based, multi-national businesses are powerless to stop its implementation and certain success.

- It does not require union assistance, which is good, since unions have become impotent in the extreme.

- Lobbyists are completely powerless to stop it.

Only one thing can stop the solution proposed here from being successful. That would be if American middle-class working turtles decided not to implement it. Make no mistake, problem number two must be solved, or the American middle-class will continue to decline, and will become totally extinct over the next two to three decades, and the American Dream will not be reborn.

American middle-class turtles may choose to ignore it, and, in so doing, let the Dream die forever. Or they may choose to solve it, and in so doing, cause the Dream to be reborn for them and their families. But every American middle-class working turtle must choose to either be part of the solution, or be part of the problem.

Fair warning: after reading what follows, the option will no longer exist for you to claim that you didn't know what you could have done to solve the problem of devaluation of the labor of American middle-class working turtles…

Just say no!

That's the foolproof solution to this problem. Here's why:

Paradoxically, the same companies that are routinely exporting the most (good) U.S. jobs to foreign countries, are still among those that are the most dependent on the American middle-class worker turtles to continue supporting them, to keep buying their products produced by foreign workers, and, in fact, to keep them alive. On the one hand, the companies exporting American jobs are stabbing their former employees in the back, while, at the same time, asking their victims to be understanding of their problems on a "global scale", and to please continue buying their products, produced by the foreign workers that their jobs were given away to. The bottom line is this: at this point in time, the U.S. companies involved in exporting jobs to foreign countries, still need the American middle-class worker, more than the American middle-class workers need them.

While American-based businesses are free to build factories and/or contract for third party assembly wherever the labor is cheapest, they still can only sell their products in countries where the citizens have enough disposable income with which to buy them. Right now, and for the next few years (only) that means that they must sell between thirty and fifty percent of their total worldwide output to workers in the United States of America. If their American market dried up, and sales to workers in America weren't there to provide them the revenues with which to pay off their huge global-expansion-based debts, many of these companies would fail. Very quickly.

The average U.S.-based multi-national company faced with a sudden, total loss of the U.S.-worker market, could not survive for a single year.

The American middle-class worker can win back his or her livelihood and a decent standard of living, and restore opportunity for his or her children, by simply refusing to buy the products of companies that are exporting their workforce to other countries, and refusing to buy the products of foreign companies that have driven American industries out of business by undercutting their prices. If it isn't made in America, just don't buy it. Just say no.

Look at the "made-in" label on manufactured goods before you buy them. If it doesn't say "Made in the U.S.A. ", just don't buy it. Find one that is made in America if you can, and buy that one instead, even if it costs a bit more. If you can't find one that is made in America and there is any way at all that you could get along without it, do without. You may even save some money by not buying a few things you don't really have to have to get by.

It's not as hard as it might sound. Life can go on without $90 tennis shoes with special soles. Life might even be improved if we went without TV for a while. There are still a (very) few American made pocket calculators and watches. Kids hearing would be better if there were no Walkman radios and CD players. American made cars are just as good as foreign cars. Better even, if you count the fact that American workers were used to build them. The same goes for most other kinds of electronic equipment from phones to computers. If you own a construction company, insist on American-produced building products. We can rebuild our steel industry and electronics industry if we try. Heck, we invented these industries. We should be able to re-invent them and take them back if we really try.

Well, that's it. That is all that has to be done. No elections are needed. No legislative actions are required. No waiting period has to be observed. No-one's permission has to be obtained in advance. You don't even need to write a letter to American businesses telling them you have stopped buying their products until they start making them back here in America. They will know when they see that sales aren't enough to cover expenses, and that they are going bankrupt. They will figure it out quickly enough.

And they will move to restore sales by (quickly) moving manufacturing operations back to America. If they don't, they will perish.

What's the catch?

There is just one catch. **Time**. The large multi-national companies are betting that laziness and apathy (remember "the nothing" from The Never Ending Story) on the part of middle-class American working turtles, combined with a reluctance on the part of American middle-class working turtles to accept any temporary inconveniences, no matter how small, that might occur during the struggle, will buy them enough time to build up disposable income in some other countries, to the point that they no longer will have to rely on the American market to keep them alive.

It might not take all that long to accomplish such a change in market dynamics. Consider China, where living standards are very poor when compared to those in the United States. There are almost five times as many Chinese citizens as there are American citizens.

It stands to reason that if China's average standard of living were only to be improved by 20%, the net effect would be to create a new market as great as presently exists in the USA. Once that point is reached, the American-based multi-national companies will no longer feel threatened by the loss of the American middle-class worker market, and will have little incentive to do anything at all in terms of acting to improve the economic well-being of America's middle-class working turtles and their families.

Time is, therefore, of the essence.

Nothing in this solution to the problem of American middle-class workers seeing their labors devalued bodes ill for workers in other countries. American multi-national businesses would still be free to invest their profits, made from selling goods worldwide (including in the U.S.), in whatever other country they wished, and in the process help that country improve its lot in life too. That's how the U.S. got its start, and it's only fair that U.S. companies now help some of the "emerging" countries get started on a path out of poverty too.

But, American-based, multi-national companies should not expect to have American's whose jobs they are giving away to workers in other countries, willingly sacrifice themselves and their families, and their futures, in order to just help the multi-national companies build up worker standards of living, and markets, in other countries, 20-30 years sooner than they otherwise might.

China is a large enough market, that once its average citizen standard of living is the equal of ours today, they will not need the American Market to any extent. So is India. So is Russia. And, there are others. And, we should wish them all well in bettering themselves. At the same time, we should not allow the example that was the American Dream, and the American middle-class to be sacrificed toward that end, just for the sake of expediency, and to satisfy the immediate greed of a few.

Predictable Effects of Just Saying No

If every American middle-class worker, employed, unemployed, and especially the under-employed, would just do this one thing (just say no), without exception, for a maximum of 36 months' time, all starting on July 4, 2016, here are the predictable effects on a number of symptoms of decline now troubling our society:

The benefits accruing from solving problem number two, would be significant. These same benefits would also define the acceptance criteria to be applied once the solution was implemented. If these benefits did not accrue the solution would be considered invalid, and we would then go back to step one, and start over.

(1) The good paying manufacturing jobs that have been exported to other countries would begin quickly returning to America, providing a way for The American Dream to be fully

restored by July 4, 2026, regardless of what else might happen in government circles.

(2) The national debt (now about $7 trillion dollars) would be able to be completely eliminated within fifteen years' time, with or without a balanced budget amendment. As the total amount of the nation's debt is reduced, tax dollars now used to pay interest on the debt can be diverted to other, more productive, uses.

(3) Taxes, as a percent of gross national product could eventually be permanently lowered between 15% and 20% since there would be no recurring payments needed for either principal or interest after the debt was paid off.

(4) Total tax revenues to government at all levels would increase, even as tax rates were lowered, due to significantly higher wages being earned by millions of middle-class American workers.

(5) Tax payments needed to pay for welfare might be reduced, but would certainly stop increasing, since millions more workers who are now being paid so little that they are still below the poverty level, would finally be able to raise themselves out of poverty. Welfare of some kind will remain necessary so long as technology continues to displace more workers than it is capable of creating new jobs (at equal or better pay) for.

(6) Sufficient money would be available to provide for meeting the needs relating to expected growth in the retirement and healthcare areas for older citizens (by some means) which will inevitably occur as medical breakthroughs continue to expand average life expectancy.

(7) Sufficient money would become available to provide a safety net for millions more working citizens who have already been displaced through past government actions that resulted in their jobs already having been given away to someone in another country, or merged out of existence, and for whom, in the short term, and possibly also in the longer term, there will still not be enough jobs

available to lift them out of poverty. (This could take ten to twenty years to complete, maybe more).

(8) Sufficient money would become available to pay for effective enforcement measures relating to stopping illegal in-migration into America. This would, over time, reduce the glut of illegal in-migrant labor now available to fill "first job" opportunities, and some ongoing manual labor jobs, which has served to drive pay for these jobs to an all-time low.

(9) Criminal activities would be reduced significantly on a per-capita basis, due to America again being able to offer many more of its least advantaged citizens an alternative to crime, as a way out of poverty.

(10) Costs related to law enforcement would be reduced significantly on a per-capita basis, freeing up tax revenues for other, more productive uses.

(11) Single parent homes would decline significantly on a per-capita basis, since for millions of families the possibility of two high-enough paying jobs would finally provide a real basis for holding a home and family together.

Speaking of jobs, here are some questions about whose JOB it is to see to it that the solutions to the problems facing us (including this one) get implemented:

Question Number One

Just whose job is it anyway, restoring the American Dream for your family, protecting your family's income, and restoring opportunity for your children, and your grandchildren?

Question Number Two

Are you willing to let a small group of elected officials, part of an elitist government, most of whom were endowed at birth and continually thereafter with significant unearned advantages in life, and most of whom have no first-hand experience, understanding, or appreciation of the problems visited upon the working middle-class in America over the past forty years' time by the Federal government; and who individually receive significant sums of money for voting in a manner that is diametrically opposed to the interests of most of their constituents; to be the sole determiners of the economic well-being of your family, and the outcome of your future, and the future of your children and your grandchildren?

Question Number Three

Aren't some decisions just too important to be left up to a very small handful of elite elected officials, the majority of who have repeatedly shown themselves to be completely out-of-touch with your personal circumstances?

Question Number Four

And, if so, isn't this one of them?

Necessary but not Sufficient

Enacting the previously described Constitutional amendments is also a necessary, but not sufficient, element in solving problem number three, that being the systematic exclusion of ordinary citizens from the decision making processes most relevant to determining the outcome of their lives.

Enactment of the Constitutional amendments is necessary from the standpoint that once the middle-class has acted to restore the American dream on other fronts, those with a thirst for power could, and probably would, otherwise act to restore the conditions that caused the Dream to come undone earlier (as they have now done), unless somehow precluded from doing so by law. That is to say that the new elected leaders of the majority (Mid-American) party might not be themselves beyond becoming corrupted, once in office. They might well just ultimately replace one elitist-oligarchy with another elitist-oligarchy.

The Constitutional amendments suggested here would provide an ongoing barrier against the few again being able to make the most important decisions completely on behalf of themselves and their friends, and completely at the expense of the many, once the Dream was restored. As noted in the discussion of alternatives that might be employed relating to problem number two (just say no) there are actions that average citizens can take at other levels to improve things. Even at the federal level, citizens have a non-binding measure of recourse through petitioning congress, and American middle-class citizens now also have the tools needed to form and operate a third political party that has their interests at heart.

Limitations in technology available to previous generations made it difficult, if not impossible, for citizen initiatives, at the Federal level, to be successfully accomplished. The constraints of distance, and communication difficulty, previously put all the cards in the hands of elected officials. It was simply not feasible to try coordinating a national drive to petition Congress. The logistics would be roughly the equivalent of carrying on an election for the Presidency.

However, within the past ten years' time, while the rules relating to petitioning Congress haven't changed, just about everything else in the world has. Specifically, there is now a nationwide and global electronic mail system in place (actually there are several) that allows individuals all over the world to interact easily.

Conducting a national campaign for any purpose has now been made not only possible, but economically feasible for the average middle-class citizen. Of course it still takes a lot of time, on someone's part, but otherwise, just about anyone with a PC and a modem can set up a national bulletin board, and communicate easily with other citizens having similar interests, wherever they may be located.

These technological changes have now made it possible, for the first time in our country's history, for citizens to directly unite to petition congress, and in the process begin taking (back) a greater measure of control over the outcome of their lives. Technology has, in the past several years' time, been used in some ways that benefited us, and also in some ways that have had disastrous effects on the lives of many American middle-class turtles. But the biggest potential advantages of technology have been ignored.

The ignored advantages have to do with how everyday citizens can use technology to improve their economic well-being, and to positively influence the outcome of their lives, and the lives of future generations. The best way to do this would be for average American middle-class citizens to now employ existing technology to organize a political party that represents their interests. Currently, the Republicans represent the interests of between five and ten percent of the wealthiest American citizens, and the Democrats represent the interests of between ten and twenty percent of the poorest American citizens. There is currently no political organization that represents the remaining seventy to eighty-five percent of the American citizens in the middle.

America on Line, Google, Microsoft, and the Internet and its Worldwide Web, combined with the time of a few "bulletin board administrators" contributing their time and expertise in each state, would allow a national organization to be formed virtually overnight.

Meetings could include everybody in the country, without anybody having to leave home to attend. "Web Pages" can be easily established for those desiring to serve as elected officials under the banner of the new party, at all levels of government. Questions can be asked one-on-one by any member, of any prospective candidate, with the questions and answers made available to everybody who is interested (blogs). It would be the equivalent of a nationwide town hall. Of course, some "local and regional" electronic bulletin boards could also be established to handle "town meetings" at other levels too.

This is not meant to be a precise blueprint for action. Rather it is here being suggested as a viable alternative solution to problem number three, and some of the others we are facing right now. In order to get the Constitution amended in a way that restores the ability of middle-class citizens to directly impact the decision-making process (without their thoughts first going through either a Democrat or Republican "filter"), it will be necessary for the turtles in the middle to have their own political party.

When confronted with the possibility of a third party that actually represents the turtles in the middle, both the Democrats and Republicans can be expected to quickly (but temporarily) "morph" into centrists themselves, and in the process try to represent themselves as champions of those in the middle. Turtles in the middle would be wise to not trust either Democrats or Republicans when they promise to represent the interests of the turtles in the middle. They have repeatedly lied in the past in this regard. Remember the turtle motto: "fool me once, shame on you, fool me twice, shame on me".

Once the turtles in the middle have their own political party, and it is (will be) the majority party, it will not so often be necessary to petition Congress on a massive, nationwide scale. Until the turtles in the middle have their own party, and are in the majority, at all levels throughout government, petitions to congress will be necessary if legislation is to have any chance at all of being enacted that treats the turtles in the middle fairly. Remember too, that petitions can be used to overturn laws enacted below the level of the U.S. Constitution What this means is that American middle-class turtles already have available to themselves, through the petition process, the means to possibly affect a lot of legislation that has already been enacted that is to their detriment.

Realistically, Petitioning Congress may be <u>a long shot option</u>. Even though technology now exists to electronically gather names on a petition nationwide quickly, (securely and without possibility of abuse in terms of invalid signatures), congress may well choose to ignore the petitions on the grounds that the signatures were electronically recorded, rather than by having citizens signing in ink on paper. Congress has the option of ignoring even citizen petitions signed in ink on paper. Congress has often chosen in the past to ignore the wishes of those who sent them there, and they can always do so again.

Even if the congress were to act on a petition and pass a law based upon it, the law would still have to be signed by the president, who could refuse to do so. Were any of these things to happen after submitting a citizen petition to congress, the citizens would be back at square one, having as an alternative only replacing the congress and president. That game is, as we have seen, presently stacked in favor of the two existing political parties (Republicans and Democrats).

On the other hand, a petition for redress of what citizens see as a problem, signed by any means (electronic or ink) by over 50% of all eligible voters, would, whether officially acceptable as to form or not, be damned hard to ignore. A Congress that chose to ignore such a petition, or a President that chose to ignore such a petition, would likely become a "lame duck" Congress, or President, almost immediately. The media would continue to keep the matter of the Congress and/or President thumbing their nose at the public alive. Cartoonists would have a heyday illustrating the arrogance of government, and following the next election, the chairs in Congress and the White House would probably have a lot of new names on them.

Petitions would be very difficult, if not impossible, to ignore or refuse to act on. So, at least as an interim measure, it might be a good idea to implement a technologically advanced system for gathering petition names on a nationwide basis, and petition congress relating to some of the most pressing areas needing reform.

Some examples follow. Again, the examples are designed to be just that, examples, rather than being a complete list. I've just picked a few here that are well known enough to easily make the point.

1. Most current tax policies, including the collection methods for taxes, were established through legislation at a level below the U.S. Constitution. Amounts are set by the government for things like Medicare and Medicaid, and Social Security cannot be changed except by congressional action, since only congress may appropriate money. Citizens could absolutely act, through petitioning congress, to amend them or abolish them completely.

2. American middle-class turtles can act through petitioning Congress to pass laws at the Federal level (and other levels too) that require the government to establish an electronic government activity monitoring system and vote tabulating system like that described in proposed Constitutional amendment number eight; thereby bringing the lobbyist's activities out into the full light of day, and easing citizens' ability to effectively petition Congress on matters of redress.

3. American middle-class turtles can, through petitioning congress, direct Congress to act to modify the laws relating to enforcement of labor-management laws, acting to again make it mandatory that "struck" businesses restore the jobs of striking workers, once the strike is ended, thereby restoring for production workers some ability to have a say in their own destiny.

4. American middle-class turtles can, through petitioning congress, act to have Congress set the standard work week for worker turtles, and establish the minimum wage at whatever they believe it should be.

5. American middle-class turtles can, through petitioning congress, act to have congress amend the enforcement requirements of anti-trust laws relating to mergers and acquisitions, and in the process determine the rate at which employees can be rendered

"redundant" and their jobs eliminated when mergers and acquisitions occur between mega-businesses.

6. American middle-class turtles can, through petitioning congress, direct congress relating to how they wish environmental laws to be enforced, perhaps even mandating that for significant cases the decision be reached by way of a national referendum voted on by all turtles.

7. American middle-class turtles can, through petitioning congress, direct congress to enact laws regulating things like awards for product liability and malpractice cases (tort law) and limiting attorney fees to some percentage of the total award. Such an action would have the effect of reducing insurance premiums and costs of living in general substantially for all of the turtles in the pond.

8. American middle-class turtles can, through petitioning congress, direct the congress to pass laws that mandate the legal system to provide competent attorneys for individuals who feel they have been wronged in civil matters, as they do to defendants in criminal matters. Currently, government and moneyed organizations can win in all civil suits over non-moneyed individuals or groups of individuals, regardless of which party is in the right, since they have the money for lawyers and filing fees. Currently, unfair civil actions, and the inability to protect oneself from wrongful civil actions by government and moneyed interests because of lack of funding, can (and often does) result in damaging citizens lives to at least as great an extent as if they were robbed at gunpoint and beaten and crippled.

American middle-class turtles could act through petitions to congress to level this playing field. (And, there might finally be something for all those extra lawyers to do that was constructive).

9. American middle-class turtles could, through petitioning congress, direct congress to limit the ability of the Federal Reserve and Treasury to inflate the currency supply to a level consistent with growth in the population and the private sector GDP, and to limit the amount of currency that the government could take from circulation

for its own use by borrowing or otherwise. (This one is a real long shot. It is likely that both the Congress and the President would ignore such a petition, even though they would be thrown out at the next election if they did so. Who controls the money, controls the power, and both the Presidency and Congress are mostly about power. They would probably rather go out swinging, than see their spending power reduced in any way).

10. American middle-class turtles can, through petitioning congress, direct the Congress to amend the constitution and/or otherwise act in a manner to limit some powers of Congress and the Executive branch members, or at least share them with the people at large. The ability to appropriate the ways in which taxes (and borrowed money) is spent by the government is reserved (right now) solely to the Congress. Without amending the Constitution, Congress will retain that right. However, if citizens petitioned congress indicating what the majority wished to see done in the way of spending on things like welfare programs, defense spending, Medicare, Medicaid, or whatever; and the congress ignored the wishes of the majority, and it was made part of the public record, their chances at getting re-elected would be about zip, in the next election. And, remember, petitions are not just a form of polling. Petitions would represent an official vote by the whole of American society. (polling doesn't count ... voting counts).

11. The American middle-class turtles can, through petitioning Congress, act to direct Congress to pass non-binding resolutions regarding things like deployment of military forces around the world and intervening in other countries civil wars. Absent a Constitutional amendment limiting the president's and congress' abilities to declare and finance wars, the executive branch of government would retain the ability to commit troops to action anywhere in the world as he or she saw fit. However, if this was done contrary to the wishes of a majority of the citizens, as indicated by a legitimate petition to Congress, endorsed by a majority of Americans eligible to vote, congress would be very careful about appropriating money for such purposes, and the President who ignored the resolution would immediately be rendered a "lame duck" on the spot, and incapable of

governing for the rest of his or her term, since he or she would almost certainly be ousted at the next election, whenever that occurred

12. American middle-class citizens can act, through petitioning Congress, to direct Congress to modify established elections laws that mandates that petitions to Congress, like those described here, are handled through an electronically aided system that allows citizens to sign petitions to Congress, and vote, from the comfort of their homes, as well as maintaining a quick deployment of petition signing and election booths (and staffing) for those who can't (yet) vote from home electronically; and further, mandates that the government provide one or more government cable channels for use only by opposing parties to all measures being voted on at the federal level, with all parties mandated to have equal time allocated to them. It is not possible to justify logically, the government's continuing adherence to, and perpetuation of, an election process that so clearly tilts the playing field in favor of those with money to advertise on commercial TV. It can only be rationalized by the incumbents and spin doctors who benefit from keeping things as they are.

Public television is already in place (PBS) that would allow all candidates equal time for expressing their views, but it is currently limited to a single channel committed to providing a limited alternative to commercial television shows. PBS could be expanded, relatively cheaply to PBS2 and PBS3 (or more) in a manner that provided equal access to all candidates and all initiative measures, at a relatively low level of taxpayer expense.

Of course, the established networks would cry foul, since some lucrative campaign advertising revenues would be lost to them, and elected officials already in office might vote against it, since they already have the money available to them to play by the existing rules which favor money over ideas.

But, by taking the petitioning route, citizens can perhaps provide congress with the backbone to do the right thing.

13. American middle-class turtles can, through petitioning Congress, direct the Congress to act to modify enabling language in the Civil Rights laws most recently passed in a manner that does away with "reverse" discrimination. Both the original Civil Rights act of the 1960's and a later "expanded" Civil Rights Act enacted in the late 1970's were passed by Congress and were not the result of an amendment to the Constitution. They can therefore be modified by congressional action alone. Keep in mind, however, that any law passed or modified by way of petitioning congress, can be later nullified by a later congressional action. That is why the Constitution also ultimately has to be amended - to keep Congress from later undoing citizen initiated actions that are not to the liking of the next congress and/or president.

This, if we think about it, is why the most of the amendments to the Constitution were drawn up in the first place. A primary intent of the U.S. Constitution, at the time it was constructed by the founding fathers, was to put into place a system of government that provided the citizens a way of protecting themselves from bad acts committed against them by their own government. The main body of the Constitution provides checks and balances between the three internal powers of the government. Most of the amendments (including all of the first 10) provide another check and balance system between the overall government and the citizens themselves.

There are admittedly more opportunities than have been presented here for using petitions to congress to both undo bad laws put on the books in the past, and to pass some new ones that would help average citizens regain control of their lives and economic well-being. But I have on purpose limited the examples to some that directly speak to one or more of the eight problems defined earlier.

Acting to put into place a political party dedicated to furthering the interests and well-being of the average middle-class American turtles, when combined with acting through petitions along the lines suggested here, when further combined with a massive educational effort aimed at keeping population growth within long term sustainable levels, and voting with our pocketbooks by refusing to buy goods made outside the United States, would, I think, provide at least one "solution set" that would enable the American Dream to be restored.

Once restored, the new Constitutional amendments would maximize the probability that it would stay alive.

Actually, though these represent five logical "steps" in the problem solving process, and each "step" has more than one component in its makeup, this "solution set" may represent a fairly elegant one.

We need to keep in mind that over the past seventy-five years' time, the government has taken literally hundreds of actions (perhaps thousands) many of which can, in the light of hindsight, now be seen to have been harmful to the majority of American middle-class workers. If a five step solution set, can possibly be used to successfully rescind the acts that hindsight shows were more detrimental than beneficial to most Americans, and in the process cause the restoration of the great American Dream, perhaps it deserves some consideration.

There will certainly be other solutions proposed as well. Hopefully lots of them. Those solutions coming from Democrats and Republicans may be considered the most suspect with regard to their real intentions, and with respect to the probability of their ever working at all. Neither of these (minority) parties has done all that much of lasting value over the past seventy-five years, and when they have done something worthwhile, it has often been an unintended outgrowth of something they intended to work out differently than it actually did.

It was mentioned earlier, but it's worth repeating again. When solutions to longstanding problems defy conventional wisdom applied to solving them, It will usually be the case that the conventional wisdom of the day is, itself, fatally flawed. It is advisable to remain open to "unconventional" solutions that are proposed. Unconventional proposals may, or may not, ultimately bear up under closer scrutiny, but it is inadvisable to simply reject them out of hand just because they are "unconventional". The wiser approach would be to treat ALL proposed solutions as if they might be equally valid at the outset.

Later applying the acceptance criteria against all proposed solutions will cause some proposed solutions to be discarded as either completely invalid or unworkable, or perhaps just too unwieldy. But, we are wise to let the process work objectively toward that end. Maybe an example could be used here to illustrate the point. Mind you, I'm not proposing this as a solution (it might work though). I'm just putting it down here to help you switch gears a bit, over from "conventional" thinking, to "unconventional" thinking. For my example I've picked a topic that got a lot of press back in 1992, 1993, 1994, and 1995, and has more recently surfaced again.

The topic is healthcare.

Conventional thinking holds that the primary problem with healthcare is that not enough people are adequately covered by medical insurance. The proposed solutions have therefore centered finding a way for everybody to have an adequate level of insurance, so that when a need arises, regardless of age or ability to pay, all citizens get a "reasonable" level of medical care, and don't have to dip into their own pockets to pay for (much of) it.

Let's see if you have been paying attention. First step, has the problem been defined properly?

The answer of course is (big surprise) no. Inadequate insurance (and healthcare) for some citizens is not a problem. It is a symptom. Inadequate insurance (and healthcare) is the result of six problems coming together to create a group of symptoms, one of the most noticeable of which is some citizens not getting needed medical treatment. So, let's look at what the real problems are that are resulting in a lack of healthcare for some citizens.

First, the population continues to expand faster than we can create properly scaled health facilities to treat people.

Second, advances in medical technology and the treatment of diseases have expanded the average lifespan of people in our country (and some other countries too).

Third, government has assumed what used to be the personal responsibility of people to take control of their own lives, and has also taken from the citizens, in the way of taxes, the money needed for them to pay their own way and control their own lives (including paying for their own healthcare).

Fourth, the government has helped large businesses devalue the labor of American middle-class workers, by way of endorsing job-killing mergers, by siding with management over workers during strikes, and by making American workers compete directly with workers in countries who have terrible standards of living, thereby lowering the American workers' standard of living and leaving them still less money with which to take care of themselves.

Fifth, the government's policies relating to inflating the amount of currency in circulation has caused the average cost of living, including healthcare costs, to grow at a rate that is more than twice the average growth in wages paid to workers, over the past forty years' time.

Sixth, the government's attempts to guarantee outcomes for some, at the expense of both money and opportunity for everybody else, has had an immensely detrimental and costly effect on this symptom in particular.

Insurance (by any means) is not the sole answer to this problem.

In fact, insurance may well be seen as part of the problem itself. In 1940 less than 25% of the people in this country had health insurance. A visit to the hospital might run $60 a day, including drugs and doctor visits. Aspirin, which the hospitals got free from Mr. Beyer, were free to patients in the hospital. Doctors made house calls, and a house call cost an average of $6. Office calls were less. There was no such thing as "malpractice" insurance. Some incompetent physicians occasionally hurt a few people before they were drummed out of the community, and people asked other people about a prospective doctor's qualifications before electing to go to a particular practitioner.

Now, we fast forward to 2005. Over 70% of the people in the country have health insurance by some means (government, at work, or private). A visit to the hospital averages $2000 a day for less serious treatments, and up to $20,000 a day for more serious work. That doesn't include drugs, or doctor visits. In the hospital, a single Tylenol tablet, which Mr. Tylenol gives free to the hospitals, now costs a patient in the hospital $25. Doctors no longer make house calls at any price, and the average price of an office visit is $60+.

Malpractice insurance now represents about half of all amounts paid for medical treatment at every level. Incompetent physicians still occasionally hurt a few people, but they are no longer drummed out of business. Instead, the doctor's insurance company pays the injured parties a few million each, which the insurance company (and the doctor) later recover by raising their premiums and prices for subsequent office visits, and the incompetent doctor keeps his or her practice just like nothing ever happened. People are charged extra for being allowed to pick their own physician. In some forms of insurance patients don't get to pick their doctor at all.

In theory, the principal of insurance is that all contribute and share the risk of great loss, so that when a great loss occurs on the part of the few, the money of the many contributed in advance, can be used to meet the losses as they occur. Insurance was originally intended to cover only catastrophic losses. It was not originally intended to cover miniscule losses.

Ships like those bringing goods to America during our early years often had both the ship and its goods insured; the ship by the ship's owner, and the goods by the business promising delivery to America. In these instances, one of the major insurance providers like Lloyds of London would, on an individual basis, agree to accept the risk for a negotiated fee.

In 1940, very few people in this country had medical insurance of any kind. In those days "insurance" was more typically provided by large employers by way of engaging the services of a physician on a full or part time basis, as a "company doctor", for a set fee. Hospital bills were also covered by large employers out of (tax exempt) "sinking funds" compiled to meet these needs. The fees paid to salaried physicians were generally enough that physicians who were "company doctors" were among the better paid in whatever community they lived in. Most enjoyed high status and Country Club memberships.

Most communities had hospitals owned and operated by local businessmen and doctors. There was no such thing as "malpractice" insurance. Local hospitals accepted whatever the patient could offer in the way of monthly payments when a bill could not be paid in full upon discharge from the hospital, and local hospitals were, in fact, one of the few sources of "credit" available for any purpose outside of buying a home back then.

Now, fast forward to 2016. In 2016, when you check into a hospital, more time is spent making sure that the hospital won't have to extend credit, and that you can pay your bill through insurance, than is often spent in treating your health problem once you are admitted. Some hospitals even refuse to admit patients who can't pay through an insurance company. The same thing happens when you visit a doctor's office for the first time. Most small communities no longer have hospitals or treatment clinics.

The emphasis in healthcare has undergone a paradigm switch of huge proportions over the past fifty years. Medical service providers are still in it supposedly for the purpose of helping others, but the emphasis is now on "getting paid", getting paid more, getting paid more quickly, improving profits for the hospital chain's stockholders, and avoiding bankrupting lawsuits, more than it is serving the medical needs of the patient.

The conventional approaches to alleviating the symptoms (uninsured and therefore un-treated people) all center on deciding what kind of insurance system, we should have. Some advocate all government payments (socialized medicine). Others advocate an entirely private system (capitalistic). Still others advocate a hybrid part government - part private system where patients pick their own doctors, (capitalistic), but which is based upon government setting the standards and prices for treatment and payment of all bills (socialistic). Over the past thirty years, a lot of discussion relating to these three alternatives has taken place. All to no real avail.

These three alternatives have all been tried to varying degrees over the past thirty years' time. The "problem" that they are attempting to address remains in place, and is growing daily. The proponents of each of the alternatives believes that if just given more time and money, their proposed alternative would work out, even though there is no hard evidence whatsoever to support this contention on any of their parts. All right turtles, let's again see to what extent you have been paying attention. When the proposed solution fails in practice, what is the proper thing to do in the problem solving process? Right. Go back to step number one, and see if the "problem" has been properly defined. Give yourself a "way to go" award, if you got this one right.

The "conventional" wisdom being that the problem is that more people need insurance, than already have it, may be fatally flawed. It is certain that those involved in "solving" this problem have failed to define the problem. Perhaps even more disturbing is the obvious fact that even if their "diagnosis" of the "problem" was correct, they have already showed themselves to be failures in the step that calls for proposing alternative solutions. One alternative nobody is considering is the one that goes like this:

"Do Nothing".

But, given that the "solvers" don't even know what the real problem is, automatically applying the "do-nothing" alternative to it wouldn't necessarily get the desired results either. It's just disappointing to have to note that nobody involved even thought to include it as a possibility at any time over the past thirty to forty years when looking for solutions.

So, what might constitute an "unconventional" approach to alleviating this symptom of a society in decline? Well, for starters, we could go back to the beginning and work on getting a full definition of the problems causing the symptoms, including breaking them down into their individual elements, as we've done here. Then we could prepare a complete list of all possible solutions to each sub-problem. While doing it we would define the acceptance criteria for each sub-problem solution that the implemented solutions could later be objectively measured against. Then we could pick a "solution set" and implement it, and then later go back and see if we were right or not.

Believe it or not, using the scientific formula for problem solving would be considered "unconventional" at this point in time.

But, just for fun, let's take it a step further. Let's suppose we've studied until we arrived at a good definition of the problem and broken it down into its various elements. Let's further postulate that we've been brave enough to face up to reality insofar as abandoning failed solutions tried in the past. And let's go really all out here, and assume that we have not only looked at all the conventional possibilities, but that we have also purposely looked for solutions to the sub-problems that are contrary to conventional thinking.

Why? Because we know that when conventional thinking continually fails to provide valid solutions; the solution is probably only to be found by defying the conventional wisdom of the day. We have defined one of the "sub" problems, the government's meddling in the marketplace in general, and in the marketplace relating to providing healthcare in particular. The government's ineptness at negotiating prices, for anything, is well known and well documented.

Only in government would someone pay $400 for a simple hammer, or $700 for a toilet seat for an airplane, or $25 for a single Tylenol tablet that they could have for <u>free</u>. Government does this kind of thing all the time.

In three areas of health insurance that the government involves itself in (there are more than three) the government effectively sets the standards for prices charged and paid, by way of it's being both the biggest provider at the government level, and the biggest payer to the private level.

The three most notable health insurance areas that the government sets the standards for are hospital insurance, treatment at doctor's offices, and prescriptions. The government's skillful bargaining ability in these areas has really been responsible for putting health insurance on the map over the past forty years' time.

Prior to the government getting into the business, medical treatment was far more affordable than it now is, and an insurance company paying the bills was the exception, rather than the norm. The government now takes approximately 3% of <u>everybody's</u> gross income for purposes of providing limited insurance to <u>some</u>, and, arguably, they do this in a manner that is not very cost effective.

Now for the unconventional proposal: What if, instead of trying to have everybody covered under health insurance, for all kinds of medical expenses, we were instead to consider not allowing anybody to have bills for any kind of health treatment paid for by an insurer of any kind? Nobody has health insurance. No government insurance. No private insurance. No medical related insurance of any kind, for anybody.

When somebody gets sick, everybody shares the risk. Family, hospitals, doctors, prescription fillers, everybody. (It should be noted that this is only unconventional thinking by present day government standards). No insurance means no insurance. That would include insurance covering "malpractice". If there were no malpractice insurance, medical costs could drop by almost half, overnight.

Lawyers would have to take their chances when suing health providers. They might spend a lot of time, and collect nothing for their efforts. Hospitals could of course decide not to treat patients without money enough to pay at the time they were admitted, but then most mega-hospitals would go out of business overnight. When a mega-hospital closed down, local hospitals and clinics would re-emerge to take its place, owned and financed by local doctors and business people in communities that now have no hospitals or clinics at all.

This level of provider was driven out of business over the past twenty years by the mega-corps that now control over 95% of all hospitals in the country. Incompetent doctors would again be run out of town, and be penalized personally and financially for hurting people. There would be additional side benefits for those who stayed well. Every citizen could immediately begin to keep 3% more of his or her earnings, and could save it up for when it might be needed, whether for healthcare or other things.

Fraud and abuses by medical providers who have learned how to cheat the government's healthcare systems, that presently cost the taxpayers tens of billions of dollars each year, would stop overnight, and the money would go into taxpayer's pockets and the pockets of honest providers instead.

There would be no higher cost penalties for choosing your own doctor.

All of this is, of course, just a variation on the "do nothing" alternative, but at least within the last forty years, it has not once been considered, and it may well have some merit. If nothing else, it would provide a direct contrast in terms of measurable results down the road that could be directly compared with what has happened over the past four decades when trying the three "conventional" approaches.

The high cost of health treatment today is a classic marketplace cause and effect (supply and demand) study. The government's willingness (really insistence) relating to becoming an insurer of last resort for everything in the world that could possibly go wrong, from crop failure, to insuring home and business loans, to rebuilding homes lost in floodplains, to paying off depositors who put their savings in a risky business when the business goes belly-up, to paying $45 for a prescription in the United States, that is routinely sold across the counter in Mexico (by the same drug company) for $1, combined with the government's ability (and willingness) to just print up some more currency to pay for these kinds of things, has effectively removed all incentives for any business that gets paid by a government check to ever do anything except continually raise their prices.

The entirely predictable effect of this has been that prices relating to healthcare costs paid for by insurers, whether public or private, have skyrocketed completely out of control. Insurance companies have no incentive whatsoever to act to hold prices down. Regardless of statements to the contrary, the government has put up a target in the way of a COLA, a year to five years in advance of when it goes into effect, that primarily serves to tell insurance companies and medical service providers in advance, how much to raise their prices each year. Insurance companies are expert when it comes to hitting these targets.

The government, remember, profits <u>directly</u> from the increased costs of healthcare, since it gets to tax the growing income of the service -providers. The service -providers are unhurt long term, because next years' price increases for their services will reimburse them for last years' taxes-paid to the government.

Winners and losers

Under the present system, spawned by the conventional wisdom of the day, the Government wins, the Insurance companies win, and the Medical service providers win. Guess who loses?

Winning, Losing, Competition, and Valuing Work

Darwin's theory re: the evolution of species holds that all life at every level is essentially reduced to a single type of activity. Competition. In Darwin's view, this included all humans, and all human activity. There is some evidence to support this view, especially at the individual level, and even more especially among species lacking the ability to reason.

When it comes to individuals as members of groups having a common purpose, the Darwin view is seen not to be provable, in the mathematical sense. In mathematics, a single exception invalidates a proposed proof of a theory. In a relative few arguably successful human societies it can be seen first-hand that individual competition has been voluntarily placed second in importance to the goals of the society.

Perhaps the most successful society still on the planet is that constituted by the aboriginal tribes of Australia. They have had a single form of government and lifestyle for approximately 50,000 years, so far as we know. Their numbers are small, but they are remarkable in that no other society on earth, or style of government, has lasted much over a few hundred years. They have learned to exist in what many would think an inhospitable climate and terrain, disdaining material things, opting instead for what we would today term a "minimalist" lifestyle, in the extreme.

Of course, it depends on one's values, whether the aboriginal tribes are a "success" or not. If wealth is judged by how much currency one has, and other material measures, the aboriginal tribes are certainly failures. If other measures of wealth are used, they may perhaps be looked at as being quite successful.

What is not in dispute is that they have lived much as they do now, for about 500 centuries, and their average lifespan is believed to be about 100 years. They have few of the diseases most humans dread, and seem to have learned how to completely avoid things like stress.

Their society is based upon a high level of cooperation between members, and they have no formal government structure (or written laws) at all. In this, they are unique, and they are further unique in that they have avoided the "inevitable cycle" of government pondered by some of the greatest thinkers of the past three thousand years.

The Greek philosophers Plato and Aristotle viewed the battle between individual competition, and the need for societies to band together for the benefit of all members, as one which resulted in a predictable, naturally-evolving, "inevitable cycle" of government types. Anarchy led to monarchy, which led to Tyranny, which led to an Aristocracy, which led to Oligarchy, which led naturally to Democracy, which led naturally back to Anarchy.

Plato believed that the cycle could be interrupted by designing a government that made the cycle unnecessary. Aristotle believed that human nature was inherently so selfish and competitive, that the cycle could not be broken, and that mankind would always be subject to the wars and revolutions mandated by the struggle (competition) for wealth and power.

The "inevitable" natural evolution of government, through the cycle of government types noted by Plato and Aristotle, is, itself determined by competition.

In anarchy, each individual competes against all other individuals for whatever spoils are available. In a monarchy a charismatic individual exerts will over others by getting others to work for him or her and do his or her bidding, again competing for all available resources.

In a tyranny, the monarchy reaches to excess and ignores the suffering of those over which will is exerted, but is otherwise the same as a monarchy.

In aristocracies, the monarch (or tyrant) is forced to share power with other powerful leaders (aristocrats), while competing for control of all available wealth and resources.

Aristocracies tend to become oligarchies where the few profit at the expense of the many.

In Democracies, the powerful elite leaders (lords and aristocrats) are further forced to share power and resources with all other members of society. The most charismatic and capable individuals in democracies eventually refuse to have their will bent to serve others, or to share when they can through competition gain more wealth than average, and become anarchists. And so the cycle repeats itself.

Since the time of the Magna Carta, when British lords and aristocrats forced the monarchy to share power with them, based upon what they declared to be "inalienable" rights given by God to men, a series of formal governments hoping to "break the cycle" have come and gone around the world. Most have not lasted more than a couple of centuries. The United States, as a constitutionally ordered government has now been in place almost 230 years. The United States is officially labeled a "Republic".

The "Republic" was an idea put forth by Plato in his work by the same name. The idea behind a Republic is that once the stage of oligarchy is attained, benevolent lords and aristocrats who share power with the monarch <u>voluntarily</u> elect to also share wealth and power with all other members of society (workers). In this model, the need for citizens to overthrow the oligarchy and install in its place a Democracy is made unnecessary. In Plato's Republic, average citizens feel valued and participate in sharing the material wealth of the society, thus making further (r)evolution both unnecessary and undesirable. It being understood that once oligarchy gives way to Democracy, anarchy will not be far behind.

The United States originally operated as an aristocracy, but by 1940 had reverted to operating at the oligarchy level. The lords and aristocrats (congress and big business) still have control of all wealth and power. Even citizens owning property are typically indebted to those in power in significant ways.

Most homes and autos are mortgaged, rather than owned outright. The government takes over half of all income produced by citizens in the way of various "taxes" and "fees", while big business takes the rest in the form of allowing citizens to maintain a particular "standard of living" Most citizens retain little if any wealth for themselves. Many citizens have no real material wealth at all, after struggling a lifetime to obtain some. Then, when a well-off citizen dies, the government assesses a "death tax" (inheritance tax), and takes even more of whatever might be left from the estate of the deceased citizen.

Of course, the monarch and the lords and aristocrats are provided with ways to exempt themselves from most such taxes and treatment, in the laws that they pass. As "formal" governments go, the United States is already well advanced in age. The average length of time a major world power lasts, based on some formal system of government, is less than three hundred years.

Technology has always in the past served to shorten the time between cycles wherein the kind of government (oligarchy to democracy, etc.) changes. Within the next fifty years' time, the great American experiment will prove either Plato or Aristotle right. The smart money right now would probably be on Aristotle.

It may be that the greatest contribution made by the aboriginal tribes of Australia will be having set at least one example to illustrate that the "inevitable cycle of governments" is not really inevitable at all. Plato's view, combined with some hopefully voluntary, but if necessary forced, attitude adjustments on the part of some citizens, might allow the United States experiment in "republic"-based, free-enterprise capitalism to continue on indefinitely.

Without doubt the capitalistic economic- market model has shown itself to be the most effective at rapidly generating material wealth at all levels. Perhaps this occurs in some part because the capitalistic model simply accepts as axiomatic, Aristotle's (and Darwin's) view that individuals are by nature both selfish and competitive, and seeks to build on that.

However, Darwin's theory at the individual level represents anarchy in its truest form, and time and history tell us that social systems based upon anarchy cannot be long sustained. Tyrants, monarchs, and oligarchies can be overthrown by the masses of ordinary citizens, if the citizens ever decide to unseat them. History is replete with examples to show how true this is. The Magna Carta, the U.S. revolution in 1776, the overthrow of the czars in Russia in the early part of the 20th century, the Vietnamese kicking both France and the United States out of South Vietnam, and the dissolution of the USSR, are all fairly recent examples of ordinary citizens forcibly seizing control from those above them.

Toward the end of helping those with property keep it safe from seizure by the un-propertied masses, governments are instituted among peoples. The sole reason for ever forming any kind of government is to provide a system by which citizens at large are precluded from seizing property from the monarch or the lords. That includes the document that underlies our government, the U.S. Constitution. The trick is, of course, to be one of the Lords.

The U.S. Constitution is, among documents defining governments relation to the people it serves, unique. Its uniqueness lays in the fact that the framers provided in the original document, the means for ordinary citizens to periodically re-determine the balance points of power between the lords and aristocrats and the average citizens. Without resorting to force of arms through the elective and voting process being the most desirable option; but providing citizens with the ability to arm themselves and protect their interests forcibly if other measures failed.

The framers were propertied people, and were in the main seeking to protect themselves and their property from being taken by both the king of England, and ordinary citizens representing the poorest class in America at the same time.

The genius of the framers is that they recognized the inevitability of losing everything if the system of government did not legitimately hold out the opportunity for poor people to rise out of poverty based upon some combination of hard work and good fortune. They recognized that hope must remain present for all, or the government would not last, and that, from a selfish viewpoint, their wealth would disappear along with the government if it should fall. Better to allow some increase in the number of Lords, than to keep the number of Lords fixed at a low level, and risk losing everything through another revolution.

The framers were, as Darwin would agree, both competitive themselves, and as individuals perhaps about as selfish as any of us. But more importantly, they were men of reason and intellect. They wisely accepted as axiomatic that Plato's "inevitable cycle of government" would also occur in the United States, absent a mechanism in the Constitution itself that assured ongoing hope and opportunity for all citizens, and the ability for them to control the outcome of their own destinies, perhaps rising to the level of Lords themselves one day.

The framers of the Constitution, for the most part, were elitist in their views. Most considered the majority of citizens both lazy and unintelligent. They assumed (correctly as it turns out so far) that most citizens would be too lazy to often use the provisions in the Constitution put there expressly to allow them to take more control over their own destiny.

The framers were not only smart, they were clever. By making it possible (though a bit difficult) for citizens to take over the government by way of using Constitutionally mandated tools available to them; and relying on apathy and indolence on the part of the masses, the framers were at the same time able to hold out hope for all, by way of providing the legal means for citizens to override the wishes of the lords and aristocrats; but, realistically, with very little risk that the citizens would ever use the tools provided to them for doing so.

The Constitution defines our system of government as that of a "Republic", loosely modeled after Plato's dream of a utopian society, and further provides citizens with the tools needed to bend the will of the lords and aristocrats to that of the masses whenever they deem it necessary. When the government is deemed by the public at large to be corrupt, citizens have legal redress provided in the Constitution, through both non-violent and violent means.

The first choice is (or should be) the non-violent path. There is still sufficient time that, through using the elective process to put into place a government responsive to the will of the turtles in the middle, and amending the Constitution to provide for a somewhat greater sharing of power and decision making in government, with citizens becoming more directly involved in making the most important decisions affecting our society, that Plato's ideal society can be realized and preserved long term here in America.

But changing laws, and amending the Constitution, are only part of the solution to restoring the health of our country in either the long or short terms. Plato's view of a utopian society depended on the most privileged cooperating by voluntarily sharing wealth and power with the less fortunate (the benevolent aristocracy). Both Plato and Aristotle held the view that enacting laws that forced the privileged class to share with the less fortunate, was ultimately an exercise in futility. The privileged, they postulated, would always be able to avoid sharing, if they chose to, and laws enacted to force them to share would be somehow rendered unenforceable. Were these smart guys or what? Nevertheless, voluntary sharing was a necessary ingredient of Plato's utopian "Republic". Both agreed that, absent voluntary sharing of the wealth and power, the "inevitable cycle of governments" was unavoidable.

Aristotle just assumed that human nature being what it is, that the privileged ever deciding to voluntarily share their wealth and power with those less fortunate, would never happen. So far,

Aristotle has shown himself to be a pretty smart fellow. More than two thousand years have gone by since Plato and Aristotle discussed these matters, and not once, in all that time, has any propertied class voluntarily elected to share their wealth. The "inevitable cycle of government" defined by the Greeks 2300 years ago has continued unabated, as governments continue to come and go every three hundred years or so. (Sometimes less. The USSR only lasted about 70 years).

Laws passed to force privileged and propertied members of society to share with less fortunate members of society have been circumvented 100% of the time. All governments formed on the principle of forced sharing of the wealth have failed.

Measuring and Valuing work

The advent of the "industrial revolution", spawned in England, but developed to its fullest here in America, brought with it a new concept in valuing labor. A workers value was decided by two things:

First was how many people there were available that were capable of doing the task.

Second, how many units of time were required to accomplish the task a single time.

Supply and demand in terms of available qualified laborers set the base pay-level, and whoever could perform the task most quickly got the job. At the production level two primary methods of paying for labor evolved:

"Piece work" called for a worker to be paid a set amount for each time a task was performed. This allowed workers to "set their own pay level" so to speak. By working faster, and performing the work task more often than other workers, a worker could act to increase his or her pay (within physical limits of course).

"Hourly pay" was another popular option. When paid "by the hour" a worker received the same amount of pay for each hour worked, regardless of how many times a particular task was performed in any given time period.

The common ingredient in both pay methods is time. In "piece work" the number of operations per hour is the measurement of productivity. In the "by the hour" system, the measurement is the same.

In "industrialized" countries the term "productivity" came into being. Efficiency experts broke overall operations out into a series of simple steps, and, using one of the above pay methods, assigned an average time, and therefore an "average cost" to perform each task performed in the business. The concept of measuring labor efficiency by "man hours" needed to perform individual tasks is now standard practice.

Concurrent with this, technology has, as always, continued to march forward, feeding on itself, and always shortening the time required to transform ideas into reality. In the process, recent technology advances have made it possible for ever fewer numbers of technologically aided workers to accomplish all the production work necessary to meet the needs of all other members of society. In the extreme, a single worker could theoretically provide (backed by sufficient technology) for meeting the needs of everybody else on the planet.

Unrestrained growth in the number of people on the planet has mandated a way to find work for ever more people needing a way to support themselves and a family; and business mobility has increased competition between workers worldwide for the few jobs available.

We appear to be on the horns of a dilemma here. These appear to be mutually contradictory elements. But as our old friend Aristotle has taught us, contradictions cannot exist. When a contradiction seems to exist, we must examine our major premises to see which hypothesis is false. The presumption that we will encounter a point in time when most citizens cannot have jobs or support themselves due to technology making human labor obsolete, may be based upon one or more false premises.

One such false premise may be that we must always continue to value work by one of the present means (hourly or piece work). Another may be the assumption that competition and self-interest cannot ever be moderated in mankind.

All work can be broken down into simple tasks and measured against time. Not just production workers are evaluated against the time standard, <u>everybody</u> is. Executives are evaluated by how much profit the company makes, in a quarter of a year. A professional basketball player is evaluated by how many average points he scores in less than an hour's playing time. An entertainer is evaluated by how many times his or her song is played each hour, worldwide. And so on.

In the short term, but not necessarily in the long term, there will continue to be a huge gap between jobs and the number of workers available to fill them. Currently, the confluence of population growth, and technology, and ability of businesses to move operations around the world easily, has resulted in a huge glut of labor over jobs on a worldwide scale.

Business driven solely by the maximum profit motive has moved quickly, and correctly, given the present profit model, to take advantage of the labor glut, for purposes of enhancing profits for the company owners.

If these shadows of the future remain unaltered (to borrow a phrase from C. Dickens); the future will be bleak indeed for workers all over the world. But it is nowhere written that the present model can't be changed. A couple of things come to mind.

First, if our fledgling utopian society is to continue long term, and be a beacon for other countries to follow, we must do whatever is necessary to restore the American Dream. Secondly, those with great wealth need to see the wisdom of perhaps sharing more of it than they now are, voluntarily. This includes stockholders of mega-corporations. Rather than insisting on the absolute maximum profit possible, they might instead direct their boards to settle for a bit less, if it will cause jobs and lives to be saved in the process.

Third, we must look at new ways of valuing work. It is perhaps very efficient to reduce all work down to the time it takes to perform some task. It may (or may not) be necessary to do so in a competitive environment. But, it is also de-humanizing. At minimum, some attempt needs to be made to compensate for the impact of technology making human labor obsolete.

People need to feel necessary in order to remain worthwhile members of any group, whether it is a factory workforce, a school choir, a professional sports team, or a national society. Just look at the athletes who would rather be traded and play for less, than warm the bench. We all need to feel necessary. Welfare is not an answer to this need, and neither is unemployment. Welfare and unemployment payments are acknowledgements that the recipient is, in fact, unnecessary.

Here too, we must consciously look for unconventional approaches. The conventional ones just aren't working for too many people in our country, and too many people in other countries all around the world. Telecommuting, work sharing, and flextime have been positive, but incomplete, steps toward addressing the needs of some workers who are already employed.

They have little, if any, effect on those who don't have jobs. Since 1950 it has been treated as axiomatic that a "full time job" constitutes working at some task for a minimum of 40 hours each week. It was not always so. Right after the civil war, the average work week was in the neighborhood of seventy hours. At the end of WWII, the average work week was 48 hours.

It may be time to take a hard look again at what an "average work week" should entail in terms of hours worked. Of course it wouldn't accomplish anything to reduce the work week to thirty hours, and in the process put a lot of people to work that don't now have jobs, unless working 30 hours a week provided the same standard of living that 40 hours a week used to provide. That should probably be one of the acceptance criteria of any-proposed solution.

The solution to problems caused by the confluence of population growth, technology, and business mobility will itself be multi-faceted. It will require cooperation between government, citizens, and business at levels never before seen on Earth. If that level of cooperation is not forthcoming, the "inevitable cycle of governments" will work its magic on the United States of America long before the end of the current century.

Wrapping up

Well, that's about it for this chapter. There has been no attempt here to compile a complete action list, or to even try to list all the possible alternatives that might be considered when trying to solve all of our problems, and the many sub-problems which make them up. The goals of this chapter have been to help middle-class turtle's view the problems facing them from a perhaps different perspective, and to argue the importance of seeking out and seriously considering ALL possible alternatives, including considering unconventional approaches, when thinking about possible solutions to them.

Part 5 - Implementing Mechanisms

At this stage of the problem solving process, we move out of the comfortable realm of theory and planning, into the much less comfortable realm of practice. Theories and plans on paper can neither help nor harm people. Putting them into practice can do both.

It has been said, probably truly, that nothing worthwhile is ever accomplished without the assumption of risk. It has further been said, also probably truly, that nothing would ever get done if all possible objections had to first be overcome.

It is in the implementation phase of problem solving, especially when attempting to solve socio-economic problems, that risk enters the picture. It can't be avoided. Only by implementing a proposed solution to a problem can we ever empirically determine whether the proposed solution was valid or not. Conscientious government leaders (there <u>are</u> a few out there) agonize over implementing planned solutions to problems (symptoms?) they are attempting to solve, just like ordinary citizens agonize when implementing solutions to problems at the personal level.

It's not easy being a conscientious government official. If a government official shows any hesitation at all relating to implementing a proposed solution, he or she is immediately labeled (by pretty much everybody) as a "waffler" or "wishy-washy". If, on the other hand, a government official refuses to show evidence of any self-doubts at all, ever, the official is labeled "inflexible" and "arrogant". But, the anxiety relating to implementation is almost certainly there.

Conscientious government officials just have to always <u>exaggerate</u> their facts and feeling of certainty, in order to emphasize how sure they are that a given problem solution being tried at the government level, will work. Otherwise their approach never gets tried.

Especially when dealing with problems affecting the outcome of real people's lives, implementing solutions is both a tricky business, and one fraught with opportunities for failure. One never knows at the outset how citizens will ultimately react to a proposed solution.

Quite often, citizens' first reactions to the government's attempting to solve some perceived problem on their behalf is to try to purposely defeat the proposed solution. Remember prohibition? And, what about the 55MPH speed limit? And, there are hundreds of other examples. (for every government action, there is an equal and opposite citizen reaction). This is especially true if the proposed solution appears illogical on its face to affected citizens.

Egos can get in the way too. Once a government official has come out strongly for some measure, he or she feels obligated to stick with their original arguments in favor of it, for fear of being labeled "indecisive". This often occurs even when the proposed solution that was implemented fails outright to accomplish its goals (meet the acceptance criteria). When implementing solutions to socio-economic problems in a society it is advisable to keep in mind a couple of old adages that have proven themselves true (axiomatic) over time. Namely:

1. All actions have consequences…some intended, and some possibly unintended.

2. There is no such thing as a free lunch.

It is easy to say things like this, and get agreement that these statements are true. It is more difficult to get people to think about them when they are involved in the planning and theorizing stages of the problem solving process. All too often, the time when these old sayings come to mind is after an ill-conceived plan has been put into operation (implemented), and failed. Then, it becomes embarrassing, and politically risky, to admit failure, and the failed plan is too often kept in operation primarily as a face-saving measure.

If the problem solving only related to something like proving a theorem in high school Geometry, this mode of operation, while ineffective, wouldn't be otherwise all that harmful. However, when failed solutions are kept in place for these reasons when attempting to solve problems affecting the outcome of real people's lives, the effects can be disastrous on not just those individuals that are badly served in the process, but on the entire fabric of the society in question.

Over the past seventy-five years' time, and especially over the past forty years' time of that total period, elected leaders in government have routinely failed to adequately consider the consequences before implementing proposed solutions to socio-economic problems, and have further gone along with policies that openly ignore and/or defy both of the above axioms.

Unintended consequences especially have been ignored or denied, even after they materialized subsequent to implementing a proposed problem solution. Government has not only operated itself as if it believed that there really is such things as free lunches, but it has, by its actions, openly encouraged citizens at all levels to also believe in free lunches, and to ignore and/or deny unintended consequences of their own individual actions too.

I don't want to appear too critical here, but, in this turtle's judgment, that constitutes setting a bad example, and would probably fall under the category of "poor leadership".

I'll climb down off my soapbox now, and get back to the meat of the subject, which are the options available to both individual citizens and our government when it comes to implementing proposed solutions to problems. First, let's look at how the government goes about implementing solutions.

Government Implementing Mechanisms

The government's primary tool for solving problems is the enactment and enforcement of laws. It has often been said that we are a nation of laws. This may or may not be true. What is certainly true is that we are decidedly a nation of <u>lawyers</u>. And, to a significant extent it is lawyers that are responsible for the language of the laws enacted in congress. Not quite half of all congresspersons are attorneys, but when the final language of laws being considered for passage is being written, it is exclusively lawyers selected from the entire group of congresspersons that are allowed to do the writing.

It was noted earlier, that lawyers are, as a group, not known for their problem solving abilities. That becomes an especially important consideration when the language of laws is being determined. Congress typically divides the language of lawmaking into two distinct categories.

The first category has to do with <u>stating the purpose of the law</u>. It usually reads something like this:

"It being the desire of the people to have free lunches provided to them, the purpose of this law shall be to provide a means whereby free lunches shall be available to all citizens beginning on January 1, 2007, and on a daily basis thereafter. Lunches provided under this act shall be of a standard deemed healthy and nutritious and shall include no known harmful products or by-products, and shall not include parts of any endangered species. Special programs shall be provided for those with known health problems requiring specific diets. Congress shall act by June 6, 2006 to provide enabling legislation sufficient to guarantee that this objective is met. The name of this law shall be the Free Lunch Act of 2006 ".

This part is typically short and sweet.

Then comes the second part, which is typically neither short nor sweet, and which often serves to twist the original law into something quite different from what was intended. The second part concerns the "enabling" language. Enabling legislation is the part that spells out the operational details related to accomplishing the original objective stated in the law itself. It can be, and often is, the source of unintended consequences beyond imagination or belief.

For starters, by passing enabling legislation separately from the law itself, the congress creates a platform for "riders" (now sometimes called "earmarks"). In the preceding example, congress is mandated to set up an operating mechanism by June 6, 2006 to make the law operational by January 1, 2007. Pork-minded congresspersons are quick to seize on the time deadline as a means of attaching unrelated "amendments" to the enabling legislation, knowing that there will not be time for any extended debate on the amendment, and that it will therefore probably just sail through along with the main measure.

Two of the proposed Constitutional amendments suggested earlier seek to address this problem by forcing all legislation to address a single topic, and to be two pages or less in length, including all enabling language. These two Constitutional Amendments would not however be foolproof in terms of simplifying laws and rendering them less complex in the implementation, so long as congress were free to "enable" legislation through creation of a "regulatory agency".

Enabling legislation through creation of a "regulatory agency" is in fact, one of Congress' favorite ways of making the laws they pass operational. When drafting "enabling" language pertaining to a particular law, Congress often does so through creation of a "regulatory agency", (like the EPA, SBA, IRS, DOD, DOT, DOE, BATF, OSHA, SSA, etc., etc., etc.) and in the process provides them with a free hand to do whatever the agency head believes needs to be done, to make the law operate as the agency head "interprets" congress intentions.

The "enabling" language typically goes something like this:

"Congress having acted earlier to create the "free lunch law" otherwise known as H2222, or the Free Lunch Act of 2006, here acts to enable operation of that law by creating the Free Lunch Regulatory Board (FLRB). Said board to be comprised of (7) members, with there being one Chairman and six associate board members, each having one vote. The Chairman of the Board, and other board members, to be appointed by the president, and confirmed by the senate. Each board member's term shall be of eight years' duration, and board members may serve no more than two consecutive or non-consecutive terms. Pay levels for board members shall be set by the congress from time to time. The board shall be empowered to obligate the government for purposes of providing for its own operating needs and shall submit for approval an annual budget stating its requirements. The Board shall be empowered to enact rules and regulations as required to effect its objectives, as stated in the law, and such rules and regulations shall have the effect of law in the courts. Congress shall have oversight authority over all rules and regulations put into place by the Board. Funding for the operation of the agency shall be through a 1% increase in the federal unemployment tax collected by employers from all workers. Self-employed persons shall pay the 1% as an increase in federal income taxes".

This example is FAR simpler than most enabling legislation passed by congress, but I have purposely made it so to keep the length of the book under 2000 pages. I left out a lot of details typically alluded to in the enabling language, but hopefully, you get the idea of the kinds of things "enabling" language typically covers.

"Enabling" laws (making them operational) through establishment of a "regulatory agency" designed to administer the law for the congress can be a very dangerous procedure. Here is why. The enabling language that causes a new "regulatory" agency to come into being, endows the agency with the ability to make up whatever rules and regulations it sees fit to get its job done. The Supreme Court has repeatedly said through their decisions, that rules and regulations enacted by regulatory agencies authorized by the congress shall be treated in the courts as if the individual rules and regulations had been enacted by the congress itself, after taking a vote of all members of congress.

Think about that for a minute.

Unelected officials, who were put in office as part of a political payoff for helping the president get elected, and who had to agree before gaining office to go along with the president's wishes (or they wouldn't get the job) are allowed, all by themselves, to make up laws that nobody gets to vote on before they go into effect, and which affect the lives of everybody in the country. No elections. No voting. No discussion beforehand. No nothing.

These appointed bureaucrats are without question a law wholly unto themselves. Literally. The agency personnel cannot even be held personally liable for acts committed by them that result in damage to the lives and/or property of individual citizens.

Not the President and all members of Congress combined have the power of a single "regulatory agency" head. Agency heads ask no-ones-permission in advance, and are, except for "congressional oversight" completely beyond the reach of anyone's control. They typically cannot be held personally accountable for their actions by the courts, unless found to be diverting funds intended for agency use, to their own purposes.

And remember, a government program, once in motion, tends to stay in motion, unless acted on by an outside force. Even after the President and agency head are long gone that were responsible for enacting the rules and regulations, they remain the law of the land.

Congressional oversight is just that Oversight. Congress only gets involved when the rules have already worked to the detriment of the citizens, and people have already been hurt. Even then, anyone who has watched a congressional oversight committee in action is fully aware that it is seldom much more than a "venting" platform.

Whichever party was responsible for bringing the errant agency into being defends its bad acts, and minimizes the damages. The other party exaggerates the damages and says how it never would have happened if they had been in power at the time the errant agency's enabling legislation was passed. The head of the agency whose actions have been excessive claims to have been out of the loop, and promises to correct things (usually by firing underlings, but keeping his or her own job). Afterwards, they all go out together to a local watering hole in Washington, and have a few drinks and talk about their golf games.

On several occasions the Supreme Court has been asked to decide whether rules and regulations being given the weight of law in enabling legislation, which rules and regulations are promulgated by unelected officials, are contrary to the intentions of how laws were expected to be made in the wording of the Constitution. In every case (so far) the Supreme Court has ruled that such rules and regulations are as enforceable as if the rules had themselves each been separately enacted into law by a vote of a majority of the Congress.

Go figure.

It is because of the Supreme Court's tendency to support Congress' efforts aimed at assuring that "government programs, once in motion, remain in motion", that an amendment is needed to reduce the length of Supreme Court judges terms. Otherwise, this will continue until an outside force (outside of the government itself) acts to change things.

Once the turtles in the middle achieve a majority status in the congress, they may also wish to consider one more Constitutional amendment, to wit:

Amendment Number Nine

Rules and regulations promulgated by regulatory boards and agencies created through acts of Congress shall not have the effect of laws or be given the weight of law in Federal courts, unless said rules and regulations have previously been individually voted on by the Congress, and passed with a roll-call vote with 51+ % or more of the entire body of both houses of Congress voting in favor and thereafter been signed into law by the President.

Amendment number nine would render Congress, the President, and appointed agency heads directly accountable before the fact, rather than never at all.

Another drawback to the "regulatory agency" approach is that every time an agency head changes, or the majority party in congress changes, or the presidency changes, all the rules are then immediately subject to change as well.

American turtles are always shooting at moving targets, insofar as trying to stay in compliance with the various rules and regulations laid down by regulatory agencies. Planning for more than a few months is quite literally impossible for businesses in this environment. Affected businesses and individual turtles never know where they stand today insofar as rule compliance goes, let alone where they may be standing tomorrow, or heaven forbid next year.

Some agencies are worse about changing the rules frequently than others. The IRS is possibly the worst in this regard. However, the blame in the tax policy area is about equally shared by the Congress and the IRS. Congress has changed the tax code every year for at least the past thirty years, often in a significant way. About half the rule changes put into place by the IRS are related to enforcement and compliance, and about half are mandated by Congress acting to change the policies relating to who they wanted to take more money from, who they wanted to give it to, and what kinds of subterfuge they felt would be most effective at disguising the total amount taken from ordinary citizens.

But even more dangerous than congressionally mandated changes are "ad-hoc" changes. Some ambitious agency heads, with agendas of their own, simply "wing it". They do as they please, and wait to get reined in by a congressional oversight committee. In the meantime, some have done widespread damage to the public. In Vietnam, Department of Defense personnel made up "ad hoc" rules for spreading defoliants, using a chemical called "agent orange". It caused cancer in our troops who were sprayed with it (on purpose) while in the field. The DOD originally denied that they did it. Then they denied that they thought it was harmful. Then they admitted they knew it was harmful, but denied that it caused cancer. Then they admitted it caused cancer, but denied that they were responsible.

Ultimately they were let off with a "reprimand" The government quietly paid off some victims and families of victims who died as a result. The government never admitted blame for the damage done.

More recently two agency heads were taken to task for overstepping their bounds in some law enforcement actions in Waco, Texas, and Ruby Ridge, Idaho. In each instance, innocent lives were lost when agency heads took it into their minds to initiate new policies relating to the use of deadly force, on the fly. Afterwards, Congress took them to task and "reprimanded" them for their excesses, but, of course, that didn't bring back the lives of those killed by ad-hoc policies implemented by the agency heads.

There are lots more instances like that that we could dredge up for purposes of emphasizing the point, but you get the idea. The "regulatory agency" approach to enabling legislation is one fraught with danger. The danger is always to the citizens. .... Never to the government.

Enforcement at the Government Level

Rules and regulations are impotent unless accompanied by some means of enforcement. Government typically relies on coercion, threats of violence, deadly force, confiscation of property, and imprisonment as the tools by which the laws they pass are enforced.

Ultimately, all laws have as the ultimate enforcement tactic, a government employee ready and willing to kill a fellow citizen, based upon orders from his or her superior.

Every one of these enforcement options is used many times each day by government at all levels. In the majority of instances, these types of actions are taken with the concurrence of most citizens. As noted at the outset of this book, there are some bad turtles out there.

However, there are also thousands of instances wherein government officials have used the coercive forces at their command to extort unwilling citizens to follow their directives, in ways that were clearly outside the letter or intent of the laws they were sworn to enforce. Corrupt government officials who use illegal coercive measures against citizens for their own benefit, or for the benefit of some agency that they serve, are the minority at present, but an alarming increase in such misguided actions has occurred over the past twenty years' time. Such corrupt uses of government enforcement measures are still the exception to the rule, but the exceptions are no longer nearly as rare as they once were.

What is rare, is for government employees who violate the rules relating to enforcement, and use of deadly force against citizens, to be prosecuted and incarcerated like they would be if they were not government employees. Government at all levels is (very) sensitive to charges of abuse of power, and invariably deals with the abusers in a very lenient manner, when they are caught, prosecuted, and punished at all.

The second amendment of the Constitution sought to provide citizens a measure of ability to resist coercion and threats of deadly force, from any source, by allowing citizens the right to arm themselves, and form into militias for their own protection, especially from their own government, if necessary. Those who would seek to disarm criminals by way of abolishing the second amendment, perhaps fail to understand the possible ramifications of disarming the public in total.

History teaches that the most dangerous treachery typically originates from within. American turtles would be well advised to retain the right to arm themselves. It is not inconceivable that the U.S. government might someday cause the country's economy to deteriorate to a point that open rebellion against the government became the only viable alternative for citizens' intent on protecting themselves and their families. In fact, unless a significant turnabout in government direction is effected within the next decade or two, such an alternative may very well become the most workable one open to the majority of citizens at large, at some not too distant point in time in the future.

The government at all levels now takes a little over 50% of all middle-class citizen income. At some point, (i.e., when the government takes 60%, 70%, 80%, 90%, or more), the government's relentless march toward controlling all money, and every aspect of every citizen's life, will reach a level wherein ordinary citizens who have never knowingly broken a law in their lives, will simply elect to withdraw from the whole process, regardless of the consequences to themselves.

No-one knows when such a critical mass might be achieved, but it is a safe bet that, if the present direction of government remains unaltered, it will occur within the next 40 years for a majority of citizens, within 20 years' time for a significant minority of citizens, and a lot sooner than that for some citizens who have already been pushed to their limit, and are already desperate in the extreme.

Violence begets violence. It has always been so. When the U.S. government acts to approve job destroying mergers for profit only, and American-based businesses giving away millions of jobs of American workers to someone else in another country where living standards are incredibly poor by comparison, these are acts of violence in the extreme.

When the U.S. government knowingly takes such violent actions against the citizens it purports to serve, the government loses all rights to thereafter complain about violence committed by others, or to complain about citizens operating outside the law when the law breaking is expressly for purposes of keeping some citizen and his or her family from starving, whose job has been given away, with the government's blessing. The question is not just "why we are becoming a more violent society (it's not all the fault of television), but also how long the majority of citizens can last without resorting to violence as a means of just getting by.

The bottom line is that government enforcement of laws is achieved through confiscation of property, and the threat of violence and imprisonment, or through setting examples by translating the threat of violence and imprisonment into practice. These alternatives, the only ones open to the government, have their limitations.

Government cannot put everybody in prison. Not even close.

Anytime a majority of citizens choose to ignore the law, there is not much the government can do about it. The Prohibition Amendment to the Constitution is a good example of how government acts when confronted with this reality. A miniscule number of the most egregious offenders are singled out and made examples of. The rest are ignored. There was probably more hard liquor consumed in America per capita during the time prohibition was in effect, than at any time before or since.

There are currently well over ten million working individuals that don't file income tax returns, or pay income taxes. The government knows who they are, but can't do much about it.

Government seeks out people who have a high profile, and who are well known in their communities, for prosecution, as a way of "making an example" of them. For every individual prosecuted for failure to pay income taxes, an estimated 10,000 either fail to pay all that is owed, or anything at all, and other than suffering through an occasional audit, no harm comes to them.

And, who drives the speed limit? Again, only the most egregious offenders are prosecuted. Same for driving while intoxicated. Etc., etc., etc.

Confiscation of property without due process is on the increase, as government seeks to find ways other than taxes to pay for its expansion. Confiscation of property under the rules of due process takes time, so government often just ignores due process and the Constitutional protections for personal property when it suits their purposes.

Since government property confiscation is a civil process, citizens are at the mercy of the government when this happens, unless they are wealthy enough to pay for a lawyer to combat the government's violations of the law in these respects. In criminal actions the defendant is guaranteed legal representation by the Constitution. No such guarantee for civil actions is provided by the Constitution.

The government can commit rape of the first magnitude in terms of confiscating property, against those unable to protect themselves in court. And, for the most part, it is those who are the weakest that the government picks on in this regard. In part, this is why an amendment to the Constitution is needed relating to guaranteeing representation in civil matters in court. Not only the government, but all big businesses continually take advantage of the inability of average citizens to defend themselves in civil suits, as a way of implementing coercive actions that benefit them.

This is not to suggest that all government confiscation of property is excessive, and/or unwarranted, or that all civil actions by mega-business are unwarranted. There are some bad turtles out there, who undoubtedly deserve to see their property, gained through breaking the law and hurting others, confiscated, and citizens who mistreat corporations too.

However, the abuses in this area are sufficient (and have been for some time) to warrant providing average citizens with the means to protect themselves when such abuses occur.

The best way to assure fairness in terms of civil actions would be by Constitutional amendment:

To wit:

Amendment Number 10

"It shall be the right of every natural or naturalized citizen to be provided with fully competitive legal representation in all civil actions brought against them by a government body or by any other corporate entity which has substantially greater financial resources with which to pursue civil litigation. Payments by citizens for legal representation in civil actions covered by this statute shall be fixed at a level not to bring undue financial hardship on the citizen during the tenure of the action, including all related appellate actions, if there be any."

There are even limits to how effective government can be when using deadly force. It is a complete unknown as to how police or military units would behave if faced with really large body of concentrated resistance on the part of a group of their citizen neighbors who armed themselves in defense against perceived mistreatment by their government. It is one thing to ask armed forces to forcibly turn aside extremists who have armed themselves for purposes of imposing their will on other citizens, or citizens who have organized to deny some citizens of their rights under the law (like slavery).

It may be quite another to expect military forces to coerce friends and neighbors at gunpoint whose stated purpose is protecting themselves and their families from government imposed tyranny.

No-one wants, or should want, to see a confrontation between American military forces, and other American citizens. The outcome would be uncertain at best, and possibly violent in the extreme. It is not a given that American military forces would win such an encounter, even assuming they were willing to confront their friends and neighbors with deadly force. The air force's smart bombs would be useless, and American big game hunters are greater in number, possibly better armed, more practiced, and typically better shots than are most military personnel, and, they know the terrain better. A force like that, motivated by the need to protect their homes and families, would be a formidable force indeed. (Imagine a situation like Iraq, but where <u>every</u> single citizen was fully armed).

In significant measure, it may be knowledge of that fact that has served to strictly limit the times and places where the government has chosen to deploy military troops on home-ground in the past. And, Lord willing, it will prove a deterrent in the future as well.

None of this is meant to suggest confrontational actions between citizens and their government as being either necessary or desirable at this point in time. It is to say that all government enforcement mechanisms have built in limitations that have served Americans pretty well in the past, and hopefully will continue to do so in the future.

It is further to suggest that the Constitutional right to keep and bear arms, and to form militias for purposes of protecting the citizens of each state is a necessary, but not by itself sufficient, element in keeping government at all levels in check; and that citizens have now been confronted with a litigious government and corporate mentality that puts citizens unable to defend themselves in civil actions at great, and unfair, risk of seeing their property taken from them.

When the first ten amendments to the Constitution were put into place, we didn't have thousands of civil laws on the books (and almost 1,000,000 lawyers) that could be used by moneyed entities to intimidate and financially ruin citizens. Now we have both. We now therefore also need to provide a level playing field in this arena for all American citizens.

Implementing Options for Citizens

The implementing methods open to citizens depend on the type of solutions being implemented. If the solutions selected relate to passing, changing, or cancelling laws, the implementing options will be different than if the solutions do not relate to laws and lawmaking.

Elections are the primary conventionally (and constitutionally) provided means by which citizens' attempt changing of laws through changing elected representatives. Presently, two political parties (Democrats and Republicans) have pretty much monopolized Congress and lawmaking. These two parties together represent between fifteen and thirty percent of Americans. The remaining seventy to eighty-five percent of Americans are presently unrepresented in the Congress.

It has been suggested that another party be organized to represent the turtles in the middle. In fact, if the turtles in the middle are to have any chance at all of having their views represented in the congress, a third party representing their interests will have to be implemented, and fairly soon.

Petitions to congress are another way of getting citizen ideas into the lawmaking process. It has been suggested that a national electronic bulletin board be established to serve this purpose. Ideally, the government could take on this responsibility, since working the will of the people is (supposedly) their primary reason for being. However, Congress has often hidden comfortably in the past behind a veil of ignorance, and may choose to avoid helping citizens express their wishes along these lines as a way of retaining the option to claim that they just weren't certain what the people wanted them to do. If the government elects not to enable citizen petitions on a national scale, it can probably be handled by others in the private sector.

Recall of elected officials also remains an option. Citizens do not have to wait until a scheduled election to remove an official they feel is acting contrary to their interests, and install another in his or her place. Recalls occur at the state level, and (again) require gathering names of dissatisfied citizens on petitions in order to prompt the state to hold a "recall election". Of course, during a recall election, the incumbent gets another chance to recapture the office, and incumbents typically have a widely disproportionate amount of money to spend, contributed by those whose interests are improved by keeping them in office.

Realistically, petitioning government for purposes of amending past actions on their part, is not as effective as electing representatives who are more likely to do the right thing in the first place.

"Pocketbook Voting"

At least as effective as voting in election booths for a continuing stream of "lesser of evils" choices offered by the democrats and republicans is "pocketbook voting". Pocketbook voting entails citizens endorsing policies they favor, and voting against policies they don't like, by way of directing their spending to only those types of activity they favor. Pocketbook voting is one of the most coercive actions available to either government or citizens.

Government uses it constantly by way of favoring groups with which they agree with lots of taxpayer dollars, while not directing any spending toward those types of activities they disapprove of. Congress, for example, approves of borrowing and debt. Congress therefore acts through the tax laws to subsidize these types of activity by allowing amounts spent for purposes of paying off interest on various kinds of debts to be deducted before calculating total taxes for individuals and businesses.

There are quite literally hundreds of examples that could be given to show how Congress uses the power of their purse strings to coerce citizens and businesses to act in ways they (the Congress) wants them to act.

The congress, however has to first pass "appropriation" laws to enable pocketbook voting by the government, while citizens don't have to ask anybody's permission before spending their money as they please. An example of this implementing mechanism was offered earlier (Just say No), as it related to coercing mega-businesses to restore American production jobs previously given away to workers in other countries where standards of living are very poor.

Another way citizens could effortlessly help in the fight to save jobs for themselves and their friends and co-workers would be to use pocketbook voting to coerce mega-businesses into reconsidering rendering workers "redundant" through mergers. Most mergers nowadays are solely for purposes of increasing profits. Typically, the merger is not a prerequisite for the survival of either of the two merging entities. It is just for increasing profits. In some instances, the profits of the two merging companies are already at very good levels before the merger. Stockholders allowing their boards to consider mergers for purposes of increasing profits, when workers' lives are literally at stake, would probably act to vote against the mergers if it was clear that by so doing, a majority of their present customers would leave them.

If, the next time two mega-banks announce a proposed merger that will eliminate between two and five thousand jobs, fifty percent of their customers voted with their pocketbooks to take their account to another bank, the boards and stockholders might reconsider the merger.

If, the next time two profitable airlines announce a merger that will eliminate a lot of jobs, and destroy a lot of family's lives, average citizens voted to show their displeasure by boycotting the merging airlines; they would probably reconsider the merger real quick. In the process saving a lot of jobs.

The beauty of pocketbook voting by average citizens is how quickly it works its magic. When the folks at Coca Cola tried dictating to their customers how their product would taste and be packaged (differently) in the future, their customers voted with their pocketbooks to keep things as they were. It took less than two weeks for the stockholders, board, and executives at Coca Cola to get the message and restore the taste and packaging that their customers wanted.

Pocketbook voting is decidedly free-enterprise, so no-one can object to it in any way. At the same time, it should be noted that using boycotts to effect policy changes is decidedly a coercive type of action. Previously, I surmised that if Plato's utopian society (the Republic) were to ever have any chance of being achieved in the first place here in the U.S., or to have any chance of succeeding long term, once established, that some behavior modification would have to occur at the lord and aristocrat (Congress and big-business) level of our society. Such attitude adjustments being made by these groups voluntarily if possible, but, if necessary by forced means. Pocketbook voting would be one very successful (forceful) way to modify Congress' and mega-business' actions relating to exporting American workers' jobs to other countries, and to merging the jobs of their fellow Americans out of existence.

Strikes

Negative actions (anti) can be as effective as positive actions (pro) in accomplishing objectives Within the past twenty years we have been conditioned to "always think positively" and to be "pro-active" Those coming out "against" an idea are labeled "anti's" and are generally denigrated, without respect to the merit of their ideas. Therefore, part of the job of "spin-doctors" is to "frame" their arguments along "pro" or "positive" lines. Considerable effort is spent arguing over who should have the advantage of having their side of an argument labeled by the media as the "pro" or "positive" side of the argument.

We have been conditioned to think that anything "negative" should be avoided, and that all thinking should be channeled along "positive" lines. Those who fail to understand the benefits of seizing the high ground and having their side of an argument labeled "pro" by the media, are at a real disadvantage. The benefits, in a "conditioned" society of being on the "pro" side of an argument can be significant.

Those on the receiving end of a strike or boycott are quick to label the strikers or boycotters as "anti-" something of other, as a means of getting public support, and media support, on their side. In the dispute over abortion, those in favor of abortions were first to seize on this tactic in terms of gaining an advantage in the public eye for their point of view. They labeled their side "pro-choice" and the other side "anti-abortion". It worked really well from a tactical standpoint. Later on the "anti-abortion" side realized the error of letting the other side "frame" the debate by attaching negative labels to their side, and made a big push to have their argument side labeled "pro-life", instead of "anti-abortion". But from the beginning, the side originally labeled "anti" was playing catch-up ball, and was generally on the defensive.

Out west boycotts were used to withhold a super bowl game from a state that failed to bow to pressure to enact a state holiday honoring a fallen civil rights leader. While the boycott was itself a decidedly negative and coercive tactic, those favoring it were quick to label themselves "pro-civil rights" rather than "anti-discrimination". The tactic worked, and the state in question immediately held a special election and voted in the new state holiday.

Real estate developers too, use the labeling tactic very effectively in fighting and defeating citizen objections to uncontrolled growth in and around metropolitan areas. Opponents are labeled "anti-progress" while their own views are presented as "pro-growth". Using this tactic, (and greasing some political palms) has allowed housing development in many areas to grow to a point where the existing infrastructure is insufficient to meet the needs of the original citizens of the community. The original citizens are then forced to pay for infrastructure improvements suitable for accommodating the new developments, which nobody but the developers and government wanted in the first place. Another great example of government serving the will of the citizens.

Tobacco companies argue that American government should follow their "pro-free-choice" agenda, rather than "caving in" to the arguments of the "anti-smoking" fanatics. So far, the tobacco companies appear to be winning the fight. Millions of young children benefit each year from the "pro-free-choice" advertisements of the tobacco companies, and, without a doubt, medical suppliers benefit too from all the business that the tobacco company's products continue to bring their way each year.

There are other examples of course, and, again, I apologize, in advance, if by limiting them, I have failed to include one of your favorites.

All of this by (long) way of introducing strikes, as an implementing mechanism for citizens. Strikes are, by their nature, negative. So, if we are conditioned to think anything negative must also therefore be "bad", readers will be predisposed to think negatively about the subject, even before it is discussed. The foregoing is by way of showing that all things "negative" are not "bad" For example, if someone is "anti-cancer" or "anti-child pornography" that should not have a negative connotation. Similarly, if someone is "anti-violence" it should not necessarily place them in an unpleasant light.

It will be important to understand going in that any turtle who even suggests strikes or boycotts must be quick on the draw in labeling themselves "pro" something or other, or risk suffering a lost cause.

Language and labels can be very powerful things, often showing themselves to be more powerful than the ideas being discussed. This is especially true when most of the turtles in the pond have been carefully psychologically "conditioned" to think in terms of labels, rather than to use reason to examine the merits of ideas.

Therefore, I hereby label the calling for of occasional strikes and boycotts as being the "pro-American, pro-Jobs, pro-family, pro-democracy, pro-free-enterprise, and pro-everything else" position whenever it is employed toward any of these ends.

The "just say no" alternative called for boycotting products made in other countries, to the greatest extent possible. Opponents and their spin doctors would be quick to attach a label of "anti-progress", and/or "anti-free market" to such a movement. Fortunately, I have already defeated this tactic on their part, by claiming the high ground in advance.

It should be noted that the "anti-free market" label that opponents will be quick to seize on would be an accurate one. Free markets are generally undesirable while free-enterprise is generally desirable.

Typically strikes have, in the past, in America, been limited to workers striking against a particular company or industry (air traffic controllers, auto-workers, etc.). In the relatively recent past, business first used the "divide and conquer" tactic to get union workers at different auto makers to agree to negotiate separately, rather than as a united group.

Hindsight has shown it to have been a huge tactical mistake for the auto-workers to go along with this idea. Once the auto-workers in general were divided by company, business working behind the scenes in Washington, used government changes in the institutional protections previously awarded to auto-workers (and striking workers in general), to dismantle the UAW unions completely. Other industries quickly went to school on this case study, and as this is written, all American workers' unions have now pretty much been reduced to impotent groups, forced to take whatever crumbs management is willing to throw their way.

That being the case, it probably wouldn't serve much purpose to suggest that union members try, at this stage of the game, to enforce their will on companies through holding strikes or work stoppages.

One lesson here, is that there is strength in numbers. While just the auto workers by themselves could not influence management of the auto makers, if all American middle-class turtles whose interests were affected chose to boycott all auto manufacturers, until changes to their liking occurred, the auto manufacturers would have no choice whatsoever but to go along, and to do so very quickly.

Similarly, if all American middle-class working turtles were to go on an all-out purchasing strike, and refuse to buy (or pay for) anything at all that was not absolutely needed for survival, the government and big-business would be forced to come to the table in earnest.

In one large population center the police employees, who as civil employees have already suffered the loss of their right to strike, (for any reason), elected to "just say no" by way of calling in "sick", thereby leaving the criminal element free to roam the streets without regard to getting caught. First, of course, the powers that be denigrated them for being "anti-public service", but they stayed "sick" and unavailable for work. Within 48 hours' special committees were called to hear their complaints, and act on them.

The lesson here is that if strikers have real leverage available to them in terms of withholding services or pay; that strikes don't necessarily have to last a long time. It might be surmised that if the American middle-class were to demonstrate displeasure with big-business and government (at any level) by simply electing not to spend a penny that wasn't absolutely needed for survival, that the impact on the U.S. economy (business) and tax collections at every level (government) would quickly (within a few days or weeks) clarify who was really running things.

This wouldn't work much of a hardship on American's at all, but the negative impacts on business and government would be enormous. Of course, business would react by laying off workers when business fell sharply, but would have no real choice but to call them back when the "strike" ended. Scabs wouldn't be available to help either management or government in a strike of this kind. Business would be faced with outright failure, very quickly, if the "strike" went on more than a few weeks. Workers could, in this instance hold out a lot longer than either business or the government could. Workers might lose some hourly pay, and have to struggle a bit with some past due bills before recovering fully from the effects of the "strike", but they would definitely be hurt less than business and\or government.

The government however, would be devastated by such a strike, very quickly, since the government needs every cent of taxes collected from both business and citizens (all paid for in the end by citizens only) just to keep its doors open on a daily basis. Government's bills are fixed, including COLA's, and any reduction at all in income would be devastating. Of course they could print up some more money to cover their expenses (inflation), but if they did so, citizens could react by stretching out the strike even more. In this environment, the individual citizens would hold all the cards, and time would, for a change, be on their side.

Payments relating to bills for things like auto payments, and house payments might have to be put on hold for a while, if the "strike" stretched out more than a month or so, (unlikely) and lenders might not like it much, and threaten foreclosures, but foreclosure actions take time, require due process (court hearings) before they can be taken, and the courts would quickly become so overburdened that few legal actions could occur against striking customers. Lenders would just have to go along. Of course threats would be made, but they would, for the most part, be toothless threats.

Strikes are a very powerful coercive weapon, if properly conducted. Proper conducting of strikes requires that the strikers have the capability to withhold something that the other side can't get along without for long. When workers strike against a single company (like Caterpillar) management can usually outlast them by way of replacing them with scabs, and living off the company's cash reserves. But when <u>customers</u> strike against either single companies, or government, the <u>customers</u> actions cannot be defeated by any means.

There is no such thing as "scab customers" that management or government can employ to replace the striking cash paying customer of business or government services.

Strikes are, in the end, always a contest of wills. Things like running out of food to eat, or money to pay the rent, are simply means of breaking down the striker's will to continue, in "worker-based" strikes. But, in "customer-based" strikes, the customer holds all the cards.

The beauty of "customer-based" strikes, is that the customers get their way by not doing <u>anything</u>. No other actions are needed on the striking customer's part. They don't have to write any letters, march around with picket signs, worry about someone replacing them even temporarily, or otherwise involve themselves in any of the kinds of things striking workers have to do when conducting strikes. All striking customers have to do is stay home, not spend money, and wait (not very long) for an acceptable offer to come their way.

Is that a powerful tool for citizens to have for shaping the will of government and business, or what?

Peaceful Civil Disobedience

Government enforcement mechanisms depend on voluntary compliance, and can't work without it. Anytime a majority of turtles in the pond choose to ignore a law, the government is largely powerless to do anything about it. This is not to say that government can't act to make some turtles pay a price for disobeying the laws, but it is to say that government's abilities in these areas are limited.

If everybody decided not to pay taxes, or to cheat and dummy up a return asking for a refund of all taxes already paid in through withholding, the IRS systems would overload in about an hour. The citizens ignoring of DUI laws, prohibition, abortion, highway speed limits, and so on reveals the natural constraints on government imposing their will through threats of arrest and incarceration.

Similarly, government can foreclose on your property if you don't do things their way. However, property foreclosures take time; require you to be given a chance to have your day in court first, and citizens claiming these rights en masse could clog up every court in the country for ten years, all in less than a week's time.

During the Vietnam "conflict" a lot of young citizens, including a future U.S. President, just decided not to play the game. Some moved out of the country. Some found other ways to beat the game. In the final analysis, the government had to look the other way, and offenders were not jailed *en masse*, or otherwise punished for skipping out.

But, be advised that even peaceful civil disobedience may carry a potential price with it, even if the probability that the price will be exacted in full, may be relatively low. At least a few citizens who elect to "peacefully" disobey laws probably will be caught and punished, as a way of making an example of them to instill fear in others.

If very many are so doing, the risk to any single member (of being prosecuted) may be low, but, if you don't like the odds, doubt your courage, or otherwise aren't willing to pay the price if you happen to be one of the ones they choose to make an example of, don't do it.

Armed Resistance

In America, unlike most other countries around the world, citizens have the right to arm themselves for purposes of protecting themselves and their property. This includes defending oneself from tyrannical acts committed by the government, if necessary. In fact, the principle reason for the second amendment to the Constitution was to provide individual citizens a means of defending themselves from tyrannical measures inflicted on them by their own government. The founders were well aware of how easy it is for any government with an army to subjugate citizens unable to defend themselves when confronted with deadly force.

The government dislikes turtles talking about the possibility of citizens ever having to forcibly protect themselves from their own government, but it has happened in the past, and may well happen again in the future. At a place called Ruby Ridge in Idaho, a family recently had to arm themselves against a government bureaucrat who ordered their lives terminated without due process. The bureaucrat, of course, attempted to later convince the public that those killed were desperados engaged in dangerous crimes against society. The evidence clearly showed otherwise, and the government eventually paid the "desperado's" survivors a few million dollars for violating their civil rights by murdering some of them. (The government denied that the multi-million-dollar payment to the victims was in any way an admission of guilt).

If these "desperados" had not had the ability to arm themselves, and through use of armed resistance, hold off the government "agents" until the Press could find Ruby Ridge, and begin televising the goings on, it is arguably the case that the government agents might have continued the "enforcement" action until all of the "desperados" were dead and couldn't tell any tales, rather than having to stop after just killing an unarmed pregnant woman and a boy and a dog.

The "Ruby Ridge Incident" should not be construed as a typical government operation. It was clearly an exception to the rule. It is presented here only to illustrate the point that force of arms is sometimes a rational, legal and viable alternative, in extreme circumstances, and is protected through the U.S. Constitution, for just that reason.

The founding fathers expected use of deadly force to be the last alternative resorted to by law-abiding citizens. A legitimate means, but the means of final resort. We are well advised to keep it that way.

Limits on Citizen Implementing Mechanisms

Government's implementing mechanisms have built-in limitations, and implementing mechanisms by citizens also have some built-in limits. However, it may be argued that the greatest limiting factor in terms of citizens bending either business (aristocrats) or government (lords) to their will, is, the strength of their collective will itself. Paraphrasing a past president, we might say that "the only thing we have to fear, is fear of not trying".

Part 6 - Proving the Solutions

Proving out solutions, once they have been implemented, is a straight forward process. The results are measured objectively against "acceptance criteria" established at the time the problems were being defined, broken down into their smallest parts, and possible alternative solutions were being proposed by those working on the problem.

The "if-then" statements comprising the acceptance criteria are later used to objectively measure how effectively the implemented solution has achieved its goals. The operative word here is "objectively".

This part of the process has been ignored by politicians, almost to the same extent they have failed at defining the problems in the first place. Rather than taking an objective look at whether a government program or law has worked as planned, and letting the chips fall where they may, politicians typically "bend the facts" to suit a determination that the program or law in question has (big surprise) always worked out pretty much as planned.

Laws and programs that have failed utterly and completely are declared effective but "in need of some adjustments". Politicians are loath to ever admit they were just flat out wrong. This character flaw works to render most politicians completely <u>useless</u> when it comes to problem solving. Inability to admit failure prohibits them from moving on through to the end of the problem solving process. They always declare victory at step six, usually by lying to themselves and everyone else, and therefore never go on to, or use, step number seven.

The end result of politicians taking this approach is that failed laws are kept operational, more (inflation provided) money is thrown at them, more "adjustments" are made by bureaucratic rule makers, and the system continues to crumble under its own weight. It will be a requirement of restoring the American Dream that whoever is responsible for restoring it, will have to have the courage to objectively measure implemented solutions against previously laid down acceptance criteria, and if the solution fails the test;

    1) admit that the selected alternative was a failure
    2) abandon the failed solution, and
    3) move on to step number seven

….and be willing to go back to step one in the problem solving process.

It doesn't sound so hard, but it's tougher than it sounds to do. That's why it typically doesn't get done. Tough or not, it's necessary, and without the will to do it, the entire process fails. Which brings us to the next, and final, chapter of this work.

Part 7 - Free Will

Well, we are nearing the end of the book. In this final chapter, my goal will be to offer some thoughts about why it is not just important, but essential, for the turtles in the middle to move <u>now</u> (and quickly) to change the balance points of power that exist between worker turtles and leader turtles.

I'm reminded of the story about the small turtle who, when finding himself in trouble with is parents, sought lenient treatment by way of responding to their indictments with the following reply:

"Don't be so hard on me. God isn't done with me yet".

God isn't done with America yet, either. But God, it is said, only helps those who try to help themselves. If America is ever to achieve Plato's dream of a utopian society, and set an example for all the other countries of the world to follow, the turtles living in America will have to solve <u>one more problem.</u>

I saved this one for last, because it is the hardest. Plato couldn't solve it. Aristotle couldn't solve it. Aristotle, in fact, believed that it could never be solved. Saint Thomas Aquinas, John Locke, John Calvin, Baron Montesquieu, John Adams, James Otis, James Madison, and Thomas Jefferson combined couldn't solve it. No government in the history of the world has solved it, including the government of the United States of America, though America arguably came the closest of any country to doing so when the great American Dream was still alive and well.

The problem is how to reconcile the fiercely selfish and anarchical nature of Capitalism and free-enterprise, which are necessary to create wealth.... With the voluntary sharing of wealth and power by the lords (Congress) and aristocrats (commercial interests) governing from the oligarchy level... as called for by Plato in the establishment of a utopian (Republic) society. Anarchy and Oligarchy are by definition mutually exclusive concepts.

Plato argued that man had it within him, through reason and free-will, to voluntarily overcome self-interest for the betterment of the whole of society. Aristotle disagreed, and held the position that selfishness and self-interest would always win out in the end, making the long term establishment of a utopian society unattainable.

Along about 1930 AD, we turtles in America had come about this close (hold your thumb and index finger about a quarter inch apart) to making it happen. We weren't there yet, but we were getting close. We still denied some their God-given rights, but the public commitment was there to correct these wrongs; and the critical mass of public opinion was building rapidly on the side of justice and fair play.

Then, rather suddenly, tough times came, self-interest kicked in, and it started going away. It's still going away today. Each year since, we have traveled farther and farther down the road to self-interest, and farther and farther away from Plato's utopian society. I'd swear I could hear Aristotle laughing.

Among documents committed to paper, the United States Constitution will, whether America ultimately survives or not, quite probably be regarded by history as the first roadmap to the utopian society. Whether or not we American turtles have the will and the courage to follow the map to the pot of gold at the end of the rainbow remains to be seen. But, we do have a map that will lead us there if we choose to follow it.

The U.S. Constitution belongs in the same category of documents as the Bible, the Koran, the teachings of Confucius, the Torah, the Ten Commandments, the Magna Carta, and Plato's Republic.

The history of the United States Constitution is itself, a story of biblical proportions. In fact, the United States Constitution is a culmination of the ages old desire of man to provide a written formula for existing in harmony with his fellow man, along the lines of Plato's Republic.

It's most basic premise is that man is endowed by his creator with certain inalienable rights, and that government is bound to accept that fact in its actions. At the root of the United States Constitution, as was the case with the Magna Carta, the (partially unwritten) British Constitution, the Declaration of Independence, the Articles of Confederation, and the first Constitution of Virginia, which all preceded the U.S. Constitution; was the premise that God's laws relating to inalienable rights of individual men and women, should not (and could not long) be set aside by any government conceived by man.

This view allowed the American Colonies to justify using force of arms to break away from England. American colonists were convinced that their God-given rights were being usurped by the King's agents, and that God would be on their side in resorting to force of arms to restore them.

In those days, as now, there were several religious beliefs accommodated in America. But, regardless of which faith denomination the early Americans followed, their interpretation of "inalienable rights", as defined in all of the above-referenced documents, was the same.

Over the past hundred years' time, and especially within the last fifty years of that span of time, some Americans (and some citizens of other countries too) have chosen to equate some additional "entitlements" recently conceived by the mind of politicians (to buy votes), with the "inalienable rights", granted by God, as enunciated in all of the most significant documents ever written for purposes of defining the lines between government and those being governed.

Arguably, the present day politicians thumping for "entitlements" may not be the same quality of thinkers that typified a Plato, Aristotle, Aquinas, Locke, Calvin, Montesquieu, Adams, Otis, Madison, or Jefferson.

This has served to muddy up the waters considerably. It is not a question of wanting to do the right thing. Most turtles want to do the right thing. It is a question of which things are really (permanent) God given rights of men and women, no matter which society they might be a part of; and which things are (perhaps temporary) citizen granted privileges gained by living in a given society having a given total amount of wealth available for distribution, at a given point in time.

Difficulty arises when a citizen granted privilege, granted when society's wealth level was high, has to be later reduced or withdrawn when society's wealth level is reduced for some reason.

And material wealth does change hands and even changes countries at times. Between 1970 and 1980 the greatest single transfer of material wealth in the history of the world occurred relating to mineral wealth. The U.S. was on the losing end of that one, and the government of the U.S. is still trying to figure out how to continue providing increased levels of money, originally intended to be temporary citizen granted privileges, to groups of citizens who had come to feel permanently "entitled" to a certain level of living, without regard to how well off (or not) the whole society might be at the time.

At the same time, the citizens who originally granted the privileges (and paid for the benefits), and many of whom are now doing less well, are being un-consulted in the matter.

Currently, yet another transfer of wealth is underway. America's manufacturing wealth is being transferred to a whole slew of other countries around the world who have gained the blessing of the United States Government, and, apparently the majority of turtles in America, to allow the manufacturing jobs that American middle-class turtles used to hold with pride, to be given away to citizens of other countries. The transfer of manufacturing jobs and wealth is ongoing, and the velocity of the transfer is very high.

Concurrent with the transfer of manufacturing jobs and wealth out of America, our government has acted, incorrectly many would say, in trying to continue providing an improved standard of living for some previously "entitled" citizens, while, at the same time acting on other fronts, to cause the standard of living for most other turtles in the pond, including those who are paying all of the bills, to become significantly worse.

The fable of Robin Hood tells of a hero figure who forcibly took from the rich to give to the poor. In the Robin Hood fable, most of the taking was done at the expense of Prince John and the Sheriff of Nottingham. It should be noted that Prince John and the Sheriff of Nottingham were, in fact, synonymous with the government. Heck, they <u>were</u> the government. Prince John and the Sheriff of Nottingham got their money from taxing the people, and Robin Hood and his band of Merry Turtles took it away from the government, and gave it back to the people.

The author must have been an Aristotle fan. Aristotle would probably suggest that (that) was the only way the average citizens would ever get anything of value back from the powers that be; and that Prince John, being the tyrant he was, it would only be a matter of time until the landed aristocracy would rise up to unseat him. This, as we are told, is what happened when King Richard returned from the Crusades with his knights and nobles (the aristocrats).

Of course the Robin Hood story is just that, a story.

What is fact is that the landed aristocrats of England, by way of the Magna Carta, did later force the King to consent to their sharing in the powers of government, and the wealth of the kingdom, through a form of constitutional government.

What is also fact is that the Magna Carta first defined "inalienable God-given rights" of the kind now found in our Declaration of Independence and Constitution.

What is also fact is that these individual rights are now being usurped by our government.

What is also fact is that the U.S. Constitution provides the turtles in the middle with the tools needed to regain their rights, their country, and the fulfillment of their dreams.

What seems also to be fact is that the turtles whose rights are being taken from them by their government don't appear to be willing to act to take back their rights, and restore the dreams made possible when they had them. Were the founding fathers of America right when they assumed that the majority of citizens would be too lazy to act in their own best interests?

Only time will tell.

The great gift of the U.S. Constitution, to the citizens of the United States of America, and indeed to all citizens of the world, was that it distilled all prior work relating to governments and those being governed, based upon God-given rights, into a single, workable, written formula that really could be used in a fluid manner to reconcile the mandatory self-interest of capitalism and the necessity of cooperation and sharing required by oligarchies, and in so doing allow Plato's utopian society (The Republic) to not only be achieved, but to continue on indefinitely.

That is some gift!

But, turtles take note: The Constitution's powers can also be used by government to (legally) confiscate the rights of citizens, and their income, and their property, and even their dreams. It is a two edged sword, and it can cut either way.

It is ours to do with as we wish, individually, and collectively. What we choose to do with it is entirely up to us. Of course, we can always choose to do nothing at all. That's always an alternative. But choosing not to accept and use the gift would be ungracious in the extreme, especially considering the very high price in time, effort, and lives, paid by citizens of the world over the past twenty-three hundred years creating it on our behalf.

Not to mention foolhardy.

In the final analysis, it comes down to a matter of will. If the turtles in the middle have the will to recover the rights taken from them by their government, and to use the powers of the Constitution to fairly and equitably re-establish the balance points of power between ordinary citizens and their government and commercial interests, in a way that is somewhat more inclusive of the turtles in the middle; our fledgling republic can be fully restored, and the dreams of its citizens with it.

Fairly and equitably are the operative concepts. It is probable that most politicians who have in the past acted in ways that damaged the American Dream, initially went to congress to try and help out average citizens. But power has a tendency to corrupt, and most succumb to the corrupting effects of power within a few years of gaining office. Sometimes the corrupting process doesn't take years, only months.

The turtles in the middle must constantly be on guard not to fall into the same trap, once they are in power. If the turtles in the middle succumb to self-interest at the expense of civil servants and commercial leaders, the Dream will be no better off than when civil servants and commercial leaders succumbed to self-interest at the expense of the turtles in the middle. Our goal should be to prove Plato right, not Aristotle.

The Constitution provides the necessary tools for the turtles in the middle to model the government and our society in their image. In order to prove Plato right, the image of the turtles in the middle must be one of courageous individuals, always working to balance the competing interests of free-enterprise capitalism, the needs of the worker citizens, and the benevolent oligarchy, fairly and equitably for <u>all</u> the turtles in the pond.

Right now, that's not the way it is working out. But, with God's help, and some effort on the part of the turtles in the middle, it can be made to work out that way. It's a matter of <u>will</u>. God's and ours. Mostly ours, at this point. The founding fathers, and the many preceding them acknowledged earlier, gave us a most precious gift in the form of the United States Constitution. But they never could have done so unless they, themselves, had first been given three even more precious gifts.

As turtles go, I'm not all that big on most forms of organized religion. I'm reminded of Ray Walton's line in the movie Paint your Wagon, "I don't give a bloody damn how a man prays ... there's room enough in hell for all of us". But we know there is a God, because Newton was right: "For every action, there is an equal and opposite reaction."

As we have repeatedly seen throughout this work, every cause has an effect. That is the overriding universal law. It's axiomatic. There can be no effects without causes. Nothing in the physical universe we know makes sense otherwise. It's not just a matter of faith. It's a matter of looking at the universe around us and using our reasoning abilities to understand that it all came from somewhere…even when we don't really yet know enough to fill in all of the details.

And I believe that God intervenes personally sometimes in the affairs of men, and was holding the founding fathers of this country in his (or her) hands and guided their actions during the convention whose efforts resulted in the birth of the Constitution of the United States. It was not the first time God acted to help us find the way, and it hopefully won't be the last.

The Ten Commandments, carried down from the mount by Moses, were not complex, as laws go, and were meant to apply to all men and women absolutely equally. Like many laws now made in our congress, God's laws came in two parts. The first part was the purpose of the law (i.e., thou shalt not kill). The second part was made up of the "enabling" legislation. Again, similar in this respect to many current man-made laws. To "enable" mankind to keep his laws, God provided mankind with three tools sufficient for all enforcement:

Reason, opposable thumbs, and free-will.

Those too, were some gifts!

And, they made possible everything else that followed, good and bad. One of the really good things that they made possible was the Constitution of the United States. American turtles now have all the tools needed to effect their own salvation. Reason, opposable thumbs, free-will, and the Constitution. The question is whether we will exercise our free-will to use the gifts given to us for good, for evil, or not at all.

At the time our Constitution was being thought up, there were only a quarter of a billion people inhabiting the entire planet and only about three million people on the whole North American Continent. Now there are over seven billion on the planet and 290 million in the U.S. alone.

Think about that for a minute.

Within the past two hundred and twenty-nine years, Mother Earth has become home to more than twenty four times as many people as inhabited her for over a million years before that. Given present growth in the human population, our planet will have forty times as many people as existed when the Constitution was being written, by the year 2040. That is just 24 years from now.

By the year 2070, if the human population continues to grow as it is now doing, there will be eighty times as many people as when the Constitution was written. That is just 54 years from now.

This is significant from several standpoints, not the least of which is that there is probably no way that this planet could withstand the effects of 20 billion humans living on it at one point in time. Even if it could, life as we now know it would almost certainly not be possible.

In the shorter term, the huge growth in population has served to significantly shorten the time available to us to solve our problems. If we had the luxury of solving our problems in a world where our country consisted of only 3 million or so citizens, and the world overall only had a quarter of a billion population, we could afford to let a lot of years pass between recognizing a problem, and implementing a solution.

If we choose to take several years pondering things at this stage of the game, we will certainly lose the game. And, we can so choose if we wish. After all, we still have free-will to use as we please. We can just twiddle our opposable thumbs, and choose to do nothing.

But that would require that we abandon reason. And that we must not do.

For abandoning reason is the cardinal sin. There is no redemption from cardinal sin. One may break God's laws, and man's laws, and expect to be forgiven by man and by God. But one may not simply throw the greatest gifts of God back in God's face, and expect to be saved by man or by God.

The future of America and the world depend on mankind using reason to solve the manmade problems facing us today. Promptly. We have the tools. We have the talent. We don't have a lot of time, but we do have enough time. Just barely.

But, do we have the <u>will</u>?

In 1979, the man who would become our president asked the following question. "If not us, who, and if not now, when?" At the time he said that, about twenty-seven years ago, the planet had about four and a half billion people living on it. The answer to his question from the turtles in the middle at that time was:

"Somebody else, and some other time".

Our planet now has more than seven and a half billion people living on it, and our problems are now more than <u>four times</u> as serious as they were when the question was first asked. The time left to us to solve our problems is now <u>less than half</u> of what was available when the question was first asked. We now have less than twenty-five years left to save America. There is only one possible rational answer to the question now.

"If not us, nobody, and if not now, never."

Within the next two to three decades the great question debated by Plato and Aristotle, and many great thinkers that followed them, relating to governments and those governed will finally be answered. America will prove one of them right, and the other wrong. Time has run out for waiting. This has been said before, and in the past it has always turned out that there was more time available than the prognosticator thought. That could be true now too. But, it's probably not. This time the threat is real, and this time we must act. Here is why.

Many of the turtles reading this may already be familiar with the "technology driven curve". For the benefit of those who aren't I'll sketch one out here, and show how it works.

The "technology driven curve" is a graph of points along a curved line that results from plotting advances in some field affected by technology, against time, according to a mathematical formula. I won't go into the details of the equation here, but instead will try to interpret what the equation and the plotted graph resulting from plugging in different variables (technical advances and time) tell us.

Graph Number 1 depicts how technological advances relate to man's ability to move faster through space. As you can see by looking at the graph, the curve is what math-types call a "double asymptotic" curve. That is, at each end of the curve, the curve gets ever closer to a limit defined by one of the lines representing the two crossing axes (x-axis and y-axis), but never quite touches it. The two intersecting axes are called asymptotes. Don't ask me why.

For the first million or so years, man's speed was limited to how fast he (or she) could walk or run. The speed goes up when man figures out that domesticated animals can be used to carry people faster than they can themselves run or walk. (Horses, Camels, etc.). Speed is again increased when man discovers through invention, ways to convert energy stored in plants and minerals into mechanical energy for purposes of further increasing the speed at which man can travel.

Once invention takes hold as the primary means by which progress is achieved, the rate at which changes occur continually accelerates. Steam engine driven locomotives lead to the automobile which leads to the propeller driven airplane, which in turn leads to jets, which leads to rockets, which leads to spaceships, and so on.

As the graph shows, the time between advances shortens inversely compared to the magnitude of the advance. Near the end of the time-cycle, large advances occur very rapidly, as inventions feed on other inventions to greatly shorten the amount of time necessary to effect change.

In this example we can see that mankind has advanced more in the past 100 years, in terms of his ability to move faster through space, than he and she were able to advance in all the time preceding that combined, since man appeared on the Earth. Actually, I think that the example used here was among the first developed to use mathematics to predict, in advance, when technology could be expected to reach a given level of advancement, in a given field, by a given point in time.

An interesting thing about the "technology driven curve" is how closely it parallels the exponential curve representing growth in the human population. In retrospect, this probably makes sense, since the more people there are available to work on expanding technology (invention) at any point in time, the more often someone will come up with an idea that advances the state of the art in a given field.

Graph #1 - Human Speed of Travel

This chart illustrates how technology has accelerated the ability of man to travel through space over (especially) the past 100 years' time.

Within the past 150 years of time, man has advanced more in this regard than in all the time before that since man first emerged on Earth as a separate species.

If the present trend continues, man may expect to achieve light speed before the end of the current century.

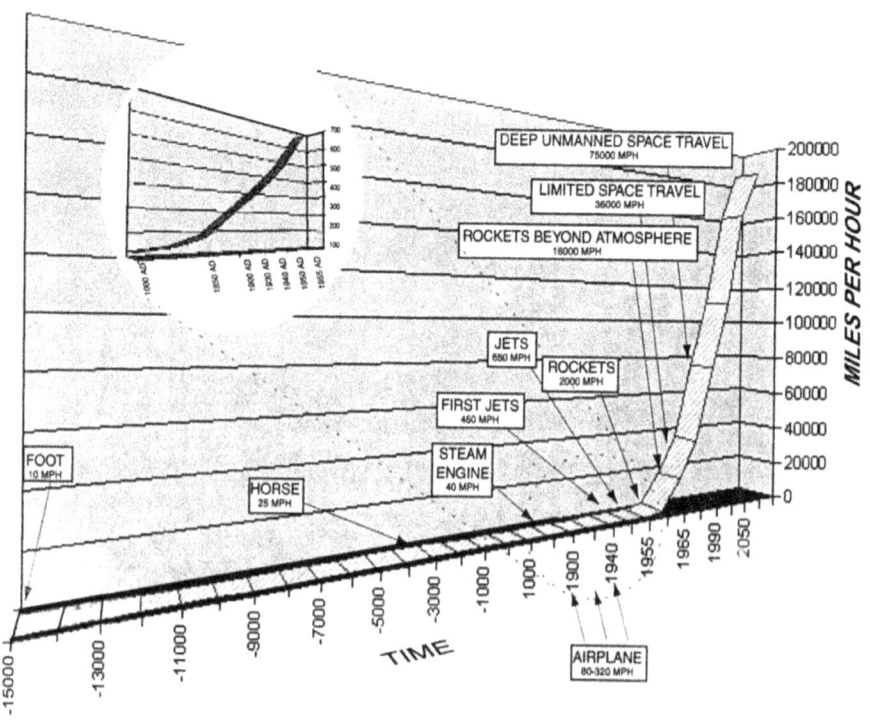

Graph #2 - Population Growth

This chart depicts the growth in worldwide population from about 1600 (AD) through the year 2070 and beyond. The population figures from 1600 through the present time are based upon actual past experience. The population estimates from now through the year 2070 are projections based upon the present growth rate in population. In just the last 90 years, the worldwide population has grown to be approximately 15 times greater than it did in all the time before that combined, going all the way back to when man first appeared on Earth.

It is highly unlikely that planet Earth could withstand the detrimental effects of housing the 20 billion people that would exist by the year 2070, if present population growth were left unchecked. It is even more doubtful that if the Earth were ever somehow to accumulate a human population of 20 billion people, that the majority of those inhabiting the planet at that point in time could ever hope to have a standard of living equal to what we enjoy today.

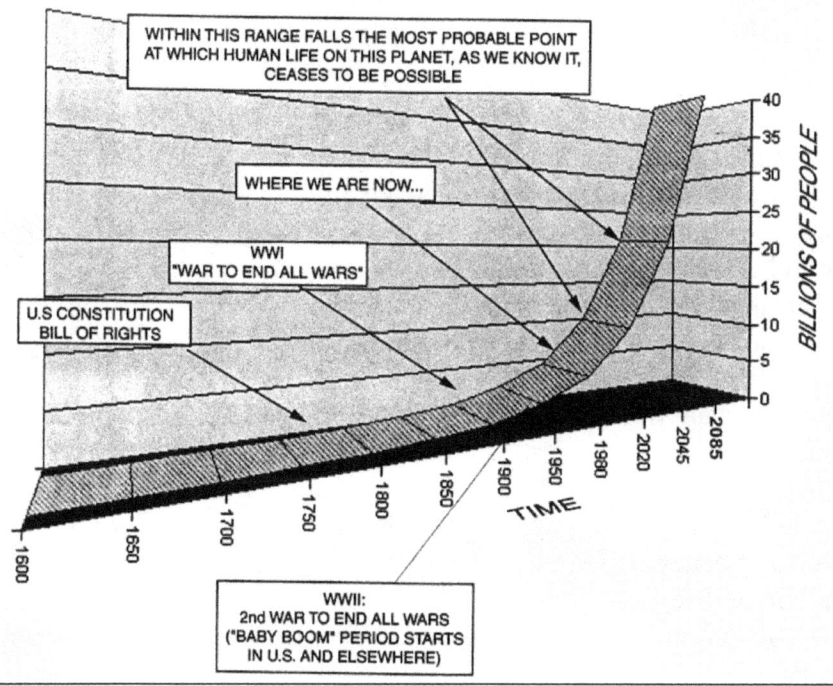

By the end of the 21st century, if population expansion continues at the present rate of increase annually, the Earth would expect to be home to approximately 40 BILLION people. We currently have approximately 7.5 billion people living on our planet, and the population is growing at a "net" rate of approximately 4 new humans each second. That's 240 per minute, 14,400 per hour, 345,600 per day, 126,144,000 per year, another billion approximately every 7 years (compounded rate of growth).

The "nature" of technological advance always falls along the exact same type of curve. By putting the curve on a piece of paper, and plotting past advances in a given field, against the time between past advances, scientists are able to predict with remarkable accuracy when future advances will come on line. Mind you, the curve is not accurate enough to predict the actual year, day, and hour that a technological breakthrough will occur, but it has invariably been accurate to within a decade or two, which is pretty good, considering how much time there is out there to guess about.

Graph #3 - Advances in Pneumatic Tire Durability

This graph shows how scientists working for tire manufacturing companies were able to predict that by the turn of the 21st century, they would need to be able to make tires that lasted for 100,000 miles. Why? Because technology (invention) feeds on itself in entirely predictable ways. For tire company managers, knowing when they would have to have a tire that lasted 100,000 miles in order not to be swept aside by another company who did have such a capability, provided them with an incentive to not rest on their laurels when tire mileage doubled from 10,000 miles to 20,000 miles.

When tires only lasted 10,000 miles, tire companies were probably better off because we had to buy them more often. But each individual tire manufacturer realized that even if they didn't achieve the 100,000 mile tire by the year 2000, that someone else probably would, and customers would then leave them to buy the better tires offered by their competitor.

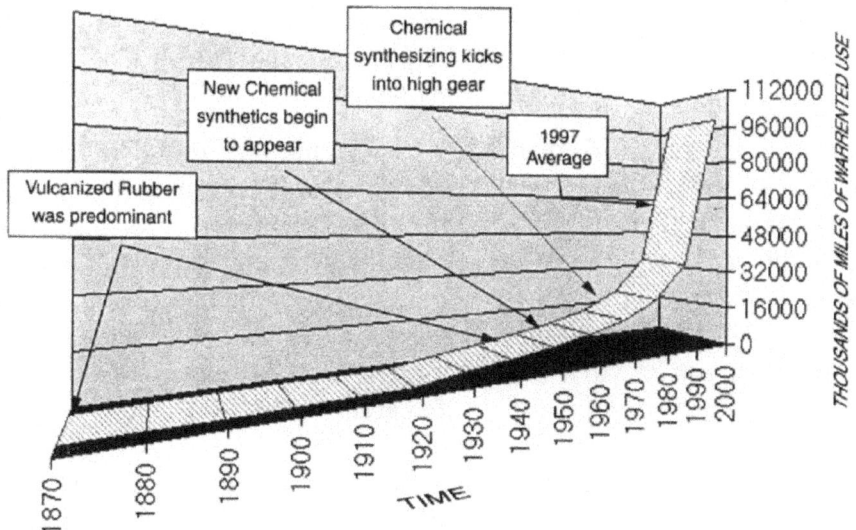

So, maybe this is interesting, but what does it have to do with what we were talking about? Good question. Here is the answer. Technology and population are not the only trends that can be represented by a double asymptotic curve. It appears that Plato's "inevitable cycle of governments" may also proceed along similar lines.

Not every stage in the cycle of governments occupies the same amount of time. Monarchs, tyrants, aristocracies, oligarchies, democracies, and anarchies all have tendency to rise and decline at different rates, along a predictable curve related to time.

Further, the time between changes is affected by the technology available at the time that can be used to accelerate the rate at which the changes within government can be made to occur, and according to the population affected at the time by government actions. So the curves for technology and population are similar to the graph noting changes in government forms insofar as the establishment of both timelines and population are concerned.

Graph #4 - Government Forms Overlaying Population Growth Trends

Graph Number 4, relating to Plato's and Aristotle's "inevitable cycle of governments", is the same as the curve used to predict technological changes and breakthroughs. The legend indicates how government types have changed in the past and projects forward expected future changes from oligarchy (where we are now) to democracy, to anarchy, and finally back to becoming subjects of another nation capable of restoring order and economic stability when citizens tire of the effects of anarchy.

The graph postulates that as is the case with population and technology, changes in government types will become increasingly frequent as both technology and population explode over the next few decades, and government fails to face up to or adequately address the eight fundamental problems facing us today.

As can be seen by looking at the graph, our present power structure is well along the timeline that predicts a change from oligarchy to democracy, and changes in government type (form) may be expected to accelerate due to population growth and technology.

That is legitimate cause for alarm, since democracies are typically even shorter lived than oligarchies, and relatively quickly deteriorate into anarchies. Monarchies and anarchies may (or may not) be relatively long lived, (even if uncomfortable for most citizens) since they occur very close to one of the asymptotes, and are limited only by the patience of the majority of citizens in general to live with their shortcomings.

This chart postulates that changes in government forms will continue in the United States as the needs of an ever-increasing population fail more and more to be met. The past government forms of the United States shown on the chart for the period from our Revolutionary War with England up to the present time reflect historically accurate changes from Monarchy (where we started) up through Oligarchy (where we are now). The changes between now and approximately 2060 may or may not occur, depending upon what American citizens decide they want to do with their country going forward.

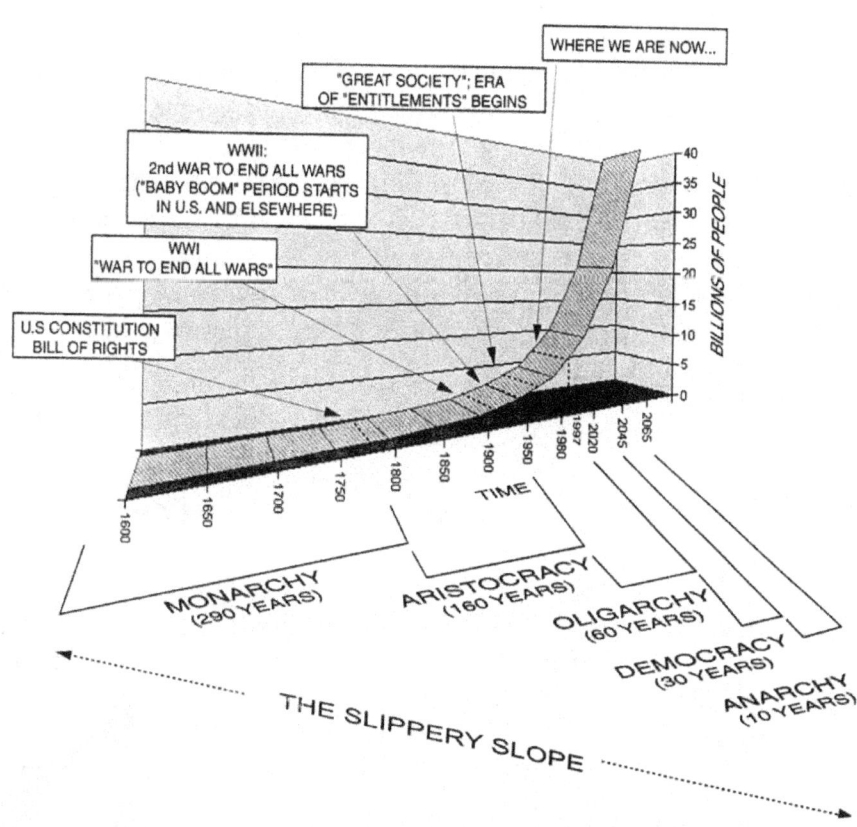

The thing is this fellow turtles, societal decline is entirely predictable, when the majority of members comprising the society choose self-interest over reason. Reason must prevail if our society is not to crumble around us.

The challenge facing the turtles of America, across all levels of our society, is to somehow find a way to break the "inevitable cycle of governments" while we are still in the "benevolent oligarchy" stage. If we are successful in that attempt, the possibility exists that we might have a chance to finally realize, in the American Republic, Plato's utopian society; and pass along the fruits of our achievements to future generations of turtles here in America, and in so doing to become a beacon for other countries to follow.

I have suggested that the best way to do this would be for the turtles in the middle to organize politically and act to re-establish the balance points of power between the citizen turtles, and the turtles in government and business, in a manner that gives working citizens more say in deciding the most important matters that affect the outcome of their lives. For the past forty to fifty years the balance points of power have been set entirely for the benefit of government, single interest groups, and business, with arguably poor overall results. We are now facing rapid decline in our society, because the self-interest of these groups has been left unchecked by the turtles in the middle.

The price of freedom, economic well-being, and an American Dream worth holding on to is eternal vigilance, and the willingness of <u>every</u> generation to work hard to become and stay free.

America has come a long way in the struggle to be a beacon to its citizens and all of the other citizens of the world. But, freedom and opportunity are never free, and they can't be bought and paid for by one generation for another generation. They may only be borrowed, and they always impose a debt on those who would enjoy their benefits.

Ours is a debt of honor. It is a debt that we owe to ourselves, and we most assuredly owe it to those who preceded us and gave their lives that we might have a chance to complete the task of building a free Republic. We owe it to Plato, and Aristotle, and Aquinas, and Locke, and Calvin, and Montesquieu, and Adams, and

Otis, and Madison, and Jefferson. We owe it to those who fought to establish on this continent a new nation. We owe it to those who in our civil war fought both to defend the sanctity of states' rights <u>and</u> the guarantee of individual freedoms; and to those who defended our country's values in every war since then.

Most of all we owe it to those who follow us in time. Our children and grandchildren.

Repaying our debt will be a task worthy of the best in us, and that is what we must be ready to summon up and give. Time and the odds are now against us. But, that has never stopped Americans before. We have always answered the call before when our country's future was at stake. We must not fail to do so now. Now is the time to declare to ourselves, and the rest of the world, what we are made of, and what we stand for. It's time for the Americans in the middle to stand up and be counted. Without regard to race, creed, age, sex, or prior national origin.

Regardless of prior lineage, we are all **Americans** now. All by God and all by choice. And, it's our <u>Country</u> that's at stake. It's our future and the future of our <u>children</u> that's at stake. And it's our Dreams the politicians are dismantling. Now is the time to act. While we still can. Time is of the essence.

The whole is always equal to the sum of its individual parts. The idea that is America is equal to the sum of the actions of its individual citizens. Previous generations of Americans worked, fought, and paid dearly to establish and maintain this country and its freedoms for our benefit.

Their legacy will be that of devoted, courageous citizens willing to pay the full price of citizenship. We inherited the benefits of their efforts. These are the unearned advantages bestowed upon us by our forefathers and ancestors.

We didn't fight to establish this country. They did. We didn't protect it when it was threatened. They did. We didn't debate the great questions of citizens and government, and construct a living document by which Plato's Republic could be achieved. They did. These were the gifts passed down to us by those that came before.

It remains to be seen what our generation's legacy will be. It will, in the final analysis, be whatever we <u>will</u> it to be.

I began this work with the question: Whatever happened to the American Dream? Now, many pages later, with sincere thanks for your taking the time to read what I felt compelled to write down, I end with the most important question posed within. The answer you give, will ultimately determine the outcome of your life, and the lives of future generations of American's, some not yet born; so please consider carefully before you give it.

Once again:

Just whose job is it anyway, restoring the American Dream for your family, protecting your family's income, and restoring opportunity for your children, and your grandchildren?

Jack

Appendix - The Constitution

Read it through. It's only 12 pages long, and it is the starting point for understanding what the framers had in mind when they declared independence from England. Read this document and you will come to understand the promise that is (can be) America.

Dozens of great nations have come to the point where we are now, being the richest and most powerful on the planet, only to quickly come apart and be reduced to once great nations, with visions of past glories lost, inhabited by citizens whose dreams didn't matter anymore. In retrospect, none of them really ever had a chance of succeeding long-term. But in America's experiment in freedom and self-government we have been given just such an opportunity.

In all of the recorded history of man on this planet, only <u>one</u> Government was ever established for the sole purpose of insuring that every citizen was provided with the right to life, liberty, and the pursuit of happiness.

And, in all of the recorded history of man on this planet, America is the only nation that reached the point of being the richest and most powerful with a real chance to <u>finish</u> the building of a utopian society, and not be relegated to the scrap heap of once great nations.

Coincidence? I think not. Our fate is truly in our own hands in no small part because of this document. It's the map to the pot of gold at the end of the rainbow.... If we choose to follow it.

Constitution for the United States of America

We the People of the United States, in Order to form a more perfect Union, establish Justice, insure domestic Tranquility, provide for the common defense, promote the general Welfare, and secure the Blessings of Liberty to ourselves and our Posterity, do ordain and establish this Constitution for the United States of America.

Article 1.

Section 1

All legislative Powers herein granted shall be vested in a Congress of the United States, which shall consist of a Senate and House of Representatives.

Section 2

The House of Representatives shall be composed of Members chosen every second Year by the People of the several States, and the Electors in each State shall have the Qualifications requisite for Electors of the most numerous Branch of the State Legislature.

No Person shall be a Representative who shall not have attained to the Age of twenty five Years, and been seven Years a Citizen of the United States, and who shall not, when elected, be an Inhabitant of that State in which he shall be chosen.

Representatives and direct Taxes shall be apportioned among the several States which may be included within this Union, according to their respective Numbers, which shall be determined by adding to the whole Number of free Persons, including those bound to Service for a Term of Years, and excluding Indians not taxed, three fifths of all other Persons.

The actual Enumeration shall be made within three Years after the first Meeting of the Congress of the United States, and within every subsequent Term of ten Years, in such Manner as they shall by Law direct. The Number of Representatives shall not exceed one for every thirty Thousand, but each State shall have at Least one Representative; and until such enumeration shall be made, the State of New Hampshire shall be entitled to choose three, Massachusetts eight, Rhode Island and Providence Plantations one, Connecticut five, New York six, New Jersey four, Pennsylvania eight, Delaware one, Maryland six, Virginia ten, North Carolina five, South Carolina five and Georgia three.

When vacancies happen in the Representation from any State, the Executive Authority thereof shall issue Writs of Election to fill such Vacancies.

The House of Representatives shall choose their Speaker and other Officers; and shall have the sole Power of Impeachment.

Section 3

The Senate of the United States shall be composed of two Senators from each State, chosen by the Legislature thereof, for six Years; and each Senator shall have one Vote.

Immediately after they shall be assembled in Consequence of the first Election, they shall be divided as equally as may be into three Classes. The Seats of the Senators of the first Class shall be vacated at the Expiration of the second Year, of the second Class at the Expiration of the fourth Year, and of the third Class at the Expiration of the sixth Year, so that one third may be chosen every second Year; and if Vacancies happen by Resignation, or otherwise, during the Recess of the Legislature of any State, the Executive thereof may make temporary Appointments until the next Meeting of the Legislature, which shall then fill such Vacancies.

No person shall be a Senator who shall not have attained to the Age of thirty Years, and been nine Years a Citizen of the United States, and who shall not, when elected, be an Inhabitant of that State for which he shall be chosen.

The Vice President of the United States shall be President of the Senate, but shall have no Vote, unless they be equally divided.

The Senate shall choose their other Officers, and also a President pro tempore, in the absence of the Vice President, or when he shall exercise the Office of President of the United States.

The Senate shall have the sole Power to try all Impeachments. When sitting for that Purpose, they shall be on Oath or Affirmation. When the President of the United States is tried, the Chief Justice shall preside: And no Person shall be convicted without the Concurrence of two thirds of the Members present.

Judgment in Cases of Impeachment shall not extend further than to removal from Office, and disqualification to hold and enjoy any Office of honor, Trust or Profit under the United States: but the Party convicted shall nevertheless be liable and subject to Indictment, Trial, Judgment and Punishment, according to Law.

Section 4

The Times, Places and Manner of holding Elections for Senators and Representatives, shall be prescribed in each State by the Legislature thereof; but the Congress may at any time by Law make or alter such Regulations, except as to the Place of Choosing Senators.

The Congress shall assemble at least once in every Year, and such Meeting shall be on the first Monday in December, unless they shall by Law appoint a different Day.

Section 5

Each House shall be the Judge of the Elections, Returns and Qualifications of its own Members, and a Majority of each shall constitute a Quorum to do Business; but a smaller number may adjourn from day to day, and may be authorized to compel the Attendance of absent Members, in such Manner, and under such Penalties as each House may provide.

Each House may determine the Rules of its Proceedings, punish its Members for disorderly Behavior, and, with the Concurrence of two-thirds, expel a Member.

Each House shall keep a Journal of its Proceedings, and from time to time publish the same, excepting such Parts as may in their Judgment require Secrecy; and the Yeas and Nays of the Members of either House on any question shall, at the Desire of one fifth of those Present, be entered on the Journal.

Neither House, during the Session of Congress, shall, without the Consent of the other, adjourn for more than three days, nor to any other Place than that in which the two Houses shall be sitting.

Section 6

The Senators and Representatives shall receive a Compensation for their Services, to be ascertained by Law, and paid out of the Treasury of the United States. They shall in all Cases, except Treason, Felony and Breach of the Peace, be privileged from Arrest during their Attendance at the Session of their respective Houses, and in going to and returning from the same; and for any Speech or Debate in either House, they shall not be questioned in any other Place.

No Senator or Representative shall, during the Time for which he was elected, be appointed to any civil Office under the Authority of the United States which shall have been created, or the Emoluments whereof shall have been increased during such time; and no Person holding any Office under the United States, shall be a Member of either House during his Continuance in Office.

Section 7

All bills for raising Revenue shall originate in the House of Representatives; but the Senate may propose or concur with Amendments as on other Bills.

Every Bill which shall have passed the House of Representatives and the Senate, shall, before it become a Law, be presented to the President of the United States; If he approve he shall sign it, but if not he shall return it, with his Objections to that House in which it shall have originated, who shall enter the Objections at large on their Journal, and proceed to reconsider it.

If after such Reconsideration two thirds of that House shall agree to pass the Bill, it shall be sent, together with the Objections, to the other House, by which it shall likewise be reconsidered, and if approved by two thirds of that House, it shall become a Law. But in all such Cases the Votes of both Houses shall be determined by Yeas and Nays, and the Names of the Persons voting for and against the Bill shall be entered on the Journal of each House respectively.

If any Bill shall not be returned by the President within ten Days (Sundays excepted) after it shall have been presented to him, the Same shall be a Law, in like Manner as if he had signed it, unless the Congress by their Adjournment prevent its Return, in which Case it shall not be a Law.

Every Order, Resolution, or Vote to which the Concurrence of the Senate and House of Representatives may be necessary (except on a question of Adjournment) shall be presented to the President of the United States; and before the Same shall take Effect, shall be approved by him, or being disapproved by him, shall be repassed by two thirds of the Senate and House of Representatives, according to the Rules and Limitations prescribed in the Case of a Bill.

Section 8

The Congress shall have Power To lay and collect Taxes, Duties, Imposts and Excises, to pay the Debts and provide for the common Defence and general Welfare of the United States; but all Duties, Imposts and Excises shall be uniform throughout the United States;

To borrow money on the credit of the United States;

To regulate Commerce with foreign Nations, and among the several States, and with the Indian Tribes;

To establish an uniform Rule of Naturalization, and uniform Laws on the subject of Bankruptcies throughout the United States;

To coin Money, regulate the Value thereof, and of foreign Coin, and fix the Standard of Weights and Measures;

To provide for the Punishment of counterfeiting the Securities and current Coin of the United States;

To establish Post Offices and Post Roads;

To promote the Progress of Science and useful Arts, by securing for limited Times to Authors and Inventors the exclusive Right to their respective Writings and Discoveries;

To constitute Tribunals inferior to the supreme Court;

To define and punish Piracies and Felonies committed on the high Seas, and Offenses against the Law of Nations;

To declare War, grant Letters of Marque and Reprisal, and make Rules concerning Captures on Land and Water;

To raise and support Armies, but no Appropriation of Money to that Use shall be for a longer Term than two Years;

To provide and maintain a Navy;

To make Rules for the Government and Regulation of the land and naval Forces;

To provide for calling forth the Militia to execute the Laws of the Union, suppress Insurrections and repel Invasions;

To provide for organizing, arming, and disciplining the Militia, and for governing such Part of them as may be employed in the Service of the United States, reserving to the States respectively, the Appointment of the Officers, and the Authority of training the Militia according to the discipline prescribed by Congress;

To exercise exclusive Legislation in all Cases whatsoever, over such District (not exceeding ten Miles square) as may, by Cession of particular States, and the acceptance of Congress, become the Seat of the Government of the United States, and to exercise like Authority over all Places purchased by the Consent of the Legislature of the State in which the Same shall be, for the Erection of Forts, Magazines, Arsenals, dock-Yards, and other needful Buildings; And

To make all Laws which shall be necessary and proper for carrying into Execution the foregoing Powers, and all other Powers vested by this Constitution in the Government of the United States, or in any Department or Officer thereof.

Section 9

The Migration or Importation of such Persons as any of the States now existing shall think proper to admit, shall not be prohibited by the Congress prior to the Year one thousand eight hundred and eight, but a tax or duty may be imposed on such Importation, not exceeding ten dollars for each Person.

The privilege of the Writ of Habeas Corpus shall not be suspended, unless when in Cases of Rebellion or Invasion the public Safety may require it.

No Bill of Attainder or ex post facto Law shall be passed.

No capitation, or other direct, Tax shall be laid, unless in Proportion to the Census or Enumeration herein before directed to be taken.

No Tax or Duty shall be laid on Articles exported from any State.

No Preference shall be given by any Regulation of Commerce or Revenue to the Ports of one State over those of another: nor shall Vessels bound to, or from, one State, be obliged to enter, clear, or pay Duties in another.

No Money shall be drawn from the Treasury, but in Consequence of Appropriations made by Law; and a regular Statement and Account of the Receipts and Expenditures of all public Money shall be published from time to time.

No Title of Nobility shall be granted by the United States: And no Person holding any Office of Profit or Trust under them, shall, without the Consent of the Congress, accept of any present, Emolument, Office, or Title, of any kind whatever, from any King, Prince or foreign State.

Section 10

No State shall enter into any Treaty, Alliance, or Confederation; grant Letters of Marque and Reprisal; coin Money; emit Bills of Credit; make any Thing but gold and silver Coin a Tender in Payment of Debts; pass any Bill of Attainder, ex post facto Law, or Law impairing the Obligation of Contracts, or grant any Title of Nobility.

No State shall, without the Consent of the Congress, lay any Imposts or Duties on Imports or Exports, except what may be absolutely necessary for executing its inspection Laws: and the net Produce of all Duties and Imposts, laid by any State on Imports or Exports, shall be for the Use of the Treasury of the United States; and all such Laws shall be subject to the Revision and Control of the Congress.

No State shall, without the Consent of Congress, lay any duty of Tonnage, keep Troops, or Ships of War in time of Peace, enter into any Agreement or Compact with another State, or with a foreign Power, or engage in War, unless actually invaded, or in such imminent Danger as will not admit of delay.

Article 2.

Section 1

The executive Power shall be vested in a President of the United States of America. He shall hold his Office during the Term of four Years, and, together with the Vice-President chosen for the same Term, be elected, as follows:

Each State shall appoint, in such Manner as the Legislature thereof may direct, a Number of Electors, equal to the whole Number of Senators and Representatives o which the State may be entitled in the Congress: but no Senator or Representative, or Person holding an Office of Trust or Profit under the United States, shall be appointed an Elector.

The Electors shall meet in their respective States, and vote by Ballot for two persons, of whom one at least shall not lie an Inhabitant of the same State with themselves. And they shall make a List of all the Persons voted for, and of the Number of Votes for each; which List they shall sign and certify, and transmit sealed to the Seat of the Government of the United States, directed to the President of the Senate.

The President of the Senate shall, in the Presence of the Senate and House of Representatives, open all the Certificates, and the Votes shall then be counted. The Person having the greatest Number of Votes shall be the President, if such Number be a Majority of the whole Number of Electors appointed; and if there be more than one who have such Majority, and have an equal Number of Votes, then the House of Representatives shall immediately choose by Ballot one of them for President; and if no Person have a Majority, then from the five highest on the List the said House shall in like Manner choose the President.

But in choosing the President, the Votes shall be taken by States, the Representation from each State having one Vote; a quorum for this Purpose shall consist of a Member or Members from two-thirds of the States, and a Majority of all the States shall be necessary to a Choice. In every Case, after the Choice of the President, the Person having the greatest Number of Votes of the Electors shall be the Vice President. But if there should remain two or more who have equal Votes, the Senate shall choose from them by Ballot the Vice-President.

The Congress may determine the Time of choosing the Electors, and the Day on which they shall give their Votes; which Day shall be the same throughout the United States.

No person except a natural born Citizen, or a Citizen of the United States, at the time of the Adoption of this Constitution, shall be eligible to the Office of President; neither shall any Person be eligible to that Office who shall not have attained to the Age of thirty-five Years, and been fourteen Years a Resident within the United States.

In Case of the Removal of the President from Office, or of his Death, Resignation, or Inability to discharge the Powers and Duties of the said Office, the same shall devolve on the Vice President, and the Congress may by Law provide for the Case of Removal, Death, Resignation or Inability, both of the President and Vice President, declaring what officer shall then act as President, and such Officer shall act accordingly, until the Disability be removed, or a President shall be elected.

The President shall, at stated Times, receive for his Services, a Compensation, which shall neither be increased nor diminished during the Period for which he shall have been elected, and he shall not receive within that Period any other Emolument from the United States, or any of them.

Before he enter on the Execution of his Office, he shall take the following Oath or Affirmation:

"I do solemnly swear (or affirm) that I will faithfully execute the Office of President of the United States, and will to the best of my Ability, preserve, protect and defend the Constitution of the United States."

Section 2

The President shall be Commander in Chief of the Army and Navy of the United States, and of the Militia of the several States, when called into the actual Service of the United States; he may require the Opinion, in writing, of the principal Officer in each of the executive Departments, upon any subject relating to the Duties of their respective Offices, and he shall have Power to Grant Reprieves and Pardons for Offenses against the United States, except in Cases of Impeachment.

He shall have Power, by and with the Advice and Consent of the Senate, to make Treaties, provided two thirds of the Senators present concur; and he shall nominate, and by and with the Advice and Consent of the Senate, shall appoint Ambassadors, other public Ministers and Consuls, Judges of the supreme Court, and all other Officers of the United States, whose Appointments are not herein otherwise provided for, and which shall be established by Law: but the Congress may by Law vest the Appointment of such inferior Officers, as they think proper, in the President alone, in the Courts of Law, or in the Heads of Departments.

The President shall have Power to fill up all Vacancies that may happen during the Recess of the Senate, by granting Commissions which shall expire at the End of their next Session.

Section 3

He shall from time to time give to the Congress Information of the State of the Union, and recommend to their Consideration such Measures as he shall judge necessary and expedient; he may, on extraordinary Occasions, convene both Houses, or either of them, and in Case of Disagreement between them, with Respect to the Time of Adjournment, he may adjourn them to such Time as he shall think proper; he shall receive Ambassadors and other public Ministers; he shall take Care that the Laws be faithfully executed, and shall Commission all the Officers of the United States.

Section 4

The President, Vice President and all civil Officers of the United States, shall be removed from Office on Impeachment for, and Conviction of, Treason, Bribery, or other high Crimes and Misdemeanors.

Article 3.

Section 1

The judicial Power of the United States, shall be vested in one supreme Court, and in such inferior Courts as the Congress may from time to time ordain and establish. The Judges, both of the supreme and inferior Courts, shall hold their Offices during good Behavior, and shall, at stated Times, receive for their Services a Compensation which shall not be diminished during their Continuance in Office.

Section 2

The judicial Power shall extend to all Cases, in Law and Equity, arising under this Constitution, the Laws of the United States, and Treaties made, or which shall be made, under their Authority; to all Cases affecting Ambassadors, other public Ministers and Consuls; to all Cases of admiralty and maritime Jurisdiction; to Controversies to which the United States shall be a Party; to Controversies between two or more States; between a State and Citizens of another State; between Citizens of different States; between Citizens of the same State claiming Lands under Grants of different States, and between a State, or the Citizens thereof, and foreign States, Citizens or Subjects.

In all Cases affecting Ambassadors, other public Ministers and Consuls, and those in which a State shall be Party, the supreme Court shall have original Jurisdiction. In all the other Cases before mentioned, the supreme Court shall have appellate Jurisdiction, both as to Law and Fact, with such Exceptions, and under such Regulations as the Congress shall make.

The Trial of all Crimes, except in Cases of Impeachment, shall be by Jury; and such Trial shall be held in the State where the said Crimes shall have been committed; but when not committed within any State, the Trial shall be at such Place or Places as the Congress may by Law have directed.

Section 3

Treason against the United States, shall consist only in levying War against them, or in adhering to their Enemies, giving them Aid and Comfort. No Person shall be convicted of Treason unless on the Testimony of two Witnesses to the same overt Act, or on Confession in open Court.

The Congress shall have power to declare the Punishment of Treason, but no Attainder of Treason shall work Corruption of Blood, or Forfeiture except during the Life of the Person attainted.

Article 4.

Section 1

Full Faith and Credit shall be given in each State to the public Acts, Records, and judicial Proceedings of every other State. And the Congress may by general Laws prescribe the Manner in which such Acts, Records and Proceedings shall be proved, and the Effect thereof.

Section 2

The Citizens of each State shall be entitled to all Privileges and Immunities of Citizens in the several States.

A Person charged in any State with Treason, Felony, or other Crime, who shall flee from Justice, and be found in another State, shall on demand of the executive Authority of the State from which he fled, be delivered up, to be removed to the State having Jurisdiction of the Crime.

No Person held to Service or Labour in one State, under the Laws thereof, escaping into another, shall, in Consequence of any Law or Regulation therein, be discharged from such Service or Labour, But shall be delivered up on Claim of the Party to whom such Service or Labour may be due.

Section 3

New States may be admitted by the Congress into this Union; but no new States shall be formed or erected within the Jurisdiction of any other State; nor any State be formed by the Junction of two or more States, or parts of States, without the Consent of the Legislatures of the States concerned as well as of the Congress.

The Congress shall have Power to dispose of and make all needful Rules and Regulations respecting the Territory or other Property belonging to the United States; and nothing in this Constitution shall be so construed as to Prejudice any Claims of the United States, or of any particular State.

Section 4

The United States shall guarantee to every State in this Union a Republican Form of Government, and shall protect each of them against Invasion; and on Application of the Legislature, or of the Executive (when the Legislature cannot be convened) against domestic Violence.

Article 5.

The Congress, whenever two thirds of both Houses shall deem it necessary, shall propose Amendments to this Constitution, or, on the Application of the Legislatures of two thirds of the several States, shall call a Convention for proposing Amendments, which, in either Case, shall be valid to all Intents and Purposes, as part of this Constitution, when ratified by the Legislatures of three fourths of the several States, or by Conventions in three fourths thereof, as the one or the other Mode of Ratification may be proposed by the Congress; Provided that no Amendment which may be made prior to the Year One thousand eight hundred and eight shall in any Manner affect the first and fourth Clauses in the Ninth Section of the first Article; and that no State, without its Consent, shall be deprived of its equal Suffrage in the Senate.

Article 6.

All Debts contracted and Engagements entered into, before the Adoption of this Constitution, shall be as valid against the United States under this Constitution, as under the Confederation.

This Constitution, and the Laws of the United States which shall be made in Pursuance thereof; and all Treaties made, or which shall be made, under the Authority of the United States, shall be the supreme Law of the Land; and the Judges in every State shall be bound thereby, any Thing in the Constitution or Laws of any State to the Contrary notwithstanding.

The Senators and Representatives before mentioned, and the Members of the several State Legislatures, and all executive and judicial Officers, both of the United States and of the several States, shall be bound by Oath or Affirmation, to support this Constitution; but no religious Test shall ever be required as a Qualification to any Office or public Trust under the United States.

Article 7.

The Ratification of the Conventions of nine States, shall be sufficient for the Establishment of this Constitution between the States so ratifying the Same.

Done in Convention by the Unanimous Consent of the States present the Seventeenth Day of September in the Year of our Lord one thousand seven hundred and Eighty seven and of the Independence of the United States of America the Twelfth. In Witness whereof We have hereunto subscribed our Names.

George Washington - President and deputy from Virginia
New Hampshire - John Langdon, Nicholas Gilman
Massachusetts - Nathaniel Gorham, Rufus King
Connecticut - William Samuel Johnson, Roger Sherman
New York - Alexander Hamilton
New Jersey - William Livingston, David Brearley, William Paterson, Jonathan Dayton
Pennsylvania - Benjamin Franklin, Thomas Mifflin, Robert Morris, George Clymer, Thomas Fitzsimons, Jared Ingersoll, James Wilson, Gouvernour Morris
Delaware - George Read, Gunning Bedford Jr., John Dickinson, Richard Bassett, Jacob Broom
Maryland - James McHenry, Daniel of St Thomas Jenifer, Daniel Carroll
Virginia - John Blair, James Madison Jr.
North Carolina - William Blount, Richard Dobbs Spaight, Hugh Williamson
South Carolina - John Rutledge, Charles Cotesworth Pinckney, Charles Pinckney, Pierce Butler
Georgia - William Few, Abraham Baldwin

Attest: William Jackson, Secretary

Amendment 1

Congress shall make no law respecting an establishment of religion, or prohibiting the free exercise thereof; or abridging the freedom of speech, or of the press; or the right of the people peaceably to assemble, and to petition the Government for a redress of grievances.

Amendment 2

A well-regulated Militia, being necessary to the security of a free State, the right of the people to keep and bear Arms, shall not be infringed.

Amendment 3

No Soldier shall, in time of peace be quartered in any house, without the consent of the Owner, nor in time of war, but in a manner to be prescribed by law.

Amendment 4

The right of the people to be secure in their persons, houses, papers, and effects, against unreasonable searches and seizures, shall not be violated, and no Warrants shall issue, but upon probable cause, supported by Oath or affirmation, and particularly describing the place to be searched, and the persons or things to be seized.

Amendment 5

No person shall be held to answer for a capital, or otherwise infamous crime, unless on a presentment or indictment of a Grand Jury, except in cases arising in the land or naval forces, or in the Militia, when in actual service in time of War or public danger; nor shall any person be subject for the same offense to be twice put in jeopardy of life or limb; nor shall be compelled in any criminal case to be a witness against himself, nor be deprived of life, liberty, or property, without due process of law; nor shall private property be taken for public use, without just compensation.

Amendment 6

In all criminal prosecutions, the accused shall enjoy the right to a speedy and public trial, by an impartial jury of the State and district wherein the crime shall have been committed, which district shall have been previously ascertained by law, and to be informed of the nature and cause of the accusation; to be confronted with the witnesses against him; to have compulsory process for obtaining witnesses in his favor, and to have the Assistance of Counsel for his defense.

Amendment 7
In Suits at common law, where the value in controversy shall exceed twenty dollars, the right of trial by jury shall be preserved, and no fact tried by a jury, shall be otherwise re-examined in any Court of the United States, than according to the rules of the common law.

Amendment 8
Excessive bail shall not be required, nor excessive fines imposed, nor cruel and unusual punishments inflicted.

Amendment 9
The enumeration in the Constitution, of certain rights, shall not be construed to deny or disparage others retained by the people.

Amendment 10
The powers not delegated to the United States by the Constitution, nor prohibited by it to the States, are reserved to the States respectively, or to the people.

Amendment 11
The Judicial power of the United States shall not be construed to extend to any suit in law or equity, commenced or prosecuted against one of the United States by Citizens of another State, or by Citizens or Subjects of any Foreign State.

Amendment 12
The Electors shall meet in their respective states, and vote by ballot for President and Vice-President, one of whom, at least, shall not be an inhabitant of the same state with themselves; they shall name in their ballots the person voted for as President, and in distinct ballots the person voted for as Vice-President, and they shall make distinct lists of all persons voted for as President, and of all persons voted for as Vice-President and of the number of votes for each, which lists they shall sign and certify, and transmit sealed to the seat of the government of the United States, directed to the President of the Senate;

The President of the Senate shall, in the presence of the Senate and House of Representatives, open all the certificates and the votes shall then be counted; The person having the greatest Number of votes for President, shall be the President, if such number be a majority of the whole number of Electors appointed; and if no person have such majority, then from the persons having the highest numbers not exceeding three on the list of those voted for as President, the House of Representatives shall choose immediately, by ballot, the President. But in choosing the President, the votes shall be taken by states, the representation from each state having one vote; a quorum for this purpose shall consist of a member or members from two-thirds of the states, and a majority of all the states shall be necessary to a choice. And if the House of Representatives shall not choose a President whenever the right of choice shall devolve upon them, before the fourth day of March next following, then the Vice-President shall act as President, as in the case of the death or other constitutional disability of the President.

The person having the greatest number of votes as Vice-President, shall be the Vice-President, if such number be a majority of the whole number of Electors appointed, and if no person have a majority, then from the two highest numbers on the list, the Senate shall choose the Vice-President; a quorum for the purpose shall consist of two-thirds of the whole number of Senators, and a majority of the whole number shall be necessary to a choice. But no person constitutionally ineligible to the office of President shall be eligible to that of Vice-President of the United States.

Amendment 13
1. Neither slavery nor involuntary servitude, except as a punishment for crime whereof the party shall have been duly convicted, shall exist within the United States, or any place subject to their jurisdiction.

2. Congress shall have power to enforce this article by appropriate legislation.

Amendment 14
1. All persons born or naturalized in the United States, and subject to the jurisdiction thereof, are citizens of the United States and of the State wherein they reside. No State shall make or enforce any law which shall abridge the privileges or immunities of citizens of the United States; nor shall any State deprive any person of life, liberty, or property, without due process of law; nor deny to any person within its jurisdiction the equal protection of the laws.

2. Representatives shall be apportioned among the several States according to their respective numbers, counting the whole number of persons in each State, excluding Indians not taxed. But when the right to vote at any election for the choice of electors for President and Vice-President of the United States, Representatives in Congress, the Executive and Judicial officers of a State, or the members of the Legislature thereof, is denied to any of the male inhabitants of such State, being twenty-one years of age, and citizens of the United States, or in any way abridged, except for participation in rebellion,

or other crime, the basis of representation therein shall be reduced in the proportion which the number of such male citizens shall bear to the whole number of male citizens twenty-one years of age in such State.

3. No person shall be a Senator or Representative in Congress, or elector of President and Vice-President, or hold any office, civil or military, under the United States, or under any State, who, having previously taken an oath, as a member of Congress, or as an officer of the United States, or as a member of any State legislature, or as an executive or judicial officer of any State, to support the Constitution of the United States, shall have engaged in insurrection or rebellion against the same, or given aid or comfort to the enemies thereof. But Congress may by a vote of two-thirds of each House, remove such disability.

4. The validity of the public debt of the United States, authorized by law, including debts incurred for payment of pensions and bounties for services in suppressing insurrection or rebellion, shall not be questioned. But neither the United States nor any State shall assume or pay any debt or obligation incurred in aid of insurrection or rebellion against the United States, or any claim for the loss or emancipation of any slave; but all such debts, obligations and claims shall be held illegal and void.

5. The Congress shall have power to enforce, by appropriate legislation, the provisions of this article.

Amendment 15

1. The right of citizens of the United States to vote shall not be denied or abridged by the United States or by any State on account of race, color, or previous condition of servitude.

2. The Congress shall have power to enforce this article by appropriate legislation.

Amendment 16

The Congress shall have power to lay and collect taxes on incomes, from whatever source derived, without apportionment among the several States, and without regard to any census or enumeration.

Amendment 17

The Senate of the United States shall be composed of two Senators from each State, elected by the people thereof, for six years; and each Senator shall have one vote. The electors in each State shall have the qualifications requisite for electors of the most numerous branch of the State legislatures.

When vacancies happen in the representation of any State in the Senate, the executive authority of such State shall issue writs of election to fill such vacancies: Provided, That the legislature of any State may empower the executive thereof to make temporary appointments until the people fill the vacancies by election as the legislature may direct.

This amendment shall not be so construed as to affect the election or term of any Senator chosen before it becomes valid as part of the Constitution.

Amendment 18

1. After one year from the ratification of this article the manufacture, sale, or transportation of intoxicating liquors within, the importation thereof into, or the exportation thereof from the United States and all territory subject to the jurisdiction thereof for beverage purposes is hereby prohibited.

2. The Congress and the several States shall have concurrent power to enforce this article by appropriate legislation.

3. This article shall be inoperative unless it shall have been ratified as an amendment to the Constitution by the legislatures of the several States, as provided in the Constitution, within seven years from the date of the submission hereof to the States by the Congress.

Amendment 19

The right of citizens of the United States to vote shall not be denied or abridged by the United States or by any State on account of sex.

Congress shall have power to enforce this article by appropriate legislation.

Amendment 20

1. The terms of the President and Vice President shall end at noon on the 20th day of January, and the terms of Senators and Representatives at noon on the 3d day of January, of the years in which such terms would have ended if this article had not been ratified; and the terms of their successors shall then begin.

2. The Congress shall assemble at least once in every year, and such meeting shall begin at noon on the 3d day of January, unless they shall by law appoint a different day.

3. If, at the time fixed for the beginning of the term of the President, the President elect shall have died, the Vice President elect shall become President. If a President shall not have been chosen before the time fixed for the beginning of his term, or if the President elect shall have failed to qualify, then the Vice President elect shall act as President until a President shall have qualified; and the Congress may by law provide for the case wherein neither a President elect nor a Vice President elect shall have qualified, declaring who shall then act as President, or the manner in which one who is to act shall be selected, and such person shall act accordingly until a President or Vice President shall have qualified.

4. The Congress may by law provide for the case of the death of any of the persons from whom the House of Representatives may choose a President whenever the right of choice shall have devolved upon them, and for the case of the death of any of the persons from whom the Senate may choose a Vice President whenever the right of choice shall have devolved upon them.

5. Sections 1 and 2 shall take effect on the 15th day of October following the ratification of this article.

6. This article shall be inoperative unless it shall have been ratified as an amendment to the Constitution by the legislatures of three-fourths of the several States within seven years from the date of its submission.

Amendment 21

1. The eighteenth article of amendment to the Constitution of the United States is hereby repealed.

2. The transportation or importation into any State, Territory, or possession of the United States for delivery or use therein of intoxicating liquors, in violation of the laws thereof, is hereby prohibited.

3. The article shall be inoperative unless it shall have been ratified as an amendment to the Constitution by conventions in the several States, as provided n the Constitution, within seven years from the date of the submission hereof to the States by the Congress.

Amendment 22

1. No person shall be elected to the office of the President more than twice, and no person who has held the office of President, or acted as President, for more than two years of a term to which some other person was elected President shall be elected to the office of the President more than once. But this Article shall not apply to any person holding the office of President, when this Article was proposed by the Congress, and shall not prevent any person who may be holding the office of President, or acting as President, during the term within which this Article becomes operative from holding the office of President or acting as President during the remainder of such term.

2. This article shall be inoperative unless it shall have been ratified as an amendment to the Constitution by the legislatures of three-fourths of the several States within seven years from the date of its submission to the States by the Congress.

Amendment 23

1. The District constituting the seat of Government of the United States shall appoint in such manner as the Congress may direct: A number of electors of President and Vice President equal to the whole number of Senators and Representatives in Congress to which the District would be entitled if it were a State, but in no event more than the least populous State; they shall be in addition to those appointed by the States, but they shall be considered, for the purposes of the election of President and Vice President, to be electors appointed by a State; and they shall meet in the District and perform such duties as provided by the twelfth article of amendment.

2. The Congress shall have power to enforce this article by appropriate legislation.

Amendment 24

1. The right of citizens of the United States to vote in any primary or other election for President or Vice President, for electors for President or Vice President, or for Senator or Representative in Congress, shall not be denied or abridged by the United States or any State by reason of failure to pay any poll tax or other tax.

2. The Congress shall have power to enforce this article by appropriate legislation.

Amendment 25

1. In case of the removal of the President from office or of his death or resignation, the Vice President shall become President.

2. Whenever there is a vacancy in the office of the Vice President, the President shall nominate a Vice President who shall take office upon confirmation by a majority vote of both Houses of Congress.

3. Whenever the President transmits to the President pro tempore of the Senate and the Speaker of the House of Representatives his written declaration that he is unable to discharge the powers and duties of his office, and until he transmits to them a written declaration to the contrary, such powers and duties shall be discharged by the Vice President as Acting President.

4. Whenever the Vice President and a majority of either the principal officers of the executive departments or of such other body as Congress may by law provide, transmit to the President pro tempore of the Senate and the Speaker of the House of Representatives their written declaration that the President is unable to discharge the powers and duties of his office, the Vice President shall immediately assume the powers and duties of the office as Acting President.

Thereafter, when the President transmits to the President pro tempore of the Senate and the Speaker of the House of Representatives his written declaration that no inability exists, he shall resume the powers and duties of his office unless the Vice President and a majority of either the principal officers of the executive department or of such other body as Congress may by law provide, transmit within four days to the President pro tempore of the Senate and the Speaker of the House of Representatives their written declaration that the President is unable to discharge the powers and duties of his office.

Thereupon Congress shall decide the issue, assembling within forty eight hours for that purpose if not in session. If the Congress, within twenty one days after receipt of the latter written declaration, or, if Congress is not in session, within twenty one days after Congress is required to assemble, determines by two thirds vote of both Houses that the President is unable to discharge the powers and duties of his office, the Vice President shall continue to discharge the same as Acting President; otherwise, the President shall resume the powers and duties of his office.

Amendment 26
1. The right of citizens of the United States, who are eighteen years of age or older, to vote shall not be denied or abridged by the United States or by any State on account of age.

2. The Congress shall have power to enforce this article by appropriate
legislation.

Amendment 27
No law, varying the compensation for the services of the Senators and Representatives, shall take effect, until an election of Representatives shall have intervened

www.ingramcontent.com/pod-product-compliance
Lightning Source LLC
Chambersburg PA
CBHW020728160426
43192CB00006B/151